Why Gender Matters in Economics

Why Gender Matters in Economics

MUKESH ESWARAN

PRINCETON UNIVERSITY PRESS

Princeton and Oxford

Copyright © 2014 by Princeton University Press

Published by Princeton University Press, 41 William Street, Princeton, New Jersey 08540

In the United Kingdom: Princeton University Press, 6 Oxford Street, Woodstock, Oxfordshire OX20 1TW

press.princeton.edu

Library of Congress Cataloging-in-Publication Data

Eswaran, Mukesh.

    Why gender matters in economics / Mukesh Eswaran.

      pages   cm

    Includes index.

    Summary: "Gender matters in economics—for even with today's technology, fertility choices, market opportunities, and improved social norms, economic outcomes for women remain markedly worse than for men. Drawing on insights from feminism, postmodernism, psychology, evolutionary biology, Marxism, and politics, this textbook provides a rigorous economic look at issues confronting women throughout the world—including nonmarket scenarios, such as marriage, family, fertility choice, and bargaining within households, as well as market areas, like those pertaining to labor and credit markets and globalization. Mukesh Eswaran examines how women's behavioral responses in economic situations and their bargaining power within the household differ from those of men. Eswaran then delves into the far-reaching consequences of these differences, in market and nonmarket domains. The author considers how women may be discriminated against in labor and credit markets, how their family and market circumstances interact, and how globalization has influenced their lives. Eswaran also investigates how women have been empowered through access to education, credit, healthcare, and birth control; changes in ownership laws; the acquisition of suffrage; and political representation. Throughout, Eswaran applies sound economic analysis and new modeling approaches, and each chapter concludes with exercises and discussion questions. This textbook gives readers the necessary tools for thinking about gender from an economic perspective. Addresses economic issues for women throughout the world, in both developed and developing countries Looks at both market and nonmarket domains Requires only a background in basic economic principles Includes the most recent research on the economics of gender in a range of areas Concludes each chapter with exercises and discussion questions"—Provided by publisher.

    ISBN 978-0-691-12173-4 (hardback)

    1. Women—Economic conditions.   2. Women—Employment.   3. Women—Social conditions.   4. Women in development. I. Title.

HQ1381.E89   2014

305.4—dc23   2014008909

British Library Cataloging-in-Publication Data is available

This book has been composed in Sabon, with Scala and Scala Sans display, by Princeton Editorial Associates Inc., Scottsdale, Arizona

Printed on acid-free paper. ∞

Printed in the United States of America

10 9 8 7 6 5 4 3 2 1

For Viju, Nisha, and Megha

CONTENTS

MODULE TWO **Gender in Markets**

CHAPTER FOUR **Are Women Discriminated Against in the Labor Market?**

CHAPTER FIVE **How Do Credit Markets Affect the Well-being of Women?**

CHAPTER SIX **What Are the Effects of Globalization on Women?**

PREFACE

The notion of writing this book took shape when, a decade ago, I started teaching an undergraduate course titled Women in the Economy. In preparation, I wrote down an ambitious list of topics that I thought the course ought to cover in order to do justice to the subject. Then I set about looking for a textbook that covered most of these topics. To my chagrin, I discovered that most of the books in existence were quite limited in their scope. The majority of these were texts focused on the employment of women. I could not find a book that offered a comprehensive view of the economic lives of women.

Do women and men behave differently in economic circumstances? How much of gendered behavior can be attributed to biology, and how much to socialization? What determines the bargaining power of women in a household? How did men come to make the important decisions in most societies, and how did they perpetuate this advantage? Why were women until recently relegated to doing housework and raising children? To what extent do markets determine the well-being of women? Do credit markets discriminate against women? Do labor markets? Are there reasons to believe that globalization may have hurt women? What are the economic consequences to women of marriage? How did the revolution in contraception impinge on the lives of women in the developed world and also in the less-developed world? Why are women, whose autonomy is so important to reducing fertility in poor countries, so often victimized by the very process that causes the decline in fertility? What were the economic factors that led to women gaining suffrage? What economic effects did it have? How can women be empowered?

These are some of the questions that I felt should be addressed, and *addressed at a nontechnical level that presumed only knowledge of the basic principles of economics.* After I had taught the course for the first time, I decided to write an undergraduate textbook, with a broad scope, on why gender matters in economics. As time went by, I added more topics.

The problems confronting women in rich and poor countries are not often the same. While there are some commonalities, history, culture, religion, the level of economic development, and politics inevitably render what may be minor issues in a rich-country setting serious issues in poor countries. In recognition of this fact, this book discusses women's economic lives in both settings.

I owe a great debt to my students over the years for their keen interest in the subject and for giving me comments on my course notes that became the beginnings of this book. I am deeply grateful to Nancy Folbre and Joyce Jacobsen, who read earlier drafts of the manuscript. They gave me extensive and constructive comments and alerted me to my blind spots. I thank Claudia Tufani for excellent research assistance. I acknowledge discussions with Siwan Anderson, Robert Dimand, Diane Eaton, Nicole Fortin, Nisha Malhotra, and Dilip Mookherjee. I am grateful to my editor Peter Dougherty for his patient encouragement over the years (even when progress on the manuscript was slower than expected). At Princeton Editorial Associates, I thank Peter Strupp for efficient handling of the production process and Marilyn Martin for excellent copyediting.

I thank my children Nisha and Megha for interesting discussions on some of the topics covered in this book. Above all, I am indebted to my wife Viju for her support and encouragement over the years.

Why Gender Matters in Economics

CHAPTER ONE

Introduction

This book examines the various ways in which economic outcomes differ for women and men and seeks to identify the reasons for these differences. The fact that economic activities differ by gender has traditionally been attributed—only partly correctly—to the advantages of a sexual division of labor. It has been argued that, because women perhaps have an advantage over men in looking after children when they are young, it has been beneficial for both men and women for the former to engage in paid employment while the latter concentrate on (unpaid) housework. But technology, fertility choices, market opportunities, and social norms have changed all of that in the past few decades. Women now have more freedom and more time available for education, for paid employment, and more generally for careers. Yet outcomes in the household and in the market are often markedly worse for them than for men with similar economic qualifications. In this book we seek to understand why this is so, why gender matters in the economic realm.[1] We shall see how small differences and relatively minor advantages (such as physical strength for men) can be magnified to produce striking differences in outcomes by gender. These have been translated into economic differences. But, as we shall also see, economics is by no means the sole reason for gender disparities. Socialization, culture, biology, history, and religion have played roles in bringing about gender inequities.

Although the subject matter of this book is extremely important, interest in it among mainstream economists has been surprisingly recent. Only in the past few decades have scholars in economics started addressing these issues

---

[1] *Sex* and *gender,* of course, do not refer to the same thing. The sex of an individual refers to whether the person is male or female; the gender refers to the individual's masculinity or femininity. As in most of the economic literature, we use the terms *sex* and *gender* almost interchangeably in this book, though the contents apply more broadly to gender. The context makes it clear whether a particular discussion applies only to sex.

systematically. It is not the case that there was no interest at all prior to this. Powerful voices in the past brought attention to important gender issues. Ardent feminists such as Mary Wollstonecraft, Harriet Mill and her husband John Stuart Mill, Charlotte Perkins Gilman, Elizabeth Cady Stanton, and Susan B. Anthony, among many others, sought through their writings to level the gender playing field along many dimensions. But mainstream economists did not follow their cue. However, in recent decades—partly under the influence of feminist economists who have questioned male-centered presumptions in economics—the profession has seriously turned its attention to issues pertaining to gender.

As a result, the literature on gender and its role in economics has been transformed. In the early days of formal analysis in this area, the labor supply activity of women was in the foreground and occupied almost the entire scope of the field. Recently, however, many aspects of women's economic lives have been investigated, and it has become clear that their labor supply captures only one facet—though a very important one—of their economic well-being. Today the numerous topics pertaining to the economics of gender that are being investigated almost defy classification. Nevertheless, it is possible to organize the research in a manner that communicates the core factors that determine the well-being of women. Furthermore, although it is impossible to present a single overarching model that addresses all the diverse issues, it is possible to communicate the sort of models that are best suited to analyzing them. These, in fact, are the ultimate twin goals of this book.

The problems confronting women in the developed and the developing worlds can be quite different, and so this book treats the core concerns in both. To a certain extent, some of the problems of women in poor countries today are similar to those that were faced by women in the rich countries when those countries were at the corresponding stage of development. However, culture matters, and so does history. Therefore, the lessons learned from the rich countries cannot be directly applied to poor countries. Nevertheless, at a broad level there are some similarities. For eons, the lives of women the world over have been dominated by decisions made by men—by patriarchy, in other words. In the rich countries patriarchy has certainly been retreating for at least a century, though it has hardly vanished. In the poor countries today, the pace of retreat has been much slower. In this book we shall see how crucially important economic opportunities for women are in undermining patriarchy. However, although economic development certainly improves the condition of women, it cannot by itself eliminate the gender differences in outcomes.[2]

---

[2] See Duflo, E. (2012), "Women Empowerment and Economic Development," *Journal of Economic Literature* 50, pp. 1051–1079.

This book is set out in four modules. In the first module ("Fundamental Matters," comprising Chapters 2 and 3), we deal with core mechanisms—the economic, psychological, and social factors that determine gender differences in behavior. In the second ("Gender in Markets," Chapters 4–6), we discuss how gender plays out in market activities. In the third ("Marriage and Fertility," Chapters 7–9), we discuss gender issues pertaining to the economics of marriage and family. And finally, in the last module ("Empowering Women," Chapters 10 and 11), we discuss what enhances the autonomy of women in their struggle for equality with men. In the rest of this chapter, I outline with a broad brush the sorts of issues that are dealt with in depth in the rest of this book.

When economic outcomes are different for women than for men, not all of these may be due to differences in the constraints they face, the skills they possess, or the discrimination they may encounter. It is conceivable that, in similar circumstances, the economic behavior of women may differ from that of men. For example, in the context of negotiations, Linda Babcock and Sara Laschever (2003) have documented the fact that women, in contrast to men, frequently receive less because they don't ask for more.[3] This can have serious long-term consequences. A lower starting salary would contribute to a substantial wage gap in a few decades even if salaries were to subsequently increase at the same rate. Whether women have different attitudes and behaviors in the economic realm and, if so, whether they respond to the way they are viewed and how this works to their disadvantage, is the subject matter of Chapter 2. In particular, we shall discuss the role of nature and nurture (including socialization) in determining behavior.

A large part of the gender gap in average wages is due to the fact that, across the world, the top executive positions are occupied mostly by men; relatively few women find their way to the top. See Figure 1.1 for the share of women on the boards of directors of publicly traded companies in the three dozen or so rich countries of the world, which belong to the Organisation for Economic Co-operation and Development (OECD).[4] The OECD average, shown in black (as opposed to gray), is a mere 10%. Norway owes its relatively high proportion of women on boards to legislation that mandated a minimum proportion that is very high by OECD standards.

We would expect that these top positions would be determined by competition among potential candidates based on their past performance. If it turns out that women are averse to this sort of competition, they will stay out of the fray and, naturally, will not be chosen for these positions. If this is

---

[3] Babcock, L., and S. Laschever (2003), *Women Don't Ask: Negotiation and the Gender Divide,* Princeton University Press, Princeton, NJ.

[4] The minimum sample size is 200 observations. The results for Austria, the Czech Republic, Estonia, Hungary, Iceland, the Slovak Republic, and Slovenia were dropped due to small sample sizes.

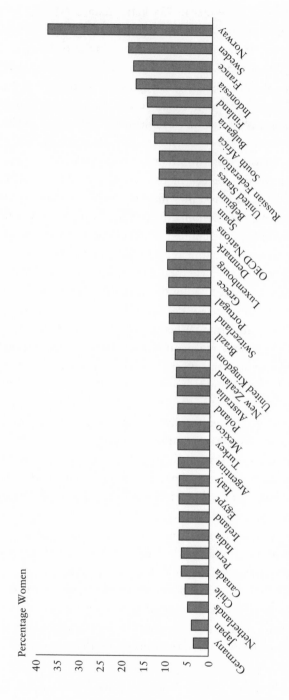

FIGURE 1.1 Proportion of women on the boards of publicly traded companies in the OECD countries, 2012 (percent)

Source: OECD (Organisation for Economic Co-operation and Development) (2012), *Closing the Gender Gap: Act Now*, OECD Publishing, http://dx.doi.org/10.1787/9789264179370-en, with permission.

the case, women may not make it to the top, not because they lack the skills, the drive, or the creativity but simply because they do not care for the means employed to select the winner. Is this true? In Chapter 2 we shall examine this issue and also survey the experimental evidence on questions of this nature. Furthermore, we shall examine gender differences in competitiveness or cooperativeness, both within single-sex groups and within mixed-sex groups. Interestingly, behavior (especially for women) can differ in the two scenarios and therefore lead to asymmetric economic outcomes.

A very important venue in women's struggle for gender equality is the household. Much of their time and energy are devoted to running their households. But how much say do they have in household decisions relative to their spouses? To what extent can they determine the goods and services on which their households' income should be spent? Can they single-handedly decide whether they should work in the labor market? And, if they do work outside their homes, how much control can they exercise over their earnings? How much control do they have (if any) over how many children they will have? Do they have any input into how much education their children should receive? Do they have the independence even to decide whether their children need to be taken to the doctor when they are unwell? The answers to some of these questions depend on whether the women in question live in developed countries or in developing ones. And the answers are quite sobering.

The core issue at the root of all of the questions raised in the paragraph above is this: what determines women's autonomy, independence, or status in their households? This is the subject matter of Chapter 3. The bargaining models used in economics are of great relevance to providing satisfactory answers. We shall first discuss the Nash bargaining model, which identifies the fundamental principle that women's status in marriage depends on how well they can do for themselves *outside* marriage.[5] We shall examine why this is so. The chapter also discusses why it is that males have the dominant say in marriage in most societies and how the changing outside options of women have been mirrored by their changing status in their households in recent times. In other words, the chapter suggests how patriarchy arises, how it is perpetuated through culture, and how it is undermined. The insights of bargaining theory will be useful in understanding many of the phenomena discussed in this book.

The second module ("Gender in Markets") examines how gender interacts with markets. Since World War II, the participation of women in the labor market has steadily increased in the rich countries, and that of men

---

[5] Throughout this book we use the term *marriage* quite loosely. It is used not to refer to a formal ceremony in a church or temple or to registration in a civil court but rather in the sense that two people have decided to form a family unit, even if it means only cohabitation. When we speak of marriage in the formal sense, the context will make it apparent.

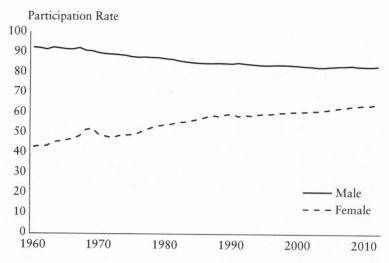

Participation Rate

FIGURE 1.2 Labor force participation rates of women and men in the OECD countries, 1960–2010

Note: OECD, Organisation for Economic Co-operation and Development.

has decreased slightly.[6] As a result, the gender gap in labor force participation (male minus female participation) has declined, though a gap still exists. The average trends in the OECD countries for the past five decades can be seen in Figure 1.2. There are many reasons that this gender gap in labor force participation has declined. Technological change has reduced the burden of housework and so has freed up the time of women (the traditional homemakers) to work in the labor market. Also, technology has opened up market opportunities for the sort of skills that women are more likely to possess than men.

Women have been having fewer children, so they have more time to work in paid employment. Divorce rates have been rising, so women have had to increasingly rely on their own earnings after divorce but also to engage in market work in anticipation of potential divorce. Another reason for the declining gender gap in labor force participation is that men have been gradually reducing their participation, partly because their spouses are earning more. For these and many more reasons, the participation of women in the labor market has increased in the developed world. In the poor countries, however, the decline in the participation gap is much gentler because women's participation rate has always been high (except in a few countries); poverty forces both spouses to generate labor income.

Despite the increasing labor force participation of women, it is nevertheless the case that their average earnings remain much lower than those

---

[6] By labor force participation we mean the proportion of able-bodied people in a group who are either working or actively looking for work.

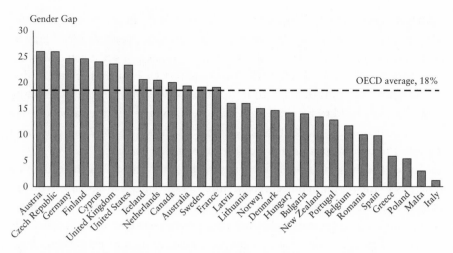

FIGURE 1.3 The gender gap in average earnings of full-time employees in OECD countries, 2009 or latest year available (percentage of gap)

Source: OECD (Organisation for Economic Co-operation and Development) (2012), OECD Family Database: Gender Gap in Average Earnings of Full-Time Employees [LMF1.5C], OECD, Paris, www.oecd.org/social/family/database, with permission.

of men. See Figure 1.3 for the gap in 2009 in the earnings of full-time employees in the OECD countries.[7] Of course there are many reasons why, on average, men and women might have different earnings: they can have different levels of skills or education, they can work in occupations with different wages, they may have different degrees of flexibility in their work schedules, they can work for different numbers of hours, and so on. One possible reason is that the wage rates are lower for women because the labor market discriminates against them. By *discrimination* we mean that different treatment is meted out to women than to men even when their relevant work characteristics (e.g., education, experience, and ability) are identical.

In Chapter 4 we ask whether women are discriminated against in the labor market. We shall discuss two forms of discrimination, the first of which is a "taste for discrimination" or prejudice, which was first analyzed by Gary Becker (1957), who argued on theoretical grounds that prejudice can persist only in the absence of competition in the labor market.[8] The second form of discrimination we shall discuss is called statistical discrimination and was first identified by Kenneth Arrow (1972) and independently identified by

---

[7] In Figure 1.3 the data for Estonia, Cyprus, the Slovak Republic, Latvia, Lithuania, Bulgaria, Luxembourg, Romania, Ireland, Slovenia, and Malta refer to all employees who work at least 15 hours per week. (Even though many of these countries are not displayed in the figure, their statistics have been used in computing the OECD average.)

[8] Becker, G. (1957), *The Economics of Discrimination,* University of Chicago Press, Chicago.

Edmund Phelps (1972).[9] This occurs when people do not have full information about an individual's relevant work characteristics (such as how likely he or she is to remain in the job) and use group averages as a substitute. We shall also discuss the empirical evidence for or against each of these types of discrimination. We shall then try to understand why women often express the view that they need to be more able than men employed in the same job. We discuss a theoretical model that shows how such perceptions can arise and identify the conditions under which they are indeed correct.

One of the most noticeable aspects of gender differences in the economic sphere is in the realm of entrepreneurship. Entrepreneurs are people who see market opportunities and go into business to fill perceived niches in the market in order to earn a profit. They are identified as self-employed people or as owners of firms and, therefore, as employers rather than as employees. A far higher proportion of entrepreneurs is male than female. Table 1.1 shows the prevalence of various types of entrepreneurship in male and female populations in the age group 18–64 years.[10] This table is derived from a survey of 42 countries around the world, divided into the three groups shown.[11] In the rich countries, entrepreneurship offers greater scope for increasing incomes and wealth than does salaried employment. Entrepreneurs comprise a much larger proportion of the wealthiest people in the United States, for example, than do salaried people.

It is usually the case that those who become entrepreneurs need access to credit. Relatively few people can start a business using entirely their own money. If access to credit differs by gender, this in itself may largely account for the gender gap in entrepreneurship. There are many reasons why credit may be less accessible by women, one of which is that, if they are less wealthy than men on average, they have fewer assets to offer as security ("collateral") to creditors when they borrow. The need for collateral arises in credit markets because creditors require some security that the money they lend will be

[9] Arrow, K. (1972), "Models of Job Discrimination," in *Racial Discrimination in Economic Life*, ed. A. H. Pascal, Lexington Books, Lexington, MA, pp. 83–102, and Phelps, E. S. (1972), "The Statistical Theory of Racism and Sexism," *American Economic Review* 62, pp. 659–661.

[10] Early-stage entrepreneurs are defined by the Global Entrepreneurship Monitor (GEM) as those involved in owning and managing a nascent business or one that has been in operation for 42 months or less. By contrast, established entrepreneurs are those involved in owning and managing a business that has successfully survived in the market beyond 42 months. (The GEM is an international consortium, and this report was produced from data collected in and received from 41 economies in 2007. I thank the authors, national teams, researchers, funding bodies, and other contributors who have made this possible.)

[11] High-income countries and areas are Austria, Belgium, Denmark, Finland, France, Greece, Hong Kong, Iceland, Ireland, Israel, Italy, Japan, the Netherlands, Norway, Portugal, Puerto Rico, Slovenia, Spain, Sweden, Switzerland, the United Arab Emirates, the United Kingdom, and the United States; low- and middle-income countries in Europe and Asia are China, Croatia, Hungary, India, Kazakhstan, Latvia, Romania, Russia, Serbia, Thailand, and Turkey; and low- and middle-income countries in Latin America and the Caribbean are Argentina, Brazil, Chile, Colombia, the Dominican Republic, Peru, Uruguay, and Venezuela.

TABLE 1.1 Proportions of male and female populations aged 18–64 who are engaged in various levels of entrepreneurial activity, by region and income, 2007 (percent)

Region and income	Owners engaged in early-stage entrepreneurial activity (nascent + new)		Established business owners		Overall business owners (nascent + new + established)	
	Male	Female	Male	Female	Male	Female
Low- and middle-income countries, Europe and Asia	11.7	7.6	8.2	4.6	19.9	12.2
Low- and middle-income countries, Latin America and Caribbean	19.6	14.4	12.2	6.6	31.8	21.0
High-income countries	8.2	4.3	7.9	3.6	16.1	7.9

Source: Allen, I. E., A. Elam, N. Langowitz, and M. Dean (2007), *Global Entrepreneurship Monitor: 2007 Report on Women and Entrepreneurship*, Table 2, http://www.gemconsortium .org/docs/download/281 (accessed July 4, 2013), with permission.

returned (with interest). So those without assets are disadvantaged in credit markets. Furthermore, it is conceivable that women may be discriminated against in credit markets, that is, they may be treated differently than men with the same economic characteristics. We address whether this is the case in Chapter 5.

In the past few decades there has been a sea change in the extent to which economies across the globe have become linked; they are now interconnected in myriad ways. This wave of globalization has had an effect on the well-being of women, mostly positive but sometimes negative. In Chapter 6 we examine two links through which globalization has impinged on the lives of women. The first is increased foreign trade. We shall ask how increased international trade has affected the well-being of women. Another effect of globalization on women works through foreign direct investment, in which multinationals from one country locate factories and subsidiaries in other countries for various reasons. We shall ask whether women are benefited or hurt by foreign direct investment. We shall also discuss some recent literature that has documented a very definite gender gap in attitudes toward trade liberalization: women are more protectionist toward the domestic economy than are men.

In Chapter 6 we shall discuss as well how globalization has contributed to undermining patriarchy in developing countries. By increasing employment opportunities for women, it has increased the bargaining power of women relative to men. Women, however, sometimes actively participate in protests against globalization. Why is this? Not all the effects of globalization on women are benign. One downside of globalization is that it has been accompanied by a substantial increase in the trafficking of women and children.

We discuss this phenomenon and the policy lessons that can be learned from the experiences of Scandinavian countries in attempting to curb this extreme form of exploitation of women and children.

We move on to the third module ("Marriage and Fertility") in Chapter 7. Marriage is a universal institution. The social, psychological, and economic conditions of married people differ from those of unmarried people. We first outline and discuss the evidence for these differences. We then ask why marriage arises spontaneously between individuals, resulting in families. We discuss an economic and an evolutionary theory of this phenomenon. Both explain why marriage is a widespread and persistent institution.

Then we address a series of very interesting questions about marriage: What economic forces lead to monogamy as the preponderant marital arrangement in most countries? Why do we observe dowries (various forms of wealth that brides' parents give their daughters when they marry) in some societies and bride prices (wealth that grooms' parents offer to brides' parents) in others? Are these related to the productivity of women in marriage relative to that of their husbands? What are the consequences of marriage in terms of the development of skills (known as human capital) that are useful in markets and in households? Married men are known to earn higher incomes than their unmarried counterparts with similar qualifications. Is marriage responsible for this income difference? Spousal violence occurs in most societies, and women are largely the victims. Why do men resort to physically assaulting their wives, and why do women remain in such abusive marriages? When marriages end in divorce, how do women fare afterward? These questions occupy us in Chapter 7.

The issue of fertility is naturally a matter of great importance to women, and not just for the obvious reason that it is women, not men, who give birth. A high fertility rate is one of the reasons that women's options have been constrained for ages. All the developed countries of today have gone through a transition from long periods of high fertility and high death rates to low fertility and low death rates. The effect of this "fertility transition" has invariably been to reduce the rate of population growth. Numerous economic benefits have accompanied this decline in fertility and mortality: greater ability to save money and greater freedom for women to pursue careers (earn higher incomes) and work longer hours, among many other benefits. In Chapter 8 we analyze the issue of fertility decline in the light of economic theory and examine why this decline has occurred and what it has meant for women. In particular, we examine what role the autonomy of women (that is, the extent to which they can act of their own volition) plays in this phenomenon. Many developing countries, too, have been undergoing the fertility transition in recent decades. Table 1.2 shows the trends in various parts of the world during the past four decades in the total fertility rate (which is roughly the number of children a women has during her reproductive life). Accompanying this transition has been an extremely disconcerting development: the ratio of

TABLE 1.2 Total fertility rates in various regions of the world, 1970, 1990, and 2011 (births per woman)

Region, country, or country group	1970	1990	2011
Least developed countries (UN classification)	6.75	5.95	4.19
Sub-Saharan Africa	6.69	6.25	4.88
Middle East and North Africa	6.62	4.85	2.65
South Asia	5.74	4.22	2.69
India	5.49	3.92	2.59
Latin America and Caribbean	5.30	3.21	2.18
East Asia and Pacific	5.17	2.50	1.75
China	5.51	2.34	1.58
Europe and Central Asia	2.82	2.33	1.80
OECD members	2.79	1.96	1.76
North America	2.46	2.06	1.87
United States	2.48	2.08	1.89
European Union	2.37	1.64	1.58

Source: World Bank (2013), Gender Statistics: (1) United Nations Population Division, World Population Prospects; (2) United Nations Statistical Division, Population and Vital Statistics Report (various years); (3) census reports and other statistical publications from national statistical offices; (4) Eurostat: Demographic Statistics; (5) Secretariat of the Pacific Community: Statistics and Demography Programme; and (6) U.S. Census Bureau: International Database, databank.worldbank.org/ (accessed July 8, 2013).

Note: OECD, Organisation for Economic Co-operation and Development.

male children to female children born has been increasing. See Table 1.3 for a snapshot of this ratio in 2011.

There is strong evidence that this increasing ratio of male to female births may be due to sex-selective abortion, among other things, because parents have a strong preference for male children. In countries where this preference is strong (for economic and cultural reasons), fertility decline may make it even more likely that, among the few children a couple now has, parents will think it is imperative that one or more be male. This discrimination against females is also pervasive after birth; they are often given less nutrition than their brothers, less education, and less frequent doctor visits in case of illness. As a result, in the population at large, the ratio of males to females is often much higher than in regions where such a preference for male children does not exist. This has led to the concept, coined by Amartya Sen, of "missing women," that is, women who should have existed but actually do not because of this male bias.[12] In Chapter 8 we shall also discuss the economics of this gender bias in the sex composition of children and its pernicious effects.

[12] Sen, A. K. (1990), "More Than 100 Women Are Missing," *New York Review of Books* 37, December 20.

TABLE 1.3 Sex ratios at birth for various regions of the world, 2011 (male births per 100 female births)

Region, country, or country group	Sex ratio
East Asia and Pacific	112.5
China	118.4
South Asia	107.2
India	108.0
Indonesia	105.0
Europe and Central Asia (developing countries only)	106.0
European Union	105.7
OECD members	105.4
Middle East and North Africa	105.1
North America	105.0
United States	104.9
Latin America and Caribbean	104.9
Sub-Saharan Africa	103.9
Least developed countries (UN classification)	103.8

Source: World Bank (2013), Gender Statistics: United Nations Population Division, World Population Prospects, databank.worldbank.org/ (accessed July 8, 2013).

Note: OECD, Organisation for Economic Co-operation and Development.

Technology has diverse effects on women's economic lives. The division of labor that we have witnessed for millennia across the globe whereby women were restricted either to housework or to work compatible with the raising of children was partly determined by biology—though the effect of socialization here cannot be overstated. What was feasible for women in the past was also constrained by the technology available to them. It has been only in recent times that technology, complemented by numerous social and economic developments, has afforded women the opportunities to have full-fledged careers at levels comparable to those of men. One of the most important technological breakthroughs from the point of view of affording flexibility for women was the contraceptive pill in the 1960s. This was accompanied by the institutional change of legal access to abortion. This change has given women far greater control over their bodies than before. In the United States, legal access to abortion began in most states with the landmark ruling of *Roe v. Wade* in 1973, and other developed countries have passed similar laws that have become increasingly liberal with regard to abortion. In Chapter 9 we study the effect of these birth control technologies on the lives of women in the developed and the developing worlds.

The impact of contraception on women in poor countries can be measured in a manner that is direct and compelling: by looking at maternal mortality (the deaths of mothers in pregnancy and childbirth). In some poor countries, the rate of maternal mortality is 20 times higher than that in the rich countries. Many of the pregnancies that result in maternal mortality are unwanted. So when contraception and abortion are made available, the incidence of maternal mortality declines substantially. This is an issue that we shall examine in Chapter 9.

One of the profound effects of contraception is that it has given women greater flexibility to choose when in their reproductive lives to have children. In the developed world, the choice of timing has enabled women to make greater investments in time-intensive professional degrees (like those in medicine or law) that give them opportunities for better careers. The ability to time the birth of children has also enabled women to acquire some work experience—which is a very important determinant of future salaries in their careers. Indeed, it has enabled women to have careers where previously they would have had none to speak of. Another far-reaching effect of the easy availability of contraception is that it has changed the bargaining power of women relative to their spouses. Women's ability to have independent earnings and careers has improved their outside options. Not only has this had implications in terms of who does the unpaid housework in a household, it has also influenced the amount of time devoted to paid work in the market by the couple. Put differently, the shift in bargaining power has changed the amounts of leisure enjoyed by men and women in marriage. We shall discuss these issues in Chapter 9.

In Chapter 10 we come to the final module ("Empowering Women"), an important focus of this book. In the past few decades it has become increasingly apparent that a large number of economic outcomes hinge on women's ability to exercise autonomy. One of the most fundamental steps toward achieving greater autonomy is acquiring the political right to vote. If women are denied this right, they are not even being recognized as independent persons whose opinions on governance and the allocation of public goods count. In most of the developed countries of today, the right to vote was acquired by women in the nineteenth and twentieth centuries. The acquisition of this right was hastened by women through activism and struggle, but the right was invariably won by peaceful means.

The attainment of women's suffrage itself had economic underpinnings. What economic factors led men to see that it was in their own self-interest to pass the legislation that gave women the right to vote? And once women earned this right, did governments start responding to their concerns? If so, how did the nature of government expenditures change? There is evidence that a "political gender gap" has been developing in Western democracies in recent decades: women tend to be more "left-wing" politically than men, which in the economic realm translates into women's desire for greater government participation in the economy than men. In terms of political

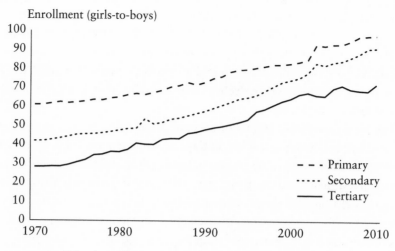

Enrollment (girls-to-boys)

FIGURE 1.4 School enrollment ratios of girls to boys in South Asia,
1970–2010

Source: World Bank (2013), Education Statistics: United Nations Educational,
Scientific, and Cultural Organization (UNESCO) Institute for Statistics, databank.
worldbank.org/ (accessed June 18, 2013).

behavior, this makes women more likely than men to vote for liberal candidates. Indeed, this left-wing bias among women appears to be so strong that
parents who have mostly daughters also tend to be more left-wing than parents who have mostly sons. In other words, parental concern for their children's well-being appears to mirror their children's (gendered) preferences.
These issues pertaining to women's empowerment through suffrage, their
political preferences, the government's response, and the economic consequences will preoccupy us in Chapter 10.

   In Chapter 11, the final chapter, we shall consider the kind of policies
that empower women and bring together the lessons we have learned earlier in the book. We shall also examine the evidence for these policies and
lessons. One of the most powerful ways of empowering women is through
education. In developing countries there is a substantial gap between the
educational attainments of women and men. See Figure 1.4 for the school
enrollment ratios of females to males (expressed as percentages) in South
Asia for the past four decades in primary, secondary, and tertiary education.[13] Although the trends over time have been in the right direction, the
ratios are well below 100%, with the highest for primary education and
the lowest for tertiary. Despite the inequity of this state of affairs, the benefits to society of having educated people are frequently higher for educated

---

[13]These are terms used by the International Standard Classification of Education. Loosely
translated, *primary* refers to primary-school education, *secondary* covers middle and high
school, and *tertiary* refers to education above the high school level.

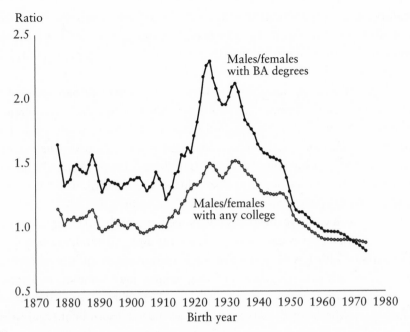

FIGURE 1.5 The ratio of male to female U.S. students who have any college and who have bachelor's degrees in cohorts born in 1876–1975

Source: Goldin, C., L. F. Katz, and I. Kuziemko (2006), "The Homecoming of American College Women: The Reversal of the College Gender Gap," *Journal of Economic Perspectives* 20 (4), pp. 133–156, with permission.

women. For example, child mortality declines when women are educated. Also, fertility rates decline more rapidly when women are educated because they then perceive a higher opportunity cost to having children. There are sound economic reasons for attempting to close the gender gap in education in poor countries.

In the developed world, the gender gap in education is almost nonexistent in the present day. In fact, female enrollments are higher than male even for tertiary education. For the United States see Figure 1.5, which is drawn from Claudia Goldin, Lawrence Katz, and Ilyana Kuziemko (2006).[14] It shows the ratio of males to females with any college at all and the ratio of those with B.A. degrees among the various cohorts born from 1870 through 1970. (This level of education would correspond to the tertiary level in the paragraph above.) This ratio was above 1 (and often well above 1) for those born before 1970; more males than females went to college. However, for those born after 1970, the ratio has fallen below 1; more women than men are going to college. This is also the trend in most of the OECD countries. This is largely

[14] Goldin, C., L. F. Katz, and I. Kuziemko (2006), "The Homecoming of American College Women: The Reversal of the College Gender Gap," *Journal of Economic Perspectives* 20 (4), pp. 133–156.

because women's participation in the labor market has increased, and this has made investing in women's college education worthwhile. The overt discrimination against educating female children seen in developing countries is not observed in the developed world.

Even in the case of education, however, women may be handicapped by poor access to credit because, as we have mentioned, they lack the collateral needed to borrow money. Making more credit available to women has to be part of any endeavor to empower women. In Chapter 11, using the example of the well-known Grameen Bank, we shall discuss how this may be accomplished. In this context, we shall also address the question of what exactly empowers women when they do gain access to credit.

Because women have been disadvantaged for millennia, an important question is whether they can be empowered through affirmative action in the labor market. This has been tried in a few countries, and it is a contentious issue because affirmative action favoring women may come at the expense of discriminating against men. In Chapter 11 we shall discuss this debate and examine whether affirmative action does indeed discriminate against the majority. We shall do so especially in the context of the United States. We shall also allude to the experience of other countries, like India, with such a policy.

Another arena in which affirmative action is potentially useful is the political realm. Women are severely under-represented in politics (Table 1.4). India's experience provides an excellent example of what may be accomplished when affirmative action is implemented in politics. In the early 1990s, India amended its constitution to reserve, among other positions, that of "village chief" for women in a third of the villages. This has been shown to have had some beneficial effects in terms of investment in the sort of public goods that women prefer, such as piped water.[15] In Chapter 11 we shall examine the evidence on the potential role of affirmative action in the political arena as a way of empowering women.

We shall also discuss the role of government expenditures on family-practice medicine and healthcare. These, we shall see, have a great impact on the well-being of women in developing countries by enabling the avoidance of unwanted pregnancies and the spacing of children, as well as facilitating investment in human capital. Finally, we shall discuss the effect of amending inequitable inheritance laws. Because inheritance provides assets that can be used as collateral, it can potentially increase the earning power of women. India's recent experiment with changing its inheritance laws to reduce discrimination against women in bequests provides a useful point of departure for analyzing such a policy. The experience also cautions us about the down-

---

[15] See Chattopadhyay, R., and E. Duflo (2004), "Women as Policy Makers: Evidence from a Randomized Policy Experiment in India," *Econometrica* 72, pp. 1409–1443.

TABLE 1.4 Percentage of national parliamentary seats in a single or lower chamber held by women, by region, 2011

Region, country, or country group	Percentage of seats
European Union	24.9
OECD members	24.2
United Kingdom	22.3
France	18.9
Latin America and Caribbean (all income levels)	23.0
Mexico	26.2
Sub-Saharan Africa (all income levels)	20.5
Least developed countries (UN classification)	20.4
South Asia	20.3
India	11.0
Indonesia	18.2
North America	20.1
United States	16.8
East Asia and Pacific (all income levels)	17.7
China	21.3
Europe and Central Asia (developing countries only)	16.1
Middle East and North Africa (all income levels)	10.1
Egypt	2.0

Source: World Bank (2013), Gender Statistics: Inter-Parliamentary Union (IPU), databank .worldbank.org/ (accessed July 8, 2013).

Note: OECD, Organisation for Economic Co-operation and Development.

side of changing policies without also implementing complementary policies to reduce the effects of a backlash. Recent research on the nature of property law, we shall see, shows that it even affects the prevalence of HIV among women in Sub-Saharan Africa.

These, then, are the sorts of issues this book deals with. Although the approach adopted is largely economic, I do not hesitate to draw on insights from other fields such as psychology, evolutionary psychology, political science, sociology, and gender studies. The subject matter of this book does not lend itself to a narrow perspective.

Before we launch into the first module, I should make clear that the partitioning of the book into modules is done purely for organizational convenience. There are substantial overlaps and interconnections between the modules. For example, what transpires in marriage (issues considered extensively in the third module) has important implications for what happens to women in markets (dealt with in the second module), and vice versa. Moreover, what happens in households is determined to a significant extent by the bargaining strengths of the spouses (an issue examined in the first module). And women's bargaining strength, of course, depends on whether they possess the factors that enhance their autonomy (studied in the fourth module). The themes of the four modules are thus intricately interlaced. The arrangement of the topics and the exposition, however, are such that the analysis and discussion at a given point in the book can be understood with the tools and concepts introduced earlier.

Fundamental Matters

CHAPTER TWO

Do Women and Men Behave Differently in Economic Situations?

I. Introduction

Market outcomes are very different for women and men, as we have briefly seen in the introduction to this book. This is true in developed countries as well as in developing countries. These differences, in part, are due to the different constraints that women and men face. Only women give birth, and, at least in the initial months of a child's life, they play a more important role than men. The raising of families has traditionally meant that women have withdrawn from the labor force for some time, and, as a result, the work experience they have accumulated has been less than that of men with similar levels of education and backgrounds. Because work experience improves productivity, women have tended to be paid less than men on this count. Besides, doing much of the housework has constrained women in terms of the time available for market work and the type of market work in which they have been able to engage. Often women have been subjected to different norms than men. For example, in developing countries women's movements are restricted, and frequently they are not allowed to work outside their homes. Naturally, externally imposed constraints like these have serious consequences for women's well-being.

In this chapter we study whether women and men *behave differently* in similar circumstances.[1] This difference in behavior could be due to socialization: women and men may be expected to play different roles in societies, and they may have been trained to behave differently from childhood. Or it is possible that evolutionary forces have shaped the preferences of women and

---

[1] A comprehensive and illuminating treatment of the subject can be found in Bertrand, M. (2010), "New Perspectives on Gender," *Handbook of Labor Economics*, Vol. 4b, Elsevier, Amsterdam, Chap. 17.

men differently, depending on what was most effective in the environment of our ancient past in promoting their respective genes. Whatever the reason, if women and men behave differently under identical economic conditions, the *outcomes* are likely different for them.

Marianne Bertrand and Kevin Hallock (2001) studied the compensation of top executives in the United States during the period 1992–97.[2] They argue that because all who qualify for such jobs are likely to be highly motivated, career-oriented, and able people, there is limited scope for unobservable differences between males and females to make a difference in the outcomes. Through the years they studied, women constituted only 2.4% of the top-level managers in corporations, and their compensation was about a third lower than that of men. A large part of this difference in compensation was due to the fact that women were less likely to occupy top positions in large firms (which also pay more). Also, women in the sample tended to be younger and to have less seniority than men. After the authors accounted for all the observable differences between women and men, the gender gap in average compensation that was still unaccounted for was only 5%. In other words, women and men with identical qualifications in identical top executive jobs received nearly the same incomes. The reasons that women received much lower average compensation were that they occupied fewer top positions (which tended to be in firms that were not large) and they were younger and had less seniority.

But why did women occupy top executive positions in only a small proportion of corporations? Is there a "glass ceiling" that prevents women from rising to the top? Apart from being younger and lacking seniority, it is possible that women's attitude toward competition is different than that of men. If intensely competitive screening processes determine successful applicants for top executive jobs, women may stay away from them. We shall pursue this explanation, among others, in this chapter.

More generally, there may be other behavioral differences between women and men. For example, it is possible that women are more altruistic than men. If so, in bargaining situations women may be at a disadvantage because they may be unwilling to drive as hard bargains as men might. Concern for others' positions could conceivably influence how strident a position they might be willing to take in bargaining situations. This tendency may be compounded by the fact that women in many cultures are socialized not to appear aggressive or pushy. It has also been proposed that women and men may have different responses to risky scenarios (ones in which outcomes are uncertain). In particular, it has been suggested that women may be more averse to risk than men. If this were true, it would mean that women would pass up lucra-

[2] Bertrand, M., and K. F. Hallock (2001), "The Gender Gap in Top Corporate Jobs," *Industrial and Labor Relations Review* 55, pp. 3–21.

tive opportunities because they are risky, whereas men might not. As a result, the average earnings of women—and, over time, their wealth—would end up being lower than those of men.

In this chapter we discuss such behavioral differences and examine the evidence for these various possibilities. If there are systematic gender differences in behavior, it means that, even if they have identical economic qualifications and experience, women and men will have different outcomes. The evidence we bring to bear on these issues comes mostly, but not entirely, from experiments done in laboratories. Males and females are brought into the laboratory and are placed in gaming situations under controlled conditions. By deliberately blotting out differences in things that are not the focus of investigation, researchers can identify gender differences in behavior when external circumstances are identical. This technique, in which social scientists adopt the methodology of physical scientists, offers valuable insights into gender differences in economic, psychological, and social behavior. It must be noted, however, that different experiments on behavior by gender sometimes seem to give contradictory results. In a survey of the experimental evidence, Rachel Croson and Uri Gneezy (2009) attributed this to the fact that women's behavior is much more sensitive to the *context* than is that of men.[3] Therefore, slight differences in the way the experiments are conducted can lead to different outcomes because women tend to pick up on these cues but men do not.

When it comes to explaining gender differences in economic outcomes, one fact that is underappreciated is that even ostensibly objective evaluation committees suffer from unconscious "observer biases" that put women at a disadvantage relative to men. Male and female evaluators might interpret the same data differently and so generate different outcomes. We discuss clear evidence of this and consider how such a bias might be reduced.

Finally, we discuss different approaches to explaining gender differences in behavior. In particular, is it nature that determines behavior, or is it nurture? Put differently, is behavior determined by evolution or by culture? We discuss three different approaches to gender issues: that of evolutionary biology and evolutionary psychology, that of feminism, and that of postmodern feminism. Because humans are largely products of evolution, clearly nature is important. But this only partly explains the pervasive oppression of women, which feminism aims to set right. We shall discuss compelling evidence that brings home the point that nurture is important, too. Through the process of socialization, culture plays a very important role in generating gender differences in behavior. This bolsters the view of postmodern feminism, which argues that most gender roles are not innate and are merely implementations of socially constructed notions.

---

[3] Croson, R., and U. Gneezy (2009), "Gender Differences in Preferences," *Journal of Economic Literature* 47, pp. 448–474.

II. Do Women Behave More Altruistically Than Men?

Do women exhibit behavior that is more altruistic than that of men? Do women care more than men for the well-being of others? If so, we would expect that, in situations that require bargaining, women would be less demanding than men. In wage negotiations with employers, for example, female employees might come away with less than otherwise identical male employees. It is important to understand whether this might be one of the reasons that economic outcomes are less favorable for women than for men.

To get an idea of gender differences in bargaining outcomes, consider a gaming scenario referred to as the ultimatum game. There are two ways to play this game. We consider these in turn.

The Ultimatum Game with Simultaneous Moves

First, consider the following setup. An experimenter contributes $10, and two people ("players") have to decide how to split this amount between themselves. Player 1, called the proposer, is told to write on a piece of paper how much she is willing to offer the other person. This is her strategy. The other player, Player 2, called the responder, is asked to write, without knowing the proposer's offer, what she deems the minimal acceptable offer; that is, she would reject any lower offer. This number is the responder's strategy.

The experimenter collects the two pieces of information from the respective players, reveals the information to both players, and declares the outcome of the game using the following rule. If the proposer's offer is at least as large as the responder's minimal acceptable offer, the players' incomes (payoffs) are determined according to the proposer's offer. If the proposer's offer falls short of the responder's minimal acceptable offer, the offer is rejected and *neither player gets anything*. The payoffs of the two players, in the latter case, are zero. Both players know the rules by which their payoffs are determined. In the above description of the game, the ultimatum game involves simultaneous choices (moves) by the players.

The essential feature of this version of the game is that the proposer does not know the responder's strategy, and vice versa; it is as if they chose their strategies simultaneously.

In such a circumstance, it is interesting to ask when neither player would have regrets about the strategy she adopted. There would surely be regrets if, given what the other player has chosen, a player could have improved her payoff by choosing something other than what she actually did. A pair of strategies such that neither player has such regrets, given the other player's strategy, is said to be a *Nash equilibrium*.[4] Let x denote the amount of money the proposer offers the responder and y denote the responder's min-

---

[4] Nash, J. (1951), "Non-Cooperative Games," *Annals of Mathematics* 54, pp. 286–295.

imal acceptable offer. Now consider the pair (x, y). If $x \geq y$, the offer of the proposer is at least as large as the minimal acceptable amount. The offer is accepted and the amount split, with x going to the responder and $\$10 - x$ to the proposer. If $x < y$, the offer of the proposer falls short of the minimal acceptable offer, and neither player gets anything.

Economists like to focus on Nash equilibria because in such outcomes neither player regrets what she has done, given the choice made by the other player. Nash equilibria are often used as *predictions* of what players would actually do in gaming situations.

We can think of lots of pairs of strategies that do not constitute a Nash equilibrium. For example, the pair ($\$4$, $\$3$) will be accepted, because the proposer's offer exceeds the responder's minimal acceptable offer. The responder will get $\$4$ and the proposer $\$6$. But this pair of strategies is not a Nash equilibrium. Given what the responder chooses, the proposer could do better by offering the lower amount $\$3$. The proposer will have regrets about her offer afterward. The pair ($\$4$, $\$5$), to take another example, will end up in a rejection, and neither player will get anything. Clearly each player could do better, given the strategy the other has chosen. For example, given the proposer's strategy, if the responder sets the minimal acceptable offer at $\$4$, both could be better off.

Now let's consider a pair of strategies that is a Nash equilibrium. The pair ($\$3.56$, $\$3.56$) is a Nash equilibrium, because neither player can do better given what the other has chosen. The proposer's offer will be accepted; the responder will get $\$3.56$ and the proposer $\$6.44$. Likewise, the pair ($\$3.57$, $\$3.57$) is also a Nash equilibrium, as is the pair ($\$6.23$, $\$6.23$). The ultimatum game, when modeled as a game in simultaneous moves, has many Nash equilibria. This is one of the difficulties when the game is played in this way, with the players making their choices simultaneously. Because there are *many* Nash equilibria, the players may target *different* Nash equilibria, and they might end up with regrets after the fact.

The above scenario is more or less the setup used by Sara Solnick (2001) to investigate gender differences in behavior in an experimental setting.[5] The game was played once between two players. In one scenario, the players were anonymous; in another, the genders of the people involved were known.

Solnick worked with 89 pairs of players; for 24 pairs the players were anonymous, whereas 65 pairs knew each other's genders. About 71% of the proposers offered to split the money evenly. In both scenarios, *the average offer of the proposer did not depend on the proposer's gender* ($\$4.67$ for male proposers and $\$4.67$ for female). But *the gender of the responder mattered*. As responders, males got better offers—especially from females.

[5] Solnick, S. (2001), "Gender Differences in the Ultimatum Game." *Economic Inquiry* 39, pp. 189–200.

Solnick found the following:

(a) *As proposers,* both men and women made *lower* offers if the responder was a woman. Male proposers offered $4.73 to male responders, on average, but only $4.43 to female responders. Female proposers offered $5.13 to male responders, on average, but only $4.31 to female responders.

(b) *As responders,* both women and men declared *higher* minimal acceptable offers if the proposer was a woman.

Solnick found that, among all possible pairings, there were more rejections (and therefore, neither player got anything) in female–female pairings. As a result, in such pairings females received the lowest average earnings. Males did well in male–female pairings.

When players' genders were unknown, males and females earned the same on average. When genders were known, men's average earnings as proposers were around 14% more than women's earnings. As responders, men's average earnings were around 18% more than women's. Solnick argues that both men and women believed that women would accept a smaller amount than men, and so women were offered less. Thus, in the experimental setting, men ended up earning more than women.

The Ultimatum Game with Sequential Moves

It is possible to play the ultimatum game as a situation involving not simultaneous but sequential moves. In this case, the proposer makes an offer that is made known to the responder and the latter decides whether to accept the offer or to reject it. If the responder accepts it, the $10 is split as proposed, and if it is rejected, neither player gets anything. The difference between this and the previous setting is that here the responder knows the strategy chosen by the proposer.

Catherine Eckel and Phillip Grossman (2001) experimented with this sort of setup of the ultimatum game.[6] They chose players of both sexes; in some rounds of the game, both players were of the same sex; in others, they were mixed. The players knew the sex of the person they were matched with but not the precise identity of the person (there were many people of each sex in the room). Each person played eight games but with different players. Because the identity of a player's partner changed from one round to the next, it was not possible for a player to establish a reputation for a particular sort of behavior. Nor could a player punish or reward rivals for their behavior in previous rounds of the game.

---

[6] Eckel, C., and P. Grossman (2001), "Chivalry and Solidarity in Ultimatum Games," *Economic Inquiry* 39, pp. 171–188.

In the sequential ultimatum game, if the proposer offers an amount $x > 0$, a rational responder will accept it because by rejecting the offer the responder gets nothing (as does the proposer). If the offer is $x = 0$, the responder will be indifferent between accepting and rejecting because in either case the responder gets nothing. In this case, suppose the responder opts to accept. Theory thus predicts that in the (sequential) ultimatum game we will observe the proposer take almost everything and offer almost nothing to the responder.

Eckel and Grossman found that offers that were consistent with the theoretical prediction were rejected with certainty. The rejection percentages for offers were 59% for $1.00, 21% for $1.50, 2% for $2.00, and 0% for higher offers.

Why were offers close to $0 rejected? One can offer a simple explanation.[7] Evolution has conditioned us to think in *relative,* not absolute, terms. In other words, what each of us considers acceptable is not an amount considered in isolation but how this compares with what others get. Why did nature hard-wire us like this? There are strategic reasons, which we need not go into much detail about. Basically, people who gauge their well-being in relative terms behave more aggressively than those who do not. As a result, in some gaming situations the former do better (that is, garner more resources) than the latter. Because they have more resources, they can have more children and also ensure that more of them survive. In other words, their genes will find greater representation in future generations. So, to the extent that behavior is genetically determined, behavior motivated by *comparisons* becomes an intrinsic part of human nature.[8] This would be an evolutionary psychologist's view of why status—which is all about relative positions—matters so much to us.

Why should this tendency lead one to reject small offers in the ultimatum game? Suppose that the responder, Player 2, has a utility function U_2. Further, suppose that this coincides with the income, y_2, the player receives. By rejecting an offer, the responder gets zero income and zero utility. So any positive offer will be accepted. But now suppose that the utility depends on the responder's income and also *negatively* on the income, y_1, of the proposer (Player 1). Suppose now that $U_2 = y_2 - wy_1$, where w is positive and measures the "weight" or extent to which the other player's income affects Player 2's well-being. If $w = 0$, the responder does not care what the proposer gets; if $w = 1$, the responder looks at the difference between his or her income and

[7] See Eaton, B. C., and M. Eswaran (2003), "The Evolution of Preferences and Competition: A Rationalization of Veblen's Theory of Invidious Comparisons," *Canadian Journal of Economics* 36, November, pp. 832–859.

[8] This is the process of natural selection that is described in more detail in Section VI of this chapter.

the proposer's. In general, we expect w to lie between 0 and 1. As long as $w > 0$, the utility of a player reflects status concerns because that player is valuing his or her income relative to that of the other.

Let us suppose, for the sake of argument, that $w = 1/3$. If the responder rejects the proposer's offer, both receive zero income and the responder's utility is zero. If the proposer keeps $9.00 and offers $1.00, and if the responder accepts the offer, his or her utility is $1 - (1/3) \times 9 = -2$, which is less than the utility of rejecting the offer. So the responder will reject it. In fact, one can verify that the responder will definitely reject all offers less than $2.50. The reason is not gender dependent, though it may be true that the weight w depends on gender.

Does this mean that the reasoning used to arrive at the theoretical prediction of the outcome of the ultimatum game is wrong? No, it does not. It means only that we are attributing the wrong objective to players by assuming that they maximize their own incomes. If we attribute a different objective but use the same principles outlined above, we will predict a different outcome to the ultimatum game.

Now let's get back to gender differences in behavior. Eckel and Grossman, like Solnick, find that there is not much difference between men and women in the role of proposers. The average offers in their study are 36.5% and 38.5% of the total amount for men and women, respectively, whereas it is 46.7% and 46.8% in Solnick's study. Why is the average offer much lower in Eckel and Grossman's study? It is probably because of the *sequential nature* of the game. In the simultaneous-move scenario, the outcome depends on both players' actions. In the sequential-move scenario, responders have full control of the final outcome when it is their turn. If responders turn down a positive offer, they get nothing, and they alone decide whether that will be the case. Because proposers know that responders will be reluctant to give up a positive payoff in exchange for a zero payoff, their offers are lower.

Eckel and Grossman, too, find that proposers of both sexes make lower offers on average when the responders are women. In Solnick's study, men and women as responders received 44% and 37%, respectively, of the total amount, whereas in Eckel and Grossman's the corresponding figures were 49% and 38%.

The average rejection rates are similar: 12% in Solnick's study and 13% in Eckel and Grossman's. However, in the former the offers made by women were rejected more often than those made by men, whereas in the latter the reverse was true. In fact, in Solnick's, woman-to-woman offers were rejected most often (23% of the time); in Eckel and Grossman's, these were rejected least often (3% of the time). It appears that when the ball is entirely in their court, as in the sequential game, women are more accommodating than men. Eckel and Grossman interpret this as showing that women are more cooperative than men. And perhaps they are seen as such, and so they receive lower offers as responders. But when the moves are simultaneous, in some sense they have less control over the outcome because they have less opportunity to be more accommodating.

Eckel and Grossman point out that there are some important differences between their study and Solnick's. One is that, in the simultaneous-move setup, neither player knows the outcome. The players are subject to both risk and the possibility of exploitation—risk because the other player's strategy is unknown and so may come as an unwelcome surprise and exploitation because after the fact a player may feel that he or she offered too much or accepted too little. In the sequential game, in contrast, the responder knows what the outcome is going to be because he or she determines it. There is neither any risk nor any scope for feeling exploited. And this difference between the experimental setups may lead to different outcomes if men and women respond differently to risk and the possibility of exploitation. One game that avoids this difficulty is the dictator game, which we now briefly consider.

The Dictator Game

Catherine Eckel and Phillip Grossman (1998) also performed experiments using the dictator game.[9] In this game, the proposer actually decides how much to allocate to each player. The responder has no role, really, because the proposer is a dictator. Furthermore, because responders do not get to make choices, their attitudes toward risk do not matter. An experiment involving the dictator game may be a good way of getting at gender differences in altruism.

In this game Eckel and Grossman had the proposer (Player 1) split $10 between himself or herself and Player 2. The dictator did not know the sex of the other player, who was in a different room. Half the dictators were women, the other half men.

One would expect to see the proposers being less generous than in the ultimatum game because in the latter they have to worry that a low offer may be rejected. In the dictator game, there is no such concern. Sure enough, Eckel and Grossman found that the contributions were much lower in the dictator game. The overall average contribution in the dictator game was $1.21 (out of the $10). The contribution of women was $1.61, whereas that of men was $0.82. Women were twice as generous as men. The authors show that this difference is significant in a statistical sense. In other words, it is highly unlikely to have been a freak random result that obtained in the sample even though there was no underlying difference in the generosity of the genders.

When the confounding factors of the ultimatum game (like risk) are eliminated, women are seen to be more generous than men. But we have to keep

[9] Eckel, C., and P. Grossman (1998), "Are Women Less Selfish Than Men?: Evidence from Dictator Games," *Economic Journal* 108, pp. 726–735.

in mind that this is a relative statement; a contribution of $1.61 (16% of the total) is not terribly generous but is generous compared to the average contribution of men (8% of the total). Both of these contributions are very far from the $5.00 mark that would constitute the ideal of "treating one's neighbor as oneself."

The Prisoners' Dilemma Game

We can gain more insight into gender differences from what is known as the prisoners' dilemma game.[10] This most famous of all gaming situations describes a whole host of social and economic problems (such as overfishing, global pollution, the buildup of nuclear arms, or shirking in the workplace—the list is almost endless). This is an example of a scenario in which all people individually do what is best for themselves but the outcome is bad for all; the outcome could have been better for all concerned if they had not behaved so selfishly.

The reason this game is interesting in the present context is that the outcome depends on the degree of selfishness of the players. If women and men have different degrees of altruism, it is conceivable that the outcome (the Nash equilibrium) will be better for one gender. Let's see why.

Suppose that two players simultaneously choose an action, which can be either C (a cooperative action) or D (a deceptive action). The monetary payoff to each player, in general, will depend on the actions of both players. In each pair of numbers in Table 2.1, the first number represents the material payoff to Player 1 and the second number that to Player 2. If the pair of actions chosen is (C, D), where the first action is Player 1's and the second Player 2's, the former receives a payoff of 1 and the latter a payoff of 6. If they both choose D, they each get 2, but if they both choose C, they each get 5.

Assume, first, that each player is interested in his or her own monetary payoff. Suppose that the players play this game only once. What will be the Nash equilibrium in this game? To determine this, let us put ourselves in the shoes of Player 1 first. If she believes that Player 2 will choose C, her best response will be to choose D because that will yield her a payoff of 6 instead of 5 (which is what she would have gotten had she also chosen C). Player 2, unfortunately, will be deceived—she will get a payoff of 1. If, on the other hand, Player 1 believes that Player 2 will choose D, it is in Player 1's self-interest to also choose D, because this will yield her a payoff

---

[10] The game has received its name from the following scenario. Two partners in crime are apprehended and are kept in separate jail cells. The police offer each criminal a very light jail term if he informs on his partner and provides them with more evidence than they currently have. If he informs, however, it will mean a stiffer sentence for the partner if the latter doesn't also inform. If neither criminal confesses, they do not get away scot-free but will end up with an easy jail term because the police evidence is limited. This puts each prisoner in a dilemma: should he or shouldn't he inform on his partner?

TABLE 2.1 Monetary payoffs in a prisoners' dilemma game

| | | Player 2 | |
		C	D
Player 1	C	(5, 5)	(1, 6)
	D	(6, 1)	(2, 2)

of 2 as opposed to 1 (which is what she would have gotten had she chosen C). Because it is in Player 1's self-interest to choose D irrespective of what she believes Player 2 will choose, we say that D is a *dominant strategy* for Player 1. Since the game is perfectly symmetric, by putting ourselves in the shoes of Player 2 we can see that D is a dominant strategy for her, too.

The outcome of this game will clearly be the pair of actions (D, D), and each player will receive a monetary payoff of 2 in this outcome. This outcome is also a Nash equilibrium.[11] Both players would have been better off had they each chosen C. But the pair (C, C) will not obtain because it is in the self-interest of each player to choose D if she believes the other will choose C. We say that the outcome (D, D) of the prisoners' dilemma is *Pareto inefficient*.[12] This game offers a simple demonstration of why it is often the case that actions that are rational from the individual point of view end up hurting everyone collectively.

How does altruism figure into the equilibrium of the game? Suppose that we allow for the possibility that each player cares for the welfare of the other. Instead of assuming that each player will maximize her own monetary payoff (income), suppose that she maximizes her utility, which we take to depend not only on her own monetary payoff but also on that of the other player.[13] Let us denote the level of altruism of both players by the number a, the meaning of which will become clear shortly. Suppose that Player 1's utility is given by $U_1 = y_1 + a y_2$ and that of Player 2 by $U_2 = y_2 + a y_1$, where y_1 and y_2 denote the respective monetary payoffs of Players 1 and 2.[14] If $a = 0$, it means that each player cares only about her own monetary payoff; there is no distinction between monetary payoff and utility. At the other extreme, if $a = 1$, it means that each player feels that a

[11] The strategy pair (D, D) is clearly a Nash equilibrium because neither player regrets doing what she did, given that the other player's choice is D.

[12] A situation is said to be *Pareto efficient* if there is no way to improve the well-being of all people concerned. Because here there is a way of improving the outcomes of both players, it is Pareto inefficient.

[13] This follows the procedure first suggested by Brew, J. S. (1973), "An Altruism Parameter for Prisoners' Dilemma," *Journal of Conflict Resolution* 17, pp. 351–367.

[14] In principle, we could allow the degree of altruism to be different for the two players. But for simplicity we assume here that they are the same.

TABLE 2.2 Utility payoffs in a
prisoners' dilemma game

		Player 2	
		C	D
Player 1	C	(10, 10)	(7, 7)
	D	(7, 7)	(4, 4)

dollar going to the other player is just as good as a dollar coming to herself. In general, we expect that a takes on a value between 0 and 1—that is, they are not entirely selfish; nor are they so altruistic that they consider their neighbors as themselves.

If the players maximize their *utility* instead of their monetary payoffs, what will the Nash equilibrium be? The answer depends on the degree of altruism, a. To see this, first observe that if $a = 0$ the equilibrium will obviously be the same as before because each player perceives no difference between monetary payoff and utility. Instead, if the degree of altruism is $a = 1$, Table 2.2 displays the combination of utility payoffs for the various possible actions.

If Player 1 thinks that Player 2 will choose C, she herself will also choose C because it will give her a utility of 10 units as opposed to 7 units (which is what she would get if she chose D). Similarly, if she thinks that Player 2 will choose D, she will again choose C because she will get 7 units as opposed to 4 units (which is what she would get if she chose D). Thus, action C is a dominant strategy for Player 1. Likewise, C is a dominant strategy for Player 2. The Nash equilibrium in this case is (C, C). This outcome will give each player a utility of 10 and, from Table 2.1, a monetary payoff of 5. The outcome is Pareto efficient.

We see that altruism can generate a much better outcome for each player in the prisoners' dilemma game. Because numerous social and economic interactions have a structure analogous to that of this game, it follows that the consequences of altruism can be quite beneficial, far-reaching, and important. One may argue that assuming $a = 1$ is a very strong requirement: who among us can dare to say that we treat our neighbors as ourselves? Fortunately, to support the outcome (C, C) as a Nash equilibrium we do not need to meet such a high standard of altruism. We require a player to receive higher utility by playing C instead of D when the other player chooses C, that is, we require that $5 + 5a > 6 + a$, that is, $a > 0.25$. Thus, when the degree of altruism exceeds a "sufficiently high" level (the critical level being $a = 0.25$ in this example), the Nash equilibrium of the prisoners' dilemma game will be (C, C). It will be Pareto efficient not only in terms of utility but also in terms of monetary payoffs.

Psychologists have done experiments to test whether altruism induces people to play more cooperatively in the prisoners' dilemma game. Daniel Batson and Tecia Moran (1999), for example, conducted such an experiment among 60 undergraduate women, some of whom were induced to feel empathy for their partners in the game.[15] The presumption here—supported by prior evidence—is that empathy for another person in difficulty induces altruism toward her. The authors found that the extent of cooperation in the prisoners' dilemma was higher among participants in whom a high degree of empathy was induced than among those in whom either no empathy or a low degree of empathy was induced.

In games in which the players make their choices sequentially, it is often the case that the player who chooses first has an advantage over the player who follows. For example, in the sequential version of the ultimatum game the proposer could appropriate almost the entire amount of money available. One advantage of the prisoners' dilemma game is that the players make their choices simultaneously, thereby eliminating any advantage or disadvantage that obtains when the moves are in sequence. Furthermore, the payoffs in the prisoners' dilemma game are symmetric: exchanging the roles of Players 1 and 2 merely exchanges their payoffs. That is, their payoffs depend only on the pair of actions chosen and not on who the players are. As a result, this game is ideally suited to examining gender differences in gaming behavior.

Andreas Ortmann and Lisa Tichy (1999) present some experimental results on gender differences in the outcomes of the prisoners' dilemma game using a table of payoffs somewhat analogous to those shown in Table 2.1.[16] They had participants play several rounds of the game in an experimental setting but not with the same players. They were interested in examining the differences in the choices that women and men made. They found that, in the early rounds, women opted for the "cooperate" option more frequently than men (41% of the time, as opposed to 30%). However, over subsequent rounds women's cooperation rate fell and the difference between the rates for women and men declined. Why was this? The authors discovered that women's and men's responses to previous experiences in the game were similar. For example, the experience of playing cooperatively and being cheated on produced similar reactions in women and men in subsequent rounds. So although women may have initially approached the game more cooperatively than men, over time their experiences aligned their behaviors.

Experiments on an interesting variant of the prisoners' dilemma game were

[15] Batson, C. D., and T. Moran (1999), "Empathy-Induced Altruism in a Prisoners' Dilemma," *European Journal of Social Psychology* 29, pp. 909–924.

[16] Ortmann, A., and L. K. Tichy (1999), "Gender Differences in the Laboratory: Evidence from Prisoners' Dilemma Games," *Journal of Economic Behavior and Organization* 39, pp. 327–339.

performed by Mark van Vugt, David Cremer, and Dirk Janssen (2007).[17] They examined how people's behavior differed when they acted as *individuals* and when they belonged to a *group*. Undergraduate students were recruited from the University of Southampton in England and were randomly assigned to either the individual or the group experiment. Each team comprised six participants. Each participant was given £2 (roughly $3.30 at the time of writing) that he or she could either keep or contribute in entirety to a group investment. If the group contributed at least £8 in total (that is, if at least four group members contributed), the investment paid off: each group member got an additional £4, whether or not he or she contributed. If the group's total contribution fell short of £8, no additional money was given out and the contributors lost what they had contributed. In this scenario, contributing was a "public good," which means that one person's contribution generated benefits for all the people in the group. But the noncontributors could get a free ride (provided that enough others contributed) because they could receive an additional £4 without sacrificing anything. The structure of this game, therefore, is exactly like that of the prisoners' dilemma except that there are now more than two players.

The participants were told that identical experiments were being conducted simultaneously at 10 other English universities (as, indeed, they were), and these universities were individually named. The difference between the group-oriented experiment and the individual-oriented one was this: In the former, the participants were told that the experimenters were looking to see how the *groups* in the various universities performed in the experiments. In the latter, they were told that the experimenters were looking to see how the *individuals* in the various universities performed in the experiments. What the authors of the study found was that the proportion of men who contributed was substantially higher in the group-oriented experiment than in the individual-oriented one. For women, however, there was not much difference in the two scenarios, though on average their contribution was higher than men's.

What these experiments reveal is that men seem to behave more cooperatively when there is *intergroup* competition than when there is none. Women's degree of cooperation, on the other hand, is less sensitive to intergroup competition. The authors suggest an evolutionary argument for this type of behavior difference: In our evolutionary past, men were mostly responsible for securing resources for their tribes by competing with other tribes, for protecting their tribes in warfare against other tribes, and so on. Women's contributions were less dependent on intertribe competition. Nature seems to have genetically programmed males to be more generous when the group is under threat than when it is not.

---

[17] Van Vugt, M., D. Cremer, and D. Janssen (2007), "Gender Differences in Cooperation and Competition: The Male Warrior Hypothesis," *Psychological Science* 18 (1), pp. 19–23.

Hannah Bowles, Linda Babcock, and Kathleen McGinn (2005) have provided experimental evidence demonstrating that women negotiate harder when they are negotiating on behalf of others.[18] In fact, they negotiated remunerations that were 18% higher for others than for themselves; the corresponding number for men was only 0.5%. This difference could conceivably be due to gender differences in altruism. However, it is also possible that part of the difference arises because women are concerned about the backlash from being seen as exhibiting the male trait of self-promotion. Hannah Bowles, Linda Babcock, and Lei Lai (2007) provided evidence showing that, in an experimental setting, male evaluators more heavily penalized female candidates than male candidates for initiating negotiations for higher compensation.[19] Men's beliefs about how women *ought to behave* may condition women's behavior and induce them to be more reticent about asking for more.

As has already been pointed out, very few women make it to top positions like seats on the boards of directors of large corporations. Renee Adams and Patricia Funk (2012) investigated whether women who do make it to the top are just like the men who are at the top.[20] For this study they surveyed all the directors and CEOs of publicly traded companies in Sweden in 2005. They found that top executive women are different from men, even though they are different from women in the general population. In particular, women in top corporate positions emphasize benevolence more, and power and tradition less, than their male counterparts.

There is empirical evidence suggesting that psychological differences between women and men play an important role in earnings differences. Nicole Fortin (2008) examined, among other things, how gender differences in the attitudes toward money and work are related to earnings differences between men and women.[21] For this she followed respondents to a high school survey conducted in the United States in 1972, in which information on attitudes toward money and work, people and family, and so on, was gathered. Data on the wages of these individuals were subsequently collected when the respondents were in their mid-twenties and early thirties. Fortin found that there were indeed gender differences in attitudes: men valued money more, and women valued people and family more. These

[18] Bowles, H. R., L. Babcock, and K. L. McGinn (2005), "Constraints and Triggers: Situational Mechanics of Gender in Negotiation," *Journal of Personality and Social Psychology* 89, pp. 951–965.

[19] Bowles, H. R., L. Babcock, and L. Lai (2007), "Social Incentives for Gender Differences in the Propensity to Initiate Negotiations: Sometimes It Does Hurt to Ask," *Organizational Behavior and Human Decision Processes* 103, pp. 84–103.

[20] Adams, R., and P. Funk (2012), "Beyond the Glass Ceiling: Does Gender Matter?," *Management Science* 58, pp. 219–235.

[21] Fortin, N. (2008), "The Gender Wage Gap among Young Adults in the United States: The Importance of Money versus People," *Journal of Human Resources* 43, pp. 884–918.

differences were correlated in the expected manner with wages (positively when money was valued more, negatively when people and family were valued more). This can arguably be interpreted as the effects of gender differences in altruism. Alan Manning and Joanne Swaffield (2008) provide evidence from the labor market in the United Kingdom of the effects on wages of gender differences in psychology.[22] When men and women enter the labor market, there is virtually no gender gap in wages, but a decade or two later, a substantial wage gap emerges. The authors show that psychological gender differences (such as attitudes toward risk, competitiveness, self-esteem, and altruism) account for a small but discernible part of the gender difference in the U.K. data.

The discussion above focuses only on *differences* in altruism between women and men. The level of altruism is itself quite important, however, and women may have had a great role in instilling altruism in both males and females. One of the puzzles in biology has been why altruism exists at all in nature. By definition, altruism benefits someone else at a cost to oneself. In evolutionary terms, altruism facilitates the survival of the recipients and their progeny at the expense of the givers and their progeny. So how can altruism persist? Nature, which is completely amoral, should do away with altruism through the process of natural selection, as described later in this chapter. In other words, the very presence of altruism in humans is something that needs to be explained.

In her most recent book, *Mothers and Others*, Sarah Hrdy has argued that the most unique feature of humans relative to other primates is their capacity to empathize with others, share resources, and generally engage in cooperative behavior with them by reading their intentions and assessing common goals.[23] Her intriguing hypothesis, which she supports with evidence from diverse sources, is that modern humans came from an ape species that evolved cooperative breeding. That is, infants were taken care of not only by the mother (and the father, to a smaller extent) but also by several "alloparents" such as grandmothers, siblings, and cousins. This enabled women to have more children, which was important for the success of *homo sapiens* as a species. More importantly, this practice enabled children to depend on others for much longer periods and so to develop larger brains—which in turn enabled the evolution of the cognitive machinery that could read the minds of others, empathize with them, and so on. Thus, in Hrdy's view, alloparenting (mostly by females) is largely responsible for empathy and the unique cooperative aspects of humans although our most closely

---

[22] Manning, A., and J. Swaffield (2008), "The Gender Gap in Early-Career Wage Growth," *Economic Journal* 118, pp. 983–1024.

[23] Hrdy, S. B. (2011), *Mothers and Others: The Evolutionary Origins of Mutual Understanding*, Harvard University Press, Cambridge, MA.

related species, the chimpanzees, are highly self-serving. Women, then, may have played a huge role in generating altruism in *both* sexes, even if the differences in the altruism levels of women and men are small. This is a point worth bearing in mind.

Now that we have examined the evidence for gender differences in altruism, we move to consider whether there are gender differences in the proclivity for competition. These, too, can have an effect on the economic outcomes in the marketplace, and if these differences in proclivity are verified to be real, it is important to understand how these differences arise and what can be done to counter them.

III. Are Women Less Competitive Than Men?

As was pointed out in the introduction to this chapter, there are relatively few women in the United States in the top and high-paying executive jobs. (This is also true elsewhere in the world.) This is one reason that the average income of working women is lower than that of working men. There is usually stiff competition for these top jobs. Because the salaries and perks of such jobs are very attractive, there normally are many possible contenders for these positions. One would expect the outcome of this competition to be determined by the choice of the person who is most competent for a job. This is not to rule out the possibility, however, that it is not merit but nepotism or cronyism or some other factor that determines the outcome in some cases. For example, the person may be chosen because he is related to some high-ranking official who has a preference for blood relatives, because he comes with the recommendation of someone in an old boys' network that discriminates against participation by women, or because the selection committee is sexist.[24] Or it may be that the successful candidate is well connected in social networks comprising people who are on selection committees. Let us set aside such cases and suppose that the most competent person does get the job.

How do committee members determine the person they deem the most competent? They do this by comparing the past performances of the contenders. They rank the potential candidates for the job according to some presumably objective criteria that indicate the candidates' ability, dedication, creativity, and other traits. Then the best candidate is offered the prized job and the rest lose out. Economists refer to such situations as tournaments because usually in a tournament the winner takes all and the losers get nothing. In a tournament, a candidate is judged not by his or her absolute performance but by comparison with the performance of others. Competition

---

[24] On some evidence for this last point, see Wennerås, C., and A. Wold (1997), "Nepotism and Sexism in Peer-Review," *Nature* 387, pp. 341–343. We shall discuss this evidence in a later section of this chapter.

tends to bring out the utmost in people, and tournaments epitomize this sort of performance-maximizing scheme.[25]

What happens if, for some reason, women are predisposed to dislike competition? What if they are psychologically averse to putting themselves into situations in which they are pitted in competition with others? If top executive jobs are allocated by tournaments, women will be disproportionately ruled out from such jobs because they will tend not to apply. And this outcome will not arise because women are less able, less dedicated, or less creative but simply because the selection process induces them to stay away. It is important, therefore, to understand whether women and men have different attitudes toward competition.

Uri Gneezy, Muriel Niederle, and Aldo Rustichini (2003) performed experiments in a controlled setting to examine this issue.[26] They used the following setup. A number of women and men (who were students at an Israeli university) were given some simple tasks, the outcome of which determined how much they were paid (their payoff) in the experiments. The tasks entailed solving some mazes on computers. The measure of a person's output was how many mazes she solved in a given amount of time (15 minutes). First the players participated in an experiment in which their compensation was determined entirely by their own output. They were paid a piece rate of 2 shekels (roughly US$0.50) for each maze they solved. The experimenters found that there was not a significant difference in the average performances of women and men. Consequently, one was assured that the average level of ability was the same in the samples of men and women who participated.

Next the participants were placed in mixed-gender groups and were told that their compensation would be determined by a tournament. The winner would be the person who solved the maximum number of mazes, and she would receive 12 shekels for each maze she solved; the others would receive nothing. Each person was given information only about her own earnings. The experimenters found that, in moving from the piece-rate to the tournament setup, the average performance of men increased substantially; that of women, however, did not. As a result, there was a gender gap in the performance in the (competitive) tournament setting, though there was none in the (noncompetitive) piece-rate setting.

The extent of competition is not the only thing that changes when one moves from a piece-rate to a tournament setting. In the piece-rate setup, one's remuneration depends only on one's own performance (which is entirely under one's own control). In a tournament, there is a considerable amount of

---

[25] Of course they also provide a strong incentive to cheat, which is why Olympic aspirants are carefully tested for performance-enhancing drugs.

[26] Gneezy, U., M. Niederle, and A. Rustichini (2003), "Performance in Competitive Environments: Gender Differences," *Quarterly Journal of Economics* 118, pp. 1049–1074.

risk because one's income also depends on other people's performance (over which one has no control). If men and women react differently to risk, it is conceivable that their behavior will diverge when they go from the piece-rate to a tournament setting. Gneezy, Niederle, and Rustichini looked into this possibility and found that risk did not play an important role in explaining performance in these experiments. The appearance of a gender gap in performance in going from piece rates to tournaments, therefore, had to do only with the competition introduced by tournaments.

The authors repeated the tournament experiment with single-sex groups. They found that men's average performance was not different from that in the mixed-group tournament (which, recall, was significantly higher than in the piece-rate scenario). But women's performance in the single-sex tournament was significantly higher than in the mixed-group tournament (which, recall, was not significantly higher than in the piece-rate scenario). In other words, women seem to exercise themselves to compete with *other women* but not with men. In contrast, the performance of men improves as a result of competition—regardless of whether they are in single-sex or mixed-sex tournaments.

A gender gap in performance arises where none existed before as a response to competition, and this is *not* because men possess any greater ability than women. When the selection process for top executive jobs is through tournaments, therefore, women may be at a disadvantage.

Experiments along somewhat similar lines to those discussed above were conducted by Muriel Niederle and Lise Vesterlund (2007).[27] Here, after the participants first performed in piece-rate and tournament settings, they were given the option of choosing which of these two settings they wanted in the following rounds. More than twice as many men as women opted for the tournament. The authors found that, relative to the scheme that would have maximized their remuneration, too many women who were high performers opted for the (noncompetitive) piece rates and too many men who were low performers selected the (competitive) tournament. Women and men appeared to have had different assessments of their relative standing in their groups and, therefore, of their chances of success in tournaments. The authors asked the participants for their own perceptions of their relative ranking. (The actual relative ranking had not been revealed to them at that point.) They found that, although women and men were both more optimistic about their ranking than was warranted by their performance, men were far more so.[28] This overconfidence of men in their ability was partly responsible for their inclination

[27] Niederle, M., and L. Vesterlund (2007), "Do Women Shy Away from Competition? Do Men Compete Too Much?," *Quarterly Journal of Economics* 122, pp. 1067–1101.

[28] Among men, 75% thought they were the best in the group; among women, this proportion was 43%.

toward the tournament. Even after accounting for this overconfidence, however, there was still a gender gap in the proportion of women and men who chose the tournament. There seems to be something in the nature of the tournament that women innately find unpalatable and that induces them to stay away from such compensation schemes.

IV. Are Women More Averse to Risk Than Men?

Many believe that women dislike uncertainty more than men. If this is true, they may pass up risky opportunities that are very profitable in favor of safer options that are less profitable. If men and women differ in their propensities to tolerate risk, the earnings of men may be higher than those of women who are equally qualified and otherwise have identical economically relevant traits. Is it true that women are more averse to risk than men?

Before we try to answer that question, let's try to formalize a little more precisely the notion of aversion to risk. Suppose that an investment project (call it A) requiring an outlay of $100 becomes available. The revenue that Project A will generate is uncertain. Suppose that it will generate $80 with a probability of 0.5 and $160 with a probability of 0.5. If many people invest in A, roughly half will receive $80 and half will receive $160. The average (or expected) revenue generated will be 0.5 × $80 + 0.5 × $160 = $120. The *expected return* on this investment is defined as (expected revenue – outlay)/outlay. For Project A, this will be ($120 – $100)/$100 = 0.20 or 20%.

Consider another investment opportunity, say Project B, which also requires an outlay of $100 but will generate revenues of $120 with certainty. The return on investment in this project will also be 20%.

When investors are asked to choose between Projects A and B, they usually choose B. The reason is that, though the expected returns to the projects are both 20%, the return in Project B is free of any risk. Project A may generate $80 or $160, but Project B will generate $120 for sure. When the expected returns are the same, most people feel that it would be foolish to choose an option that is risky. Most people (women *and* men) are typically averse to risk. To induce them to opt for the risky project, they have to be offered a higher expected return than what they will receive in their safer option. It is generally the case that people expect to be compensated for the risk they bear by an increase in expected returns. So the expected return on Project A would have to be higher than 20% for them to select it in favor of Project B. How much higher? That depends on how averse to risk people are. A person who is indifferent to risk would not require a higher return. Such a person is referred to as being risk neutral.

There is a simple measure of how one can capture the extent to which people are averse to risk. This is the concept of *certainty equivalent*. Consider a scenario in which people are in such a position that they are forced to choose the risky Project A. Suppose that we start by offering them an alternative, risk-free project (call it Project C) that requires the same outlay of $100 but offers them revenues that are *certain*. If these certain revenues are $120, people who are averse to risk will naturally prefer Project C (because this is the same as Project B in this case). Then we gradually reduce the revenues on the risk-free alternative, C, until they are indifferent between Project A and this risk-free alternative. Suppose that when Project C offers revenues of $114 for sure, a person is indifferent between A and C. Then $114 represents the person's *certainty equivalent* of Project A.

The difference between $120 and $114 (that is, $6) is the amount of money that the person is willing to forgo from the expected revenue of Project A in order to be rid of the risk associated with the outcome of this project. This difference ($6 in this example) is defined as the person's *risk premium* and is a measure of the extent to which the person finds uncertainty unpleasant. A person who is more averse to risk will be willing to forgo more than $6 to be rid of the risk. The lower a person's certainty equivalent of a given project (and therefore the larger the risk premium), the greater is that person's aversion to risk. People who can tolerate more risk have lower risk premiums. Risk-neutral persons will have risk premiums of $0 because they are indifferent to risk.

The aversion to risk that people normally feel explains why they buy insurance. No matter how carefully they may drive their cars, for example, they may still get into accidents due to circumstances beyond their control. This exposes them to risk. When they purchase insurance, what they are doing is paying a fixed fee (the insurance premium) to the insurance company, which then takes the responsibility of fixing the damage to their cars in the event of accidents.[29] The payment is for the service of ridding them of the exposure to risk. The idea is the same when people buy house insurance, health insurance, and so on.

The risk to which a situation exposes people also depends on how wealthy they are. Wealthier people find a given risk less unpleasant. In other words, aversion to risk tends to decline with wealth. One reason for this is that wealth enables them to withstand ups and downs in their fortunes.[30] An entrepreneur who runs a risky business enterprise may earn a lot in one year but very little in the next. If she has wealth, she might be less intimidated by the riskiness of her enterprise. This is because she can cope with the variabil-

---

[29]This assumes that the driver is fully insured. Usually, however, insurance companies require a deductible that the driver has to pay; the company pays for damages in excess of the deductible. The reason for the deductible is to induce the driver to exercise caution while driving; full insurance would invite reckless driving.

[30]This idea is developed in Eswaran, M., and A. Kotwal (1990), "Implications of Credit Constraints for Risk Behavior in Less Developed Economies," *Oxford Economic Papers* 42, pp. 473–482.

ity in her income by falling back on her wealth to sustain her in the years when her income turns out to be low.

A study by Nancy Jianakoplos and Alexandra Bernasek (1998) using data from the United States examined the financial decisions of women and men to see if there were gender differences in their choices.[31] In particular, the authors examined the proportion of their wealth that people invested in risky assets as opposed to safe assets. For the reasons given above, we would expect people to opt for risky assets only if they offer expected returns that are high enough to offset the riskiness of these assets. We have also argued above that aversion to risk declines with wealth; so, as one gets wealthier, one should hold a higher proportion of one's wealth in risky assets with high expected returns. The authors find that, although aversion to risk does indeed decline with wealth for both women and men, the decline is slower for women. They conclude that women exhibit more aversion to risk than men in financial decisions. As a result, women choose safer assets, and the expected returns on these assets will be lower than the corresponding returns for men.

We can readily get an idea of how much difference this would make over the long haul. Suppose, for the sake of argument, that women invest $100 each in an asset that yields an expected return of 4% per year, while men invest $100 each in a riskier asset that also yields a higher expected return of 5% a year. Furthermore, suppose that these amounts remain invested for 20 years. Over this period, the original $100 will grow to $219 when the return is 4% per annum but to $265 when the return is 5% per year.[32] Thus, over the two decades men will end up being roughly 20% wealthier than women because they were less averse to risk and so opted for riskier assets with higher expected returns. If the difference in attitudes toward risk is a robust and consistent difference across women and men, it may be one reason that women may be less wealthy than men. This is what Jianakoplos and Bernasek suggest.

It must be noted that not all researchers accept the claim that women are more risk averse than men. In an experimental study, Renate Schubert and her co-authors (1999) found that context matters a great deal in making these comparisons.[33] They first confronted males and females with an abstract gamble and elicited their preferences relative to an outcome that bore no risk. In this scenario, women seemed to be more risk averse than men. When the researchers presented them with the same gambles in the context of investment and insurance decisions, however, women revealed them-

---

[31] Jianakoplos, N. M., and A. Bernasek (1998), "Are Women More Risk Averse?," *Economic Inquiry* 36, pp. 620–630.

[32] If an amount $A is invested at a rate of return r, when compounded the amount becomes $A(1 + r)^t$ at the end of t years.

[33] Schubert, R., M. Brown, M. Gysler, and H. W. Brachinger (1999), "Financial Decision-Making: Are Women Really More Risk Averse?," *American Economic Review* 89, pp. 381–385.

selves to be no more averse to risk than men. This study cautions us about drawing inferences regarding risk aversion in the abstract; context matters in financial decisions. Nevertheless, the survey of Rachel Croson and Uri Gneezy (2009) that we alluded to earlier in this chapter cites evidence that greater risk aversion in women relative to men is a fairly robust finding in the literature.

What might explain the gender difference in attitudes toward risk? An evolutionary argument made by Robert Trivers (1972) can shed light on this question.[34] To understand this argument, we must first bring to mind the obvious fact that women have their own children, whereas men have children through women. For the genes of a man to be passed on to future generations, he has to find one or more mates. It is not enough that he should survive; he has to find sexual partners. Because the investment of the mother (during nine months of pregnancy and in the early years of the child) is so much greater than that of the father, from the point of view of men, women are the bottleneck when it comes to fertility.

The reproductive success (number of surviving children) of women shows far less variability across the population than that of men. Why is that? Because women are the bottleneck, they have relatively little difficulty finding mates who will impregnate them. Because men compete for sexual access to women, however, it is by no means guaranteed that a man will sire any children. Men who are particularly successful at finding mates will sire many children; those who are less successful will sire few. Men who more aggressively pursue women, woo them, fend off rival suitors, and so on are more successful at finding mates. This process by which certain traits attract mates and facilitate the passing on of genes to future generations is referred to as *sexual selection*. Darwin emphasized sexual selection also, in addition to his better-known natural selection ("survival of the fittest"), which we shall discuss in Section VI of this chapter. The cost to a man of not finding any mates is that his genes are completely lost to posterity. By increasing the chances that a man will attract mates when he indulges in risky behavior, nature in effect encouraged this type of behavior in men—so the argument of Trivers goes. Consequently, it has become a part of male nature to engage in risky behavior. Women, on the other hand, had little evolutionary incentive to embrace risky behavior. This could well be the reason that women may be more averse to risk than men, if indeed women are.

Finally, we should also recognize that there are limits to the extent to which experiments in a laboratory setting can unearth differences between the behaviors of men and those of women. For example, as we already mentioned in the previous chapter, Linda Babcock and Sara Laschever (2003)

---

[34] Trivers, R. L. (1972), "Parental Investment and Sexual Selection," in *Sexual Selection and the Descent of Man: 1871–1971,* ed. B. Campbell, Aldine, Chicago, pp. 136–179.

have persuasively argued that women don't fare as well as men in negotiations because women don't ask for all they could or should.[35] In real-world situations, women are more likely than men to take some things as given and nonnegotiable when, in fact, they are subject to negotiation. There are many reasons for this behavior, but a very important one is that women in most societies are socialized to behave in a manner that requires them to suppress their self-interest. So they either do not ask for what they want or try to satisfy their desires indirectly—by working harder, being more deserving, and so on—so that they will be given what they want without asking for it. This is the sort of real-world behavior that cannot be identified in experimental games because all players are carefully primed by the persons conducting the experiments, who give very precise instructions about what is possible and what is not in the experiments. We shall elaborate on this limitation of experiments in the following sections.

V. A Cautionary Note on Observer Bias

Here we briefly take a step back and note that, even though the types of experiments discussed above are carefully designed, they may still suffer from the preconceptions that well-meaning scholars may bring to their designs. Christina Günther, Neslihan Ekinci, Christiane Schwieren, and Martin Strobel (2010) performed experiments that were variations on those done by Gneezy, Niederle, and Rustichini (2003) that we described in Section III.[36] Günther and her co-authors ask why women do not perform as well in mixed groups as in single-sex groups. They attribute this tendency to the tasks chosen by the experimenters and to the "stereotype threat" that women face. The psychological concept of stereotype threat refers to the fact that, when put in a situation in which people of an identifiable group are operating under stereotypical preconceptions on the part of the majority, these groups do not perform well.[37] For example, if women are stereotyped as not being good at mathematics, when confronted with a situation in which it is explicitly made clear to them that they are up against a tough mathematical task, their performance is worse than when they receive no indication that the task is mathematically difficult. There are psychological forces at work that prevent groups from performing up to their level of skill when they are under a stereotype threat.

[35] Babcock, L., and S. Laschever (2003), *Women Don't Ask: Negotiation and the Gender Divide,* Princeton University Press, Princeton, NJ.

[36] Günther, C., N. A. Ekinci, C. Schwieren, and M. Strobel (2010), "Women Can't Jump?—An Experiment on Competitive Attitudes and Stereotype Threat," *Journal of Economic Behavior and Organization* 75, pp. 395–401.

[37] See, for example, Steele, C. M., S. J. Spencer, and J. Aronson (2002), "Contending with Group Image: The Psychology of Stereotype and Social Identity Threat," *Advances in Experimental Social Psychology* 34, pp. 379–440.

Günther et al. argue that the task of solving mazes in the study of Gneezy, Niederle, and Rustichini (2003) can be considered a "male" task because men are stereotypically viewed to be good (and women not so good) at these spatially oriented tasks. Thus, when women are asked to compete in a mixed group under this implicit stereotype threat, they underperform. So Günther et al. performed similar experiments with a "neutral" task and a "female" task. The neutral task comprised coming up with as many words as possible in a fixed time frame starting with a letter given to the participants—a task on which evidence shows that neither gender has an advantage. The female task entailed pattern recognition and verbal memory, tasks at which women are stereotypically deemed better than males. The authors found that on the neutral task, women competed just as strongly as men. On the female task, they found that women competed more strongly than men (though these results were weak in a statistical sense).

The implication of the findings of Günther et al. is that women may not perform competitively on tasks deemed "male" tasks because they are operating under a stereotype threat. If the preconceived belief foisted onto them is that they will fail, then why try? But if the task is suitably changed so that a negative stereotype is not at work, the competitive disadvantage of women disappears. This should alert us to the fact that subtle changes in experimental design can result in drastic changes in observed behavior.

This behavior under the stereotype threat is also a problem in matters pertaining to race, religion, sexual orientation, and country of origin, among others. An interesting study was done in India by Karla Hoff and Priyanka Pandey (2004) on how making caste salient undermined the performance of low-caste students.[38] Caste is an institution in India that has been in place for millennia. According to the system, society is fragmented into four broad castes (and numerous subcastes) that are hierarchical. Below these castes are people who were considered to be beyond the pale of the caste system and deemed "untouchable." Those in the high castes have had considerable status and tend to be educated. Those in the lowest castes have been looked down upon and discriminated against. A person's caste, unlike his or her race, is not apparent. So it is reasonable to expect that low-caste people might suffer from stereotype threat if knowledge of their caste were made public. Hoff and Pandey recruited equal numbers of male high-caste and low-caste ("untouchable") junior high school students from a village in the state of Uttar Pradesh. The experimenters (educated, so clearly perceived to be of high caste) had these students perform some tasks requiring skill under two controlled scenarios, with the promise that they would be rewarded with money in accordance with their performance. In one scenario, caste was not

---

[38] Hoff, K., and P. Pandey (2004), "Belief Systems and Durable Inequalities: An Experimental Investigation of Indian Caste," World Bank Policy Research Working Paper WPS 3351.

brought to the attention of the students. In the second scenario, the students were publicly identified as belonging to the high or the low caste. When caste was not made salient, Hoff and Pandey found that there was no significant difference in the performance of high- and low-caste students. However, when caste was made salient, a caste gap in performance emerged; the low-caste students' performance dropped quite significantly. The authors argued that the performance gap was due not so much to the loss of self-confidence of low-caste students as to their belief that the experimenters (high-caste persons) were not likely to be fair in disbursing the rewards, which led to a decline in their effort. This experiment reveals that context matters enormously to the behavior of even participants in experiments.

If subtle cues make so much difference in controlled experimental settings where scholars are extremely careful about possible bias, we might wonder how much more prevalent this bias might be in real-world settings where people are less conscious of such cues. A very interesting and provocative study was published by Christine Wennerås and Agnes Wold (1997) (cited earlier) on gender bias in the awarding of postdoctoral fellowships in the biomedical sciences in Sweden by the Swedish Medical Research Council. These fellowships are stop-gap transitional positions (usually for two years) that are taken up by scientists who have completed their doctoral work but have not yet acquired permanent positions. This study is particularly interesting because scientists often feel that their approach to truth is based on an objective methodology and that subjective considerations are irrelevant. Using the Swedish Freedom of Press Act, Wennerås and Wold got ahold of the names and resumes of the applicants for the fellowship in the year 1995 and, most important, the evaluations of the selection committees. These selection committees comprised highly accomplished academics in the relevant fields. The authors used six different objective measures of productivity in their analysis, revolving mostly around academic publications. By employing statistical methods they could isolate the effect of gender on the committees' evaluations of the scientific competence of the applicants, holding constant all other relevant characteristics. The authors discovered astounding evidence that evaluations of scientific competence depended on the applicants' genders. For a woman to receive the same competence score as the average man in the application pool, she had to be two and a half times more productive than he. This reflects a staggering amount of gender discrimination. Among all the nations of this world, Sweden ranks as one of the highest in terms of gender equality. Given this evidence from Sweden, no evaluation committee anywhere in the world can be sure that it is free of gender bias.

What can be done about this sort of bias, which creeps into the judgments of even reputed and allegedly objective scholars? Is it conceivable that having more women on the evaluation committees would help because they would be more sympathetic to female applicants? A recent study by Manuel Bagues and Berta Esteve-Volart (2010) addresses this issue, among others.[39] These authors used a massive data set from 1987 through 2007 of candidates who attempted to secure four different kinds of jobs in the Spanish Judiciary that can be attained through competitive public examinations. The candidates are randomly assigned to various evaluation committees, and the gender composition of these committees varies considerably. So the authors could use this variation in the committees' composition to assess the success rates of male and female candidates they evaluated. The authors' results were surprising. They found that, relative to committees with more male evaluators, those with more female evaluators assigned higher scores to *male* candidates but more or less the same scores to female candidates. Because the total number of positions available to be filled is usually restricted, an increase in male scores means that more males are hired and some females are squeezed out. In particular, the authors found that males were 16% more likely to succeed in a female-minority committee, and 34% more likely in a female-majority committee, than in a committee of all-male evaluators. Females were 10% less likely to succeed in a female-minority committee, and 17% less likely in a female-majority committee, than in an all-male committee. Thus women on selection committees appear to put female candidates at a disadvantage by favoring males.

These findings are exactly the opposite of what one might have informally expected. How do we make sense of them? Three possible reasons that Bagues and Esteve-Volart offer are (i) female evaluators may be engaging in a taste for discrimination in favor of males; (ii) because they dislike competition, as we saw earlier, female evaluators in mixed-gender committees may be conceding more to male candidates; and (iii) male evaluators may be favoring male candidates more in mixed-gender evaluation committees. Whether or not these reasons are correct, the findings make one thing clear: there is much more we need to learn about the dynamics of interactions between people in society before we can presume to have identified the underpinnings of human behavior. Findings such as these raise important questions about how society can successfully level the playing field for women. Clearly, a policy measure that ensures equal representation of women and men on selection committees (perhaps through a quota system) might not work; in fact, it can make matters worse. What is to be done, then?

A plausible answer to this question comes from the work of Claudia Goldin and Cecilia Rouse (2000).[40] They examined the effect of moving to "blind" auditions on the success and hiring of women musicians. Tradition-

[39] Bagues, M. F., and B. Esteve-Volart (2010), "Can Gender Parity Break the Glass Ceiling?: Evidence from a Repeated Randomized Experiment," *Review of Economic Studies* 77, pp. 1301–1328.
[40] Goldin, C., and C. Rouse (2000), "Orchestrating Impartiality: The Impact of 'Blind' Auditions on Female Musicians," *American Economic Review* 90, pp. 715–741.

ally, in the United States an orchestra conductor had almost unilateral power to select the members of the orchestra. Many well-known conductors have publicly revealed that they believed women's musical abilities were inferior to men's. So it is highly plausible that women were laboring under the handicaps of a negative stereotype and even overt discrimination in the selection process. In the 1970s and 1980s, the major orchestras in the United States moved, not necessarily all at the same time, toward holding blind auditions in which a cloth screen prevented the evaluators from seeing the genders of the candidates. Goldin and Rouse set about trying to identify the effect this change in procedure had on the success of women in auditions in making it to the next round of the contest and on ultimate hiring. They also used gender information in the rosters (lists) of the people in the orchestra to see whether there was any change in the representation of women. They found that moving to blind auditions explained about a third of the increase in the proportion of women hired. Blind auditions also explained around 25% of the increase in the proportion of female orchestra members recorded on the rosters. These numbers represent substantial increases.

This study by Goldin and Rouse suggests one way to level the playing field for women more generally: to suppress information about gender in the competition process. If knowledge of gender sets in motion various stereotypical prejudices and unconscious processes in evaluators, making this irrelevant information unavailable is a good way to stymie the mechanism of bias. This is a principle that would be applicable more generally: to information about marital status, sexual orientation, race, religious beliefs, and so on.

The discussion in this section should make us wary of attributing a single cause to any phenomenon pertaining to gender. The outcomes of human interactions are the result of numerous forces that are at work. The very nature of understanding requires us, on the one hand, to minimize the number of contributing factors so as to isolate the most important factors. To say that anything can happen because there are too many factors that impinge on outcomes is not useful. If we don't understand how and why things happen, we cannot redress unfairness and correct imbalances in the system. Good policy measures require a firm theoretical understanding of the processes that are at work. On the other hand, to be recklessly "reductionist" by attempting to reduce all the relevant causes to a single dominant cause is to invite trouble because it may ignore important dimensions of the issues that ought not to be ignored.

VI. Nature versus Nurture in Gender: Evolutionary, Feminist, and Postmodern Views

What are the sources of the gender differences in behavior detected in the experimental and empirical results discussed in the preceding sections? Are these differences determined by nature (genes, selected by evolution) or by nurture (the environment in which people are raised and operate)? This debate has been going on for a long time, and only recently has enough evidence emerged for us to take stock. In this section we shall take the opportunity to discuss different approaches to understanding gendered behavior. In subsequent chapters we shall have occasion to refer to these approaches. It should be noted, however, that these do not represent mutually exclusive categories; there are overlaps between the various viewpoints.

The View from Evolutionary Biology and Evolutionary Psychology

Biological evolution works largely (but not entirely) through a process known as natural selection, which we now describe in highly simplified form. Suppose that there is a population of organisms of a given species that is located in a given environment. The organisms compete with each other for resources that promote survival. Consider a trait, call it X, that can be passed on from parent to offspring, that is, a trait that is heritable. Suppose that this trait contributes to an organism's ability to access food resources and, therefore, to its survival and to the number of live offspring it can leave behind. The offspring will also possess this trait because the trait is heritable.

Consider an environment in which all the organisms within a population have trait X in the same measure and that each organism has 3 offspring. Each of these 3 offspring will also have 3 offspring, each of these will have 3 offspring, and so on. In other words, an organism's genes will be represented in 3 offspring, 9 grandoffspring, 27 great-grandoffspring, and so on. Because all the organisms are assumed to be identical, each organism's representation in the gene pool of the population will remain constant over generations.

Now allow for variation in the gene responsible for trait X. In particular, suppose that there is a single mutant that displays a superior measure of trait X. As a result, in the struggle for survival the mutant can access more resources and therefore leave behind more surviving offspring, say 4 offspring. Each of the offspring, having inherited the mutant gene, will leave behind 4 offspring, and so on. Consequently, this mutant's genes will be represented in 4 offspring, 16 grandoffspring, 64 great-grandoffspring, and so on. It is easy to see that the proportion of the mutant's genes in the population will keep increasing with each generation. After about 50 generations, almost 100% of the genes for trait X in the population will be the original mutant's. In other words, the mutant's genes will have been "selected" because of the survival advantage it conferred on the organism that possessed them.

Returning to the original scenario, now suppose that the mutant had genes for trait X that put the organism at a competitive disadvantage in the struggle for survival. Suppose that the mutant can acquire resources to leave behind only 2 surviving offspring (while all the other organisms leave behind 3 offspring). Because the offspring inherit the mutant's genes, the original mutant will have 2 offspring, 4 grandoffspring, 8 great-grandoffspring, and so on. It is easy to see that, in this case, the proportional representation of the mutant's genes will keep declining over time. After about 50 generations, this proportion will be virtually zero. In other words, the original mutant's gene will have been purged from the population.

This process by which nature selects genes that confer a survival advantage and deletes those that confer a survival disadvantage is what Charles Darwin called "natural selection" in his *Origin of Species.* As long as there is variation in the genes that translates into different chances of survival, natural selection will bring about "improvements" in the traits that enable individuals to garner more resources for themselves and therefore better *adapt* themselves to the given environment. In other words, these adaptations brought about by evolution facilitate individual survival. The evolutionary biologist explains the existence of various biological traits in terms of the function they perform in enhancing the organism's survival. The core requirement for evolution to do this work (assuming that the trait is heritable) is variation; if there is no variation in the traits across the organisms of a species, there is nothing for natural selection to work on.

Evolutionary psychology starts from the premise that many important behavioral traits in humans (and animals) are genetic and, therefore, are the products of natural selection. The tendency to ensure self-preservation, the tendency to appropriate resources for oneself at the expense of others, and the special love one feels for one's own children, to name just a few, are deeply entrenched behavioral traits that are universally observed in humans. Evolutionary psychologists offer explanations for these behaviors in terms of the functions they perform, that is, as adaptations that facilitated survival. Such explanations, when applied to gender issues, are sometimes quite insightful and can be useful—as long as they are kept in perspective.[41]

There are dangers associated with the use of explanations based on evolutionary psychology, however. These explanations rarely identify the actual genes that are allegedly at work in the phenomena under scrutiny; nor is there much hope of doing so. Furthermore, because evolution did its work on our behavior hundreds of thousands (and possibly millions) of years ago, an explanation based on evolution has to conjure up possible scenarios from our distant past that are shrouded in mystery. So such explanations cannot be taken as established beyond doubt, much less as the truth. In fact, there is often so much speculation involved in the suggested explanations that they

---

[41]What is called sociobiology is an extreme (and discredited) form of evolutionary psychology that takes the view that gender differences are innate and hard-wired by natural selection.

may at times seem like "adaptive storytelling."[42] Evolutionary psychology is nowhere nearly as firmly established by evidence as is evolutionary biology. So evolutionary explanations of human behavior—and we shall frequently offer such explanations in this book—should always be entertained with some skepticism, no matter how insightful they may seem. This is particularly the case in matters pertaining to gender, because the adaptive storytelling may be informed by male bias stemming from the fact that until recently the majority of physical and social scientists have been male. Evolutionary arguments should be used to understand how some aspects of human behavior *may* have come about but never to justify the status quo. Nature has no morality; there is no sense in which what nature has wrought is necessarily what we should consider good or decent, fair or right.

The Feminist View

Feminism takes the stand that, though women are the equals of men, they are oppressed by men, and this domination should be eliminated. Feminists have argued that, despite the claim that neoclassical economics (the standard Western economics) deems itself value neutral, its approach is fraught with unwarranted assumptions and male-centered biases that work to the disadvantage of women. For example, the very definition of a nation's gross domestic product (GDP) largely excludes women's contributions in their homes because only market transactions are counted in GDP and women spend much of their time doing unpaid housework.

Even among feminists, however, there are many divisions depending on the various approaches adopted. Feminists often view arguments from evolutionary psychology as male biased and as perpetrating the male dominance of women. Not all feminist approaches to gender issues, however, are diametrically opposed to evolutionary biology and psychology. In fact, some ardent feminists like Sarah Hrdy and Patricia Gowaty are reputed scientists who work on various aspects of evolution.

The first wave of feminism was initiated by the classical economist John Stuart Mill (1869) in the masterful book *The Subjection of Women,* which is believed to have been co-authored by his wife, Harriet Mill. The approach taken—what is now referred to as liberal feminism—is consistent with standard approaches in economics that presume individual choices are paramount. Mill found the subjugation of women by men intolerable and argued for greater freedom for women because this maximizes the happiness of the maximum number of people.

[42] For an insightful article on the dangers of evolutionary explanations, see Tang-Martinez, I. (1997), "The Curious Courtship of Sociobiology and Feminism: A Case of Irreconcilable Differences," in *Feminism and Evolutionary Biology: Boundaries, Intersections, and Frontiers,* ed. P. A. Gowaty, Chapman and Hall, New York.

The second wave of feminism, spawned in the 1960s and 1970s, took a more radical approach, drawing on Marxist ideas. In contrast to neoclassical economics (which focuses on individual behavior), Marxism focuses on class behavior, where a class comprises a group of individuals who have similar economic interests (e.g., workers, capitalists, landlords, and others form separate classes). Radical feminists viewed women as an oppressed class and so sought to employ Marxist analysis in which individual classes are deemed to apply concerted efforts to bring about outcomes consistent with their class interests.[43] This line of feminist thought sees the male domination of women (patriarchy) as going hand in hand with capitalism. Subsequently, many feminists have argued that capitalism and patriarchy are separate and distinct forces leading to the oppression of women.[44] The emphasis on economics in this approach, albeit in a Marxist framework of thought, means that to these feminists evolution is hardly the driving force behind the oppression of women. To them it is economics, politics, sociology, religion, and generally culture that are responsible for the oppression of women.

Academic feminist economists typically do not espouse the wholesale rejection of neoclassical economics.[45] Rather, they encourage the use of the analytic tools of the discipline and their application to questions that are of interest to women. Furthermore, they question the glib assumptions that (male) economists have tended to make through bias or ignorance. As a result, many feminist concerns are being increasingly incorporated and addressed in mainstream economics. In recent decades, the discipline of economics has become more sensitive to gender issues, and many feminist insights about the importance of previously ignored "noneconomic" factors (such as culture) on economic outcomes for women have been vindicated by rigorous research. The experiment discussed below is an example of this.

This interesting experiment, done by Uri Gneezy, Kenneth Leonard, and John List (2009), brings out the importance of culture on behavior under controlled conditions.[46] These authors performed identical experiments with participants drawn from two different cultures: the Maasi from Tanzania, Africa, and the Khasi from Meghalaya, India. The African Maasi are a typical patriarchal society in which males dominate important decision making, whereas the

[43] Whether all women can be placed into a separate class is debatable. Women come from families with different levels of wealth, and their interests may not all be aligned. Nevertheless, the use of Marxist analysis is useful in addressing gender issues, as we shall see in Chapter 5.

[44] Some examples of work along these lines are Hartmann, H. (1976), "Capitalism, Patriarchy, and Job Segregation by Sex," *Signs* 1, pp. 137–169, and Folbre, N. (1982), "Exploitation Comes Home: A Critique of Marxian Theory of Family Labour," *Cambridge Journal of Economics* 6, pp. 317–329.

[45] See Ferber, M. A., and J. A. Nelson (1993), "Introduction: The Social Construction of Economics and the Social Construction of Gender," in *Beyond Economic Man: Feminist Theory and Economics,* ed. M. A. Ferber and J. A. Nelson, Chicago University Press, Chicago.

[46] Gneezy, U., K. L. Leonard, and J. A. List (2009), "Gender Differences in Competition: Evidence from a Matrilineal and a Patriarchal Society," *Econometrica* 77, pp. 1637–1664.

Indian Khasi are a society that is matrilineal. In the latter, the husband moves to his wife's house on marriage and decision-making power is vested in the female line. Many of the gender roles one observes in patriarchal societies are reversed in the Khasi. Gneezy, Leonard, and List exploit this difference in culture to investigate whether there are observed gender differences in competitive behavior—a useful exercise given that, as we have seen earlier, previous experiments revealed that women may be less competitive than men.

The authors chose a task in which neither gender exhibited a particular advantage (tossing a tennis ball into a bucket kept a few meters away) and offered pairs of (same-gender) participants a choice between two options: one gets (i) an amount of money X for each successful shot (that is, when the ball drops into the bucket and stays in it) or (ii) $3X$ per successful shot if one beats the other person and nothing if one loses (and X per successful shot if both tie). The amount X was substantial and was offered in the local currency. The interesting question is how gender-dependent the choice of the competitive option (ii) was. Gneezy, Leonard, and List found that, after accounting for all observable differences other than gender, among the (patriarchal) Maasi, men were about 25%–29% more likely to compete than women; among the (matrilineal) Khasi, women were 24% more likely to compete than men.

How does one explain this? The explanation could not be genetic in this case, because evolution works over a very long time horizon, and even 1,000 years or so of these social organizations is nowhere near long enough to generate biological differences in behavior. The answer lies in the role of culture. The authors argue that, because the returns to the competitive behavior of women stay in the household in the matrilineal Khasi society, such behavior is encouraged—just as competitive behavior by men is in a patriarchal society. The results of such carefully designed experiments bring home the importance of culture in determining behavior. This suggests that earlier results (with participants drawn from Western culture) showing that women are less competitive than men were really capturing something about the effect of Western culture on the competitive behavior of women. Had we generalized from such studies, we would have erroneously claimed as a universal truth about gender something that most certainly seems to be *culture driven*.

The Postmodern Feminist View
Postmodernism has not made serious inroads into economics.[47] Nevertheless, it offers a profound truth relevant to gender issues. Postmodern feminists may take sex as more or less given, being determined by biology; typically, one is

[47] Ferber and Nelson (1993), cited earlier, provide a very readable introduction to postmodern thought as it might apply to economics. For a more general introduction to postmodernism, see Gergen, K. J. (2009), *An Invitation to Social Construction,* 2nd ed., Sage Publications, Los Angeles.

born as either a male or a female. But gender is a different matter; gender ("masculine" or "feminine") is a concept that is "socially constructed" and so depends on society's perceptions. Thus, although only women can have children and only women can lactate, it does not follow that infants should be taken care of only by women. To insist that they should is to tie gender firmly to sex. As we can see, men are increasingly taking care of babies these days, suggesting that there is no reason to believe that this is only women's work.

The contribution of postmodernism to our thinking on gender issues is that it brings home the point that society largely reacts to *its own concepts* about gender. Because these concepts have been conjured up by human minds, they do not necessarily contain any unchanging truth; our concepts do not necessarily reflect reality. Society creates gender-dependent norms and expects its members to conform to these norms. People give validity to gender-normative roles by respecting them and performing actions consistent with them. This is the sense in which Judith Butler (1990) claims that gender is a "performance."[48] It is this performance, consistently repeated by most people in society, that creates a binary masculine or feminine categorization of gender that is considered the norm. Such a social construction forces a binary choice on all the people, whereas most people actually lie on a continuum between the two extremes. And people who seek to truly live as transgendered individuals are met with hostility and a refusal to acknowledge the reality of such an existence.[49]

Another way of couching this view is to say that every society develops concepts pertaining to gender and then socializes individuals to conform to these notions. The primary influences in this regard are parents, relatives, teachers, siblings, and peer groups. To show that this is not merely an abstract argument, let us take a concrete example to illustrate its scope in explaining observations. Consider an issue we have already discussed in a previous section, namely, risk aversion. The experimental evidence we cited largely showed that women tend to be more risk averse than men. We saw that evolutionary psychology offered *one* possible explanation for this. We discuss below another analysis that demonstrates in a compelling manner the importance of socialization and its effect on risk aversion.

Allison Booth and Patrick Nolen (2012) examined the issue of gender differences in attitudes toward risk with an eye to isolating the effect of socialization.[50] They drew samples of girls and boys in grades 10 and 11 from

---

[48] Butler, J. (1990), *Gender Trouble: Feminism and the Subversion of Identity*, Routledge, New York.

[49] See Namaste, V. K. (2000), *Invisible Lives: The Erasure of Transsexual and Transgendered People*, University of Chicago Press, Chicago.

[50] Booth, A. L., and P. Nolen (2012), "Gender Differences in Risk Behavior: Does Nurture Matter?," *Economic Journal* 122, pp. F56–F78.

both single-sex and coeducational schools in the United Kingdom. They then put them into single-sex and mixed-sex groups and performed an experiment involving real money to elicit the students' attitudes toward risk. They offered the students a choice between a sure payoff of £5 and a bet in which they would get either £11 or £2 depending on a coin toss. Although the expected value of the bet was £6.5 and so exceeded the sure payoff, students could reject the bet if they were sufficiently risk averse. Thus their choices reflected their attitudes toward risk.

Booth and Nolen found that girls from single-sex schools were more likely than girls from coeducational schools to choose the risky option. Furthermore, they were just as likely as boys (from either type of school) to choose the risky option. Why the difference? The authors argue that it is basically the effect of socialization. Girls in coeducational schools are under greater pressure to establish their feminine identity in order to be attractive to boys, and they behave according to stereotype and take fewer risks.[51] Girls from single-sex schools, in contrast, are under no such pressure and so are used to acting according to their true preferences. Thus exposure to different social environments results in different behaviors. The experiment performed by Booth and Nolen nicely captures the effect of socialization and suggests that the results of previous studies that found women more risk averse than men may have obtained because the effect of socialization was not adequately accounted for. Participants may have been merely playing out gender-normative roles.

We see, then, that a premature conclusion that men are less risk averse than women could easily be used to justify why men earn more than women and become wealthier than women over the long haul. It can simply be argued that men take more risks with high payoffs and are rewarded for their boldness. Embedded in such a tendency to explain the status quo may well be preconceptions deriving from a male-centered view of the world.

VII. Summary

We started this chapter by asking whether there are gender differences in behavior that can possibly explain the differences in observed economic outcomes for women and men. To this end, we focused on some important differences: altruism, competitiveness, and aversion to risk. We saw that laboratory experiments in which women and men are asked to participate in gaming situations may be a good way to elicit gender differences in behavior.

---

[51] On the importance of identity in economic and social interactions, see Akerlof, G. A., and R. E. Kranton (2000), "Economics and Identity," *Quarterly Journal of Economics* 115, pp. 715–753. See also the following book, published in 2010 by the same authors: *Identity Economics: How Our Identities Shape Our Work, Wages, and Well-Being*, Princeton University Press, Princeton, NJ.

We first examined potential gender differences in altruism. In the ultimatum game, we saw that the average earnings of females were less than those of males. The likely reason is that women are seen as more accommodating than men. In repeated experiments of the prisoners' dilemma sort, women start out behaving more cooperatively than men, but over time their behavior, too, gravitates to the noncooperative defection option of men. In public-good games that entail more than two players, however, an interesting gender difference in behavior emerges. In competition *between* groups, men cooperate more than they do when individual payoffs are made more salient. Women's behavior, however, is the same in either case. There seems to be something in group activity that mobilizes male cooperative actions. Evidence from the labor market suggests that gender differences in altruism (with women exhibiting more altruism) do seem to be correlated with gender differences in earnings (with the more altruistic earning less).

Experiments that seek to ascertain gender differences in the degree of competitiveness show that women are willing to compete with other women in single-sex games. However, in mixed-sex games women curtail their competitiveness somewhat, whereas men do not. This suggests that the composition of the group matters in terms of how women and men compete. So the nature of the tournament set up to determine a winner may not elicit interest or effort from women even when they have the requisite skills, experience, and ability. We discussed a careful experiment on gendered competitive behavior that was conducted in a patriarchal society and also in a matrilineal one. The findings were that, although men were more competitive than women in the former, women were more competitive than men in the latter. Thus culture matters. We should be wary of attributing innate psychological characteristics to men and women because their behavior may merely be displaying gender-normative role-playing.

Experiments on gender differences in attitudes toward risk largely show that the behavior of women *appears to be* more averse to risk than men's. However, to conclude from this that women are innately more risk averse may be an unwarranted step because many factors that impinge on behavior may not be controlled for even in the best-designed experiments. We saw that high school girls in single-sex schools in the United Kingdom were no more risk averse than boys, whereas girls from coeducational schools (who would have been socialized to act "feminine" to be attractive to boys) were more risk averse than boys in their behavior. This underlines the great importance of socialization in gendered behavior.

We discussed the notion of observer bias that induces significant distortions in outcomes. Evaluators of performances and tournaments have their own unconscious biases and stereotypical views that seep into their decisions. We discussed empirical work that unearthed serious gender biases against women even in well-meaning and reputed scholars. The remedy for this, we saw, was not necessarily to insist on gender balance on the evaluation committees but rather to move toward suppressing gender (and other irrelevant) information and making contests "gender blind."

We finally discussed what all these experiments reveal about gender differences in economic behavior. We discussed three different approaches to the study of gender. The first is that of evolutionary biology and psychology. We noted that, although arguments invoking evolution are useful, they have their limits. Unless they are accompanied by a healthy dose of skepticism, they can descend into mere "adaptive storytelling." The second is that of feminists, who seek to eliminate the male oppression of women by examining its causes. Much of feminist inquiry has been conducted in the tradition of Marxian analysis, with its emphasis on class struggle. Recently, however, feminist economists have used the standard methodology of economics to address important issues in gender. Finally, we discussed the postmodern view as it applies to economics. This approach emphasizes that many of our beliefs regarding gender are merely socially constructed concepts. These concepts have no other reality except what they derive from society's adherence to them. Experiments on the effects of culture and socialization on gendered behavior reveal that the postmodern point of view has much to recommend it.

The most important lesson we must draw from our survey of the experimental literature is that *context matters* enormously. And because context matters, apart from economics (which definitely matters), culture matters, politics matters, biology matters, psychology matters, history matters, law matters, and religion matters. We cannot draw sharp conclusions about gendered behavior without consulting the appropriate context.

Exercises and Questions for Discussion

1. Consider the ultimatum game we discussed in the text.

   (a) Explain why there are many Nash equilibria in the simultaneous version of the game but only one outcome in the sequential version.

   (b) Explain what gender differences are commonly observed in the two versions of the game in experimental studies.

   (c) What explanations do you offer for these differences?

2. Consider a two-person game in which each player has two strategies (X and Y) and their material payoffs are shown in the table below.

		Player 2	
		X	Y
Player 1	X	$(1, 1)$	$(5, 0)$
	Y	$(0, 5)$	$(4, 4)$

(a) Do the players have a dominant strategy if they maximize their material payoffs? If so, which one?

(b) What would you predict the outcome of the game to be? Is the outcome Pareto efficient?

(c) Is the above outcome a Nash equilibrium? Why or why not?

Now suppose that the players maximize utility instead of their material payoffs. Player 1's utility is $U_1 = m_1 + a m_2$, and Player 2's is $U_2 = m_2 + a m_1$, where m_1 and m_2, respectively, denote the material payoffs of Players 1 and 2 and a is a number between 0 and 1 that captures each player's altruism toward the other.

(d) Construct a table that is similar to that above but shows the utility payoffs of the players.

(e) What is the smallest value of the altruism index a that will yield an outcome that improves on both players' payoffs obtained in part b above? Explain your reasoning.

(f) If women are more altruistic than men, as experimental results seem to show, what are the gender implications for the degree of cooperation that can be sustained in prisoners' dilemma–type scenarios?

3. Consider the experimental findings of Uri Gneezy, Muriel Niederle, and Aldo Rustichini (2003) on differences in the competitiveness of women and men.

(a) What were the essential findings of this study?

(b) Why might these findings be relevant to the fact that women constitute a very small proportion of top executives?

(c) Can you think of some policy implications of these findings in terms of how the playing field for top executive positions may be made more gender neutral?

4. (a) Explain what is meant by the "stereotype threat" and what it does to the performance of people in the stereotyped group.

(b) What is the importance of stereotyping in the findings of Christina Günther and co-authors (2010) on gender differences in competitiveness?

(c) Explain why these findings are important for experimental design and what we can conclude from them.

5. Consider an evolutionary environment in which all humans are identical and have genes that confer on each of them the biological ability to have two surviving offspring. Suppose that some variation develops in this population due to random mutations. Consider two sorts of mutants. Mutant 1 has different genes that facilitate the survival of only one offspring, whereas Mutant 2 has genes that enable her to leave behind three surviving offspring.

(a) By tracing what occurs over several generations, explain what happens to the proportional representation of Mutant 1's genes over time.

(b) By tracing what occurs over several generations, explain what happens to the proportional representation of Mutant 2's genes over time.

(c) In the light of a and b, explain the working of Darwin's natural selection in simplified form. In what sense can this be interpreted as "survival of the fittest"?

(d) What assumptions are required to justify the application of natural selection to the *psychology* of human behavior?

(e) Why is there a danger of "adaptive storytelling" in the use of evolutionary psychology to explain gender differences?

6. Suppose that equal-sized samples of male and female students are drawn from single-sex and coeducational high schools and that each is subjected to a bet that offers $200 if a coin comes up heads and nothing if it comes up tails. They are then asked what is the largest amount of money, received for sure, that would leave them indifferent between it and taking the bet. This amount (the certainty equivalent) is averaged for the various samples and presented in a table of hypothetical numbers.

Sex and type of school	Certainty equivalent
Male, single-sex school	$90.60
Male, coeducational school	$90.40
Female, single-sex school	$90.20
Female, coeducational school	$84.40

(a) If all males were lumped together, what would the average risk premium of a male be? And if all females were lumped together, what would the average risk premium of a female be?

(b) From part a, what conclusion would you draw about gender differences in the attitudes toward risk if you did not care which type of school the students came from?

(c) If you suspect that students drawn from different schools might socialize students differently, what do you conclude from the table above?

(d) In the light of the findings of Allison Booth and Patrick Nolen (2012), what reasons do you offer to explain the numbers shown in the table above?

(e) What lesson would the above hypothetical table offer on the "nature versus nurture" debate and the dangers of presuming innate gender differences in behavior?

7. (a) What exactly is meant by the claim of postmodern feminists that many traits that are deemed to be gendered are merely "socially constructed" ideas? Can you give examples of popular notions of gendered behavior that are socially constructed?

(b) Discuss the findings of Uri Gneezy, Kenneth Leonard, and John List (2009) on gender differences in competitive behavior in patriarchal and matrilineal societies. Based on these findings, can you make a case to justify the position of postmodern feminists?

8. (a) Explain the concept of "observer bias." What empirical evidence reveals that selection committees are inadvertently biased against women in their assessments of the ability and accomplishments of competing candidates?

(b) Does improving the gender balance of evaluation committees reduce the bias referred to above? Why or why not?

(c) What policy measures would you recommend to minimize the gender bias of selection committees? Why?

CHAPTER THREE

What Determines the Balance of Power in a Household?

I. Introduction

All over the world, men play a larger role in society's decision making than women. This starts at the level of the household: fathers ("patriarchs") generally are seen to have more authority than mothers ("matriarchs"). But the influence of patriarchs even in families is far broader than this in developing countries, where people live in extended families in which the patriarch's and matriarch's sons and their families live with them. The men of the household typically work more in the labor market than do the women. In the public sphere, men are more visible than women; in politics, the proportion of men is generally much larger than that of women. In developing countries, economic necessity may have always forced women to work in the labor market, but it is nevertheless the case that in these countries and in the rich ones, men have generally had a greater say inside and outside the household.

The very thought systems that humans have available to them to make sense of the world around them have largely been formulated by men, as Gerda Lerner (1986) has argued, and women have no means of articulating their experiences because they have been denied the education and leisure needed for this.[1] Feminists refer to this male domination as patriarchy and cite it as one of the most important reasons for the subservience of women. What are the causes of this gender disparity in power, and what can be done to redress the imbalance? This chapter is devoted to providing an understanding of the conceptual framework that economists find most useful in thinking of issues pertaining to power. After we have discussed this, I shall outline theories of patriarchy and review the empirical work that supports them.

---

[1] Lerner, G. (1986), *The Creation of Patriarchy*, Oxford University Press, New York.

Until a couple of decades ago, economists largely thought of the family as a single decision-making unit, as if it comprised only a single person. This construction, which is referred to as the unitary model of the family, has been useful for understanding some aspects of the family. It has enabled us, for example, to understand the emergence of a division of labor in the family and the formation of the traditional household based on the notion of comparative advantage. This view has rationalized why, under some conditions, in a family the husband works in the labor market and the wife concentrates on housework. This division of labor is breaking down in the developed countries but is still in place in developing countries.

Although economic theory based on comparative advantage provides compelling reasons that two people are better off forming a family rather than remaining separate, it is silent on *how* the gains to family formation are split between the two spouses.[2] Do most of the gains in marriage go to men? Is it the case that men manage to pursue or satisfy their aspirations but women are unable to? Were it possible for them, would women like to rearrange the priorities of the family? Would they prefer to alter the division of labor so that they would be better off?

In any cooperative endeavor like marriage or cohabitation, it is reasonable to presume that the partners exploit all the benefits that are available to cooperation and that no opportunity to improve the well-being of both people is ignored. This idea is captured by the notion of *Pareto efficiency* (also referred to as *Pareto optimality*). An outcome is Pareto efficient if it is impossible for both people to become better off or, equivalently, if a move that makes one person better off would necessarily make the other worse off. But there can be an infinite number of such Pareto-efficient outcomes. A situation in which one spouse receives 99% of the benefits of marriage or cohabitation, leaving the other with only 1%, can be Pareto efficient—it may be impossible to make one person better off without making the other worse off.[3] Pareto efficiency tells us nothing about how the benefits are *distributed*. Even if we agree that the outcome in marriage may exhaust all the opportunities whereby both people could be made better off, we need a theory that will tell us how the gains are distributed.

The branch of economics that provides us with useful tools for analyzing economic outcomes within marriage and the distribution of benefits is game theory. In particular, it is bargaining theory that is most relevant. One of the most helpful models in this theory is John Nash's famous bargaining model.[4]

---

[2] By the word *spouses* I do not mean only legally married people; those cohabiting are included in this term.

[3] We can see why the economist Amartya Sen remarked, "A society or an economy may be Pareto optimal and still be perfectly disgusting." Sen, *Collective Choice and Social Welfare*, Holden-Day, San Francisco, 1970, p. 22.

[4] Nash, J. (1950), "The Bargaining Problem," *Econometrica* 18, pp. 155–162.

I describe this model in this chapter. We shall see how the outcome of bargaining depends on the well-being that the bargainers can assure themselves of *in the event that bargaining breaks down*. What they can secure for themselves in this eventuality depends on their alternative (outside) opportunity, which is referred to as their threat utility. After we analyze Nash's model, we shall examine what factors determine these threat utilities. We shall go on to discuss another model of bargaining, in which the two bargainers alternately make offers that can either be accepted or rejected. Here, too, we shall see how and why the threat utilities matter.

The bargaining model was first applied to households by Marilyn Manser and Murray Brown (1980) and by Marjorie B. McElroy and Mary Horney (1981).[5] We shall end our discussion of bargaining models by looking at the evidence in their favor. The evidence is quite persuasive.

Finally, we shall examine how it is that men have come to dominate the power relations within the household, that is, how patriarchy may have arisen. We shall also study how this asymmetry in power within the household carries within it the seed responsible for circumscribing women's role in the economy and in society in order to serve male interests. We shall begin by examining Friedrich Engels's classic theory that this domination is tied to the emergence of private property and shall discuss the suggestive evidence for it.

We shall then go on to discuss the view from evolutionary biology. We shall see that a part of the domination of women—and *only a part*—can be attributed to what has evolved in nature (for example, only women give birth, only women lactate, and men have more physical strength, on average, than women). But patriarchy arose and has persisted for millennia for other reasons—reasons that have to do with the asymmetry of power that comes from controlling productive assets and also from the power of enforcing socially constructed notions that are handed down through culture. The final topic of this chapter is how culture is recruited to pass on patriarchal values and the empirical evidence that reveals this.

II. The Unitary Model

The unitary model, as we have seen above, assumes that a family can be treated as a single unit without composite parts. There are many ways of rationalizing this obviously ludicrous falsehood. One way is to presume that all members of the family agree upon what the family's objective should be, and then they all decide to pursue this common objective. Another is to

---

[5] Manser, M., and M. Brown (1980), "Marriage and Household Decision-Making: A Bargaining Analysis," *International Economic Review* 21, pp. 31–44, and McElroy, M. B., and M. J. Horney (1981), "Nash-Bargained Household Decisions: Toward a Generalization of the Theory of Demand," *International Economic Review* 22, pp. 333–349.

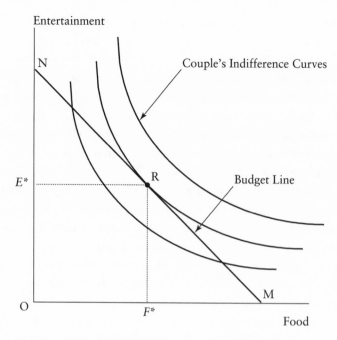

FIGURE 3.1 Resource allocation in the unitary model

assume that there is a benevolent dictator who makes all the decisions of the family. Yet another is to assume that all members of the family have identical preferences for various goods and services so that for all practical purposes the family behaves as a single individual.

To see what such a construction implies, consider a couple deciding how to spend their income between food and entertainment. Suppose that the husband's annual salary is $40,000 and the wife's $30,000. Assume that they pool their income instead of maintaining separate accounts. An individual's preferences can be represented by indifference curves—that is, curves along which an individual is indifferent between the various combinations of food and entertainment. If the two individuals discussed here are assumed to have identical preferences, they will have identical indifference curves. Figure 3.1 illustrates the couple's (common) indifference curves and the budget line, MN, as determined by their total income.

Suppose that the husband makes the decisions regarding how the couple's joint income should be allocated. As indicated in the figure, the couple will achieve their highest level of (common) well-being at point R, where they allocate their joint income so as to consume an amount F^* of food and E^* of entertainment. What would happen to this allocation of their income if it was the wife who earned $40,000 and the husband who earned $30,000? Nothing would happen. This is because the couple are pooling their income, and only the total income matters. What would happen to the allocation of income if the decision maker was the wife? Once again, nothing would happen. This is because the two people have identical preferences, so regardless of who makes the decisions, the allocation they will opt for will be the same. This is the essence of the so-called unitary model, in which the family is treated as a unit. In this model the identities of the decision makers do not matter because they have common preferences. Nor do their individual incomes matter; it is only their joint income that matters.

In reality, as most people would suspect, the identity of the decision maker *does* make a great deal of difference in terms of how income is allocated. Two people rarely have identical preferences. Although the assumption that a family operates as a single unit is a useful fiction to posit for many purposes, it is not something that can be maintained when the well-being of women is the subject of investigation. For their well-being certainly depends on who makes the decisions in the household and how these decisions are made. There is considerable evidence to suggest that the unitary model of the household is incorrect. Two examples will suffice to make the point, one from a developed country and another from a developing country.

It has traditionally been assumed that mothers have more to do with children's welfare than fathers. In the United Kingdom, changes made in a child benefit program afforded some insight into how the expenditure pattern of a household changes when income is transferred from fathers to mothers. Prior to April 1977, the British government reduced the taxes that were automatically withheld from fathers' paychecks. The reduced taxes were a benefit intended for the children. Between April 1977 and April 1979, however, the government instituted some changes in the child benefit program. In essence, after April 1979 it eliminated the tax break for fathers and replaced it with a weekly nontaxable payment to mothers. Basically, this switch *redistributed income* from fathers to mothers. If the unitary model of the household were correct, this redistribution "from the wallet to the purse" should have made no difference to the expenditure patterns of households. Shelly Lundberg, Robert Pollak, and Terence Wales (1996) found that, in reality, it did make a difference: expenditures on women's and children's clothing went up, as did expenditures on domestic services; expenditures on men's clothing and tobacco went down.[6] This demonstrates that the *identity* of the person controlling the income does matter.

In the West African country of Burkina Faso, married men and women cultivate separate plots of land even though they may help each other with their labor. The men and women often cultivate the same crop. Christopher Udry (1996) found that the yield on women's plots is lower (by about 20%) than that on the plots of men cultivating the same crop, even though they

[6] Lundberg, S., R. A. Pollak, and T. J. Wales (1996), "Do Husbands and Wives Pool Their Resources?: Evidence from the United Kingdom Child Benefit," *Journal of Human Resources* 32, pp. 463–480.

both belong to the same household.[7] Almost all of the fertilizer used by the household is devoted to men's plots. The optimal fertilizer allocation may be defined as that which would maximize the joint incomes of husbands and wives. Because the increase in output made possible by applying fertilizer to a given plot of land is likely to exhibit diminishing returns, it would make economic sense to allocate some fertilizer to women's plots, too. Why don't men allocate some of the fertilizer so as to maximize joint income? It is because men and women control only the income generated from *their own plots*—incomes are not pooled. Furthermore, if their preferences as to how income should be spent are different, it is not only total income but also individual incomes that matter. Naturally men want most of the fertilizer for their own plots, even if diverting some of it to their wives' plots would increase the family income. If they have the power to decide how the fertilizer should be allocated, they will allocate most of it to their own plots.

The two examples above reveal that the identities of the income earners and of the decision makers matter. In any household, it is rarely the case that all decisions are made by one person. For example, in the Burkina Faso case, if the husbands were dictators, they would allocate fertilizer so as to maximize the joint incomes of the families because they would have the assurance that they could spend these incomes in any manner they wanted. They don't allocate fertilizers in this manner because they obviously do not have dictatorial decision-making authority. Typically both spouses in a household have some say in the decision making, though not to the same extent. What determines the extent of an individual's influence in the joint decision-making process, and how does that impinge on the outcome? This is the focus of bargaining models, to which we now turn.

III. The Nash Bargaining Model

The Nash model of bargaining belongs to a class referred to as cooperative bargaining models. The idea is that the two parties involved cooperate in the process of bargaining to arrive at a solution by which they split the gains to come up with an agreement. In other words, the final bargain they arrive at is such that it is impossible to improve the well-being of one party without hurting the other; that is, the bargaining outcome is *Pareto efficient*. In such an outcome, all the gains possible through bargaining are exhausted; that is, no possibility whereby both people could benefit is thrown away.

Suppose that two individuals, Anne and Brett, can participate in an arrangement that can potentially make both of them better off. Can we predict what arrangement they will come up with? How will they split the bene-

[7] Udry, C. (1996), "Gender, Agricultural Production, and the Theory of the Household," *Journal of Political Economy* 104, pp. 1010–1046.

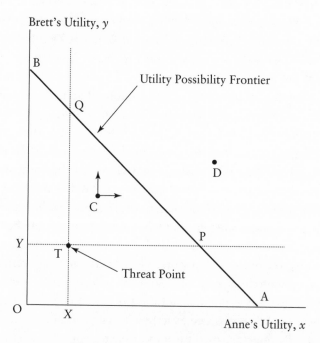

FIGURE 3.2 The basic setup for the Nash bargaining model

fits that the arrangement can generate? Who is going to benefit more from the arrangement, and why? The framework proposed by John Nash is designed to answer these questions. The framework is quite general—it can apply to the bargaining between the two members of a married or an unmarried couple, between the management of a firm and its labor union over wage increases, between two politicians who can strike a mutually advantageous bargain, between a parent and a child over the weekly allowance, and the like. In order to be concrete, in what follows we shall assume that the context is marriage or a common-law relationship.

Let x denote the level of Anne's well-being or utility in the relationship and y denote Brett's. In Figure 3.2, every point represents a combination of Anne's and Brett's utility. Every arrangement they wish to enter into will have as its limit a frontier denoted by AB in the figure, which defines the limit of the possibilities. In other words, it defines the limits of the combinations of well-being that can be achieved by the couple. (If Anne and Brett were bargaining over how to divide a pie, for example, the possibilities would be limited by the size of the pie.) We refer to AB as the utility possibility frontier. Any combination like C, which lies inside the frontier, is achievable within the arrangement. However, a combination at a point like D that lies outside the frontier is not feasible—the arrangement cannot generate sufficiently large benefits.

We shall assume that each person would like to maximize his or her own level of well-being. In Figure 3.2, Anne's most preferred outcome is point A, where she achieves the highest level of utility that the arrangement is capable of generating. However, at point A Brett's utility is minimized. On the other hand, Brett's most preferred outcome is point B, where he achieves the highest level of utility that the arrangement is capable of generating for him. But at point B, Anne's utility is minimized.

What combination of utilities will Anne and Brett actually achieve? We can be sure that, if we assume that the outcome is Pareto efficient, they will never end up at a point like C in Figure 3.2. Why? Because at C there are benefits from the arrangement that remain unexploited. The outcome C is one in which both people can be better off if they are moved in a northeasterly direction (in between the indicated arrows) toward the frontier AB. It is clear that any point that lies inside the frontier AB is not Pareto efficient because it can be improved on by making both parties better off. Only outcomes on AB can be Pareto efficient, because once they are on AB the only way one person can be made better off is by making the other person worse off (because moving outside the frontier is not an option that is available). So if we believe that the outcome of the bargaining process between Anne and Brett is Pareto efficient, they must end up somewhere on AB. But where exactly will they end up? Notice that every point on AB is Pareto efficient—it is impossible to make one person better off without making the other one worse off.

In order to identify the outcome of the bargaining problem, we need more information. In particular, we need to know how Anne and Brett would fare if negotiations between them broke down. What level of well-being would they achieve if they abandoned the possibility of coming up with a mutually acceptable arrangement? In Figure 3.2 this level of well-being is represented by X for Anne and Y for Brett. These utility levels, X and Y, are referred to as the *threat utilities* of Anne and Brett, respectively. They represent their respective outside options, which indicate the opportunities that are individually available to them outside the present arrangement they are bargaining over. We shall take these threat utilities as given, for they are determined by considerations that lie outside the present arrangement. Later on we shall discuss what factors determine these threat utilities. In Figure 3.2, the point T with coordinates X and Y, respectively, is called the threat point.

In the cooperative arrangement that Anne and Brett are bargaining over, Anne would find a level of well-being below X unacceptable; she would be better off walking away from it and settling for her outside option. Therefore, those outcomes on the segment of AB that lie above Q are ruled out as possible outcomes of the bargaining scenario, because these points are no longer Pareto efficient when Anne's outside option is considered. These points offer Anne a level of well-being that is less than her threat utility. Likewise, Brett would find a level of well-being below Y unacceptable; he would be better off walking away from it and taking up his outside option. So those outcomes on the segment of AB that lie below P are ruled out as possible outcomes of the bargaining scenario because these points offer Brett a level of well-being that is less than his threat utility. Therefore, the outcome of the bargaining will be somewhere on the segment PQ of the utility possibility frontier. The question is where on PQ, because that will determine the ratio in which the gains to the couple's cooperation will be split between Anne and Brett.

Notice that there are cooperative *and* competitive aspects to the resolution of the bargaining scenario. On the one hand, unless Anne and Brett cooperate, they will not realize the possible gains to their project. Once they have decided to cooperate, however, any surplus that Anne receives above her threat utility will come at the expense of Brett's surplus over his threat utility, and vice versa. Thus a tension between cooperation and conflict is inherent in the bargaining situation.

Suppose that Anne could single-handedly determine the outcome of the bargaining. She would want to maximize her own well-being, x. Equivalently, she would want to do as well as possible for herself compared to what she could do in her threat option. In other words, she would maximize the surplus of her utility over her threat utility, namely, $x - X$. However, in this she would be constrained by the fact she cannot push Brett below point P on the segment AB. If she tried, he would walk away, and the potential benefits of the arrangement would not materialize. So Anne would opt for point P, thereby holding Brett down to the minimal utility (Y) necessary to elicit his cooperation. Similarly, if Brett could single-handedly determine the outcome of the bargaining, he would want to maximize the surplus of his utility over his threat utility, namely, $y - Y$. But he cannot push Anne above point Q on the segment AB because she would then walk away. So he would opt for point Q, thereby holding Anne down to the minimal utility (X) necessary to elicit her cooperation.

In reality, however, we would expect that neither Anne nor Brett would have the power to single-handedly determine the outcome of the bargaining. Both would likely have some say in the matter, though perhaps not an equal say. As a result, we would expect the outcome of the bargaining to lie somewhere between P and Q on AB.

The Bargaining Solution Proposed by John Nash

Under some technical assumptions, John Nash demonstrated which allocation would obtain in the outcome.[8] He proved that the allocation that would obtain in the bargaining situation is the one for which the *product* of surpluses,

$$(x - X)(y - Y)$$

---

[8] The three assumptions he made may be translated in this context as follows: (1) The outcome depends only on the threat utilities of Anne and Brett, not on the fact that one person is called Anne and the other Brett. To put it differently, if we switch the threat utilities of Anne and Brett, the utilities they achieve in the bargaining outcome will also switch. (2) If we change the units in which we measure utility, the solution will be the same (except for the change in units). (3) If an outcome that did not obtain as a bargaining solution is removed from the realm of possibilities, the original bargaining scenario will still obtain in the new bargaining scenario.

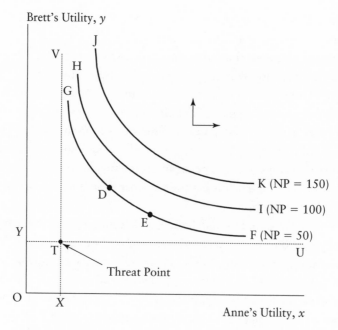

Brett's Utility, *y*

FIGURE 3.3 Illustration of contours along which the Nash product is constant

achieves its *largest possible value,* provided that the following conditions are satisfied: (a) x is at least as large as X, (b) y is at least as large as Y, and (c) the point (x, y) lies on or inside the utility possibility frontier. Conditions a and b merely state that Anne and Brett must receive at least what they can obtain in their threat options. Condition c says that the allocation must be feasible for the given bargaining situation. In other words, what ends up being maximized in the bargaining outcome is neither Anne's surplus $(x - X)$ nor Brett's surplus $(y - Y)$—so neither Anne nor Brett unilaterally determines the outcome—but rather the product $(x - X)(y - Y)$, which is referred to as the *Nash product.* The proposed solution to the bargaining situation is called the *Nash bargaining solution.*

A Geometrical Exposition of the Nash Bargaining Solution

Let us first represent the Nash bargaining solution geometrically before we attempt to provide intuition for it. Suppose that Anne's threat utility is 10 and Brett's is 15 (that is, $X = 10$ and $Y = 15$). Suppose that in the bargaining situation Anne and Brett both achieve a utility of 20 (that is, $x = y = 20$). This allocation is denoted by point D in Figure 3.3. The Nash product (NP in the figure) for this allocation is $(20 - 10)(20 - 15) = 50$. Now we can conceive of many other allocations (x, y) for which the Nash product will also be exactly 50. Starting from D in the figure, if we increase x we need decrease y by only so much that the Nash product will remain 50. Point E is another allocation with the same Nash product of 50. In a similar manner,

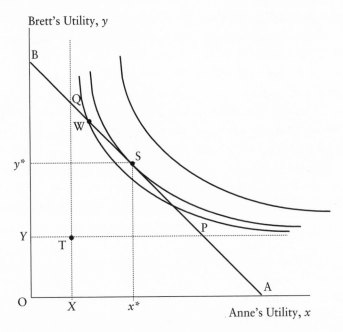

FIGURE 3.4 Illustration of the Nash bargaining solution

we can find an infinite number of allocations with the same Nash product. If we join all these points, we get the downward-sloping curve GF shown in the figure. For convenience, we shall refer to this curve as an *isoproduct contour*. This curve necessarily slopes downward because an increase in x must be accompanied by a decrease in y if the Nash product is to remain 50. Likewise, the isoproduct contour corresponding to a Nash product of 100 will lie on the higher curve HI, the contour for a Nash product of 150 will lie on the even higher curve JK, and so on. In fact, any movement in the northeasterly direction (in a direction between the perpendicular lines with arrowheads) will take us on to contours with higher Nash products.

As in Figure 3.2, in Figure 3.3 we use T to denote the threat point, whose coordinates are the threat utilities of Anne and Brett. No allocation below the horizontal line TU will be acceptable to Brett, and no allocation to the left of the vertical line TV will be acceptable to Anne. The isoproduct contours may approach the lines TU and TV, but they can never quite touch or cut across them.[9]

We are now equipped to geometrically represent the Nash bargaining solution, and this is done in Figure 3.4. In this figure we bring together the threat point, the utility possibility frontier, and the isoproduct contours. We have

[9]To see that this must be true, suppose that the isoproduct curve for NP = 50 cuts the horizontal line TU. At the point of intersection, the value of y must be equal to 15 (Brett gains no surplus), implying that the Nash product must be zero. This contradicts the assumption that the Nash product is 50 everywhere on the curve.

seen above that conditions a through c require the Nash solution to be somewhere in the triangular region TPQ. Furthermore, if the outcome is to be
Pareto efficient, we have seen that it must lie on the segment PQ of the utility possibility frontier AB. We can identify the Nash bargaining solution if
we can figure out where on the segment PQ the Nash product is maximized.
According to Nash's theoretical result, this is the point that puts Anne and
Brett on the contour corresponding to the *highest* Nash product. From Figure
3.4 we see that this point is S, where an isoproduct contour is *tangential* to
the utility possibility frontier. A point like W, where the contour cuts the utility possibility frontier, has a lower Nash product than S. The coordinates of
S, indicated by x^* and y^* in the figure, are the utilities achieved by Anne and
Brett in the Nash bargaining solution.

The Effect of the Threat Point on the Nash Bargaining Solution

Notice that at point S both Anne and Brett are better off than they would
have been at the threat point. Furthermore, the allocation of utilities at S
is Pareto efficient: it is impossible to make Anne better off without hurting
Brett, and vice versa. These features have been built into the Nash bargaining solution by the requirements that the players do at least as well as in their
threat options and that they exhaust all the benefits to cooperation.

A crucial question remains: what determines the split of the benefits that
Anne and Brett receive in the Nash bargaining solution? The answer is this:
their relative threat utilities. Understanding how this comes about provides
some intuition for the Nash bargaining solution and reveals why this is such
a useful framework for understanding bargaining outcomes.

If a person's utility in the outside option increases, he or she gets a better deal in the Nash bargaining solution. To see this, suppose that Anne's
threat utility increases from its original value X to a new, higher value, X'.
We represent the new situation in Figure 3.5. Here T and S denote the original threat point and Nash bargaining solution, respectively, and T' the new
threat point. The isoproduct contours are now different than before because
the Nash product associated with the allocation (x, y) is now $(x - X')(y - Y)$.
So we will now have a *different set* of isoproduct contours.

The Nash bargaining solution will be given by that point on PQ that is
on the highest of the new isoproduct contours. These new contours will now
approach (but never touch) the horizontal line through T', which is the same
as before, and the new vertical line through T'. The vertical line through T' is
shifted to the right relative to the vertical line through T. As a result, the new
contour passing through any point is steeper than the old contour through
the same point because these curves are now being squeezed to the right.
This pushes the new point of tangency in the *southeasterly* direction relative
to the old point of tangency. The new Nash bargaining solution, denoted in
Figure 3.5 by S', lies on PQ to the southeast of the original solution, S. This

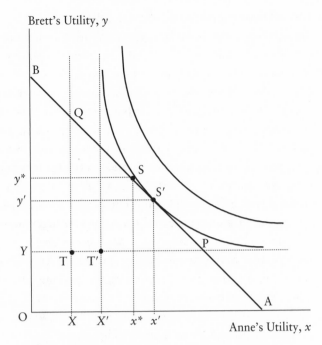

FIGURE 3.5 Illustration of how the Nash bargaining
solution changes when Anne's threat utility increases

new solution, which is also Pareto efficient, offers Anne a higher level of utility and Brett a lower level of utility than before. As indicated in the figure,
Anne receives a utility x' and Brett y'.

This simple exercise in which the threat utility of Anne is increased illustrates one of the most important properties of the solution to the bargaining
situation. When Anne has better outside options, she is assured of a better
agreement in the arrangement with Brett. The fact that she now can do better
for herself in the event that negotiations between her and Brett break down
guarantees Anne better treatment in the bargain. This situation, of course,
is symmetrical. If it is Brett whose threat option improves, it is his share that
increases in the bargaining solution. *The most important determinants of
how the gains to cooperation are split are the relative threat utilities of the
bargainers.*

All this is not to say that Anne and Brett necessarily bargain across a table
as the management and union of a firm might. Rather, their bargaining is at
a psychological level. How assertive a person is likely to be in a bargaining
situation depends on his or her fallback options, that is, how well the person can do in the event that bargaining breaks down. It is this that credibly
communicates to the other party the person's willingness to walk away if he
or she doesn't receive a reasonable share of the benefits to cooperation. What
can legitimately be deemed reasonable depends on the person's threat utility.

A Simple Method for Computing the Nash Bargaining Solution

How does one determine the Nash bargaining solution in a handy manner? To draw the set of isoproduct contours and then pick the point of tangency with the utility possibility frontier appears to be an involved and tedious procedure. Fortunately, when this frontier has a simple shape, there is a straightforward procedure that enables us to determine the Nash bargaining outcome. One needs only to draw a simple graph. To illustrate this we shall suppose that the utility possibility frontier is a straight line. Suppose that, along the utility possibility frontier, Anne's and Brett's utilities sum to some known constant, M, that is, $x + y = M$. For example, M may be the amount of the total benefits (say, \$1,000) that would be received from their cooperative endeavor, and the bargaining is over how Anne and Brett might split this amount. It is important to understand that M is something that is given in the bargaining situation and is not to be determined by Anne and Brett. At point A in Figure 3.4, $x = M$ and $y = 0$. As we move up along AB, Anne's utility decreases and Brett's increases until, at B, $x = 0$ and $y = M$. Thus along AB we can express Brett's utility in terms of Anne's: $y = M - x$, which simply says that Brett gets what is left over after Anne gets her share.

We know that the Nash bargaining solution lies on the segment QP in Figure 3.4 because it is Pareto efficient. So we can restrict the search for the solution to this segment. At any point on this segment, by expressing y in terms of x, the Nash product $(x - X)(y - Y)$ can be rewritten as $(x - X)(M - x - Y)$. Expressed in this way, the Nash product depends only on Anne's utility, because X, Y, and M are known quantities that are given. Suppose that we start from point Q in Figure 3.4 and move along AB toward P and compute the Nash product at each point. We can then plot a graph of the Nash product in terms of the value of Anne's utility, x. This is done in Figure 3.6.

At point Q in Figure 3.4, Anne receives a utility that is exactly equal to her threat utility $(x = X)$, so the Nash product is zero. Likewise, at point P Brett receives a utility that is exactly equal to his threat utility $(y = Y$ or $x = M - Y)$, so the Nash product is again zero. As we move from Q to P, however, the Nash product first increases and then decreases. This is shown as the hill JKL in Figure 3.6. Because the Nash product is highest at point K in this figure, the corresponding value of Anne's utility, x^*, can be read directly from the graph. Brett's utility, y^*, can then be obtained as $y^* = M - x^*$. Thus this simple procedure enables us to compute the Nash bargaining solution with relative ease.

The Relevant Threat Point in Household Bargaining

We have seen that the outcome of bargaining depends on each person's threat point. In household bargaining, what should we take as the threat point? In some cases, it might be divorce that defines the appropriate threat utility. In such cases a breakdown of bargaining is identified as the breakdown of

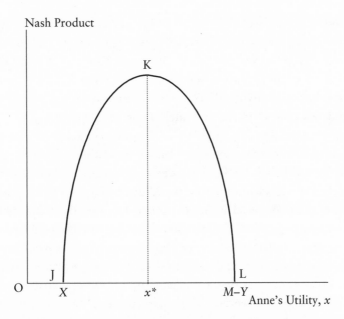

FIGURE 3.6 A simple way to determine the Nash bargaining solution

the relationship. How well Anne and Brett can do for themselves in the event that they break up and go their separate ways may seem the natural choice for their threat utilities. This is the view espoused by some scholars, such as Marilyn Manser and Murray Brown and Marjorie McElroy and Mary Horney.[10] In the developed world, divorce may indeed be a reasonable threat point in many circumstances.

It has also been argued, however, that the utility that each person derives by behaving *noncooperatively within marriage* may define the relevant threat point. This has been the viewpoint of scholars such as Frances Woolley (1988), Shelly Lundberg and Robert Pollak (1993), and Zhiqi Chen and Frances Woolley (2001).[11] In other words, if negotiations break down Anne and Brett may ignore the fact that their actions impinge on the well-being of the other person. They may act in their individual best interest, taking the other person's actions as beyond their control. In that scenario, when negotiations break down Anne does the best for herself, taking as given the actions of Brett. Likewise, Brett does the best for himself, taking as given the actions of Anne. The noncooperative outcome whereby neither

[10] Manser and Brown (1980) and McElroy and Horney (1981).

[11] Woolley, F. R. (1988), "A Non-Cooperative Model of Family Decision Making," Trinity International Development Initiative Working Paper 125, London School of Economics, London; Lundberg, S., and R. Pollak (1993), "Separate Spheres Bargaining and the Marriage Market," *Journal of Political Economy* 101 (6), pp. 988–1010; and Chen, Z., and F. R. Woolley (2001), "A Cournot–Nash Model of Family Decision Making," *Economic Journal* 111 (October), 722–748.

can choose actions different from his or her current choice that could make him or her better off, given the other person's action, is referred to as the *Nash equilibrium,* as we saw in the previous chapter.[12] It is important to note that this noncooperative behavior is occurring *within* marriage; the two people have not divorced. This threat alternative may be more appropriate in developing countries in which divorce is relatively rare.

It is quite possible that, in this noncooperative mode, both people may retreat into their *separate spheres* as defined by traditional norms, as argued by Lundberg and Pollak (1993). Let us be more specific. Suppose that Anne is more efficient at housework than Brett and that he is better than Anne at market work. In their cooperative endeavor, they may split their activities according to comparative advantage. Anne may do a larger share of the housework, recognizing that this has to suffice for two people, and take up only a part-time job outside the home. Brett may do much less of the housework and spend most of his nonleisure time earning an income. In a noncooperative situation like that alluded to above, however, Anne might curtail some aspects of her housework (such as cooking and laundry) so that it suffices only for her. In her time that has been thus freed up, she might take up full-time employment outside the home. And Brett, needing some of these household services that Anne has ceased to provide, may need to curtail his market activity and spend more time doing housework. Furthermore, traditional norms may dictate that Anne is responsible for housework and Brett for the income necessary to run the household. So when they retreat into their separate spheres, Anne may contribute only her labor for the upkeep of their household, withholding any financial resources (even though she can afford to contribute these, too). The utility that each person derives from this noncooperative scenario defines the threat point in the "separate spheres" view. The couple is still married—they are not separated or divorced—but in choosing their actions each person is looking only to his or her own well-being (ignoring the beneficial or costly effects of their choices on the partner), and that only in his or her traditional sphere of activity.

Does it matter whether it is divorce or the noncooperative outcome within marriage that is the threat point in the bargaining solution? Yes, it does. To see why this is true, consider two events:[13] (a) Anne gets a good job that she can take up in the threat scenario, and (b) Anne receives as an inheritance some real estate that earns her rental (nonlabor) income. Both of these events increase her threat utility, but which would yield a better bargaining outcome for her? The answer depends on whether it is divorce or the noncooperative outcome within marriage that is the threat point. To draw a comparison, suppose that the increase in Anne's utility in scenarios a and b

---

[12] Note that the Nash equilibrium is distinct from the Nash bargaining solution.

[13] The argument that follows is drawn from Anderson, S., and M. Eswaran (2009), "What Determines Female Autonomy?: Evidence from Bangladesh," *Journal of Development Economics* 90, pp. 179–191.

is the same. If divorce is the threat scenario, both events will increase Anne's bargaining power by the same amount and will not affect Brett's threat utility because the individuals are going their separate ways. There is nothing to choose between the two events. In other words, one will obtain the same Nash bargaining solution in both scenarios.

If noncooperative behavior within marriage is the threat scenario, however, the two events might generate very different bargaining outcomes by affecting Brett's threat utility differently. Some household goods and services are public goods in the sense that one cannot prevent one's spouse from enjoying their benefits. When Anne receives rental income, as in event b, she will spend part of it on the household (e.g., buying paintings for the living room), and this public good will benefit Brett even in the noncooperative scenario. So when Anne's nonlabor income increases because of her inheritance, Brett's threat utility also increases. What happens in event a, when Anne gets a good job? In this case Anne will divert some of her time from doing housework to working in the market. As a result, Brett (who consumes these household services) will be worse off. So Brett's threat utility will decrease in event a. In other words, event b increases the threat utilities of both Anne and Brett, whereas a increases Anne's threat utility but decreases Brett's. Consequently, when the couple's noncooperative behavior within marriage is the threat point, scenarios a and b will generate different Nash bargaining solutions. So it matters which scenario defines the threat point.

At this point we should recognize that this approach to bargaining within the household—as useful as it is—has its drawbacks. Amartya Sen (1990) has argued that one drawback of such models is their presumption that individual self-interest is a well-defined concept.[14] This is not necessarily the case, especially in developing countries. Society often downplays some activities, especially those undertaken within the household, as "unproductive." If they are perceived as such by women, it will undermine their perception of what is their just desserts. As a result, they may not perceive the household allocation as unfair despite the fact that they are deprived in a real sense to an outside view. Put differently, socialization may mold preferences that are detrimental to women in a bargaining situation, and bargaining models take these preferences as given. (Nevertheless, *given* these preferences, the models can accurately predict the outcomes.)

There is evidence on the kinds of socialization that are damaging to women. As mentioned in Chapter 1, Linda Babcock and Sara Laschever (2003) have shown that women may not ask for what is their rightful due in bargaining situations, and consequently they may receive less than men. Both men and women may be playing out socially constructed roles, so the out-

---

[14] Sen, A. (1990), "Gender and Cooperative Conflicts," in *Persistent Inequalities: Women and World Development*, ed. I. Tinker, Oxford University Press, New York, pp. 123–149.

comes may be very asymmetric even if their outside options are not very different. Although they are very important, outside options are not everything. An alternative way of thinking about this is to recognize that the payoff in outside options must include the negative reactions that women may face from society when they violate gender-normative roles, as shown in the work by Hannah Bowles, Linda Babcock, and Lei Lai (2007) that we discussed in the previous chapter. Because these negative reactions are usually dependent on culture, the perceived payoffs are context dependent.

IV. Determinants of Threat Utility

In a bargaining situation, a woman's threat utility is the utility she can assure herself of in the event that bargaining breaks down. We have seen that her threat utility crucially determines how well she will do in the bargain. The greater her threat utility, the greater will be her utility in the Nash bargaining solution. The better her outside options, the better the deal she can achieve within the bargain. In the bargaining outcome both players typically do better than in their threat options, so it is in their mutual interest to come to a cooperative agreement. However, the threat utility is more fundamental to their well-being than the bargaining outcome, for it is the threat utility that determines the bargaining outcome. It is in each person's interest to possess the highest possible threat utility before entering into a bargain.

But what determines a woman's threat utility? Many factors impinge on this important entity. One of the most important is her human capital. The higher her education level and the more her work experience, the greater will be her productivity and the higher her income should she work. Even if she chooses *not* to work in the cooperative outcome, her utility will be greater in the Nash bargaining solution as a result of her human capital. Ownership of other assets will also increase her threat utility. Ownership of land, financial wealth, and so on, by generating nonlabor income, will increase her threat option in household bargaining.

The laws of the society in which a woman lives are also important. Whether women are seen as equal to men in the eyes of the law matters. In many countries, women received voting rights only a few decades ago. Until then, they had no political voice to improve their lot; they had limited means through which they could increase their resources for things that met their needs. But other laws, such as inheritance laws and divorce laws, also matter. In many countries, inheritance laws are such that parents' bequests are not equally divided between sons and daughters. To the extent that daughters are discriminated against in inheritances, women will have fewer assets and, therefore, lower nonlabor income.

Divorce laws are important, too, because they determine how well a married woman will do in the event her marriage breaks up. If the household's assets are divided equally, even though she may have specialized in being a housewife, a woman will come out better than when the assets go mostly to her husband. Likewise, custody laws that favor mothers in the event of divorce increase a woman's threat utility. Her greater threat utility will embolden her to demand a more reasonable share of the surplus within marriage.

A woman's social network is also important. Those she can rely on in times of serious trouble (such as a separation or marriage breakup) will certainly impinge on her threat utility. The strength of one's family ties and the physical distance to one's close relatives are important. Someone who has no close relatives or friends and no other support groups will have a low threat utility on that count. She will usually be more timid in her approach to bargaining than if she had strong familial and social ties.

In market economies, however, by far the most important factor impinging on a woman's threat utility is her human capital—her ability to command a good labor income. Human capital is not something that can be taken away from her. A crooked relative may appropriate her land, she may lose her house in a flood or an earthquake, and she may lose her financial wealth in a stock market crash. But her human capital is inalienable; it cannot be separated from her. As long as she maintains her health, she can put her education and work experience to use in the market. Even if the laws of the land are not supportive and even if she does not have close relatives or strong support groups, she can manage to be independent using the income she earns with her human capital.

We must note, however, that even if she earns an independent income, a woman may not always be able to exercise control over how it is spent. In some of the highly patriarchal societies of developing countries, a wage-earning woman has to hand over much of her earnings to the patriarch of her household. Earning ability in such situations is limited in its scope to empower women. It is *control* over the income earned that empowers them. Siwan Anderson and Jean-Marie Baland (2002), for example, found that in the slums of the Kenyan city of Kibera, women often joined forced savings institutions just to get income out of the reach of their husbands, that is, to maintain control over their income.[15] It is nevertheless still true that women with education can exercise greater control over their earnings than those without education.

V. Noncooperative Bargaining

In the Nash bargaining solution we considered above, Anne and Brett cooperated in the bargaining process even if they behaved noncooperatively in

---

[15] Anderson, S., and J. M. Baland (2002), "The Economics of Roscas and Intrahousehold Resource Allocation," *Quarterly Journal of Economics* 117, pp. 963–995.

the threat outcome. An alternative way of analyzing bargaining situations is to assume that even the *process of bargaining* is noncooperative. In this instance, we cannot explicitly assume that the bargaining outcome is Pareto efficient.

In models of noncooperative bargaining, it is typically assumed that the bargainers can alternately make offers and counteroffers about how the gains from their cooperative endeavor are to be split. The classic paper on noncooperative bargaining is that by Ariel Rubinstein (1982), but the exposition below follows somewhat the treatment in Avinash Dixit and Barry Nalebuff (1991).[16] To get the flavor of how this works, suppose that Anne and Brett can earn a total of $100 in the event that they agree to cooperate on a one-day project. For the moment, suppose that their threat utilities are zero. We begin by assuming that only Brett can propose how they should split the amount. Anne can either accept the proposal or reject it. If she accepts it, the $100 will be split in the manner proposed by Brett. If Anne rejects Brett's proposal, they will both gain nothing from the project because it will not be undertaken. This scenario is that of the ultimatum game that we encountered in Chapter 2. How will the money be split?

As before, we assume that Anne and Brett each wants to maximize his or her own well-being. We further assume that this well-being is captured by the amount of money they receive and by nothing else. Even though Brett is the one making the proposal, he has to worry about whether Anne will accept or reject his offer, for if she rejects it, neither of them will receive anything because the project will not be undertaken. So he has to put himself in Anne's shoes and ask himself how she will behave in response to his proposal. In other words, before Brett makes his proposal, he has to solve Anne's decision problem first.

How will Anne decide when confronted with a proposal from Brett? She will recognize that if she rejects his offer, she will gain nothing from the project and, because she has no outside option, will receive nothing elsewhere either. Therefore, she will be better off accepting any offer from Brett that gives her at least one cent. Brett, wanting to maximize his own share, will want to give her just enough that she won't reject his offer but no more. He will give her no more than one cent. So he will propose that he should receive almost everything ($99.99) and that she should receive almost nothing ($0.01). Anne will accept the proposal. Of course, we might believe that Anne will be incensed by this extremely unfair distribution and reject his offer. But that would amount to saying that Anne is motivated by something other than the amount of money she will receive, contradicting our

---

[16] Rubinstein, A. (1982), "Perfect Equilibrium in a Bargaining Model," *Econometrica* 50, pp. 97–109, and Dixit, A., and B. Nalebuff (1991), *Thinking Strategically*, W. W. Norton, New York, Chap. 11.

assumption. In fact, if Anne is motivated only by the amount of money she will receive, Brett can even propose that he should receive everything and Anne nothing. If she rejects the offer, again she will receive nothing. If she is indifferent between accepting and rejecting the offer, suppose she chooses to accept. In this case, Brett will receive the entire $100 and Anne nothing. This is the noncooperative bargaining outcome.

Now let us give Anne a chance to propose a split and see how the bargaining outcome changes. Suppose that she and Brett can undertake the project on each of two days, earning a total of $100 each day if they can come to an agreement. As before, suppose that they have no outside options. Furthermore, suppose that each person would like to receive the maximum possible total earnings over the two days. On the first day, suppose that Brett gets to make a proposal as to how they should split the money. If Anne accepts the proposal, the proposed split will be implemented for both periods. If Anne rejects the proposal, they both will receive nothing for that day. But the following day, Anne will get to propose how they should split the second day's earnings. If Brett accepts her offer, they will work on the project and split the money as agreed. If Brett rejects it, on the second day, too, neither of them will earn anything.

In making his proposal on the first day, Brett will have to make sure he doesn't offer Anne too little. For if he does, she will reject his offer and do better for herself when she gets to propose the split the next day. How will she choose the split on the next (and last) day? Using the same argument as before, we know that Brett will accept any share on the second day—no matter how small—because by rejecting it he will receive zero and, because he has no outside option, zero elsewhere. So on the second day, Anne will propose that she take everything, leaving Brett nothing. That is, Anne's total earnings over the two days will be $100 (zero on the first day and $100 on the second). So when Brett makes his proposal on the first day, he will have to ensure that Anne receives a total of at least $100 over the two days. Therefore, he will offer a 50-50 split. Because this will be implemented on both days, Anne and Brett each will receive a total of $100 over the two days. Anne will accept this offer because she can do no better by rejecting it. The noncooperative bargaining outcome now is a 50-50 split.

The first thing to notice about the above outcome is that having the opportunity to reject Brett's offer and making a counteroffer gives Anne bargaining power. Compared to the earlier situation in which Anne had no such option, she now earns $50 on each of the two days. The very fact that Anne can reject Brett's offer and do better for herself by proposing the split the next day puts a limit on how selfish Brett can be. In any bargaining situation, each person has to seriously take account of the options available to the other person. The freedom to reject an offer and to make a counteroffer is a vehicle of empowerment.

However, a person may also have an *outside option*. If Anne has the option of earning an income outside of this project, how will it affect the bargaining situation with Brett? To see this, suppose that Anne has an outside option (threat utility) of $20 a day but Brett, as before, has none. So if they do not undertake a project on any day, she can earn $20 doing some other job but he cannot earn anything. How will this affect Brett's proposal on the first day? He will realize that, if Anne rejects his offer, she will earn $20 elsewhere on that day, and on the next day she will make him a counteroffer in which she will receive everything from the project. In other words, she can assure herself of a total of $120 over the two days. So if Brett's offer on the first day is to be accepted, he has to make sure that Anne will receive at least $120 over the two days. Therefore, he will offer a 40-60 split, $40 for himself and $60 for Anne, on each of the two days. And Anne will accept.

We see that when Anne's outside option increases from zero to $20 a day, her total earnings in the bargain will increase from $100 to $120. She does not actually go out and exercise her outside option. Simply having such an option affects the bargaining outcome, because Brett has to respect the fact that she has this option. The situation, of course, is symmetric: if Brett has outside options, this will generally improve his earnings at Anne's expense.

VI. Evidence for Bargaining Models

We have already discussed some evidence suggesting that the unitary model of household allocation is not supported by data. Duncan Thomas (1990) has provided additional compelling evidence of this and of the different preferences of women and men with regard to household expenditures.[17] He examined data from a national sample of Brazil as to how income in the hands of mothers and in those of fathers impinges on spending on the health and nutrition of children. He first found that, judging from the outcomes, it *does* matter whether income accrues to the mother or the father, that is, the data reject the unitary model of the household. This suggests that the individual preferences of husbands and wives are different, and for this difference to be manifested in the outcomes, the wives must have income to spend.

In examining the effect of income on bargaining outcomes such as a household's demand for various goods, it is better to focus on *unearned* income rather than total income. Unearned income refers to income from pension, social security, and financial assets, whereas total income includes labor income. Labor income may itself depend on the bargaining powers of the members of the couple. For example, whether a wife has labor income may depend on whether she has any bargaining power to assert her right to work

---

[17]Thomas, D. (1990), "Intra-Household Resource Allocation: An Inferential Approach," *Journal of Human Resources* 25, pp. 635–664.

in the first place.[18] Unearned income does not have this problem, at least not to the same extent. Thomas found that when a mother's unearned income increased, the household's demand for nutrition rose by more than 4 times the rise in nutrition demand when the father's unearned income increased by the same amount. Furthermore, the effect on child survival of increases in unearned income was almost 20 times larger for the mother than the father. This finding has enormous policy implications for poor countries that are seeking to reduce child mortality: income in the hands of mothers is much more efficacious than income in the hands of fathers.

Esther Duflo (2003) has used data from South Africa to demonstrate that the gender of a grandparent who receives cash is important to determining the health status of girls in a family.[19] In the early 1990s, after the dismantling of apartheid, the South African government expanded its pension program to include blacks. Because extended families are quite common in that country, many pensioners live in the same households as their grandchildren. Duflo found that the health status of female children, as captured by weight-for-height and height-for-age measures, is significantly better if they are living with their pension-earning grandmothers. No such effect is observed for male children. Furthermore, when children are living with their pension-earning grandfathers, there are no discernible health effects on the children. This shows that the identity of the pension recipient (male or female) has an important effect on the grandchildren's health status.

Using data from the African country of Côte d'Ivoire, John Hoddinott and Lawrence Haddad (1995) provide more evidence that the identity of the income earner makes a difference to a family's spending patterns.[20] They find that an increase in the share of women's income increases the budget share allocated to food and decreases that devoted to meals eaten outside the home, as well as to alcohol and cigarettes. If the share of the family income accruing to the wife doubles, the share of income spent on food consumed in the home increases by about 2%, whereas the shares of alcohol and cigarettes decline by about 25% and 15%, respectively. Somewhat surprisingly, this study also found that there is a decrease in the shares spent on children's and adults' clothing.

Agnes Quisumbing and John Maluccio (2003) examined the effect of the assets wives bring with them to marriage on the spending patterns of their

[18] A man with bargaining power may recognize that in the future this power may be reduced if his spouse starts working, so he might prevent her from taking a paying job. See Basu, K. (2006), "Gender and Say: A Model of Household Behaviour with Endogenously Determined Balance of Power," *Economic Journal* 116, pp. 558–580.

[19] Duflo, E. (2003), "Grandmothers and Grandfathers: Old-Age Pensions and Intrahousehold Allocation in South Africa," *World Bank Economic Review* 17, pp. 1–25.

[20] Hoddinott, J., and L. Haddad (1995), "Does Female Income Share Influence Household Expenditures?: Evidence from Côte d'Ivoire," *Oxford Bulletin of Economics and Statistics* 57, pp. 77–96.

households in four countries (Bangladesh, Ethiopia, Indonesia, and South Africa).[21] They used these assets as proxies for women's bargaining power within their households. They found that in three out of the four countries the unitary model was rejected. Furthermore, in all four countries the allocations were seen to be consistent with Pareto efficiency (which is what the cooperative bargaining models presume). In two of the countries (Bangladesh and South Africa), an increase in women's bargaining power increased the shares of income allocated to children's education. The authors, however, are cautious to point out that this need not have been because women are more altruistic than men. Because wives are considerably younger than their husbands, on average, the women may have been ensuring better care for themselves in old age via more educated children.

We have seen that, according to bargaining theory, what empowers women is greater threat utility. This was shown to be the case in a stark manner in the Matlab area of Bangladesh by research conducted by Siwan Anderson and Mukesh Eswaran.[22] In the data from this area, married women had essentially three options open to them: (i) specializing exclusively in housework, (ii) helping their husbands on their farms, and (iii) earning an independent income by raising chickens and ducks. One might have expected that the autonomy of women in option ii would have been greater than that of women in i and that the autonomy of women in iii would have been even greater. This is because in ii women helped their husbands earn income and in iii they earned independent incomes. A surprising finding of Anderson and Eswaran is that, although women in iii did have greater autonomy than women in i, those in ii did not. Why? Because women who merely helped their husbands earn money did not increase their outside options. Purdah restrictions (whereby women have to veil their faces and sometimes their whole bodies) prevented them from working with men who were not their husbands. So women without the skill to work for themselves had only two options: specializing in housework or helping their husbands in their farm work. Purdah restrictions eliminated outside options for these women. So, by working on their husbands' farms, they garnered no additional bargaining power relative to specializing in housework. It is only by working for themselves and controlling the income they earn that women gain greater say in household matters. Bargaining power depends on outside options, and if these remain unchanged, bargaining power remains unchanged. The empirical finding using Bangladeshi data is a stark confirmation of this prediction of bargaining theory.

---

[21] Quisumbing, A. R., and J. A. Maluccio (2003), "Resources at Marriage and Intrahousehold Allocation: Evidence from Bangladesh, Ethiopia, Indonesia, and South Africa," *Oxford Bulletin of Economics and Statistics* 65, pp. 283–327.

[22] Anderson and Eswaran (2009).

An interesting verification of the bargaining model has been conducted by Lixing Li and Xiaoyu Wu (2011) using data from China.[23] They argue that because couples have a strong preference for male children in China, women who have sons enjoy more status than women who have daughters. As a result, the bargaining power of the former is greater and they have greater say in household decision making. One might think that, if a son preference is strong, couples will ensure that they have mostly male children (through selective abortion and so on). However, the evidence shows that the proportion of *first-born male children* is no different in China than in countries where there is no gender preference. Sex preference shows up only in second and subsequent births. (We shall discuss preferences as to the sex of children in developing countries and their consequences in Chapter 8.)

To ensure that their measure of bargaining power was not contaminated by the possibility that the genders of children have been manipulated by parents, Li and Wu focused their attention on only first-born children. They investigated whether mothers of male first-born children have more bargaining power than mothers of female first-born children after accounting for all other relevant factors. Using Chinese data for the period 1993–2006, they found that the former enjoyed a greater say of about 4 percentage points in household decision making than the latter. They also found that the former were able to consume more nutrition and, therefore, were less likely to be undernourished. One might suspect that this is due to the fact that when the children start earning, boys earn more than girls, so their family income may be higher. But Li and Wu show that they obtained the same finding even when they restricted themselves to mothers of young children (who wouldn't have started earning). This strongly suggests that it is the bargaining power of the mothers of first-born males that is higher than that of mothers of first-born females.

Evidence for the relevance and importance of bargaining models is certainly not restricted to research done in developing countries. For example, Shelley Phipps and Peter Burton (1998) use Canadian data to show that the unitary model fails.[24] Furthermore, they find that although husbands and wives may not pool their incomes for all goods, they may pool them for some goods (such as housing). On goods that they consume privately, they tend to spend their own incomes. However, on goods that are jointly consumed, the spending is dictated by gendered norms about whose sphere of responsibility they are in: wives tend to spend on child care, for example, husbands on transportation.

[23] Li, L., and X. Wu (2011), "Gender of Children, Bargaining Power, and Intrahousehold Resource Allocation in China," *Journal of Human Resources* 46, pp. 295–316.

[24] Phipps, S. A., and P. S. Burton (1998), "What's Mine Is Yours?: The Influence of Male and Female Incomes on Patterns of Household Expenditure," *Economica* 65, pp. 599–613.

Some interesting, if indirect, confirmation of the predictions of bargaining theory has been provided by Joshua Angrist (2002).[25] He examined how sex ratios affected the bargaining power of women in the marriage market in the United States. (Angrist defines the sex ratio as the number of males per female.) If the sex ratio is higher than 1 in the age group of marriageable adults, it means that there are more men than women. This tends to improve the bargaining power of women in the marriage market. As a result, women can choose to marry men with higher incomes, insist on working less when married, and so on.

The difficulty with testing these predictions is usually that the sex ratio is very stable and does not vary enough to be informative about changes in bargaining power. However, Angrist creatively exploited the fact that there have been episodes in U.S. history when the sex ratios of various ethnic communities have changed considerably because U.S. immigration policies have assigned quotas to immigrants of different ethnic groups. In particular, he focused on the period 1910–40 and examined whether there is evidence that changing sex ratios affected the marriage rates of women and men in the next generation. The logic is that, if the sex ratio of Italians, say, changed during the period because of immigration (as it did), the marriage rates among Italians of the *second* generation would have been affected. This is because marriages tend to be endogamous, that is, there is a tendency for Italians to marry Italians, Germans to marry Germans, and so on.

Angrist found that when the sex ratios of ethnic communities increased during the period, more women tended to get married. In addition, these women participated less in the labor market, and their husbands' incomes were higher. Furthermore, the marriages that resulted from higher sex ratios were more stable. These findings are consistent with the implications of bargaining theory. When women are scarce, men will have to try harder to get wives—they will have to invest more in themselves, work harder, earn more, and so on—and will be more careful to avoid marital failure.

All in all, the evidence we have surveyed above in favor of models of bargaining within the household is quite compelling. We now turn to why bargaining theory is relevant to understanding one of the most important institutions responsible for oppressing women, namely, patriarchy.

VII. Origins of Patriarchy

In most contemporary societies, it is men who hold the power to make decisions in society at large and in households. Such societies are referred to as *patriarchal*. Societies in which, by and large, women make the decisions—

[25] Angrist, J. (2002), "How Do Sex Ratios Affect Marriage and Labor Markets?: Evidence from America's Second Generation," *Quarterly Journal of Economics* 117, pp. 997–1038.

matriarchal societies—are relatively rare. Why is this? We now address some theories of the origins of patriarchy and the evidence that supports them.

The View from the Social Sciences

Among economic theories that suggest the origins of women's oppression, Marxian theories are among the best, in particular that of Friedrich Engels (1884–1986).[26] Engels proposed what is now a classic analysis in his *The Origin of the Family, Private Property, and the State*.[27] In his view, the oppression of women has not existed from time immemorial; rather, it began with a specific change in the production technology that humans used for survival. Drawing on the work of an anthropologist, Engels argued that for much of our evolutionary history, humans were organized in clans (called *gentes*, singular *gens*) comprising individuals related by blood. Engels attributed only to men the task of providing subsistence, a view that evidence has subsequently shown to be erroneous. Clans' survival needs were met by meat acquired largely but not exclusively by the hunting of men, and vegetables were gathered largely by women. In fact, the contribution of women to clans' subsistence needs was quite considerable.[28] Nevertheless, Engels argued that the work that women did was of a public character: it was done for their entire clans, not for specific individuals. In this organization of society, all property was commonly owned and, although there was a division of labor by gender, women had as much say in community affairs as men. Engels called this egalitarian state *primitive communism*. Marriages were *group* marriages; a man and his brothers were all married to a woman and all her sisters. Paternity of a child was uncertain (it would be impossible to tell who the biological father of a child was), but, as always, it was certain who the mother was. So blood lines were traced through the mother, that is, these societies were matrilineal. However, personal property (to the extent that there was such property) was passed on by a man to his *sister's children*. Why was that? Because, if paternity was uncertain, it was possible that there were no common genes between a man and his wife's children if she had sexual relations with men unrelated to him. However, there would have been at least some common genes between him and his sister's children (because he and his sister had the same mother).

[26] Readable commentaries on Engels's book can be found in Brewer, P. (2004), Introduction to *The Origin of the Family, Private Property, and the State*, Resistance Books, Chippendale, Australia; Harman, C. (1994), "Engels and the Origins of Human Society," *International Socialism* 2 (65); and Smith, S. (1997), "Engels and the Origin of Women's Oppression," *International Socialist Review* 2, Fall.

[27] Engels, F. (1986 [1884]), *The Origin of the Family, Private Property, and the State*, Penguin Books, New York.

[28] This is especially true in regions with latitudes below 40°. See, for example, Hunn, E. S. (1981), "On the Relative Contribution of Men and Women to Subsistence among Hunter-Gatherers of the Columbia Plateau: A Comparison with *Ethnographic Atlas* Summaries," *Journal of Ethnobiology* 1, pp. 124–134.

In this setting arose "pair-bonding," in which a single male was tied to a single female in a special relationship. This relationship, Engels claimed, became permanent when the technology for survival changed from hunting and gathering and the owning of cattle became productive. He did not exactly explain how animal husbandry and the ownership of animals became privatized and animals came to be owned by men. But his logic presumably was that, because in order to graze cattle women could not stray far from their homes if they had young children, men had the comparative advantage in herding cattle. Thus men acquired the ownership of animals, and this gave them a form of wealth that they could bequeath to future generations. But in the matrilineal system, they gave inheritances to the children of their sisters. Furthermore, unless sexual relations were strictly monogamous, the children of men's wives were not necessarily their own. Thus, to be more certain of passing on their wealth to *their own children,* men would have insisted on having control of bequests through pair-bonding. Thus lineage came to be traced through fathers rather than mothers, that is, matrilineality gave way to patrilineality. Engels claimed that this was a momentous change in the status of women: "The overthrow of mother right was the world historical defeat of the female sex. The man took command in the home also; the woman was degraded and reduced to servitude; she became the slave of his lust and a mere instrument for the production of children."[29] It was the emergence of the ownership of private property in goods facilitating production that was responsible for the oppression of women, in Engels's view. He predicted that only when private property was abolished (in a socialist state) would women be freed from their servitude.

Engels did not have the evidence we do today and so got some aspects of prehistoric social organization and specialization wrong. He was incorrect in presuming that matriarchy was universal before the transition described above. Also, he concentrated on the transition from hunting and gathering to pastoralism as the crucial event that undermined women's status. As we shall see below, it is possible that it was the switch to agriculture that had this effect. Direct evidence for Engels's theory is hard to come by because it refers to events that occurred thousands of years ago, and hunting and gathering societies are very rare today and so cannot be observed. Nevertheless, his theory does receive some support from indirect evidence. Patricia Draper (1975) studied the !Kung communities at the western edge of the Kalahari Desert in Africa—one of the few hunting and gathering societies that still exist.[30] She

[29] Engels (1986 [1884], p. 87).

[30] Draper, P. (1975), "!Kung Women: Contrasts in Sexual Egalitarianism in Foraging and Sedentary Contexts," in *An Anthropology of Women*, ed. R. R. Reiter, Monthly Review Press, New York, pp. 77–109.

compared the status of women relative to men of a group that still hunts game and gathers wild vegetables with that of another !Kung group that is more sedentary. Draper found that there is considerable egalitarianism between men and women in the former group; both sexes are quite mobile, and both contribute substantial amounts of food to the community, though that of men is more variable. Women retain control over what they have gathered and exercise considerable autonomy. In contrast, in the more sedentary group, Draper observed a greater stock of durable goods, less mobility among women, greater access of men to domestic animals (mostly goats), and a decline in women's autonomy. All this is consistent with Engels's theory.

More recently, evidence consistent with Engels's theory as to how patrilineality may have emerged has been provided by Clare Holden and Ruth Mace (2003).[31] They examined 68 Bantu-speaking populations of Sub-Saharan Africa to test whether societies that were matrilineal tended to become patrilineal after they acquired cattle. In other words, when the economic activity shifted from horticultural to pastoral, did patrilineality begin to take over? (Horticulture is the precursor to agriculture and requires much lighter equipment, such as a digging stick or hoe.) Why is it that across the world in contemporary times roughly only a fifth of the societies are matrilineal, two-fifths are patrilineal, and the rest are both? This is not an easy question to answer empirically because it may be the case that patrilineality and pastoral activities have arisen together ("co-evolved") by sheer accident. One has to ensure that this co-evolution is not likely to have been an accident, and to determine this we need to examine the frequency with which patrilineality and matrilineality have occurred together.

Holden and Mace documented 24 of the 68 Bantu cultures as matrilineal and 37 as patrilineal; 30 of the 68 cultures were pastoral. They found, using sophisticated statistical procedures, that the societies that had adopted cattle owning were less likely to be matrilineal. Surprisingly, however, there was little evidence that cattle owning and patrilineality co-evolved. Nevertheless, they found that although cultures may have gone from being matrilineal to patrilineal, the reverse did not happen. In effect, the transition to patrilineality appears to have been irrevocable.

Holden and Mace offer an evolutionary explanation as to why matrilineality may not be as appropriate in pastoral cultures as in horticultural ones. We can explain this as follows. In cultures that are horticultural, women participate in economic activity because the hoe does not require much upper body strength. Parents will naturally invest in their daughters' skill (human capital). Also, families with able daughters will do better in terms of survival. It makes sense

[31] Holden, C. J., and R. Mace (2003), "Spread of Cattle Led to the Loss of Matrilineal Descent in Africa: A Coevolutionary Analysis," *Proceedings of the Royal Society of London* B, 270, pp. 2425–2433.

in this sort of society for women to pass on property through females because they know who their children are and because daughters have inherited their mothers' ability. An able woman who has the genetic makeup to survive better will pass her property on to her own children (who will share these genes). If property were to pass through the husbands, it would reward *their* children— and these are not always their wives' children, too. As we have seen, this is the case if sexual relations are not monogamous or if they are serially monogamous. So the resource abundance made possible by the superior skill of a woman in horticulture may be frittered away by being bequeathed to those who do not carry her genes and, therefore, her ability. The representation of her genes in future generations will be maximized if descent is traced through her, because her (able) children will benefit from her resources. A similar argument applies in reverse in pastoral societies, where men have a comparative advantage in herding activities. In the latter type of cultures, it makes more evolutionary sense for lineage to be traced through men.

Before we leave the discussion of Engels's theory, we should note that Marxian literature on women's oppression subsequently adopted a political and ideological emphasis—it largely saw the subordination of women as arising from the class system, with each class (such as workers, capitalists, and landlords) defined by a common collective interest. An important early exception, however, is the work of Nancy Folbre (1982), who recognized that the oppression of women started within the household and so existed before the class system arose.[32] She argued that this oppression sprang from asymmetric bargaining power within the household and saw women's employment outside the home as redressing this imbalance. Accounting for this difference in the bargaining power of women and men in formal economic models would also go a long way toward addressing Heidi Hartmann's (1981) influential critique of the Marxian literature.[33] Hartmann argued that, in an unhappy marriage with feminism, Marxism subsumes patriarchy within the class struggle between labor and capital and thereby undermines feminist objections to patriarchy. Marxian analysis of oppression based on the class system has tended to be gender neutral and therefore is not the most appropriate avenue for addressing oppression based on gender.

The View from Evolutionary Biology

Evolutionary biologists have a different take on how patriarchy arose. Barbara Smuts (1995), who analyzed the evolutionary origins of patriarchy, pro-

---

[32] Folbre, N. (1982), "Exploitation Comes Home: A Critique of Marxian Theory of Family Labour," *Cambridge Journal of Economics* 6, pp. 317–329.

[33] H. Hartmann (1981), "The Unhappy Marriage of Marxism and Feminism: Towards a More Progressive Union," in *Women and Revolution,* ed. L. Sargent, Black Rose Books, Montreal.

vides considerable insight into this question.[34] In essence, she argues that patriarchy arose out of the need for men to control the sexuality of women. Although evolutionary biologists and feminists generally do not see eye to eye, on this issue they agree. However, they may ascribe different reasons to why men feel the need to exercise this control.

The view of evolutionary biologists is as follows. It is in the reproductive interests of both men and women to have many children. Because children embody their parents' genes, the greater the number of surviving children, the greater will be the prevalence of their parents' genes in future generations. So anything that increases the number of children or improves their chances of survival is to the advantage of parents in that it improves their representation in the future gene pool. This is not to suggest that parents consciously think in this manner. The evolutionary principle of natural selection automatically rewards, in this sense, parents who have large numbers of surviving children relative to other parents.

Beyond that, however, the reproductive interests of men and women diverge. Women must bear their own children, but men do not have to. Given that a child has to be in the mother's womb for nine months, this limits how many children a woman can have. A man, on the other hand, can have many more children—through several women. In fact, if a man is assured that the mother will take care of a child, it is in his reproductive interest to maximize the number of children he has through other women. Men do not think like this, of course, but rather nature accomplishes this outcome through their desire for sex.

The desire for sex gave men the motive for controlling women. Men wanted to ensure that women were readily available to them but outside the reach of other men. This gave rise, in Smuts's view, to the institution of *patrilocal residence,* in which a wife leaves behind the natal family with which she grew up and moves to the family of her husband. The move to a completely alien environment reduces a woman's resistance to control.

To the extent that women could find food by themselves, they would have retained considerable autonomy for themselves. This is because being able to survive on their own gave them, in the language of economists, a good threat option. However, Smuts argues that things changed for the worse when, in the evolutionary history of humans, two events occurred.

First, when humans shifted to meat eating women were placed at a disadvantage. Because men are physically stronger on average and because they did not have to carry their children, they were more adept than women at catching and killing game. This made women dependent on men for protein. Anthropologists have proposed that this dependence led to the so-called meat-for-sex exchange, whereby women were forced to trade sexual access

---

[34] Smuts, B. (1995), "The Evolutionary Origins of Patriarchy," *Human Nature* 6, pp. 1–32.

for protein.[35] This dependence would have undermined women's bargaining power. Whether the meat-for-sex argument is correct with regard to humans is debatable. In hunting and gathering societies, women may have been responsible for providing the bulk of the nutrition on a daily basis because the rewards to hunting were very uncertain.

Second, around 10,000 years ago, humans moved to settled agriculture. Prior to that, humans had the nomadic lifestyle of hunters and gatherers, who moved from place to place when the local resources in an area were exhausted. Women had the freedom to hunt small game and to gather vegetables from commonly owned resources to which they had free access. But with the advent of settled agriculture, this nomadic lifestyle came to an end and women's economic dependence on men increased. The fact that women no longer had the opportunity to move freely decreased their autonomy even further because it gave men the opportunity to monitor their activities.

Why might men have wanted to monitor the actions of women? Because men are never sure of the paternity of their children. Men who unwittingly expended resources to bring up children who were not their own would have promoted the survival of other men's genes, not their own. So the representation in the future gene pool of men who were indifferent to the paternity of their children would soon have dwindled to nothing. Preserved would have been the genes of only those men who jealously guarded the sexual access to their spouses. The move from hunting and gathering to settled agriculture would have greatly reduced the autonomy of women by restricting their mobility.

If this line of argument is correct, the role played by agriculture in undermining the bargaining power of women is ironic. A great deal of the increase in the standard of living of humans in the past 10,000 years can be traced back to settled agriculture and the increase in agricultural productivity. As long as the entire population was required to work to produce the food needed for subsistence, there was neither any demand for other goods and services nor any supply (because no worker could be spared from gathering or hunting). But once agriculture became sufficiently productive that one person could produce a surplus of food (more than was necessary for his or her subsistence), a fraction of the population could feed the whole population. Then there came to be a demand for other goods and services that could be produced by the people released from having to contribute to the population's subsistence. With the appearance of this agricultural surplus arose the possibility of producing handicrafts, textiles, industrial products,

---

[35] This meat-for-sex hypothesis is originally due to Symons, D. (1979), *The Evolution of Human Sexuality*, Oxford University Press, Oxford, UK, and Hill, K. (1982), "Hunting and Human Evolution," *Journal of Human Evolution* 11, pp. 521–544. For recent evidence of this sort of exchange among chimpanzees, our closest cousins, see Gomes, C. M., and C. Boesch (2009), "Wild Chimpanzees Exchange Meat for Sex on a Long-Term Basis," *PLoS ONE* 4 (4), p. e5116, doi: 10.1371/journal.pone.0005116.

the arts, cultural activities, and everything else we believe constitutes developed societies. But the appearance of settled agriculture may have decreased the autonomy of women relative to what it was in the hunting and gathering regime of human evolution.

VIII. Culture and the Perpetuation of Patriarchy

We have reviewed the major arguments that have been proposed to explain the origins of patriarchy. But how did it perpetuate itself right down to contemporary times? To understand this, we begin with the work of Ester Boserup (1970, Chap. 1). She offered an important insight into how different farming systems affected women's employment in contemporary agriculture.[36] As we shall see, this had consequences for the emergence of patriarchy. Boserup compared societies based on shifting agriculture with those based on settled agriculture. In shifting agriculture, land is set up for cultivation through slash-and-burn techniques, and cultivation is done with a hoe. The hoe is an implement that is relatively light and easily handled by women. Because the soil is dug up only lightly using this technology, however, the nutrients are exhausted within a few years. An agricultural society based on this technology needs to frequently leave the land fallow and move to new land, which is possible only when land is abundant. Settled agriculture came with plow technology. The plow is a relatively heavy implement that digs deep into the ground and is usually pulled by draft animals. The soil does not become depleted as quickly under this technology, and this facilitates settled agriculture; that is, societies do not have to keep moving every few years. Operating the plow and managing draft animals, however, requires a considerable amount of upper body strength, so men have a comparative advantage in operating plow technology.

Examining data over five decades from African countries, Boserup concluded that female (hoe) farming was the predominant form of agriculture there. In contrast, in Asia the technology used was predominantly the plow, and therefore male farming was the norm. Furthermore, because the plow requires less weeding (an activity usually performed by women), there was little need for female labor except perhaps during harvest times. Contributing to the reduced demand for female labor was the fact that, in Asian regions using the plow, there was usually considerable landlessness, so land could be cultivated using hired labor. For these reasons, women in areas of plow agriculture tended to be secluded in their homes and often wore veils when appearing in public.

Specialization by comparative advantage as determined by technology and physical strength is one thing, but why have women been secluded? Seclusion implies that women are prevented from (or refrain from) participating

---

[36] Boserup, E. (1970), *Woman's Role in Economic Development*, Earthscan, London.

not merely in agriculture but also in many other activities outside the home. Why couldn't they participate in industrial or entrepreneurial activities? Is it conceivable that, over time, agricultural technology generates a *culture* that may prevent women from engaging in all or most of the activities outside the home? This is precisely the question that has recently been answered in an interesting paper by Alberto Alesina, Paola Giuliano, and Nathan Nunn (2013).[37]

If one were to use current data, it would be virtually impossible to find many regions in the world that do not use the plow, because most of agriculture around the world has converted to plow farming. Alesina et al. base their analysis on ethnographic data on over 1,200 ethnic groups across the world in preindustrial times. This data set contains information on plow use by these groups from the earliest time that written records were available about them. In other words, the data have information on plow use in the groups in ancient times. The question they ask is how the use of the plow in history impinges on female labor force participation today, accounting for other relevant factors. They find that those regions that historically used the plow tend to have less female labor force participation even today. Not only do women participate less in agriculture in these regions, they also participate less in nonagricultural sectors and also engage less in politics.

A skeptic might argue that the above findings do not necessarily establish that plow technology facilitated the perpetuation of patriarchy. It is conceivable that those societies that were patriarchal did not develop the kinds of institutions (like markets) that would have enabled women to work. If this were the case, female labor force participation today would be low even in the presence of current attitudes that are open to the idea of women working outside the home. To test whether this is so, Alesina et al. examine the labor force participation among immigrant women in the United States. All immigrants face the same institutions (those that are common across the United States). If past use of the plow in their countries of origin is irrelevant, the labor force participation should be the same across all immigrants. What the authors find instead is that those immigrant women who hail from countries that historically used the plow are less likely to participate in the U.S. labor market than are immigrant women from countries that historically did not use the plow. To be even more certain of the effects of plow cultivation, the authors repeated the exercise using only second-generation immigrants, because these would have been truly exposed only to the institutions in the United States, and in this case, too, they find that historical plow cultivation in the country of origin of their parents has a negative effect on the labor force participation of women.

[37] Alesina, A. F., P. Giuliano, and N. Nunn (2013), "On the Origins of Gender Roles: Women and the Plough," *Quarterly Journal of Economics* 128, pp. 469–530.

These are very interesting and important findings. What do they suggest? That *culture* plays a very important role in undermining the full participation of women in the labor market and in activities outside the home. It may be true that the plow originally offered a good reason for a division of labor by comparative advantage. But that division of labor became fossilized in the minds of people in the form of culture, which appears to have a long life. And cultural beliefs play themselves out in contemporary times and constrain women even when there are no sound economic reasons for them anymore. In other words, women are constrained to act according to socially constructed notions of appropriate behavior that have been culturally handed down. This contributes to the perpetuation of patriarchy.

These findings fit well with some of the arguments made by Gerda Lerner in her thought-provoking book *The Creation of Patriarchy* (1986). In particular, she has argued that patriarchy has been perpetuated because men have monopolized the creation of the symbols that give meaning to our lives. They have foisted on women male-centered conceptual systems that have marginalized women's experiences and left them with no alternative formulations for articulating these experiences. The feminist struggle against subjugation by men, in Lerner's view, is largely a struggle to shake free from the thought systems they have been exposed to for centuries.

Drawing on the ideas from bargaining theory, Torben Iversen and Frances Rosenbluth (2010, Chap. 2) have proposed that the prevalence of patriarchal norms in society is determined by whether the skills that women and men have are specific to the family or are generally applicable outside the household.[38] This notion corresponds exactly to that of threat options. If women have skills that are general, they can readily sustain themselves in the event that they break up with their partners. Because their threat utility is high, they will have considerable bargaining power within the household. This was the situation of women in hunting and gathering societies. In this organization of society, as we have seen, men provided the protein by hunting and women provided the bulk of the calorie intake by gathering. In these societies, women and men were deemed to have more or less equal bargaining power.

If women's skills are specific to the family, they cannot easily sustain themselves by walking away from their spouses, and their low threat utility will undermine their bargaining positions within their households. This was the situation of women after the agricultural revolution. Men's greater physical strength allowed them to specialize in farm work, whereas women specialized in raising children. Because the latter is considerably family-specific, women became dependent on men. Social norms gradually responded to this difference in bargaining power, and societies reflected patriarchal values.

---

[38] Iversen, T., and F. Rosenbluth (2010), *Women, Work, and Politics: The Political Economy of Gender Inequality,* Yale University Press, New Haven, CT.

When societies industrialized, the bargaining power of women remained low because they could not readily participate in the labor market. This was because working in factories was inconvenient to women with families. Furthermore, industrial work required highly specialized skills as opposed to general skills. (The acquisition of these specialized skills was more difficult for women than men because it is reinforced by continuous labor market participation.) As a result, patriarchal norms persisted during the industrialization of societies. Iversen and Rosenbluth argue that it was only in the postindustrial stage that women started regaining bargaining power. This is because the service sector expanded rapidly and work in this sector required general skills. This expansion coincided with women's greater participation in the labor market in most developed countries. The increase in women's threat utility led to a corresponding increase in their bargaining power. Patriarchal norms started giving way to norms that gave more equal weight to women and men. Thus male obsessions with things like women's chastity started eroding; men who still insisted on marrying women with these old-fashioned virtues had very limited choices. The insistence on such virtues is found nowadays mostly in those developing countries in which women do not yet have full freedom to operate in the labor market.

IX. Summary

The purpose of this chapter has been to help us understand what determines the bargaining power of women and men within the household. We began this chapter with an assessment of the unitary model of the household, which presumes that the household can be treated as a monolithic unit. We saw that this model is not supported by fact. Women and men within the household typically have different preferences. This led us to study Nash's bargaining model. The distinguishing feature of this model is that the payoff to a player in a bargaining situation is dependent on what her payoff would be if negotiations were to break down. When a woman's threat option improves, she achieves a better bargaining outcome.

We then went on to discuss a different approach to bargaining, the so-called noncooperative bargaining model, in which the players make alternate offers. We saw that for a player to have the option of rejecting an offer and then responding to it with her own offer is itself empowering. Furthermore, having an outside option that she can exercise in the event that she rejects an offer is also empowering. Thus we see that, whichever model we invoke, what empowers women is the ability to make choices and having good outside options.

We went on to discuss empirical evidence supporting bargaining models of the household. Data from both developing and developed countries show that women and men have different preferences regarding household expenditures and children's health and education. The extent to which these preferences are observed in the real world depends on the relative bargaining powers of the spouses. We saw that a study using data from Bangladesh revealed that if a woman's threat option does not change, her bargaining power does not change either—exactly as predicted by bargaining theory. We then discussed evidence from China showing that, in a culture that exhibits a preference for sons as opposed to daughters, women who have sons enjoy a greater say in household decisions than those who have daughters. In sum, the evidence supporting bargaining models is quite strong.

We finally launched into a discussion of the origins of patriarchy. Engels argued that societies that were originally matrilineal became patrilineal after they became pastoral and men acquired private property in the form of cattle. Men's desire to bequeath their inheritance to their children motivated the switch to patrilineality. Engels's point that private property drove a wedge between the bargaining powers of men and women is a deep insight. We saw that there is empirical evidence linking the move toward pastoralism and the switch to patrilineality, giving credence to the theory.

We further discussed empirical evidence showing that women in ethnic groups that historically used the plow are less likely even today to participate in work outside the home and in politics. The reason for this is culture. Cultural beliefs are durable, and they are passed on from generation to generation through the socialization of children. Much of the gender-normative behavior that is expected in contemporary times is merely based on socially constructed notions that have little validity in the present environment.

Exercises and Questions for Discussion

1. Sarah and Josh are contemplating marriage, and in the event that they marry their utility possibility frontier is given by $x + y = 12$, where x and y, respectively, denote the utility levels that Sarah and Josh attain in their married state. Their respective outside options generate a utility of $X = 0$ for Sarah and $Y = 4$ for Josh.

(a) Graph the region of feasible utility combinations in marriage, which presumably is a cooperative endeavor.

(b) Define the notion of Pareto efficiency. Why might we expect the outcome here to be Pareto efficient?

(c) If Sarah could unilaterally decide the allocation of utilities, what allocation would she choose? And what allocation would Josh choose?

(d) Describe (with the help of a diagram) the nature of the Nash bargaining solution (NBS), where *both* Sarah and Josh influence the outcome.

(e) Compute the utilities of Sarah and Josh in the NBS by graphing the Nash product. Based on your solution, can you predict whether Sarah and Josh will opt to marry?

(f) Redo part e when $X = 4$ and when $X = 8$ (assuming that Y is fixed at 4).

(g) Using the solutions you have computed, graph Sarah's utility in the NBS as a function of her threat utility. On the same figure, also graph Josh's utility in the NBS. What do these graphs say to you?

2. On each of two days, Alan and Daisy can jointly undertake a project that yields a profit of $150 per day. They *alternately* make proposals (at most one per day), starting with Daisy, about how to split this amount. If a proposal is rejected, they don't work on the project that day; if it is accepted, the agreement applies to *that day and the remaining day (if any)*. Suppose, first, that both Alan and Daisy have no outside option (they can earn nothing outside). They both want to maximize *their own total income* over the two days.

(a) Determine the outcome (how they will split the profit) of this bargaining situation, carefully explaining your logic.

(b) Now suppose that Daisy can earn $70 a day outside (but Alan still cannot earn anything outside). Determine the bargaining outcome now.

(c) Explain why the bargaining outcomes are different in parts a and b above.

3. In the study of Udry (1996) in Burkina Faso, spouses cultivated separate plots of land, and these had unequal productivities because different amounts of fertilizer were applied.

(a) Explain why this outcome is Pareto inefficient.

(b) Explain why such an outcome is not consistent with the unitary model of the household.

(c) What is your explanation for the observed outcome?

4. In the Anderson and Eswaran (2009) study on the bargaining power of women in the Matlab area of Bangladesh, they found that (i) women who helped on their husbands' farms had no more autonomy than women who did only housework, whereas (ii) women who earned independent income had greater autonomy.

(a) Explain whether i is consistent with Nash's bargaining theory. What aspect of the labor market in the Matlab area do you need to invoke to explain this outcome?

(b) Explain whether ii is consistent with Nash's bargaining theory.

5. Outline the theory of Friedrich Engels about the emergence of patrilineality. What evidence is there for this theory? Relate the emergence and asymmetric ownership of private property to what Engels referred to as "the historic defeat of women."

6. Summarize the arguments made by Barbara Smuts in her view of the emergence of patriarchy, with special emphasis on its evolutionary origins and the contributions of the transitions from gathering to hunting to settled agriculture. What economic measures would you recommend to counter hangovers of patriarchy in the present day?

7. Both feminists and evolutionary biologists argue that men seek to control the sexuality of women. Explain the main reasons behind this desire for control.

8. Outline Ester Boserup's theory about the roles of the types of agriculture on women's employment. Outline as well the empirical evidence in favor of Boserup's hypothesis. How do you relate women's employment to their bargaining power within the household?

9. To what extent can patriarchy be explained by evolution? Explain the role of socialization and, more generally, culture in perpetuating patriarchy.

10. Suppose that a couple in a patriarchal developing country find a way to augment their family income by undertaking a joint economic activity. This activity requires one input that cannot be purchased in the market and can be supplied only within the household and another input that is undertaken outside the home (such as marketing). Because the wife is restricted by patriarchal norms to work only within the home, she specializes in the former task while her husband specializes in the latter. With this new activity, the couple earns an extra $100 a month. Using your understanding of bargaining theory, answer the following questions:

(a) Will the wife be necessarily better off in utility terms with the couple's higher income?

(b) Do you think the proportion of the budget spent on goods preferred by the wife will increase?

(c) How might your answer change if the husband and wife reversed the activities in which they specialize?

Gender in Markets

CHAPTER FOUR

Are Women Discriminated Against in the Labor Market?

I. Introduction

Women, on average, earn lower wages than men. Is this possibly due to discrimination against women? Before we can answer this question, we have to ensure that we have accounted for all other factors that might contribute to wage differences between women and men. Part of this "gender wage gap" is due to differences in human capital (skill). Even if women and men have the same amount of education, the human capital of men tends to be higher because they have, on average, more experience in the labor market. To the extent that work experience contributes to skill, men would tend to demonstrate greater productivity and therefore earn higher wages than women. Human capital differences, therefore, explain part of the gender wage gap. Men and women tend to work in different occupations (which pay different wages) and also in different industries (which also pay different wages). These factors, too, explain part of the gender difference in average wages. Furthermore, men in North America (and likely everywhere else in the world) are more likely than women to be represented by unions. Because unions usually bargain for wages that are higher than market rates, men tend to have higher wages than women on this count, too.

Yet, after accounting for all these characteristics alluded to above, there still remains a "residual" gender wage gap. For example, this is on the order of 9% to 17% (depending on the data set used) in the United States and around 10% in Canada.[1] Is this residual gap explained by discrimination against women?

---

[1] For the United States, see Blau, F. D., and L. M. Kahn (2007), "The Gender Pay Gap," *Economists' Voice,* June. For Canada, see Baker, M., and M. Drolet (2010), "A New View of the Male/Female Pay Gap," *Canadian Public Policy* 36, pp. 429–464.

Before we launch into theories of discrimination, it is necessary to be aware of some additional factors that contribute to the gender wage gap that have nothing to do with discrimination. One is the possibility that women and men like different kinds of work. If people have an aversion to Job A compared to Job B, in order to compensate for the unpleasantness of the job, firms will have to pay identical workers more for Job A than for Job B. This difference in wages is referred to as a "compensating differential." So if we compare the average wages of identically qualified women and men, and if the men are engaged in jobs that are deemed more unpleasant (such as garbage collection or mining), part of the gender wage gap should be correctly attributed to compensating differentials and not to discrimination. Using U.S. data from 1977 that include information on job characteristics (how pleasant or unpleasant the jobs were), Randall Filer (1985) found that roughly two-fifths of the gender wage gap in the sample could be attributed to compensating differentials.[2] This indicates that differences in the working conditions of men and women are partly responsible for the gender wage gap.

Francine Blau and Lawrence Kahn (2003) conducted an analysis of the gender wage gap in 22 countries using data for the period 1985–94.[3] They found that countries that have more egalitarian wages among men also have lower gender wage gaps. Some of the factors that explain more egalitarian wages are institutional. These include centrally set wages, as in many of the Eastern European countries; greater union representation (for women, too), so that wages are bargained over instead of being determined by the labor market; or laws, such as minimum wage laws. In all such cases, the lower end of the spectrum of wages is lifted up. And because women are more concentrated at the lower end of this spectrum than men, these institutional factors raise the wages of women disproportionately relative to men and thereby reduce the gender wage gap.

With these important determinants of the gender wage gap in mind, in this chapter we address the issue of discrimination against women in the labor market. *Are women given different treatment than men by employers simply because they are women?* Even if they have economic qualifications identical to those of men and perform the same jobs, are women paid less? If so, under what conditions does such discrimination occur? What are the mechanisms through which such discrimination might work, and how are women's wages affected as a result? How do these factors impinge on women's career opportunities? In this chapter we study theories about the nature of the discrimination to which women might be subjected and then examine the existing evidence for them.

[2] Filer, R. (1985), "Male–Female Wage Differences: The Importance of Compensating Differentials," *Industrial and Labor Relations Review* 38, pp. 426–437.

[3] Blau, F. D., and L. M. Kahn (2003), "Understanding International Differences in the Gender Pay Gap," *Journal of Labor Economics* 21, pp. 106–144.

It should be noted at the outset that the theories that economists have proposed to address labor market discrimination certainly do not cover all aspects of discrimination; they are relatively narrowly focused. One glaring omission, emphasized by Kenneth Arrow (1988), is discrimination based on social networks.[4] When hiring by firms or organizations is done through social networks and contacts, there is considerable scope for discrimination to come into play. Jobs may be obtained and given through referrals from people in one's own social group. The noneconomic benefits that may accrue from such avenues may make it difficult to uproot discrimination.

Another point to be noted is that discrimination against women may start long before they enter the labor market. (We discuss some aspects of this in later chapters.) Especially in patriarchal societies, girls may receive less education and less access to healthcare and enjoy fewer opportunities than boys.[5] So by the time they are old enough to participate in the labor market, women are already handicapped relative to men. The narrow definition of *discrimination* we employ in this chapter, which is in line with current usage in economics, is that women are deemed to be discriminated against in the labor market if firms treat them differently than men *even when women have the same qualifications and productivity.*

Because the focus here is on interactions in markets—assumed to be competitive for the most part—there is little scope for individual bargaining. (The latter is relevant in one-on-one interactions.) The constraints on each individual's behavior here are imposed not by another individual but by the market as a whole. For example, firms cannot pay a worker less than what other firms are willing to pay. Likewise, a worker cannot demand a higher wage than she can earn elsewhere. Thus the analytic tool that is most useful for analysis in this chapter is not bargaining theory but the theory of how prices and quantities are determined in markets.

II. A Taste for Discrimination

In principle, it is conceivable that employers discriminate against women simply because they are prejudiced against women. They may prefer not to hire women, if possible, even though women may be just as productive as men. The consequences of this form of discrimination—a "taste for discrimination," as it is called—were first formally investigated by Gary Becker (1957), whose work we referred to in Chapter 1. The analysis uses a simple supply–demand framework to draw important inferences.

---

[4] Arrow, K. (1988), "What Has Economics to Say about Racial Discrimination?," *Journal of Economic Perspectives* 12, Spring, pp. 91–100.

[5] For a fascinating feminist overview of the patriarchal ideas of philosophers and economists in the West, see Nancy Folbre (2011), *Greed, Lust and Gender: A History of Economic Ideas,* Oxford University Press, New York.

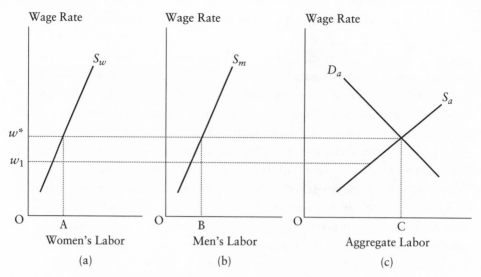

FIGURE 4.1 Labor market equilibrium in the absence of discrimination

Suppose that the production of output requires labor that can be provided equally well by men and women—in other words, women's labor and men's labor are perfect substitutes from the point of view of production. Suppose that w is the market wage rate of a person with the requisite skills for the job. Becker captured the notion of a taste for discrimination in the following way. If an employer has a taste for discrimination, the cost to him of hiring a woman is more than w, say $w(1 + d)$, where d is a positive number that denotes the intensity with which he dislikes (and so discriminates against) female employees. The amount wd that is in excess of the market wage w is not a monetary cost the employer incurs but rather a "psychic" cost or disutility stemming from his prejudice. The larger the value of d, the greater his taste for discrimination. The employer can hire men for a wage rate of w. Given that female employees are a source of disutility to him, he would be willing to hire women only if they were willing to accept a wage rate $w/(1 + d)$. For then the effective cost to him of hiring a woman, including the disutility cost, would be the same as that for a man, namely w.

What effect does employer discrimination have on the wage rate and employment of women in equilibrium? In order to isolate the effects of discrimination, we begin with a situation in which there is no discrimination. We presume that the labor supply of men and women increases with the wage rate. These supply functions are shown in the first two panels of Figure 4.1. At any wage rate, say w_1, the amount of labor supplied by women is given by the horizontal distance to the schedule S_w in panel a; that supplied by men is given by the horizontal distance to the schedule S_m in panel b. The aggregate (or total) labor supplied is given by the sum of these two and shown by the horizontal distance to schedule S_a in panel c. By repeating this exercise for every wage rate, we can construct the aggregate labor supply curve, S_a.

Panel c of Figure 4.1 also displays the aggregate labor demand function of firms, D_a. In deciding how much labor to demand at a given wage rate, a firm compares the wage rate with the value of the marginal product (that is, the dollar value of the increased output that would be produced by an additional worker). If the latter is larger, the firm will hire the worker and will keep hiring more workers as long as every additional worker more than covers his or her wage cost. For given levels of other inputs (like capital), as more workers are hired, however, the marginal product of workers ultimately declines because of diminishing returns. With additional hiring, sooner or later a point will come when the value of the marginal product of a worker will be exactly equal to the wage rate. At this point, the firm will stop hiring more workers. Thus a firm in a perfectly competitive labor market will hire workers until the value of the marginal product of the last worker is exactly equal to the wage rate given by the market. By adding up the demand for labor from all firms at each wage rate, we obtain the market demand for labor that is shown as the downward-sloping schedule D_a in Figure 4.1.

The wage rate at which the quantity of labor demanded is equal to that supplied is shown as w^*. At this equilibrium wage, the amount of labor provided by women is OA in panel a and that by men is OB in panel b. The aggregate amount of labor supplied is OC in panel c. In this equilibrium, men and women are both earning a wage rate that is equal to the value of their (common) marginal product.

Now let us consider what happens when employers have a taste for discrimination against women. To see this, suppose for the moment that *all* employers discriminate in the manner described earlier and to the same extent. If w is the actual wage rate received by women, employers will perceive that they are paying a higher wage $w(1 + d)$, with the excess wd incurred in utility, not monetary, terms. Consider Figure 4.2. Let us interpret the wage rate along the vertical axes in all the panels as the wage rate as *perceived by the employers*. If w is the cost of hiring a female worker as they perceive it, the worker receives only $w/(1 + d)$. Thus the labor supply that would be forthcoming from women will be shifted to the left (relative to S_w), to the position S'_w. The aggregate labor supply will also be shifted to the left (relative to its old position), to S'_a. The consequence of this is that the equilibrium wage, w', as determined in panel c of Figure 4.2, will be higher than before.

Because there is no discrimination against men, they will receive w' as their wage, and they will provide an amount of labor shown as OE in panel b of Figure 4.2. Women, however, will not receive w' as their wage; w' is the effective cost to employers of hiring a woman. The wage an employed woman will receive is the (lower) amount $w'/(1 + d)$, at which rate the labor supplied by women is reduced to the amount OD shown in panel a of Figure 4.2.

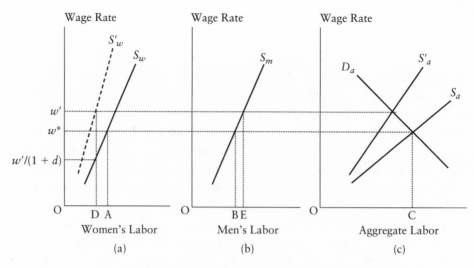

FIGURE 4.2 Labor market equilibrium in the presence of discrimination

Thus, if all employers have and indulge a taste for discrimination against women, in the new equilibrium the wage rate received by women decreases, and so does the labor supplied by women (from OA to OD). This discrimination works to the advantage of men: because it curtails the supply of women's labor, the wage rate that men receive is higher, and that results in an increase in their labor supply (from OB to OE). The value of the marginal product of a woman is identical to that of a man and is given by w'. But she receives only $w'/(1 + d)$. Therefore, *a woman earns less than the value of her marginal product in this equilibrium.*[6]

In this analysis we are assuming that the market for labor in the industry in question is perfectly competitive. Each employer perceives his demand for labor as so small that it cannot influence the wage rate. Consequently, he has no option but to take the wage rate as given. If he indulges his taste for discrimination against women, he pays a male employee the market wage but a female employee less than that wage. So employers are indifferent between the two types of labor because women are being paid less by precisely the amount needed to compensate the employers for the assumed disutility they incur (for whatever reason) by employing women. However, the individual decisions of the employers all add up to determine the wages of males and females in the labor market. As a result, in equilibrium the wage paid to women ends up being lower (and to men, higher) than when there is no discrimination. The equilibrium employment of women decreases, and that of men increases.

---

[6]This was first demonstrated in the context of racial discrimination by Kenneth Arrow (1973) in his "The Theory of Discrimination," in *Discrimination in Labor Markets,* ed. O. Ashenfelter and A. Rees, Princeton University Press, Princeton, NJ.

What happens to the profit of a firm as a result of discrimination? It is hard to tell for sure, because the price of male labor goes up but that of female labor goes down. Depending on the amount of male and female labor a firm uses, its profit may go up or down. An employer who uses only female labor would make higher profits than one who uses some male labor because the wage rate of women is lower.

Here we have to draw a distinction between the short run and the long run. The short run is defined as the time period during which a firm can change some of the inputs it uses, but not all. In particular, the amount of labor hired by a firm can usually be changed in the short run by letting go existing workers or hiring more. But the size of the factory, for example, cannot be changed. The long run is defined as a time period of long enough duration that all inputs can be changed. In particular, existing firms that cannot cover their costs can leave the market, and new firms that expect to make positive profits can enter by building factories. Becker (1957) demonstrated that the effects of a taste for discrimination can be dramatically different in the short run and the long run.

In the equilibrium of a perfectly competitive market, the price of a good is equal to the cost of producing an additional unit of the good, that is, its marginal cost. For if the price is higher than the marginal cost, firms have an incentive to increase their profits by producing more, and the increased supply will collectively lower the price. On the other hand, if the price is lower than the marginal cost, firms have an incentive to increase their profits by cutting back production, and the reduced supply will collectively raise the price. In either case, the process stops when the price equals the marginal cost. But if firms use different proportions of men and women in their production, their marginal costs will differ: firms using a higher proportion of women will have lower production costs. In the short run, the price will fall to a level at which it equals the marginal cost of production of these firms. Consequently, different firms may earn different profits in the short run, with some even incurring losses.

In the long run, however, firms incurring losses will not be sustainable. They will exit the industry. The firms that make positive profits, that is, more than cover the opportunity costs of all the inputs used, will attract entry by imitators. Which type of firm will exit the industry, and which type will enter? Clearly, the high-cost firms will exit, and the lowest-cost ones will enter. The high-cost firms will be those that use some male labor (because men have a higher wage), and the lowest-cost ones will be those that use all-female labor. Thus firm owners who have a preference for hiring male labor will be put out of business by firm owners who have no such preference, and the wedge between male and female wages will decline. *Thus we arrive at Becker's insight that a taste for discrimination will not survive perfect competition in the long run.*

This does not mean that a taste for discrimination by employers will never be manifest in the market. Whenever there is a firm that either is a monopoly or wields some market power due to the absence of competition, there is scope for it to practice such discrimination—if the owners have an inherent taste for it. This is because such firms can earn profits that are above normal, that is, their revenues more than cover the costs of all inputs (including the opportunity cost of the entrepreneurs). These above-normal profits provide a cushion against which these firms could forgo some profits to indulge a taste for discrimination. Competition takes away this cushion. If one is looking for evidence of gender discrimination, industries requiring such large investments that only a few firms can serve the market would be good bets. Firms that are protected from competition by government regulations that prevent entry might also be able to exhibit gender discrimination. Firms that are the sole employers in small towns are in a position to pay workers less than the value of their marginal product; potentially, they can use this market power with regard to hiring to treat women differently simply because they are women.

Evidence of a Taste for Discrimination

We now discuss the evidence for Becker's theory of discrimination. Orley Ashenfelter and Timothy Hannan (1986) provided some strong evidence of a taste for discrimination in the employment of women in the banking industry.[7] They examined data from 120 banks in the states of New Jersey and Pennsylvania for the year 1976. They chose this particular year because affirmative action pressures (to employ more women and blacks) increased in subsequent years, and those would have muddied any evidence of discrimination. The data were useful for testing the hypothesis of discrimination by taste because the markets of these banks were quite limited geographically. As a result, different banks in the sample faced varying degrees of competition, enabling the authors to investigate how lack of competition made it possible for banks to discriminate against women. Focusing on the occupational category "officials and managers," the study found strong evidence to support the contention that banks in less competitive environments employed *fewer* women relative to men.

Sandra Black and Philip Strahan (2001) conducted an interesting investigation of Becker's theory by further examining the U.S. banking industry.[8] Until the mid-1970s, the banking industry had been highly regulated. In particular, most of the states had in place regulations that prevented banks from

[7]Ashenfelter, O., and T. Hannan (1986), "Sex Discrimination and Product Market Competition: The Case of the Banking Industry," *Quarterly Journal of Economics* 101, pp. 149–173.

[8]Black, S., and P. Strahan (2001), "The Division of Spoils: Rent-Sharing and Discrimination in a Regulated Industry," *American Economic Review* 91, pp. 814–831.

having multiple branches in a state or from owning banks in other states. One would expect that these regulations constrained the extent of competition between banks and enabled them to earn above-normal profits (or *rents,* as they are called). Using statistical techniques, Black and Strahan first investigated whether these rents were retained by the owners of the banks or shared with the employees. They also sought to examine, in the event that the latter were true, whether the rents were shared evenly by gender.

They examined what happened to the earnings of bank employees after deregulation. One would expect that, by increasing competition, deregulation would have lowered the rents to banks and the earnings of bank employees if the rents were being shared. After accounting for the fact that the average skill level of bank employees increased after deregulation, the authors found that the average earnings of employees fell by around 9.6%. This decline, they found, was not due to a fall in the demand for labor in banking after deregulation—suggesting that the employees were sharing rents with the banks.[9]

Black and Strahan then investigated whether there was discrimination by gender in the banking industry. If women were being discriminated against, one would expect that the decline in their wages following deregulation would have been less than that for men because they were not being paid as much above their opportunity wage as men. The authors found this to be the case: the decline in women's wages was around 3%, whereas that in men's wages was 12%. What is more, the proportion of women in managerial positions increased by about 10% after deregulation. This suggests that, because it was not necessary to minimize costs by choosing the most efficient person for the job when banks were protected from competition, before deregulation women were being relegated to lower-level jobs than those for which they were qualified.

Sandra Black and Elizabeth Brainerd (2004) conducted a statistical investigation into gender discrimination by observing that exposure to international trade puts competitive pressure on industries that are concentrated, that is, have some monopoly power.[10] In particular, the authors sought to inquire whether increased international competition in the 1980s increased the wages of women relative to men in the United States because the scope for discrimination would have been curtailed. They ascertained the extent to which the gender wage gap was reduced in concentrated industries because of competition from imports

---

[9] This finding is interesting in itself, for it is unclear why the owners of banks would pay their employees more than their opportunity wages. In unionized firms the unions would negotiate higher wages for their members, but the banking sector in the United States is not unionized. In any event, it was the absence of competition that enabled managers to pay their employees more than their competitive wages.

[10] Black, S., and E. Brainerd (2004), "Importing Equality?: The Impact of Globalization on Gender Discrimination," *Industrial and Labor Relations Review* 57, pp. 540–559.

by comparing it to the wage gap reduction in industries that were competitive to begin with.[11] If there were discrimination against women, one would expect the gender wage gap in concentrated industries to have declined by more.[12]

Black and Brainerd computed the *residual* gender wage gap after accounting for employees' education and experience. This residual wage represents that component of the wage gap that is not explained by differences in the education and work experience of men and women. The authors found that this residual gender wage gap increased in industries affected by trade relative to the wage gap in industries less affected by trade. At first blush, this might seem to contradict Becker's theory. Before one can conclude that, however, one must take account of the fact that discrimination is *not* the only factor that impinges on wages. One must also be concerned about the independent effect of trade on wages.

A developed country like the United States has a comparative advantage in producing goods that require highly skilled labor and a comparative disadvantage in producing goods requiring unskilled labor. Therefore, greater exposure to international trade would reduce the wages of unskilled workers and increase the wages of skilled workers in America. If women were over-represented among the unskilled workers, their wages would decline. Thus there are two opposing effects on women's wages: the increased trade works to *reduce their wages,* and the increased competition tends to *increase their wages* through a forced reduction in discrimination. The observed change in wages would be the net result of both these effects.

How does one separate the two effects so as to isolate the effect of reduced discrimination? Black and Brainerd tested whether the gender wage gap in *concentrated* industries affected by trade fell relative to that in *competitive* industries affected by trade. This would have happened because, although trade affected both sets of industries, it would have reduced discrimination in concentrated industries by more (because they would no longer have the freedom to discriminate that they had enjoyed before). The authors found strong evidence of this. In fact, they found that an increase in the share of imports (which captures the extent of increased competition from imports) of 10 percentage points reduced the residual gender wage gap by 6.6%. Furthermore, they also found evidence that, with greater international competition, concentrated industries increased the employment of women by larger percentages than did competitive ones.

The evidence summarized above indicates that a taste for discrimination against women *does manifest* in industries that are protected from compe-

---

[11] An industry was defined as being concentrated if the sales of the largest four firms accounted for at least 40% of the total sales in the industry.

[12] Competition from imports was captured by an index that measured the "import share" (defined as the ratio of the value of imports to the value of U.S. output in that industry).

tition for whatever reason. The rigorous statistical tests from which these findings were inferred provide clear evidence that these were not likely to be random accidents: not only were women paid less, they were hired in positions below what they were qualified for.

The analysis and evidence presented above focuses on employers' discrimination. In the context of racial discrimination, Kenneth Arrow (1972)—whom we first encountered in Chapter 1—has pointed out that the implications are quite striking if one assumes that it is employees who discriminate. His analysis can be readily adapted to discrimination against women. Suppose that firms require workers and supervisors and that male workers are averse to being supervised by women but female workers are indifferent to whether they are supervised by men or women. If a woman were employed as a supervisor, the male workers would have to be compensated for their disutility with a higher wage. If the firm's work force were quite large, the expense of this could be substantial. Even if the firm's owner had no prejudice against female employees, purely in the interest of minimizing costs he would hire a male supervisor. In fact, even a female owner would do this. One would then expect to observe that the labor force in that industry was *segregated*. The labor force in a firm would tend to be either all male or all female. More precisely, any firm with a female supervisor would tend to have an all-female labor force. Thus segregation of the labor force within a given industry would emerge as a consequence of employee discrimination.

Before we leave our discussion of the evidence for a taste for discrimination, we should observe that the theory is also relevant to other forms of taste for discrimination. For example, there may be discrimination by sexual orientation of employees in the labor market. By examining incomes from a small but national sample in the United States (from 1989 to 1991), Lee Badgett (1995) has shown that, after accounting for education, work experience, and occupations, men who are gay or bisexual earn up to 25% less than heterosexual men with similar backgrounds.[13] This suggests that a taste for discrimination may be at work. The evidence she finds for lesbian women is in the same direction (though somewhat weaker than for men).

More recent work by Dan Black, Hoda Makar, Seth Sanders, and Lowell Taylor (2003) using a larger sample of American men and women (from 1989 through 1996) shows that gay men earn substantially less than heterosexual men, but lesbian women in fact earn *more* than heterosexual women.[14] The latter is a paradoxical finding, for one would expect lesbian women to face the brunt of two forms of discrimination: discrimination against their sex

[13] Badgett, M.V.L. (1995), "The Wage Effects of Sexual Orientation Discrimination," *Industrial and Labor Relations Review* 48, pp. 726–739.

[14] D. A. Black, H. R. Makar, S. G. Sanders, and L. J. Taylor (2003), "The Earnings Effects of Sexual Orientation," *Industrial and Labor Relations Review* 56, pp. 449–469.

and discrimination against their sexual orientation. Among possible explanations, the authors offer one that is consistent with discrimination and is based on the work of Claudia Goldin (1990).[15] After examining the experience of American women at the turn of the twentieth century, Goldin argued that working women faced a "marriage bar" when they got married; they were paid less than unmarried women, and they were sometimes fired when they got married. If married women still faced this marriage bar in the 1990s, lesbian women might have done better than married heterosexual women because relatively few of the former were married (given the laws against same-sex marriages in most states of the United States at the time). As the authors acknowledge, their results may be saying less about discrimination by sexual orientation than about the nature of the prevalent norms in the labor market regarding marriage and gender roles.

III. Statistical Discrimination

As I pointed out in Chapter 1, the pioneering contributors of the idea of statistical discrimination are Kenneth Arrow (1972) and Edmund Phelps (1972). The term *statistical discrimination* is applied to a situation in which people make decisions based on the statistical characteristics of a *group* in the absence of individual information. So, for example, if the average characteristics of one group are different from those of another, the market may treat them differently. Strictly speaking, this may not be thought to be discrimination in the sense in which we have defined the term. Here two people may be identical in every economic aspect that is relevant to performance. However, this fact may be unknown to an employer. Faced with this situation, an employer may find it worthwhile to use as a cue some characteristic, such as race or sex, on which to base his decisions. To the extent that these cues contain at least some information that distinguishes the average performance of the groups, the employer may be making sound economic decisions. He will be making errors in individual assessments, because he does not have complete information on each individual's characteristics. On average, however, these errors will cancel out, and the employer will be making "correct" decisions.

To see this mechanism in a concrete setting, consider a situation in which an employer is hiring for a job that requires some "firm-specific" on-the-job training. This means that whatever is learned on the job is useful at this specific firm only and has no value elsewhere. Because learning usually takes time away from production, however, there is a cost associated with it. Because the training is firm-specific, the employee would be unwilling to pay for it all by

---

[15] Goldin, C. (1990), *Understanding the Gender Gap: An Economic History of American Women*, Oxford University Press, New York.

herself because she will lose her investment in the event she is laid off. Suppose that the firm shoulders some of this cost. The firm will recover this cost in the future if the worker continues with the firm but will lose it if she quits for any reason. To clarify how this works, suppose that, net of training costs, the contribution of a worker (the value of the marginal product) to the firm is $5,000 a month ($60,000 annually) if he or she stays for a full year. If the worker quits halfway through the year, the contribution is only $3,333 a month ($40,000 annually) because the firm does not get to recoup its investment in the worker's training. Furthermore, suppose that both these productivity figures are independent of gender—there is no difference between the abilities and innate skills of males and females. If he knows for sure that an employee will stay for a year, the employer will offer a salary of $60,000 a year (or $5,000 a month); if he knows for sure that the employee will quit midyear, he will offer a salary of $40,000 a year (or $3,333 a month). This will be true whether the employee is male or female.

The employer, however, is typically not privy to information about whether a worker will stay or quit. Suppose that the employer's past records reveal that the probability that a male employee will quit before the year is out is 20%, whereas the probability that a female employee will quit is somewhat higher, 40%. For the moment, suppose that these quit rates are given. The employer finds that the gender difference in quit rates reveals information that will enable him to cut costs. So he will use gender as a cue to infer the *expected* productivity of a potential employee.

There is an 80% chance that a male employee will stay for the whole year and a 20% chance that he will quit midway, and a 60% chance that a female employee will stay for the whole year and a 40% chance that she will quit midway. Therefore, the expected productivity of a male worker will be 0.8 × $60,000 + 0.2 × $40,000 = $48,000 + $8,000 = $56,000, that is, $4,667 per month. Likewise, the expected productivity of a female worker will be 0.60 × $60,000 + 0.40 × $40,000 = $36,000 + $16,000 = $52,000, that is, $4,333 per month. The employer can observe the sex of the worker but does not know whether he or she will stay for the year or quit midway. So the employer will offer a male worker an annual salary of $56,000 ($4,667 per month). Any more than this would be unprofitable to the employer, on average, because this is the average productivity of a male worker. The worker will not accept any less because, under competitive conditions, he can earn $56,000 a year elsewhere. To a female worker, however, the employer will offer a salary of only $52,000 ($4,333 per month). Any more than this will be unprofitable to the employer, on average, because this is the average productivity of a female worker. She will not accept any less because, under competitive conditions, she could earn $52,000 a year elsewhere.

In effect, one will observe a gap of $4,000 in the annual salaries of male and female workers, despite the fact that they have identical abilities and skills.

The difference arises because the employer is using gender as a cue in forming an opinion of the extent to which he will lose his firm-specific investments in workers. Clearly he is going to be wrong about many people, but if he has correctly computed the probabilities from the historical records of quit rates of male and female workers, he will be right on average. This phenomenon is referred to as statistical discrimination because the employer is using statistical—not individual—information about quit rates to make inferences about productivity. We have assumed that male and female workers who do not quit are equally productive and that male and female workers who do quit are also equally (but less) productive. In a world where employers had perfect information about who was going to quit, the gender of the worker would be irrelevant. So why do employers rely on gender to inform their decisions? It is because gender contains information about the chances of workers quitting and, in a world where knowledge regarding individuals is imperfect, employers find this information economically useful.

If all employers engaged in statistical discrimination, it would be disastrous for a single employer not to do so. Paying men and women the same wage (say, $56,000 a year) would result in a firm's incurring greater training costs for women—costs that they could not retrieve. If the market for their output was perfectly competitive, such firms would be at a disadvantage and their losses would ultimately force them to go bankrupt. So the market would force these firm owners to statistically discriminate. This situation is in sharp contrast to that of indulging a taste for discrimination, which is costly to a firm owner in terms of profit, as we have seen. In this case, it is costly for the firm owner *not* to engage in statistical discrimination.

It is important to understand that, *as long as the probabilities of quitting are given* and are correct, there is no discrimination against any group. A woman who intends to work for a whole year will be paid $52,000 per year ($4,333 per month). This is less than the value of her marginal product of $60,000 a year ($5,000 a month). She is being treated unfairly because of statistical discrimination. But a woman who is hired and leaves midway through the year is also paid at the rate of $52,000 per year ($4,333 for each month before she quits). This is more than the value of her marginal product of $40,000 a year ($3,333 a month). In other words, the labor market treats women who quit overly generously. Women who quit benefit at the expense of women who stay. The higher value of the marginal product of women who stay raises the average productivity of female workers. And because employers cannot distinguish between women who will stay and those who will not, all women are paid their average productivity. In this scenario, the labor market does not discriminate against women as a *group*—on average, they are paid what their productivity warrants. In a sense, the women who stay are subsidizing the salaries of the women who quit.

In exactly the same manner as above, we can argue that male workers who stay are underpaid; they receive $56,000 a year ($4,667 a month), whereas their productivity is $60,000 a year ($5,000 a month). Male workers who quit are overpaid; they receive $56,000 a year ($4,667 a month), whereas their productivity is $40,000 a year ($3,333 a month). The male employees who stay benefit the male employees who quit. As a group, there is no discrimination by the labor market against men, either.

However, a male employee is paid $56,000, whereas a female employee is paid $52,000. Even if there is no discrimination *within* groups, isn't there discrimination *across* groups? Are not men unfairly favored over women? In the assumed setting, this is not so. Each member of a group is being paid the average productivity of that group. Because we have assumed that the probability of quitting is higher for women, their average productivity is lower from the point of view of the firm. Even though individual male and female workers are identical in terms of abilities and skills, because their chances of quitting are different, employers will perceive them as belonging to nonidentical groups. Hence there will be a difference in treatment.

The qualification that the chances of quitting be *given* is important to the argument. If the probability of quitting is itself determined by statistical discrimination, the argument needs modification.[16] Suppose that, for whatever reason, all employers have preconceived notions that women are not as likely to remain employed as men. Based on this notion, they will statistically discriminate against women in the manner described above. As a result, those women who plan on long-term employment might find that the salary they are earning is too low to attract their long-term loyalty. They may abandon their commitment to the labor market and become more receptive to quitting. In such a case, statistical discrimination may *bring about* the very thing that employers presume. In this situation, the probability of women employees quitting is not given; rather, it is determined by employers' perceptions, however unjustified they may have been to begin with. This sort of effect is very difficult to detect because employers may feel justified in believing that, say, 40% of recently hired women will quit because their historical records reveal precisely this probability. What the record does not reveal is whether the 40% quit rate was the result of statistical discrimination to begin with.

Even if the quit rates can be taken as given, however, it is important to realize the extent to which the outcomes depend on the combined effects of evolutionary biology and socialization (discussed in Chapter 2). For women, quitting jobs may be related at least partly to the needs of a young family; evolution may have conferred on women a comparative advantage relative to

---

[16]This point was first formalized in a slightly different context in Coate, S., and G. C. Loury (1993), "Will Affirmative Action Eliminate Negative Stereotypes?," *American Economic Review* 83, pp. 1220–1239.

men in the raising of very young children. Furthermore, socially constructed notions asserting that a woman's duty is to be with her children when they are young may induce many young mothers to quit their jobs. If this is so, to a significant extent statistical discrimination against women in the labor market may be conditioned, on the one hand, partly by what evolution has wrought and, on the other, partly by what socially constructed ideas have promoted.

Evidence of Statistical Discrimination

Before we embark on a discussion of the evidence on statistical discrimination, we note that the evidence presented below on the phenomenon does not come from labor market studies per se. But that is not in itself a problem either for the theory or for our understanding of the mechanism. The essence of statistical discrimination is that decision makers use group averages as a proxy for individual information to which they are not privy. If there is evidence of such behavior in everyday life, we may reasonably surmise that similar processes may be at work in the labor market when employers are missing information about individual characteristics pertinent to the labor market.

Ian Ayres and Peter Siegelman (1995) provided persuasive evidence for statistical discrimination in the activity of bargaining for new cars.[17] For this study the authors recruited and trained market "testers" of different genders and races but of similar educational and work backgrounds. These testers were randomly assigned to car dealerships in the Chicago area and were asked to bargain for new cars. They were trained to reveal similar information and proceed in a manner identically scripted for all the testers. Summary information regarding the initial and final offers (after bargaining was completed) is shown in Table 4.1.

In Table 4.1, *initial profit* refers to the profit the car dealership would have made had the car been sold at the initial offer made by the salesperson to the tester. *Concession,* in the third column, refers to the amount by which the initial offer made by the salesperson was reduced after bargaining. *Final profit,* indicated in the last column, is the profit the dealership would have made had the car been sold at the final offer of the salesperson. As can be seen, women and blacks were made higher initial offers than white males. (Furthermore, blacks were even offered lower concessions in the final offer.)

Ayres and Siegelman argue that the difference in treatment across groups could not have been due to a taste for discrimination. Female testers did not fare worse at the hands of male salespersons, nor did black testers fare worse in white dealerships or with white salespersons. The difference could have been due to possible differences in bargaining power, though it is usu-

[17] Ayres, I., and P. Siegelman (1995), "Race and Gender Discrimination in Bargaining for a New Car," *American Economic Review* 85, pp. 304–321.

TABLE 4.1 Car dealerships' potential profit in bargaining for cars (dollars)

Tester type	Initial profit	Concession	Final profit
White males	1,019	455	564
White females	1,127	471	657
Black females	1,337	362	975
Black males	1,954	289	1,665
All nonwhite males	1,426	381	1,045

Source: Ayres, I., and P. Siegelman (1995), "Race and Gender Discrimination in Bargaining for a New Car," *American Economic Review* 85, pp. 304–321. The figures are drawn from Table 1, p. 308, with permission.

ally hard to infer bargaining power from the sex and race of a customer. The most likely source seems to have been statistical discrimination. The authors argue that women and blacks are *less well informed* about the cost of a car to the dealership. If this fact were well known among salespeople, they would tend to exploit it by quoting higher prices to women and blacks.

John List (2004) provided some experimental evidence of the existence of statistical discrimination.[18] He examined the market for the buying and selling of sports cards.[19] He found that, between negotiating individuals in actual markets, dealers tended to discriminate against minorities (women and black males) relative to the majority (white males). In the experiment, agents participating as buyers were assigned a reservation price, which was the maximum they would be willing to pay for a particular sports card. The earning they received from a purchase was the difference between this reservation price and the amount they actually ended up paying for the card. Sellers were not told that these buyers were participating in an experiment. Similarly, sellers participating in the experiment were assigned a reservation price that was the minimum price they would accept, and their earning was the difference between the price for which they sold the card and this reservation price. Buyers were not told that these sellers were participating in an experiment. Buyers in the experiments negotiated only with actual sellers in the market, and sellers in the experiments negotiated only with actual buyers in the market. In other words, experimental buyers never negotiated with experimental sellers.

List found that buyers in the minority were quoted higher initial prices and were made higher final offers in the bargaining that followed than those

[18] List, J. (2004), "The Nature and Extent of Discrimination in the Marketplace: Evidence from the Field," *Quarterly Journal of Economics* 119, pp. 49–89.

[19] Sports cards, which are very popular in North America, are collectibles featuring sports stars and some of their game statistics. Cards that are rare and in good condition can command high prices among collectors.

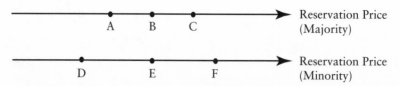

FIGURE 4.3 Why statistical discrimination can rely on variance

in the majority. Compared to sellers in the majority, sellers in the minority were offered lower initial prices for their sports cards and lower final prices in the bargaining that followed. Experienced buyers and sellers in the minority, however, managed to receive final offers similar to those in the majority but only at the expense of greater amounts of time devoted to negotiation. The author then demonstrated that this difference in the treatment of minorities was due neither to a taste for discrimination nor to any inferiority in their bargaining powers. The difference was due to statistical discrimination.

The reason for statistical discrimination in these experiments is interesting. List demonstrated that, although people in the minorities had *average* reservation values that were similar to those in the majority, these values exhibited greater *variance* or "spread." Loosely speaking, the maximum reservation values among the minorities tended to be higher than those among the majorities, and the minimum reservation values among the minorities tended to be lower than those among the majorities. Why would this fact lead people to discriminate statistically? It was because it is profit maximizing to do so. This can be readily seen with the help of Figure 4.3.

The upper line in Figure 4.3 shows the range of values of the reservation prices of buyers from the majority (young white males, say). In the figure, point A denotes the minimum reservation price in the group, C the maximum, and B the group average. Likewise, the lower line in Figure 4.3 shows the range of values of the reservation prices of buyers from the minority (women and blacks, say). In the figure, point D denotes the minimum reservation price in the group, F the maximum, and E the group average. The average values in the two groups are shown to be identical. However, the spread of possible reservation prices was greater among the minority (from D to F) than among the majority (from A to C).

A seller would naturally like to charge a potential buyer as high a price as possible, that is, the buyer's reservation price. However, he normally would not know this reservation price. All he can observe is whether the buyer is from the majority or from the minority. A seller negotiating with a buyer from the majority would quote an initial price near C to begin with in the hope of selling the card for the highest feasible price. On the other hand, were the seller dealing with someone from the minority, he would initially quote a price near F. This difference in asking price would be due to statistical discrimination. It is interesting, however, that the two groups in List's experiment had the same average reservation price; they differed only in the extent of the variation (spread) in the reservation prices. This argument shows that statistical discrimination can occur even when two groups have identical averages but different *variances*.

A similar argument can be made if we are considering the behavior of buyers with regard to potential sellers. Suppose that the reservation prices in Figure 4.3 represent the sellers' valuations. A buyer negotiating with a potential seller would quote an initial offer near A if the seller was from the majority but close to D if the seller was from the minority. In other words, buyers and sellers would use membership in minority or majority groups as cues for assessing their range of reservation values.

To the extent that women exhibit higher variances in their reservation values than men, they will be quoted higher prices by sellers and lower prices by buyers. Sellers and buyers do this because it is profitable for them to use statistical information about the various groups, not because they have a taste for discriminating against some groups relative to others.

IV. The Efficiency Wage Theory of Discrimination

We shall briefly describe another theory of discrimination, which is due to Jeremy Bulow and Lawrence Summers (1986).[20] These authors start from the premise that the labor market is characterized by roughly two sorts of jobs. There are the "good" jobs, which pay well, entail individual responsibility, offer prospects for promotion, have good working conditions, and so on. And then there are the "bad" jobs, which pay poorly, are routine, entail little individual initiative, and are dead-end jobs with few prospects for advancement. Thus the labor market is "dual" in the sense that it has two sectors: a primary sector consisting of good jobs and a secondary sector comprising bad jobs. In this context, is there any reason to believe that women would be largely relegated to the bad jobs and men to the good jobs? There is a view that this is indeed the case.[21]

The efficiency theory of discrimination argues that in the primary sector, workers have to be paid more than the going market wage. This might seem, at first blush, unprofitable for firms. Why pay someone more than what is necessary? But, as it turns out, this is economical in some circumstances. The good jobs require considerable individual initiative and effort, which means that workers can also shirk on the job. If they are going to earn a given wage

---

[20] Bulow, J. I., and L. H. Summers (1986), "A Theory of Dual Labor Markets with Application to Industrial Policy, Discrimination, and Keynesian Unemployment," *Journal of Labor Economics* 4, pp. 376–414.

[21] Barbara Bergman made an early attempt to understand how this might come about. See Bergman, B. R. (1974), "Occupational Segregation, Wages and Profits When Employers Discriminate by Race or Sex," *Eastern Economic Journal* 1, pp. 103–110.

anyway, why would they do their jobs unless they were supervised by some-body? Supervision is costly to firms, however, because someone has to be keeping an eye on the workers instead of producing something themselves. From the point of view of the firm, the cost of employing workers is not just the wage it has to pay them but also the cost of supervising them.

If the cost to the firm of supervising workers is very high, it may opt for a different strategy to reduce the need for supervision. The firm may choose to pay the workers more than the market wage and restrict their supervision to occasional, random spot checks. If in the spot checks workers are found to be shirking, they will be fired. Because they are receiving more than the market wage in these jobs, workers have a stake in keeping their jobs and will curtail their shirking. So, on balance, paying workers more than the market wage— what is called an "efficiency wage"—may be worthwhile for the firm.[22] The higher wages in these good jobs discipline workers by inducing them to abstain from shirking—as long as there are some less-well-paid workers waiting in the wings for their good jobs.[23] The bad jobs, in contrast, do not require an efficiency wage because they are routine and are easily supervised. Workers in this sector are paid just their market wages. This explains why the primary-sector jobs are indeed good and the secondary-sector jobs are bad. Even though the workers in the two sectors may have the same produc-tivity, they earn different wages.

Bulow and Summers (1986) propose that such a dual labor market as the one described above may explain gender discrimination in the labor market. Verifying that this is so would entail demonstrating that a larger proportion of women than men will find themselves in the secondary sector. How could this come about? One way is if women are more likely to obtain higher utility than men in the secondary sector. This is conceivable if women are more likely than men to perceive the secondary sector as more compatible with household pro-duction. For example, they may find it easier to split their time between house-hold work and work in the secondary sector. If so, women will not perceive being fired from a primary job to be as much of a disaster as men might, so a given efficiency wage will have less of a disciplining effect on women. The effi-ciency wage for women, in other words, will have to be higher than for men. Firms, then, will opt to hire mostly men in the primary sector because they are less expensive. The same outcome will obtain if women are more likely than men to discontinue employment (largely to raise a family) in the primary

---

[22] It was precisely for this reason that, in 1914, Henry Ford of the Ford Motor Company adopted a policy of paying workers $5 a day when other motor companies were paying between $2 and $3 a day. See Bulow and Summers (1986).

[23] The first papers to model the idea of an efficiency wage are Eaton, B. C., and W. D. White (1983), "The Economy of High Wages: An Agency Problem," *Economica* 50, pp. 175–181, and Shapiro, C., and Stiglitz, J. (1984), "Equilibrium Unemployment as a Worker Discipline Device," *American Economic Review* 74, pp. 433–444.

sector. For then, too, the required efficiency wage will have to be higher for women because the loss of high wages in future periods will be less ominous for them. The latter reason is the one offered by Claudia Goldin (1986) to explain the historical employment segregation by sex in the United States in the twentieth century (discussed below).[24]

It is not easy to empirically verify the claims of the efficiency wage hypothesis. It predicts that workers with high wages will be more productive because they shirk less. But this is precisely what would obtain in a competitive labor market in the absence of supervision problems: those workers who are more productive will be paid more. To verify the efficiency wage theory, one has to examine the cost of supervision. The prediction to be tested is that, everything else being the same, workers with less supervision will be paid more than other workers. Usually data on supervision are hard to obtain, so few statistical studies have sought to verify the hypothesis. The results from these are mixed: some find little evidence in favor of the hypothesis, but others find evidence consistent with it.

One study shows that, when supervision is more intense (the supervisor checks the work of subordinates more frequently), the wage is lower.[25] Another study undertaken with data from the petrochemical industry for its particularly convenient statistical advantages finds that, when there is more supervision, wages are lower.[26] Yet another study conducted on the reasonable assumption that larger work groups have less supervision per worker finds that workers in larger groups tend to have higher wages.[27] This makes sense because, if shirking is easier in larger groups, workers need to be paid a higher (efficiency) wage to curb shirking. On the issue of whether the efficiency wage hypothesis explains gender differences in wages, there is even less evidence to date. One investigation attempts to see if there are gender differences in the trade-off between supervision costs and wages using U.S. data from 1996.[28] The measure of supervision cost that it employs is the hourly wage of the supervisor divided by the number of workers supervised. Although this study finds that there is a trade-off between supervision costs and wages (that is, that less supervision goes with higher wages), it also detects no gender differences in this trade-off.

[24] Goldin, C. (1986), "Monitoring Costs and Occupational Segregation by Sex: A Historical Analysis," *Journal of Labor Economics* 4, pp. 1–27.

[25] Kruse, D. (1992), "Supervision, Working Conditions, and the Employer Size–Wage Effect," *Industrial Relations* 31, pp. 229–249.

[26] Rebitzer, J. B. (1995), "Is There a Trade-Off between Supervision and Wages?: An Empirical Test of Efficiency Wage Theory," *Journal of Economic Behavior and Organization* 28, pp. 107–129.

[27] Ewing, B. T., and J. E. Payne (1999), "The Trade-Off between Supervision and Wages: Evidence on Efficiency Wages from the NLSY," *Southern Economic Journal* 66, pp. 424–432.

[28] Ewing, B. T., and P. V. Wunnava (2004), "The Trade-Off between Supervision Cost and Performance Based Pay: Does Gender Matter?," *Small Business Economics* 23, pp. 453–460.

Goldin (1986) offers a plausible story as to why occupational segregation by sex (that is, the employment of women and men in different occupations) prevailed in the manufacturing sector of the United States in the early decades of the past century. Looking at employment and the mode of payment in the early 1900s, she finds that not only were women and men employed in different industries, even when they were employed in the same industry, they were paid in different ways. Men tended to be paid by time (that is, per hour or at a wage rate), but women tended to be paid at a piece rate (that is, by how many "pieces" of output they produced). Why? Goldin argues that in those decades, employed women tended to quit after they got married, so the expected duration of their employment was lower than that of men. As a result, an efficiency wage that offered the carrot of high wages in future periods as an incentive for not shirking was not as effective an inducement for women. Consequently, men were paid at a wage rate, presumably an efficiency wage, whereas women were paid at piece rates. Because, under a piece rate scheme, workers are paid an amount that exactly corresponds to what they produce, such a scheme prevents shirking. In effect, women were largely relegated to those jobs for which individual outputs could be identified so that piece rates could be paid.

V. Why Women Are Held to Higher Standards Than Men in Some Jobs

Is it conceivable that women and men are held up to different standards in the jobs they are assigned to? Edward Lazear and Sherwin Rosen (1990) have observed that much of the gender gap in average wages is due to the fact that men and women tend to perform different jobs, not because they are paid differently for the same job.[29] They argue that a difference in the quit rates of men and women could cause *higher* ability standards to be required of women than men. Their theory provides a reason for the firm conviction women often have that they have to be more able than men to fill a position. The highly simplified treatment below gives the flavor of the argument.

Because ability is essential to the discussion, let us suppose that workers can be of either low ability or high ability. Let us also assume that half the male workers are of low ability and the other half are of high ability, and likewise, that half the female workers are of low ability and the other half are of high ability. So we are assuming that there is no difference between males and females regarding the distribution of their abilities.

To keep the exposition simple, we shall assume that employers can assess the ability of their potential employees but that there is no objective measure of ability that both workers and employers can agree on. So even though

---

[29] Lazear, E. P., and S. Rosen (1990), "Male–Female Wage Differentials in Job Ladders," *Journal of Labor Economics* 8, pp. S106–S123.

TABLE 4.2 Productivity in jobs with and without learning (dollars)

Ability level	Job A (investment required)		Job B (no investment required)	
	Period 1	Period 2	Period 1	Period 2
Low	20,000	80,000	40,000	40,000
High	40,000	160,000	80,000	80,000

employers believe they can assess workers' abilities (at least to their own level of satisfaction), they cannot offer wages that are based on their perceptions of workers' abilities. In other words, different people working the same job cannot be paid different wages. The wage is tied to the *job*, not to the *individual* doing the job.

Suppose that firms are hiring workers for two jobs, which we shall call Job A and Job B. We shall assume that both sorts of jobs need to be done in the firm. Suppose that Job A is better in that the value of the marginal product of a worker is higher. However, this job requires some firm-specific investment, whereas Job B does not. To capture the nature of this difference, consider the outputs of a worker in each of two periods.[30]

The value of the marginal output of a worker is the same in each of the two periods in Job B: it is $40,000 for a worker of low ability and $80,000 for a worker of high ability. In Job A, the value of the marginal output is different in the two periods because learning is involved. For a low-ability worker, it is $20,000 in period 1 and $80,000 in period 2; for a high-ability worker it is $40,000 and $160,000, respectively, in the two periods. Furthermore, suppose that all these productivity figures are independent of gender. These figures are summarized in Table 4.2.

On scanning Table 4.2 we see that a worker's output in the better Job A is lower than that in Job B in period 1 (because of the costs associated with learning) but higher in period 2. For a low-ability worker the total output over two periods is $80,000 in Job B but $100,000 in Job A. This captures the fact that a worker is potentially more productive in Job A. This potential will be realized, however, only if the worker remains with the firm in period 2. Likewise, for a high-ability worker the total output over two periods is $160,000 in Job B but $200,000 in Job A. By assigning a worker to Job A instead of Job B, the firm loses output in period 1, but it will be compensated for this loss in period 2 if the worker stays with the firm.

In this scenario, any difference in the treatment of men and women will arise from differences in the quit rates of men and women. To make the point as simply as possible, suppose that the probability that a male worker will

---

[30] For simplicity, we shall assume that the firm hires only once in two periods in order to minimize the costs involved in the process of hiring.

stay on for period 2 is 100%, whereas the corresponding probability for a female worker is only 75%. Suppose, too, that all men are assigned to the better job. The total expected output of a low-ability male worker in Job A is $100,000, whereas that of a high-ability male worker is $200,000. Furthermore, because half the male workers are of low ability and the other half are of high ability, the average total output expected of a male worker in Job A is ($100,000 + $200,000)/2 = $150,000. If the firm makes no profit on the worker and pays each male worker the average productivity of males, each male worker will earn a total of $150,000 over the two periods in Job A.

Now consider female workers. Suppose, first, that all women are assigned to the better job. The total expected output of a low-ability female worker in Job A is $20,000 + 0.75 × $80,000 = $80,000, whereas that of a high-ability female worker is $40,000 + 0.75 × $160,000 = $160,000. On average, then, the total expected output of a female worker in Job A is ($80,000 + $160,000)/2 = $120,000. If the firm makes no profit on a female worker and pays her the average productivity of females, it can pay each woman a total of $120,000 over the two periods in Job A.

A competitive firm that hires male workers of both low and high ability in Job A will offer them a total of $150,000 over the two periods. (Recall that the firm cannot provide objective evidence on its assessment of individual abilities, and so it cannot offer different wages to high- and low-ability workers doing the same job.) If it hires female workers of both low and high ability in Job A, it can offer them a total of $120,000 over the two periods. If the firm pays female workers $150,000 over the two years in Job A, it will incur losses on its investment in the firm-specific human capital of the average female because the chance that she will quit is greater (by assumption) than that for the average male. But this disparity in wages may be perceived as discrimination by gender because workers doing the *same job* are being treated differently.

When confronted with this situation, instead of offering different wages, firms may avoid violating the law by being discriminatory in the *standard of the ability* that they set for Job A. They may opt to set higher ability standards for women. To see how this could arise, suppose that firms assign, as above, all men (of low and high ability) to Job A. But now suppose that they assign only high-ability women to Job A, relegating the low-ability women to the inferior Job B. As before, the expected output of the males in Job A is $150,000 over the two periods. The expected output of the (high-ability) females in Job A is now $160,000 over the two periods. Thus, if the firm assigns only high-ability women to Job A, it can afford to offer them the same wage that it offers the men in this job.

Are low-ability women productive enough in Job A to warrant being assigned to this job instead of Job B? Yes. Their expected output in this job over the two periods is $80,000, whereas their expected output over the two

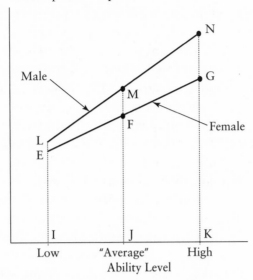

Total Expected Output

FIGURE 4.4 Why women may be of greater
ability than men on the same job

periods in Job B is $40,000 + 0.75 × $40,000 = $70,000. Yet they will not be
assigned to Job A if women and men are to be paid the same wage. *Low-ability
women will be denied the better job, even though low-ability men will not.*

To see the reason for this, note that there are two factors that are responsible for reducing the expected wage in Job A: (i) low ability, and (ii) high
quit rates. Reason i applies to both men and women, but reason ii applies to
women more than to men because women's quit rates (as assumed) are higher.
Therefore, if all men and all women are assigned to Job A, the average productivity of men will be higher than the average productivity of women. If
women and men are to be paid the same salary for the same job, the firm will
incur a loss due to the higher quit rate of women. The firm can circumvent
this loss by selecting only high-ability women for the better job.

The point can be seen more readily with the aid of Figure 4.4. On the
horizontal axis we plot the ability of the worker, which takes on two values, "Low" and "High." On the vertical axis we plot the expected total output over the two periods of the worker in Job A. The vertical distance IL
represents the output of a low-ability male worker. The total output, IE, of
a low-ability female worker is less because women have a higher quit rate
by assumption. Similarly, KN and KG denote the expected total outputs of
high-ability male and female workers, respectively. Because half the workers
of either sex are of low ability and the other half are of high ability, the vertical distance JM, where M is midway between L and N on the line LN, gives
the average value of the expected total output of males. Likewise, the vertical distance JF, where F is midway between E and G on the line EG, gives the

average value of the expected total output of females. We can think of JM and JF as the expected output, respectively, of a fictitious male and a fictitious female with an ability level labeled "Average" in the figure.

In competitive labor markets, males will have to be paid an average of JM for the two periods, which is higher than the corresponding value, JF, for females. If women in Job A are also paid JM, the firm will incur losses. But notice that KG, the expected total output of high-ability females, is higher than JM. So if only high-ability women are selected for Job A, the firm can afford to pay them JM. In other words, the firm will relegate low-ability women but not low-ability men to the inferior job. Therefore, if we examine the ability of workers doing Job A, we will find men of both low and high ability but women of only high ability. Consequently, the average ability of women in Job A will be *higher* than that of men in Job A.

This difference in the treatment of men and women will show up when their average earnings are computed. The average earnings of a man over the two periods will be determined by the average productivity of men in the better job because *all* men will be assigned to the better job. On the other hand, only half of the women—the high-ability ones—will be assigned to the better job; the remaining women will be relegated to the inferior job. The average earnings of women in this firm, therefore, will be less than those of men. Thus there will be a gender disparity in the average earnings of the employees. This disparity sneaks in via the back door (through a difference in job allocations) when there is legislation that requires the wage rate for the same job to be independent of gender.

The analysis presented above has been silent on why the quit rates are higher for women. One plausible reason is that women are better than men in nonmarket work and are more needed at home—at least when the children are very young. It follows, then, that low-ability women earn less than low-ability men in the above analysis because women are better at something other than market work while being just as good at market work. Having a comparative advantage in nonmarket work is financially disadvantageous to women even when the distribution of their abilities for market work is the same as that of men.

VI. Summary

We began this chapter by noting that there is typically a gender gap in wages in all countries and that many factors other than discrimination contribute to this gender gap. Discrimination potentially applies only to any *residual* gender gap that remains after the effects of all these other factors have been accounted for.

We first considered the theory of discrimination based on taste formulated by Becker (1957). We saw that discrimination of this sort may prevail in the short run but cannot persist in the long run if labor markets are competitive. If a labor market is not competitive, however, this outcome need not obtain. We then discussed empirical evidence from the U.S. banking industry, showing that deregulation (which increased competition) reduced the gender wage gap and also increased the proportion of women who were hired as managers, just as Becker's theory would have predicted. We also discussed evidence showing that greater exposure of the U.S. economy to international trade reduced the gender wage gap in concentrated industries relative to that in competitive industries. The evidence for the existence of a taste for discrimination, however, should not lull us into always waiting for market forces to eliminate workplace discrimination. Elimination would be hastened if governments took a proactive role by legislating and implementing antidiscrimination laws so that those who are discriminated against will have legal recourse.

We also briefly discussed some empirical evidence for another form of taste for discrimination, namely, that against gays and lesbians. We saw that there is statistical evidence that gay men earn less than heterosexual men with similar backgrounds but that lesbian women earn more than heterosexual women of similar backgrounds.

We then went on to discuss the theory of statistical discrimination, which is attributed to Arrow (1972) and Phelps (1972). We saw that, if women quit their current jobs at higher rates than men, firms use this statistical fact to minimize the cost of training their personnel by giving preference to hiring men instead of women even though both may be equally qualified. We saw that this sort of discrimination cannot be rooted out by competition even in the long run, because not discriminating statistically would put a firm at a competitive disadvantage. Drawing on experimental work that entails bargaining situations, we then saw that there is behavior in the real world that is explainable by the theory of statistical discrimination.

We next discussed a theory of discrimination based on efficiency wages that economize on the need for supervision. When such wages are paid and workers' performance is monitored only through occasional spot checks, they will curtail their shirking because they have a lot to lose in case they are fired. But if women anticipate shorter employment durations, this mechanism is not very effective for them. Goldin (1986) offered this theory as a persuasive rationale for the fact that, in the early decades of the past century, American women in manufacturing were paid at piece rates, whereas men were paid at wage rates.

Finally, we considered the puzzle of why women working in some jobs perceive that they have to be more able than the average man doing the same job. We discussed a model in which, when the quit rate of women is higher than that of men, for some jobs firms may hire both high- and low-ability men but only high-ability women.

In sum, this chapter has shown how simple economic models can be constructed to cast light on the mechanisms through which discrimination against women can arise in the labor market. We have also shown how empirical evidence can be brought to bear to verify the implications of these models.

We must emphasize, however, that many forms of discrimination in society are *not* captured adequately by the sort of economic models presented here. In patriarchal societies, there are numerous pervasive and deep-rooted biases that blight the prospects of women even before they enter the labor market. The fact that we have excluded consideration of such forms of discrimination by opting for a narrow definition of the term *discrimination* should not mislead us into presuming that they are unimportant.

Exercises and Questions for Discussion

1. Explain why, in the theory of a taste for (employer) discrimination, the effect of discrimination on the profit of a firm is ambiguous in the *short run*. What role does competition play in achieving the outcome that Becker predicts in the *long run*? Can you think of examples in which there can be discrimination by taste against women even in the long run?

2. In the villages of rural India, landlords are known to frequently treat landless workers with considerable contempt and inhumanity, especially if these workers are from the lower castes. Suppose that we characterize this behavior as discrimination by taste. What assumption of Becker's model do you think is violated by the fact that such behavior of the landlords can persist for centuries, as it has in India? What do you think will be the effect on landlords' behavior of globalization when it reaches village life in India?

3. Barbara Bergman was one of the earliest economists to suggest a model that might explain gender discrimination and occupational segregation. This exercise is based on her model. There are two jobs (Job A and Job B), and the total demand for labor (in hours) for each job is given by $L_A^d = L_B^d = 20 - w$, where w is the wage rate of a worker hired for the job. The supply of labor (in hours) of a *single* worker (be that a male or a female) for any job is given by $l^s = w/20 - 1/10$.

   (a) Suppose that there are 200 workers in total, 120 of them women. Suppose further that, initially, a person can work in either job at the going wage rate. How many workers will be hired in each type of job, and what will the wage rates be (assuming that the labor market is competitive)? Explain your answer.

(b) Now suppose that women are discriminated against in Job A and are excluded from it. In the new equilibrium, what will the wage rate be for each type of job? How many workers will be employed in each job? Of what gender?

(c) If there were equal numbers of women and men (100 each), in what ways would the outcome be different from those in parts a and b above?

(d) Would you expect the outcome in part b above to persist in the long run? Why or why not?

4. Consider the empirical findings of Black and Brainerd (2004) on the effect of international trade on gender discrimination in the United States.

(a) Explain why, to test Becker's theory, the authors had to take into account the effect on the gender gap of the country's comparative advantage in trade.

(b) Explain why the authors had to compare the effect of trade on the gender gap in concentrated (monopolized) industries with that on the gender gap in competitive industries.

(c) Were their findings consistent with the prediction of Becker's model? Explain.

5. Suppose that firms need to incur some unrecoverable expense to train their workers for a job and that women and men are equally productive when they work. Suppose also that women have a higher quit rate than men in this job.

(a) Explain how statistical discrimination against women can arise in the salaries they are offered by firms.

(b) Are all women employed by a firm discriminated against, or only some? Explain who among the women benefits from statistical discrimination and who gets hurt.

(c) Now suppose that, over several decades, women decide to participate more and more in the labor market because couples are having fewer children and because household gadgets are relieving women of some of their household chores. Explain why statistical discrimination may make it difficult for women to implement their desired increase in labor market participation.

6. Suppose that all workers have the same skill level and that, if they work for a whole year, the value of their marginal product to a competitive firm (net of training costs incurred by the firm) is $8,000 per month ($96,000 per year). If a worker quits halfway through the year, the above figure is reduced to $5,000 per month ($60,000 per year). Suppose that the historical midyear quit rate for men is 25% and for women 50%.

(a) Suppose that the employer (who has no taste for discrimination) has full knowledge of whether a worker will stay for the whole year or quit halfway. What monthly salaries will the firm offer to new employees? Will you observe any salary difference that may be attributed to gender discrimination? Why or why not?

(b) Now suppose that the employer knows only the statistical averages of the quit rates by gender and has no private information about specific individuals. What monthly salary will the firm offer to (i) women and (ii) men? Will you observe any salary difference that might be attributed to gender discrimination? Why or why not?

(c) If in part b the firm is legally forbidden to offer different wage rates to women and men for the same job, what will the firm likely do?

7. Consider a job in which the output is very sensitive to a worker's effort, but that effort is quite expensive for a firm to supervise.

(a) Explain the concept of an "efficiency wage" and why the firm may consider paying workers such a wage.

(b) If jobs require different amounts of supervision, what are some reasons that men may obtain mostly jobs paying efficiency wages but women may obtain mostly jobs at market wages?

(c) How does the efficiency wage argument relate to the fact that the U.S. labor market in the early twentieth century was segregated by sex?

8. Consider the simplified version of the model of Lazear and Rosen (1990) that was presented in this chapter.

(a) Why is the average level of ability of women in certain jobs higher than that of men in the same jobs?

(b) How do you explain, in the context of this model, why the average wage of women employed by the firm is lower than the average wage of men?

CHAPTER FIVE

How Do Credit Markets Affect the Well-being of Women?

I. Introduction

Even in the contemporary societies of developed countries, many women strongly believe that they are exploited in their economic lives. Though *exploitation* is a term that has many meanings, this insistent claim warrants economic analysis. Credit markets play an important role in relegating women to positions and occupations in which they are vulnerable to exploitation in the sense that they are taken advantage of. This results from the facts that credit markets place a premium on the ownership of wealth and that, in most societies, wealth has been historically distributed in favor of men. In this chapter we shall examine those aspects of credit markets that put women at a disadvantage.

One important route through which credit markets impinge on the lives of people is by either enabling them to become entrepreneurs or preventing them. Who exactly are entrepreneurs? These are people who identify untapped market opportunities in the form of unmet needs and, by setting up business enterprises to meet these perceived needs, make a profit from these opportunities. The alternative to being an entrepreneur is to be a worker—a person who works in someone else's enterprise.[1]

Setting up business enterprises requires money, capital. This is because there are expenditures associated with building a plant or factory, purchasing machinery, and so on. Capital is also required to pay the day-to-day expenses of running a business, such as labor, electricity, and materials. People wishing to start new enterprises must have on hand the needed capital—either

---

[1] In practice, however, due to data restrictions, entrepreneurs are usually identified as people who either own businesses or are self-employed. So an individual who has inherited an enterprise from parents is also counted as an entrepreneur.

their own or that borrowed from friends, relatives, or banks and other financial institutions. Those who cannot come up with the needed capital cannot become entrepreneurs.

Why does it matter whether one has the opportunity to become an entrepreneur? It matters, for one thing, because entrepreneurs tend to earn higher incomes than workers—at least in the developed countries.[2] For another, entrepreneurs also increase their wealth at a faster rate. Wealth is generated by income that is not consumed; it is the sum total of savings from the past. Because higher incomes facilitate higher levels of savings, entrepreneurs are able to accumulate more wealth than workers. In short, entrepreneurs in the developed world not only earn higher incomes but also tend to be more upwardly mobile than workers. The main reason for this is the crucial role played by credit markets. To the extent that credit markets work to their detriment, women will be unable to avail themselves of the opportunities afforded by entrepreneurship to improve their well-being.

The potential benefits of the credit market to women go far beyond enabling them to become entrepreneurs and generally allowing them to better use their skills and talents. Better market opportunities for women improve their well-being in their households. We saw in Chapter 3 that how well married or cohabiting women do in bargaining with their partners over important household decisions depends on their outside options. By improving their outside options, access to credit increases the well-being of women in relation to their spouses. Furthermore, we also saw that women are more altruistic toward their children than men. So the benefits of improving women's earning power accrue even to subsequent generations, for their children are better fed and better educated. Given these pervasive and salutary consequences, the credit market stands as one of the most important markets that can contribute to the well-being of women and society. Studying the obstacles that thwart women from fully participating in this crucial market is the main goal of this chapter.

Are there features peculiar to credit markets that prevent women from participating in them? One important feature of credit is that the two activities of a credit transaction (borrowing and returning) occur at different points in time. In most other transactions, in contrast, the two actions of buying and selling occur at the same point in time. If the buyer does not make a payment for a product, the product is not given; if the seller does not deliver the product, the buyer does not pay. Because the completion of a credit agreement necessarily takes place over a period of time (possibly a lengthy period), cred-

---

[2] Quadrini, V. (1999), "The Importance of Entrepreneurship for Wealth Concentration and Mobility," *Review of Income and Wealth* 45, pp. 1–19. This need not be so in poor countries. See Banerjee, A. V., and E. Duflo (2007), "The Economic Lives of the Poor," *Journal of Economic Perspectives* 21, Winter, pp. 141–167.

itors need to worry about whether their money will be returned—not only the interest that is due but even the principal that was loaned.[3]

Two problems arise when there is a possibility that borrowers can get away without fully repaying creditors' principal with interest. On the one hand, borrowers may be inclined to apply less effort in their enterprises than if the money was their own, for the costs of shirking on their effort are partly borne by the creditors. On the other, even if the enterprises require no application of effort, they may differ in terms of risk. If creditors do not know the precise extent of the risk involved, borrowers may be inclined to invest the (borrowed) money in riskier endeavors. This is because they can aim for the off-chance that they may hit the jackpot because they don't have to worry that much about what will happen if their enterprise fails.

In light of the above two problems, creditors are wary of lending unless borrowers can offer some form of security (an asset such as a house, a piece of land, or an automobile). The idea is that this asset, called collateral, can be kept by the creditor if the borrower does not return the borrowed money. Those without assets of sufficient value cannot borrow. This becomes a matter that is pertinent to gender if the ownership of assets differs by gender. It becomes imperative, then, for us to examine how wealth is distributed by gender, because that determines access to credit. As we shall see, this distribution is biased in favor of men in developing countries but not to the same extent in the developed world.

The distribution of assets has other implications. For one, those without wealth are in a precarious position in the struggle for survival, and this makes them vulnerable to exploitation. Because Marxian theory is quite useful in understanding the notion of exploitation, we shall adapt a Marxian model to study how the theory of exploitation can be applied to women. We shall also see how the distribution of assets across a population impinges on the wage rate in an economy and why wage earners may prefer that the wealth be distributed in a more egalitarian manner among the owners of wealth.

We shall then review the empirical literature that compares women and men in terms of entrepreneurship. How do they compare in terms of size of firms and profitability? Are these differences (if any) due to different preferences of women and men, or do they arise because of the constraints imposed by family life and the credit market? Finally we launch into an examination of whether credit markets merely disadvantage women relative to men or actually discriminate against them for no reason other than their gender.

As in the previous chapter, the analytic tool most relevant here is that which captures the nature of market transactions, namely, the supply and

---

[3] As the well-known British economist John Maynard Keynes put it, "If you owe your bank a hundred pounds, you have a problem. If you owe a million, it has." Quoted in *The Economist,* 13 February 1982, p. 11.

demand framework. However, in view of the two special problems associated with capital markets that we alluded to above, this standard framework has to be modified to capture how the market addresses these two specific problems. In other words, by necessity the models used have to be made more sophisticated in order to handle the stated concerns. This is a point worth noting at the outset.

II. The Gendered Distribution of Wealth

It is notoriously difficult to obtain reliable information on the distribution of assets by gender. The main reason is that assets are often held jointly at the household level, and it is difficult to identify how much is owned by men and how much by women. Any division that attributes ownership of jointly owned assets using a 50–50 split is likely to be arbitrary because social norms and the law may split the assets very differently. It is much easier to acquire information on the asset ownership of single-headed households and on the joint ownership of married households. Despite the difficulty of forming reliable estimates, it is nevertheless important to inquire if there is a gender gap in asset ownership. Carmen Deere and Cheryl Doss (2006), on whose work we now draw, offer a comprehensive review of the literature.[4] As they point out, in terms of measuring poverty, being poor in terms of income is to be poor at a given point in time (possibly because of unemployment). Being poor in terms of assets, on the other hand, is likely to imply poverty over the long haul, because an important part of one's assets is built up from one's income.

In the developed world, the best data on this issue are found in the United States and the United Kingdom. Although the ownership of assets in the U.S. and the U.K. was skewed in favor of men 150 years ago, there has been movement toward an egalitarian distribution. An important reason that women owned little by way of assets in the United Kingdom was that the law gave their husbands ownership of wives' assets upon marriage and, in fact, also of their labor and nonlabor earnings. In retrospect, we can clearly see this for what it was—a patriarchal appropriation of women's wealth through laws designed mostly by men. In British common law, married women could not even write wills. (In contrast, married women in continental European countries that derived their laws from Roman law could maintain ownership and dispose of their assets.) When the first Married Women's Property Act was passed in England in 1870, married women gained control of the wealth they brought into marriage and of their own earnings; a second act that passed 12 years later gave them the same rights

---

[4]Deere, C. D., and C. Doss (2006), "The Gender Asset Gap: What Do We Know and What Does It Matter?," *Feminist Economics* 12, pp. 1–50.

as unmarried women. As we would expect, this act increased women's bargaining power within their households, and their control over even their husbands' incomes increased.[5]

English common law was exported to England's North American colonies: it dictated the property rights of women in English Canada and most of the states in the United States. In the United States, several reforms giving legal rights to married women were undertaken on a state-by-state basis over an extended period of time (starting in 1839 in the state of Mississippi and in 1848, when the state of New York adopted the Married Women's Act). The need for reforms was more urgent in the United States and Canada because many of the measures protecting women that prevailed in England (such as equity courts) were relatively absent in the New World. Despite this, the process of reform was slow. It was only in the early twentieth century that married women could own assets and their own earnings and could dispose of these as they saw fit.[6]

Recent data from the United States suggest that the share of assets held by men and women is more or less egalitarian, though it is sensitive to the assumption that marital wealth is split 50–50 between the two spouses. In single-headed households, there is not much difference between the *nonpension* wealth levels of single males and single females; in fact, depending on the data set used, women may come out slightly ahead.[7] Women, however, tend to have much less by way of pension income. This is because women do not have the types of jobs or high enough earnings to give them access to private pension plans. For example, in the United Kingdom women owned 29% of the pension wealth but 44% of the total wealth in 1996.[8] This disparity in pension wealth has to be cautiously interpreted, however, because married women do benefit from their husbands' pension wealth.

In developing countries, the disparity between the wealth of females and that of males is far greater than in rich countries. Data restrictions, however, are also far more severe than in the developed countries. In a pioneering book titled *A Field of One's Own,* Bina Agarwal (1994) examined the reality of

[5] See Combs, M. B. (2006), "Cui Bono?: The 1870 British Married Women's Property Act, Bargaining Power, and the Distribution of Resources within Marriage," *Feminist Economics* 12, pp. 51–83.

[6] For the United States, see Warbasse, E. B. (1987), *The Changing Legal Rights of Married Women, 1800–1861,* Garland, New York; for Canada, see Backhouse, C. B. (1988), "Married Women's Property Law in Nineteenth-Century Canada," *Law and History Review* 6, pp. 211–257.

[7] Women's share of nonpension wealth is 50% using the 2001 Panel Study of Income Dynamics data; see Schmidt, L., and P. Sevak (2006), "Gender, Marriage, and Asset Accumulation in the United States," *Feminist Economics* 12, pp. 139–166. This share is 53% using the 2000 National Longitudinal Survey of Youth data; see Yamokoski, A., and L. A. Keister (2006), "The Wealth of Single Women: Marital Status and Parenthood in the Asset Accumulation of Young Baby Boomers in the United States," *Feminist Economics* 12, pp. 167–194.

[8] Warren, T. (2006), "Moving beyond the Gender Wealth Gap: On Gender, Class, Ethnicity, and Wealth Inequalities in the United Kingdom," *Feminist Economics* 12, pp. 195–219.

land ownership and its consequences for women in South Asia.[9] Land is the most important productive input in poor countries (because they have largely agricultural economies), so the gender gap in assets manifests mostly as a gap in land ownership. Inheritance laws have traditionally favored males, and even though equalizing laws were passed a few decades ago (such as the Hindu Succession Act of 1956 in India, which gave equal inheritance rights to daughters and sons if the father died without writing a will), women find it difficult to control the land that they have inherited. This is because in patrilocal societies women have to move to their husbands' homes after marriage, and marriage norms (referred to as exogamy) often require that these homes not be in the same villages in which the brides' natal families live. Also, as Agarwal argues, even when governments have undertaken the redistribution of land to the poor, the policies have invariably assumed that giving land to the heads of families (typically males) is as good as distributing it to women. In effect, governments have implicitly assumed that the unitary model of the family is valid. But, as we have seen in Chapter 3, this model is not valid, so land in the hands of husbands does not necessarily ensure the well-being of women and children. For all these reasons, the land distribution in South Asia has been heavily skewed in favor of males.

Recent surveys revealed that women were only 11.0% of the farm owners in Brazil, 22.4% in Mexico, and 27% in Paraguay.[10] In 1998–99, women owned land in 10% of the households in Ghana, whereas men owned land in 16%. Furthermore, the ratio of the mean values of men's land ownership to women's was 6.66.[11] Inheritance plays an important role in the acquisition of land in poor countries, and inheritance customs and laws frequently favor sons over daughters.

More generally, one would expect that much of people's wealth comes from their own savings in the past. The earnings of women tend to be lower than those of men. One reason is that the number of hours they work in the labor market is fewer. Another reason is that their wage rate tends to be lower than that of men because their human capital is lower. Part of this, in turn, is because the labor market experience they have accumulated is less, and part is because, in anticipation of this, the education level they acquire may also be lower. These lower earnings translate into lower accumulated savings (and wealth).

Figure 5.1 shows how the proportion of people older than age 15 years who have accounts in formal financial institutions (such as banks, credit

[9] Agarwal, B. (1994), *A Field of One's Own: Gender and Land Rights in South Asia*, Cambridge University Press, Cambridge, UK.

[10] Deere, C. D., and M. Leon (2003), "The Gender Asset Gap: Land in Latin America," *World Development* 31, pp. 925–947.

[11] Doss, C. (2005), "The Effects of Intrahousehold Property Ownership on Expenditure Patterns," *Journal of African Studies* 15, pp. 149–180.

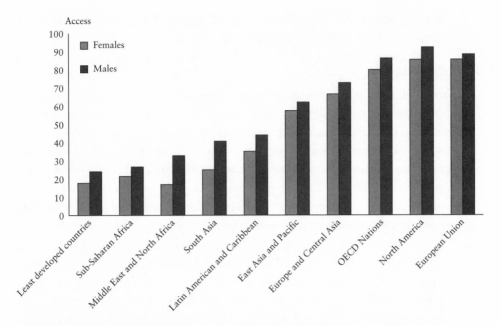

FIGURE 5.1 Access to financial institutions by gender (percent with an account at a formal financial institution), 2011

Source: World Bank 2013, Gender Statistics, Global Findex (Global Financial Inclusion Database) (accessed July 5, 2013).

unions, and cooperatives) differs by gender across the various regions of the world, covering up to 97% of the world's population. In the developing world, the proportions with accounts are quite small even among males, but the gender gap (expressed as a percentage) is very high. This is highly suggestive of the fact that wealth ownership and access to credit are highly gendered in poor countries.

We are now ready to embark on analyses that reveal several important reasons that the ownership of wealth matters and how its gendered distribution works to the detriment of women.

III. Why Asset Ownership Matters: A Marxian Model

One approach to understanding what exploitation is and how it arises is the Marxian one, especially as propounded by John Roemer. Why do we need a *Marxian* model? Because standard models in mainstream economics (called neoclassical models) are good at predicting market outcomes but are not well suited to clearly identifying how the benefits of exchange are distributed between the various parties involved in economic activities. Marxian models are particularly designed to address such distributional concerns. It is also well worth considering a Marxian model to see how various approaches to modeling can be fruitfully employed in gender analysis. We shall see that, although notions such as exploitation are somewhat alien to neoclassical models, the logic of the analysis is not very different.

The scenario described below is a slightly adapted version of Roemer's model.[12] Consider a village comprising 100 people, half of whom are women and half men. All people have available to them an independent means of obtaining their subsistence needs: they can gather food from commonly owned land. Suppose that each person needs 100 pounds of grain per year to subsist. To acquire this much grain, an individual needs to work for 300 days of the year gathering food. The implicit wage rate that someone earns in this "gathering technology" is one-third pound of grain per day. Assume, as does Roemer, that once people have acquired enough grain for subsistence they consume the rest of their days as leisure.

Farming is a more productive way of generating food than gathering; it requires less labor to produce a given amount of food, but it obviously requires access to land, too. Suppose that 1 acre of land requires, in a fixed proportion, 100 days' labor and generates 100 pounds of grain per year. The requisite land-to-labor ratio is 1:100. As Marxists write such a relationship:

1 acre + 100 days' labor → 100 pounds of grain per year.

Suppose that there are 20 acres of land in the village, distributed in an egalitarian manner: each person in the village owns one-fifth acre.

To meet the subsistence needs in this scenario where land is distributed in an egalitarian manner, each person will first use the more productive farming technology with 20 days' labor, thereby producing 20 pounds of grain. (Note that, as required, the land-to-labor ratio is 1:100.) But subsistence requires 80 pounds more. For this they have no option but to use gathering technology: they will devote 240 days of the year to generating the additional 80 pounds needed. In all, each person will need to work for a total of 260 days of the year to earn his or her subsistence requirement. This is what Roemer refers to as the "socially necessary labor time," that is, the time needed to generate the subsistence requirement when the distribution of productive assets is perfectly egalitarian.

Now suppose that the distribution of land is very inegalitarian. In particular, suppose that five men own all of the cultivable land in the village, with each landlord owning 4 acres. How will people allocate their labor across the two technologies? The landlords are in a privileged position by virtue of their land ownership. They can hire others to work their farms. Those without land have the option of working using gathering technology, which defines the opportunity cost of their time. Even if a landlord hires them, they will not be hired for a payment of more than 100 pounds of grain for 300 days' labor. Why can't

<hr />

[12] Roemer, J. (1988), *Free to Lose: An Introduction to Marxist Economic Philosophy*, Harvard University Press, Cambridge, MA, Chap. 2.

the landless people manage to do better than this? To understand why, suppose that a landlord makes a more generous offer to a worker: 100 pounds for only 200 days' labor, say. He will then receive offers from numerous other workers, who are currently using gathering technology, to work for more than 200 days (but no more than 300) for the same amount of grain. Thus the wage rate of a worker will be *bid down* by competition between landless workers and will continue to be bid down until it is equal to the opportunity wage, namely 100 pounds of grain for 300 days' work. The equilibrium wage rate of a landless person, in other words, will be one-third pound of grain for a day's labor—exactly what she can "earn" using gathering technology.

With the given farming technology, the 20 acres will need 2,000 days' labor in total. So the landlords will employ a total of 2,000/300 workers, that is, $6\frac{2}{3}$ workers. (Six people will work full time with the landlords, and the seventh will work part time for 200 days using farming technology and 100 days using gathering technology.) The total amount of grain generated using farming technology will be 2,000 pounds. Of this, the landlords will pay the workers 667 pounds (2,000 days × 1/3 pound per day) and keep the remaining 1,333 pounds. After consuming a total of 500 pounds over the year, these five landlords will accumulate the remaining 833 pounds. They can use this to hire workers from outside the village to clear more farming land from the neighboring forests.

The equilibrium wage rate is one-third pound of grain per day, despite the availability of the superior farming technology. The reason is that, because there is so little cultivable land, the demand for labor is somewhat limited. So landlords can have workers for the asking; to hire them, landlords need pay them no more than the implicit wage they can earn using gathering technology.

The important point is that the availability of farmland could reduce the amount of time workers have to work to meet their subsistence needs, but it does not because the amount of land is not sufficient to take all workers away from the gathering technology. As a result, the landless workers receive no benefit from working on a farm as opposed to gathering: in either case, they end up working the same amount of time. And the owners of land do not have to work at all. This undoubtedly would cause resentment among the workers. It is scenarios like these that constitute the basis of the claim that they are being "exploited." We have not yet seen here a formal definition of what is meant by exploitation and have been relying on a layperson's imprecise sense of the term. Roemer (1988, Chap. 2) formally defines *exploitation* as taking place if a worker has to work more than the socially necessary labor time. Because land ownership highly favors males in this example, a higher proportion of those exploited in this manner will be women. Because in reality the distribution of land ownership is indeed skewed in favor of males, this example is true to life in its implications regarding exploitation by gender.

It may be thought that there is no need for moral outrage at this outcome. After all, just as the landlords can acquire more land for cultivation by saving, so can anyone else, women included. Savings can be used to hire workers to clear forests and convert them into farmland. And saving merely requires one to forgo consumption in the present in order to increase future consumption. However, saving is easier for those who own land in the first place. Those who are close to subsistence have less scope to save than those who can earn returns on currently owned land using labor that is so abundant that its wages are held down to a pittance by backward technologies.

If women had the same options available to them as men but chose not to make use of them, the difference in land ownership would be less of an issue. However, it is doubtful whether women have ever been in this situation. With the advent of settled agriculture, land acquired significance as a productive input.[13] It is not surprising that men would have had the advantage in clearing forests for cultivation by dint of the sheer superiority of their physical strength.

Nor can it be reasonably argued that women have opted to save less than men because in the past they indulged their preference for present consumption over future consumption. There are compelling evolutionary reasons to expect that, if anything, women have a *greater tendency* to save than men.[14] This has arisen from the fact that the number of children women can have is very limited compared to the number that men can potentially have. It has to be true that, *on average,* a man and a woman must have the same number of children because every child has precisely one mother and one father. However, the maximum number of children a man can have is considerably greater than the maximum for women. The reason is that each woman must bear her own children (barring the recent and statistically negligible phenomenon of surrogate motherhood), whereas a man can have children through many women.

This biological asymmetry can be expected to have had profound effects on the way nature has contrived to propagate the genes of women and men into the future. When women reach menopause, the behavior they can engage in that can promote the survival of their genes is one in which they divert resources from present consumption toward their children (future consumption). This sort of behavior increases the survival chances of children. Women with such psychological traits would have been favored by nature in natural selection. The same argument can be made for men, too, for their genes also survive when their children survive. However, there is another ave-

[13]This happened in the so-called Neolithic Revolution, which is believed to have first occurred roughly 10,000 years ago in the Middle East.

[14]This argument is drawn from Eswaran, M., and A. Kotwal (2004), "A Theory of Gender Differences in Parental Altruism," *Canadian Journal of Economics* 37, pp. 918–950.

nue through which men can promote the survival of their genes: by impregnating more women. This additional avenue that is open to men can lead to a diversion of resources toward finding, wooing, and persuading multiple women to be their mates. Not that men necessarily think that they need to do this to perpetuate their genes—no man thinks like this—but nature "does the thinking" for them through natural selection by favoring those men who divert resources in this manner. This diversion is in the pursuit of present pleasure at the expense of future consumption. In other words, men are *less disposed* to save than women.

It follows from the above argument that the disparity between men and women in the ownership of assets cannot be explained by invoking any argument that women are more inclined to sacrifice future consumption for the present. We have to look elsewhere for the reason for this disparity. Some of the contributing factors we have already alluded to. Whatever is responsible for the lower income of women is also going to generate lower levels of wealth in the long run because wealth is saved income. The lower lifetime income of women due to lower labor market participation is certainly one contributing factor. Another is certainly their lower wage rate due to their lower levels of human capital. Yet another factor might be their lower income due to possible discrimination in the labor market. Any gender disparities in labor market earnings between women and men are likely to translate into gender disparities in wealth. In this chapter our focus is on how *credit markets* may have contributed to gender disparities.

IV. The Role of Wealth in Credit Markets

As I mentioned in Chapter 1, credit markets are peculiar in that participation in them usually requires wealth to begin with, even if one intends to be a borrower. If all borrowers invariably returned the money they borrowed, along with the specified interest, creditors would be willing to lend to all people. In reality, a creditor who lends money to a borrower has to worry about whether the borrower will return the money with interest; the borrower might default. Creditors usually ask for some security (collateral) that they can keep in the event that borrowers default on repayment of their loans. If borrowers cannot offer this collateral, they will find it hard to borrow. However, even borrowers who can offer some collateral typically cannot offer enough to cover their entire loans. Therefore, borrowers in effect have *limited liability:* if they default on repayment, creditors can extract only a limited amount of wealth from them. Even if the law specifies that borrowers are fully liable for their debts, it is often costly for creditors to retrieve what is owed them. It may be easier for them to simply write off some of their loans.

It is from the fact of limited liability that prior ownership of wealth derives its importance. There are two avenues through which this comes about. First, limited liability impinges on borrowers' incentives to apply effort. People may not work as hard when they are using someone else's money, which they don't necessarily have to return. I refer to this as the *incentive problem.* Second, people differ in their likelihood of defaulting on loans. Borrowers may have information about their chances of default, but this information may not be available to creditors. In other words, in a world in which some people have a higher likelihood of defaulting than others, creditors may not be able to separate borrowers who are "good risks" from those who are "bad risks." I refer to this as the problem of *asymmetric information,* because borrowers and lenders do not share the same information. We shall consider these in turn.

The Incentive Problem

To see how this phenomenon operates, suppose that there is a project that offers an entrepreneur a good opportunity to generate income.[15] Suppose that it requires a fixed investment, say K dollars, and that this investment cannot be retrieved after it has been undertaken (that is, K is a sunk cost). If this initial investment is undertaken and the entrepreneur works hard, the project will generate revenues that will more than justify the cost and effort. Let the required effort be denoted by E. Let the potential revenues that can be generated by the enterprise be denoted by R dollars. Suppose that a person with an amount of wealth W dollars hopes to become an entrepreneur. We assume that his wealth is either inadequate to finance the investment or is in a form that is illiquid, that is, is not in the form of the ready cash that is needed for the investment. For example, his wealth may be in the form of land or his house, which he does not wish to sell. So he approaches a creditor (a bank, say) for a loan for the amount of K dollars. The bank charges a fixed interest rate, say r. To assure the bank that he intends to return the money with interest, he offers as collateral his wealth of W dollars. Will the bank lend the potential entrepreneur the money?

To answer this question we need to examine the incentive of the potential borrower. He may well use the borrowed money for the purpose intended. But it is also possible that he may not: he may opt to embezzle this amount and consume it. To examine which option he will choose in order to maximize his well-being, we need to know on what his well-being depends. Suppose that his utility, U, is given by the difference between his consumption (denoted by c) and his effort level (denoted by e), that is, $U = c - e$. This makes sense because consumption makes one better off, whereas effort requires one to forgo leisure and so is deemed to reduce well-being. If the individual does not borrow (and so does not undertake the project), suppose that both c and e are zero, so his utility is zero.

---

[15] For a formal treatment of this problem, see Ghosh, P., D. Mookherjee, and D. Ray (2001), "Credit Rationing in Developing Countries: An Overview of the Theory," in *Readings in the Theory of Economic Development,* ed. D. Mookherjee and D. Ray, Blackwell, Oxford, UK.

If the individual borrows money, uses the credit for the intended purpose, and works hard, he will receive a revenue of R dollars. But he has to pay back the creditor the amount $K + rK$ dollars for the principal plus interest, that is, he returns $(1 + r)K$. Because he returns to the creditor what is his due, the borrower gets to retain his collateral of W dollars. If he incurs no other cost (apart from his effort), his endeavor will generate a net income of $R - (1 + r)K$ dollars, which he will consume. However, to make this possible, he has to incur the cost of E units of effort. Thus, as a genuine entrepreneur, the borrower will achieve a utility of $R - (1 + r)K - E$. We shall assume that this is positive, so undertaking the project is preferred to not undertaking it.

Now suppose that the borrower chooses instead to embezzle the borrowed money. Say he consumes it instead of investing it. The cost to him of defaulting on his loan is that he loses his collateral of W dollars that he offered to the creditor. (Obviously the borrower will choose this option only if he has not offered too much by way of collateral.) After taking into account his lost collateral, the borrower's income in this option is $K - W$ dollars. This is his effective consumption. Furthermore, by choosing this option the borrower has saved himself the trouble of applying any effort. So his utility in this instance is given by $K - W$.

Whether the borrower chooses to be an entrepreneur or an embezzler depends on which route will generate a higher level of well-being for him. He will become an entrepreneur and use the borrowed funds appropriately only if $R - (1 + r)K - E \geq K - W$. Rearranging this, we see that borrowers who will use the borrowed funds for the intended purpose are those who have offered an amount of collateral that is sufficiently large, in particular, those with wealth levels satisfying $W \geq (2 + r)K + E - R$. Suppose, for example, that $R = \$240$, $K = \$100$, $E = 50$, and $r = 0.1$ (that is, 10%). In that case, only those who have offered an amount of wealth at least as large as $2.1 \times 100 + 50 - 240 = \$20$ will actually become entrepreneurs. Those with lower levels of collateral will default on their loans.

Creditors, of course, can put themselves in the shoes of the borrowers and figure out their intentions. As a result, they will not make credit available to people with insufficient wealth. In a world in which default is a possibility, the amount of collateral a borrower can offer is a measure of what he has at stake in the success of the enterprise, because he will lose this amount in the event of default.

One real-world feature that would temper the incentive to default is the possibility that the person may need to borrow again in the future. By defaulting now, the borrower will be burning bridges, and this realization will dilute his incentive to default. Still, it is unlikely that the possible need for more loans in the future will completely do away with the need for collateral. The point here is that, in the absence of sufficient collateral, it is generally difficult for a person to credibly persuade a creditor of his good intentions. From this comes the irony that only those with wealth can borrow money; only the rich can use borrowed money to make more money.

To the extent that women own less wealth than men, their access to credit markets will be correspondingly restricted.

The Asymmetric Information Problem

Now consider a scenario in which the application of effort is not relevant to making a success of a project. People may borrow money to invest in projects, but different projects may have different chances of success. The borrowers may know the probability of success of their projects, but the lenders may not. The lenders may know only that different projects have different probabilities of success, and they may even know these probabilities. But they may not know *which* projects borrowers will undertake.

Why does the probability of success matter to a creditor? If borrowers were under full liability, it would not: whether a project were a success or a failure, the borrower would have to pay his dues to the lender. But when borrowers have limited liability, the borrower can default on the repayment of his loan if the project fails. So creditors have to concern themselves with the chances of success of the projects they are funding.

To be concrete, suppose that there are two projects, each requiring the same investment of $100 that has to be entirely borrowed. One project is a relatively safe one (S), and the other is risky (R). So that we can concentrate on the effects of limited liability, suppose further that both borrowers and lenders are risk neutral; that is, the expected value of the revenues they receive is all that matters to them.[16] Suppose finally that the average revenues the two projects generate are the same:

> S generates revenues of $90 with a probability of 1/2 and $150 with a probability of 1/2.
>
> R generates revenues of $60 with a probability of 2/3 and $240 with a probability of 1/3.

Project S has equal chances of failing (that is, generating less revenue than the cost) and of succeeding, but R has a 67% chance of failing and a 33% chance of succeeding. The expected revenue of S is 1/2 × $90 + 1/2 × $150 = $120. Because the initial investment is $100, on average S will give a 20% return on an investment of $100. On the other hand, the expected revenue of R is 2/3 × $60 + 1/3 × $240 = $120. On average, R will also give a 20% return on an investment of $100. So if borrowers were fully liable for their loans and if all they wanted was to maximize the expected returns on their investments (because they are risk neutral), they would be indifferent between projects S and R.

---

[16] In the language introduced in Chapter 2, they are assumed to be risk neutral.

Suppose that potential entrepreneurs approach one of many creditors to borrow $100 for their projects. Let us say that half of them have S available to them, and the other half have R. Assume, for the moment, that they have no collateral to offer. Also assume that a creditor can obtain a return of 10% on his funds if he invests them in projects that have no possibility of failing. That is, the opportunity cost of funds to the creditor is 10%. So if he lends to a person who will never default, competition between creditors will force the creditor to require a payment that will just about cover his opportunity cost. He will specify in the contract that the borrower should return the money with an interest of 10%, that is, the borrower should pay back a total of $100 + $10 = $110. If all borrowers are under full liability, the lender will not care whether his borrowers invest in S or in R; whether the project succeeds or fails, he is assured of getting back the $110 that each borrower owes him.

Now suppose that a lender extends credit to a lot of people and that he *knows* which project each borrower wants to invest in. Furthermore, suppose that the borrowers are under limited liability (and, recall, with no collateral to offer). If a project fails, the creditor can collect everything generated, whereas if the project succeeds he can collect enough to earn $110 on average. If he knows that a borrower will invest in S, the risk-neutral creditor will charge an interest rate of 30%. That is, when the project succeeds he will collect $130 and when it fails he will collect the entire $90 generated. Why? Because then, on average, the creditor will retrieve $1/2 \times $90 + 1/2 \times $130 = $45 + $65 = 110, which will cover the opportunity cost of his funds. If, on the other hand, he knows that a borrower will invest in R, he will charge an interest rate of 110%. That is, when the project succeeds he will collect $210 and when it fails he will collect the entire $60 generated. Then, on average, the creditor will recover $2/3 \times $60 + 1/3 \times $210 = $40 + $70 = 110, which will cover the opportunity cost of his funds. Notice that, because people investing in R will default a lot more frequently and will return less when they do, the creditor will want to charge them a much higher interest rate than those investing in S.

Now let us introduce asymmetric information. Suppose that the creditor does not know which project a borrower will invest in. He would like to charge 30% interest to someone investing in the relatively safe project and 110% to someone investing in the risky project. But he can do this only if he knows which type of project the borrower will choose. Because he cannot distinguish between borrowers, he will have to charge them all the same interest rate. Let us say that he believes (correctly) that half the borrowers will invest in each type of project. Suppose that he decides to charge everybody the average of the interest rates, that is, $(30\% + 110\%)/2 = 70\%$. This will lead to an immediate difficulty. The investors in the safe project will be required to pay $90 if the project fails and $170 if it succeeds. But the project will not yield $170 even when it succeeds. This means that the borrowers who intended to invest in the relatively safe project will realize that it is not feasible. So they will drop out of the credit market.

But what about borrowers who intended to invest in the risky project? They certainly can afford to pay $170 if the project succeeds. So they will remain in the credit market. Because these are the *only* types of borrowers who remain in the credit market, the creditor will realize that the 70% interest rate he was charging is too low, because $2/3 \times \$60 + 1/3 \times \$170 = \$96.67$, which is less than $110. So he will raise the interest rate to 110% in view of the fact that *all* borrowers will be investing in the risky project.

What, then, is the upshot of asymmetric information when borrowers face limited liability? Borrowers who are good risks (those with a low probability of default) will drop out of the market, whereas those who borrow will be the bad risks (those with a high probability of default). That is, the credit market perversely selects the bad risks while driving the good risks out of the market. This phenomenon is referred to as *adverse selection*. George Akerlof (1970) first analyzed the consequences of adverse selection in a classic paper.[17] Joseph Stiglitz and Andrew Weiss (1981) undertook the pioneering application of adverse selection to the case of credit markets.[18]

All this leads to this question: why does adverse selection matter to borrowers? It matters because people who wish to undertake relatively safe projects may not be able to borrow money from credit markets. The presence of people who are bad risks drives up the interest rate. So safe borrowers either end up paying a higher interest rate than is warranted by their risk or cannot afford to pay such a high interest charge. In either case, the good risks are put at a disadvantage.

The discussion of asymmetric information has thus far assumed that the borrowers had no collateral to offer. Here it is natural to ask whether the ability to offer collateral would make a difference. By offering some of his own wealth as security, a potential borrower may be able to credibly persuade the lender that he intends to invest the loan in a safe project. Otherwise, why would he risk his own money? Borrowers with risky projects, on the other hand, will be less willing to offer collateral even if they have wealth. When borrowers can offer collateral, creditors will offer a menu of contracts that the borrowers can choose from.[19] An essential feature of the menu is that contracts requiring more collateral will specify lower interest rates, because these will be chosen by borrowers with safe projects in mind. This will be a means by which creditors can separate good risks from bad risks. The various contracts available

[17] Akerlof, G. A. (1970), "The Market for 'Lemons': Qualitative Uncertainty and the Market Mechanism," *Quarterly Journal of Economics* 84, pp. 488–500.

[18] Stiglitz, J., and A. Weiss (1981), "Credit Rationing in Markets with Imperfect Information," *American Economic Review* 71, pp. 393–410.

[19] See Bester, H. (1987), "The Role of Collateral in Credit Markets with Imperfect Information," *European Economic Review* 31, pp. 887–899.

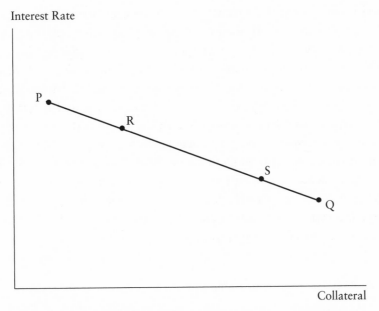

FIGURE 5.2 The relationship between interest rates and collateral

may be thought of as falling on a *downward-sloping* line like PQ in Figure 5.2. The contract R will be taken up by a borrower who is willing to offer a lower amount of collateral than a borrower who takes up contract S. Consequently, the interest rate in contract R is higher than that in contract S.

The device of offering borrowers a menu of contracts that they can choose from, however, is limited in its ability to separate risk types. It presumes that all potential borrowers have collateral available. In reality, some people with relatively safe projects may not have the collateral needed to communicate this information to creditors. They will end up paying a higher interest rate than is warranted by the risk of their projects. There is no getting away from the need for collateral.

Is there reason to believe that women may be particularly affected by adverse selection in credit markets? Yes. The problem of adverse selection arises because borrowers cannot persuade creditors of the worthiness and the relative safety of their projects. To the extent that women have had less managerial experience than men and less opportunity to deal with financial matters outside their homes due to family responsibilities, they will have greater difficulty than men in persuading creditors of the soundness of their potential enterprises. As in the case of the incentive problem, more credit will be forthcoming if borrowers can offer collateral. To the extent that women have less collateral to offer than men, they are more disadvantaged by adverse selection problems.

What evidence is there that moral hazard and adverse selection are important in credit markets? Carefully acquired statistical evidence on these theories is relatively scarce because the two effects are difficult to separate in the data. For example, people may be willing to borrow at very high interest rates because they are undertaking high-risk projects and this is private information (adverse selection). But they may also be willing to do so because they have no intention of returning the money by working hard to make a success of the project (the incentive problem). Dean Karlan and Jonathan Zinman (2009) provided reliable evidence on these theories through a carefully designed experiment in lending conducted in South Africa.[20] They found that the incentive problem can explain up to about 20% of the default rate on loans. The evidence on adverse selection was somewhat weaker but nevertheless present. Much more research to acquire empirical evidence needs to be undertaken; as the authors of the above study rightly point out, the theory in this area is far ahead of the empirical work.

V. Implications for Entrepreneurship

The manner in which credit markets work has important implications for people's choice of occupations. Suppose that there are only two occupations available: entrepreneur or worker. Only those with access to credit can become entrepreneurs; the rest have no option but to become workers in the firms of these entrepreneurs. The demand for labor will come from those who become entrepreneurs. The greater the number of such entrepreneurs, the greater will be the labor demand. The supply of labor will come from people who become workers.

How do workers fare compared to entrepreneurs? Suppose that we arrange all the people in society in the order of increasing wealth and then ask what proportion of the people in each wealth class comprises entrepreneurs as opposed to workers. In other words what proportion of people are entrepreneurs in the poorest 5% of the population, in the next-poorest 5%, and so on until we come to the richest 5%? Using data from a nationally representative sample from the United States, Vincenzo Quadrini (1999) (cited earlier) shows that, as we move into wealthier and wealthier classes, the proportion of entrepreneurs in these classes increases. The data show that in the latter half of the 1980s in the United States, entrepreneurs constituted around 75% of the wealthiest 5% of the population. Similarly, when the population is arranged in the order of increasing income (instead of wealth), as one moves into higher and higher income classes the proportion of entrepreneurs increases. In other words, on average, entrepreneurs earn more than workers. Are entrepreneurs more likely than workers to move into higher income and wealth classes than workers? The study finds that the answer to this question is yes.

[20] Karlan, D., and J. Zinman (2009), "Observing Unobservables: Identifying Information Asymmetries with a Consumer Credit Field Experiment," *Econometrica* 77, pp. 1993–2008.

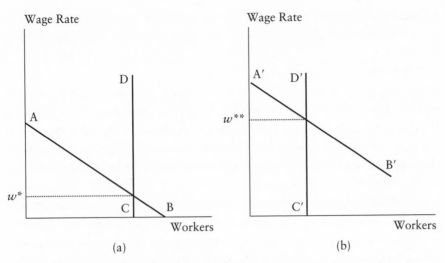

FIGURE 5.3 The relationship between distribution of wealth and wage rate

Let us see how the distribution of wealth matters. Suppose that the distribution of wealth is such that it is concentrated in the hands of very few people. This implies that, because only these people have access to the capital needed to set up enterprises, the demand for labor will be relatively low. This demand is shown by the line AB in Figure 5.3a. The line is downward sloping because higher wage rates would induce entrepreneurs to curtail their demand for labor. Suppose that each worker supplies one unit of labor (say, 8 hours a day), irrespective of the wage rate. The supply of labor is shown in the figure as line CD. The line is vertical because we have assumed that each worker supplies 1 unit of labor regardless of the wage rate. When there are many workers, the supply will be relatively abundant. The equilibrium wage rate, at which the demand for labor is equal to the supply, is shown in the figure as w^*. Above this wage rate, supply exceeds demand, and some workers will not find employment. These unemployed workers will offer to work for less than the going wage rate. This process will continue until the wage rate falls to w^*. For wage rates below w^*, the demand for labor exceeds the supply. Some entrepreneurs cannot find enough workers. These entrepreneurs will offer higher wages to workers to win them away from other entrepreneurs. The process will continue until the wage rate increases to w^*.

Now suppose that the distribution of wealth is relatively egalitarian. This will enable a lot of people to become entrepreneurs; relatively few will wish to be workers. In other words, the demand for labor will be high, but the supply of labor will be low. This situation is depicted in Figure 5.3b, in which A'B' is the demand for labor and C'D' is the supply. Notice that A'B' is shifted up relative to AB in panel a and C'D' is shifted to the left relative to CD. The equilibrium wage rate, w^{**}, is now higher than it was before. A more egalitarian distribution of wealth, by enabling more people to become entrepreneurs, has the obvious effect of enabling more people to satisfy their entrepreneurial aspirations. Less obviously, by increasing the equilibrium wage rate, it also makes better off the people who still have no option but to become workers.

To the extent that women's access to credit is undermined by lack of wealth, they are more likely to become workers (we shall discuss the evidence for this in subsequent sections). Furthermore, this very impediment to their entrepreneurial aspirations also swells the ranks of workers. The increase in the supply of workers holds down their wages—and, by lowering the price of labor, provides an additional benefit to those who can become entrepreneurs.

The distribution of wealth at a given point in time also has long-term consequences that may last over generations.[21] Typically, parents leave bequests for their children, and the amounts of the bequests they leave depend, naturally enough, on the amounts of wealth they have. Rich parents, by becoming entrepreneurs, can increase their wealth and so can leave even larger bequests than they otherwise could have for their children. This enables the children to opt for entrepreneurial activities. People who become workers because of their lack of wealth, and therefore their access to credit, cannot increase their wealth to the same extent as entrepreneurs. Consequently, workers can bequeath only small amounts of wealth to their children. In the next generation, these children are thwarted from becoming entrepreneurs. Because of the manner in which capital markets work—that is, because only those with wealth can borrow—the effects of wealth disparities across people can last for generations.

What evidence is there that people with wealth are more likely to become entrepreneurs? Earlier in the chapter we briefly alluded to some evidence for this. If credit markets did not impose the requirement that people offer collateral in order to borrow, one would find no relationship between ownership of wealth and the decision to become an entrepreneur. Using data on around 1,500 white American males between the ages of 24 and 34 years, one study examined whether entrepreneurs were handicapped by a borrowing constraint.[22] These men were wage workers in 1976, and by 1978 they either remained wage workers or switched to self-employment. The study found that wealthier individuals were more likely to have become entrepreneurs by 1978. In fact, entrepreneurs were constrained to invest no more than one and a half times the value of their own assets when starting new enterprises. Insufficient wealth constrained potential entrepreneurs in two ways. First, it prevented people from becoming entrepreneurs if they could not generate the

---

[21] The dynamic consequences of wealth distribution for occupations and economic development are examined in Banerjee, A. V., and A. F. Newman (1993), "Occupational Choice and the Process of Development," *Journal of Political Economy* 101, pp. 274–298.

[22] Evans, D. S., and B. Jovanovic (1989), "An Estimated Model of Entrepreneurial Choice under Liquidity Constraints," *Journal of Political Economy* 97, pp. 808–827.

minimal amount of funds needed. Second, even among those who could start new firms, it prevented them from doing so at a scale that would have been optimal.

Using U.S. federal tax returns, another interesting study was conducted to look at people who received inheritances between 1981 and 1985.[23] The goal was to investigate whether receiving inheritances affected the chances that the recipients would become entrepreneurs. If ownership of wealth did not matter, receiving inheritances would not have affected the probability that the recipients would become entrepreneurs during the period: the aspiring entrepreneurs could have borrowed the requisite capital. The findings suggest, to the contrary, that inheritances increased the chances that recipients would make a switch from being wage earners to entrepreneurs. Furthermore, the amount of capital invested in the enterprises that were started was also higher when inheritances were received.

VI. How Credit Markets Put Women Entrepreneurs at a Disadvantage

To the extent that the wealth owned by women is on average less than that owned by men, women are handicapped in their attempts to become entrepreneurs. What is the evidence on the extent of this handicap? Leora Klapper and Simon Parker (2011) have surveyed the evidence from many countries.[24] They find that the extent of the gender gap in the numbers of female and male entrepreneurs differs between rich and poor countries. There is certainly a gap even in the rich countries; it is greater in poor countries. This raises the question of whether this gender gap is due to women's preferences as to how they *choose* to spend their time (in housework, wage work, or work as self-employed entrepreneurs) or whether it is due to market and other constraints that *prevent* women from becoming entrepreneurs.

To understand these issues, consider the findings of Ingrid Verheul and Roy Thurik (2001), who examined data from a rich country (Holland) on about 2,000 entrepreneurs who started new enterprises in 1994.[25] In this sample, about 25% of the entrepreneurs were women. The authors looked for gender differences in the sizes of the firms started and in the composition of the start-up capital, that is, the percentage of capital coming from the entrepreneurs' own wealth and that coming from bank loans. They found that enterprises started by women, on average, had less start-up capital than those started by men.

[23] Holtz-Eakin, D., D. Joulfaian, and H. S. Rosen (1994), "Entrepreneurial Decisions and Liquidity Constraints," *RAND Journal of Economics* 25, Summer, pp. 334–347.

[24] Klapper, L. F., and S. C. Parker (2011), "Gender and the Business Environment for New Firm Creation," *World Bank Research Observer* 26, pp. 237–257.

[25] Verheul, I., and R. Thurik (2001), "Start-Up Capital: Does Gender Matter?," *Small Business Economics* 16, pp. 329–345.

Women also tend to work part time in their enterprises. As a result, their firms are smaller in size. Why? One reason is that an entrepreneur has to supervise the workers employed in her firm. A larger firm will naturally require more time devoted to supervision—time that women may not have because of responsibilities at home. This means that enterprises headed by women may have to forgo the advantages that arise from operating firms on a large scale. Often these advantages arise from the use of machinery that comes in fixed sizes.

To clarify the argument, suppose that a good can be produced using either of two technologies. One technology uses only labor, and it costs, on average, $2 to produce 1 unit of output. The other technology requires no labor other than the entrepreneur's presence. It requires a machine that costs $100,000 but that (for simplicity) is assumed to wear out in 1 year. The second technology may prove very economical if the enterprise produces a large number of units. This is because the cost of the machine is spread over more units of output. The average cost *per unit* of output when producing 100,000 units during the year with the machine is $1 per piece. If, however, the entrepreneur produces only 25,000 units per year, the average cost of output jumps to $4 per piece. A woman who splits her time between household responsibilities and entrepreneurship may find it infeasible to produce the larger quantity because her time is very scarce. Consequently, she will have to forgo the advantages of large-scale production based on the machine. She will opt to do without the machine and produce using the technology that requires only labor. Naturally this will lower the profitability of women's enterprises relative to men's, because men are typically not under similar time constraints.

As illustrated by the simple example given above, in much of modern-day production there are advantages that accrue to size. Even if wealth were the *only* factor impinging on firm size (which is not so), fewer women will become entrepreneurs, and, among those who do, the sizes of their firms will be on average smaller than those of firms owned by men. Consequently, the smaller average sizes of women's firms also means that their incomes are lower than those of their male counterparts. This is a well-established fact in the rich countries.[26] A study examining entrepreneurial performance in 13 Latin American countries found that firms owned by females under-perform relative to those owned by males in terms of many measures, such as sales, profitability, and growth.[27]

It must be noted, however, that enterprises owned by women, even if smaller than those of men, have compensating advantages: they afford women greater

---

[26] See Klapper and Parker (2011), cited earlier.

[27] Sabarwal, S., and K. Terrell (2009), "Access to Credit and Performance of Female Entrepreneurs in Latin America (Summary)," *Frontiers of Entrepreneurship Research* 29:18, Article 6. Available at http://digitalknowledge.babson.edu/fer/vol29/iss18/6.

flexibility in the management of their time. That is, women can better balance their time between market work and family. A study of people who graduated with MBA degrees from a top-tier business school in the United States documents this.[28] The study used a 1998 survey of graduates of this business school who had completed their degrees in the previous 20 years and had at least 4 years' work experience. The survey thus ensured that the educational qualifications, ages, and demographic characteristics of the male and female entrepreneurs in the sample were the same. The study restricted its attention to those from the sample who had become entrepreneurs.

Among other things, the survey asked respondents about their career motivations and preferences regarding their most recent employment. The study found that female entrepreneurs preferred careers that gave them the flexibility to balance family and career. In contrast, the male entrepreneurs were more motivated by the need for career advancement and wealth creation. This gender difference in goals was greater between married women with dependents and married men with dependents than between single or married women without dependents and their male counterparts. In other words, the presence of children at home tended to bring out sharper differences between the career goals of women and men.

This difference between the motivations of female and male entrepreneurs may perhaps be understood in evolutionary terms. In our evolutionary past, the status of a man in a tribe conferred privileged access to women, and such men, therefore, left behind more children.[29] Because status has invariably been associated with greater wealth, men with wealth have had an evolutionary advantage relative to men without. The fertility of women, on the other hand, is more or less independent of status. As a result, men seek social advancement, status, and wealth more than women. This evolutionary relic may explain the differences in preferences expressed by women and men entrepreneurs.

A different explanation is also possible. Entrepreneurial activity is inherently risky because its returns are uncertain. So people's attitudes toward risk matter in determining who will choose to become entrepreneurs. It is entirely conceivable that gender differences in attitudes toward risk have a large cultural component. In fact, in Chapter 2 we discussed an experimental study by Allison Booth and Patrick Nolen (2012) that showed how socialization shaped attitudes toward risk in women.

The reasons offered above explain why Klapper and Parker (2011) found in their review of the evidence that the gender gap in the number of entre-

[28] DeMartino, R., and R. Barbato (2003), "Differences between Women and Men MBA Entrepreneurs: Exploring Family Flexibility and Wealth Creation as Career Motivators," *Journal of Business Venturing* 18, pp. 815–832.

[29] See, for example, Buss, D. M. (1999), *Evolutionary Psychology: The New Science of Mind,* Allyn and Bacon, Boston, Chap. 12.

preneurs in the developed countries is driven partly by women's choices. But the situation is quite different in developing countries, for reasons that will become clear in what follows. Nevertheless, is the documented fact that women all over the world are less likely than men to become entrepreneurs and are seen to invest less capital in their enterprises at least partly due to discrimination by lending institutions? We address this important question in the next section.

VII. Is There Gender Discrimination in Credit Markets?

It is time now to discuss whether credit markets treat women differently simply because they are women. Would a man with precisely the same relevant economic characteristics as a woman receive different treatment when seeking credit?

In examining credit arrangements, we need to consider not only whether a person has access to credit but also the terms at which the credit is available (if at all). By *terms* I mean the interest that has to be paid and the collateral demanded by the creditor. An entrepreneur may have access to credit but at terms that are so disadvantageous to her that it is as good as having no access at all. If so, to claim that she has access to credit would be meaningless. Klapper and Parker (2011) (cited earlier) found that women across the world do receive less funds than men from external sources, but it is *not* due to explicit discrimination. What could the reasons be?

To understand these, we take a detailed look at a study by Susan Coleman (2000), who, using American data from 1993, investigated the effect of gender on access to credit and the terms of credit for small businesses.[30] She found that many characteristics other than gender impinge on the access to credit and the terms available to an entrepreneur. For instance, the age of the firm matters, because newer firms are more in need of credit than older, more established ones. Larger firms, naturally, need more credit to facilitate their larger sales. Also, as explained below, creditors may see a lower risk in lending to large firms as opposed to small ones.

If production exhibits economies of scale, large firms will have a competitive advantage, implying that smaller firms will face a greater chance of going bankrupt. A credit institution will then have greater concerns about its money being returned by a small firm than by a large one. The credit institution will consider small firms more risky than larger firms. Thus the riskiness of different firms as perceived by creditors may be different. Also, the nature of the production undertaken by the firm may matter to the creditor. A firm that uses a loan to buy durables such as machinery may be perceived as less

---

[30] Coleman, S. (2000), "Access to Capital and Terms of Credit: A Comparison of Men- and Women-Owned Small Businesses," *Journal of Small Business* 38, pp. 37–52.

risky than a firm that uses it to buy nondurable inputs. Why? Because if the former type of firm goes bankrupt, the creditor can confiscate the machinery that was purchased with the loan, sell it, and then retrieve part or all of the money owed. But the creditor cannot do the same with a firm that has spent its loan on goods that are not durable, so firms like these will be perceived as riskier.

As we have already seen, if creditors are exposed to the possibility that the money they loan will not be returned, they have to be compensated for this risk if they are to be willing to lend. In our earlier discussion we saw that creditors will seek compensation through higher interest rates. Riskier firms are charged commensurately higher interest rates on loans.

The access to credit and the terms of credit will vary across different firms because of the several factors we have enumerated above, namely, age of firm, size of firm, nature of production activity, riskiness of firm, and so on. One of the potential factors that may impinge on access to credit and the terms could be the *gender* of the firm's owner. Before anything can be attributed to gender, however, the effects of other relevant factors have to be accounted for. Otherwise, what is due to some other cause may be mistakenly attributed to gender.

To consider a concrete example, suppose that female entrepreneurs tend to own smaller firms than male entrepreneurs (which is true) and that smaller firms are deemed riskier by credit institutions (which may be true). If so, as we have seen, smaller firms will be charged higher interest rates. Now suppose that, while analyzing the data, a researcher forgets to account for the effect of firm size on the interest rate. Then it will seem that the data are indicating that some entrepreneurs are being charged higher interest rates simply because they are women and that there is discrimination by gender in the terms of credit. This, however, will be an unwarranted conclusion, because women may be paying higher interest rates not because of their gender but simply because they tend to own smaller (and riskier) firms. In other words, it may be the case that men with small firms are also paying higher interest rates. But because the majority of male entrepreneurs own larger firms, it may seem that on average the credit institutions are offering them favorable treatment because of their sex. This brings home the point that, in order to ascertain the effects of gender, it is imperative that the effects of other relevant factors also be accounted for.

What were the findings of Susan Coleman? In the data, which included nearly five times as many men's firms as women's, the latter are indeed seen to be smaller on average than the former. The firms owned by women are also more likely to be sole proprietorships (that is, owned by one person only). Furthermore, women's firms are more likely to be in the service sector. In the three years prior to 1993, women were less likely than men to have applied for loans, and of those who did apply, they were less likely than men to be granted loans. Of those who were granted loans, women paid significantly higher interest rates than men.

As we have seen, the gender differences between the outcomes with regard to credit may be due to several factors that need to be separately accounted for. When Coleman accounts for these, she finds that older firms borrowed less, larger firms (as measured by the sales) borrowed more, and credit institutions did not discriminate by gender in access to credit. However, women paid significantly higher interest rates on their loans. Firms in the service sector were required to provide more collateral than firms elsewhere in the economy, and female-owned service-sector firms were required to offer more collateral than male-owned service-sector firms.

How do we make sense of these findings? In particular, why was access to credit independent of gender even though the interest rate charged was higher for women than for men? One reason might have been that, although women and men were required to offer the same collateral when their firms were of the same size, women were less able to provide the collateral because they had less wealth than men. As a consequence, even in the case of firms of the same size, credit institutions might have seen women's firms as riskier than men's. And charging a higher interest rate, as we have seen, compensates for higher risk.

How could one make sense of the finding that, in the service sector, the collateral required of women is higher than that required of men? This may be explained by the difference in the nature of the firms that women and men tend to own. For example, it is very likely that men own a higher proportion of automotive service firms than women. On the other hand, it is likely that women own a higher proportion of day spas than men. Automotive service firms require a great deal of equipment relative to day spas. When money is borrowed from a bank by an automotive firm—whether owned by a woman or a man—most of it will be tied up in the purchase of machinery. If the firm goes bankrupt, the bank can claim the machinery and sell it to recover the money loaned. In other words, such a firm can use the equipment it purchases with the loan as collateral. So the bank will deem the loan relatively safe. When money is borrowed from a bank by another type of service-sector firm, such as a day spa—whether owned by a woman or a man—the entrepreneur will use a smaller proportion of the loan for equipment and other durable assets that can be used as collateral. If the firm goes bankrupt, the bank may not be able to recover much of its money. So the bank will deem the loan less safe than one given to an automotive service firm.

The upshot of the above argument is that more collateral will be demanded for a loan given to a day spa than for a loan given to an automotive service firm. If both types of firms are lumped together as "service-sector firms" without distinguishing between them in the analysis, the data will reveal that female entrepreneurs in the service sector are being asked to provide more collateral than male entrepreneurs in the service sector. The reality will be that one type of firm can use what it has purchased with the loan as collateral, but the other cannot. Because proportionately more women own the latter kinds of firms, it will *appear as if* they are being required to put up more collateral than men.

In the final analysis, what does the evidence suggest regarding discrimination against women by credit markets? In terms of the precise way that economists define discrimination, there does not seem to be persuasive evidence suggesting its presence. Women do not appear to be discriminated against simply because of their gender. This is also what one would expect from the point of view of economic theory: if there is discrimination, there are opportunities for credit institutions to profit from lending to women that these institutions are forgoing. Echoing Becker's argument regarding discrimination in the labor market, one could argue that banks that do not discriminate could exploit this opportunity and earn higher profits than banks that do. In a competitive credit market, this would drive out banks that irrationally discriminate against women simply because of their sex. Besides, it is hard to see why a creditor would explicitly discriminate against women on noneconomic grounds; unlike in labor markets, creditors do not interact daily or frequently with borrowers. So even if a creditor were prejudiced against women for some reason, it is hard to see why he would not lend to them when it is profitable to do so.

I should emphasize that even if there is no persuasive evidence pointing to explicit discrimination by gender in credit markets, it does not mean that the outcomes are the same for women and men. The outcomes are most definitely *not* identical. To the extent that women own less wealth than men and so can offer less collateral to creditors, credit markets are less open to women. To the extent that women have greater difficulty communicating private information about their abilities to creditors than do men, credit markets cannot serve women as well as they do men. To the extent that women own smaller and riskier firms than men, possibly because of their greater family responsibilities, they have to pay higher interest rates. All these factors work to the relative detriment of women. Furthermore, they contribute to lowering the mobility of women across income classes by making it more difficult for them to become entrepreneurs.

The difficulties confronting women in credit markets are much greater in developing countries than in the rich countries. As Bina Agarwal (1994) (cited earlier) has persuasively argued, little of the most important asset in poor countries (namely, land) is in the names of women. Credit institutions do not typically lend to them because they have little land to offer as collateral. Furthermore, patriarchal restrictions make it very difficult for women to control and manage the few assets that they do have title to. Restrictions on their mobility make it difficult for women to work in the labor market and to acquire experience that can be used to persuade institutions to lend to them. The average education level of women is usually much lower than that of men, and this works to reduce the chances that women will succeed as entrepreneurs. For all these reasons, the gender gap in entrepreneurship is wider in poor countries than in the rich.

Therefore, we see that women may not be discriminated against in the credit market, but they are certainly *disadvantaged* relative to men in their participation in this market. And this disadvantage stems largely, but not entirely, from the gendered distribution of wealth and its myriad consequences. Patriarchal control over women's lives also greatly contributes to this disadvantage, especially in the developing world.

Given the difficulty that women face in credit markets, what can be done to alleviate the situation? Because the credit market is so important, we shall discuss this at length in this book's final chapter, which deals with how women can be empowered. But here I briefly mention one novel solution that has been replicated the world over: improving women's access to capital through what is termed "microcredit." In an innovation started by Muhammad Yunus and the Grameen Bank in Bangladesh, a microcredit scheme uses the close bonds of people with their neighbors in poor countries as collateral instead of financial collateral.[31] Specifically, the institution lends to an individual from a group (typically comprising only women) on the condition that funds will be made available to others in the same group only if the first loan recipient returns the money with interest. Because people do not want to be responsible for their close friends' being denied credit, they do not default on the loans—despite the fact that they offer very little financial collateral to receive the loans. Women use these funds to undertake small entrepreneurial activities that improve their households' welfare. This and other innovative microcredit schemes are proving themselves powerful vehicles for improving the condition of women in developing countries.

VIII. Summary

I started this chapter by outlining the importance of the credit market in the choice of occupations. If credit markets preclude women's becoming borrowers, they also preclude their becoming entrepreneurs. This, naturally, also has gendered implications for income and wealth distribution.

We then examined how wealth is distributed between women and men in rich and poor countries. We saw that, in the developed countries, patriarchal societies enabled men to appropriate the income and wealth of women upon marriage. But by the twentieth century, a series of laws had slowly brought women to a position in which they could legally own and dispose of wealth. At

---

[31] Yunus and the Grameen Bank were jointly awarded the 2006 Nobel Peace Prize "for their efforts through microcredit to create economic and social development from below." U.S. Congress, "House and Senate Leaders Announce Gold Medal Ceremony for Professor Muhammad Yunus," press release.

the present time, the distribution of wealth between men and women is more or less egalitarian in the developed countries. The scenario today in developing countries, however, is quite different. In poor countries, land is the most important asset, and this is owned mostly by men. Inheritance laws frequently favor males, and even when they do not, patriarchal restrictions on women's activities curtail the extent to which they can manage their property.

We next discussed a simple but insightful Marxian model based on Roemer's (1988) work. The model introduced the idea of "exploitation" and demonstrated why an uneven distribution of wealth is essential to the manifestation of exploitation. We also saw why observed exploitation is a gendered phenomenon.

We then went on to examine why the ownership of wealth matters to credit markets. We saw that, due to the fact that borrowers face limited liability, there are two problems inherent in credit markets: an incentive problem and an adverse selection problem. First, borrowers have an incentive to shirk on effort if they use a creditor's funds. Second, different borrowers may be undertaking projects with different risks, and the level of risk may be private information that the lender does not know. We saw that, whether the problem is one of incentives or of adverse selection, having wealth to offer as collateral is beneficial to borrowers.

We then examined how credit enables people to become entrepreneurs and discussed the long-run consequences of not being able to do so. We saw that there is empirical evidence to suggest that inheritance, by relaxing the need for credit, enables workers to make the transition to entrepreneurship. But do the chances of making this transition depend on gender? We saw that this is so. The evidence suggests that female entrepreneurs prefer to balance family life and market work, so they are disadvantaged as entrepreneurs. This means that the firms owned by women are usually of smaller size and have higher risks of bankruptcy than those owned by men.

We finally addressed the issue of whether credit markets discriminate against women in the sense that these markets treat differently women and men with similar economic characteristics. By analyzing the existing evidence we concluded that discrimination is unlikely. There is no doubt, however, that women are severely disadvantaged in credit markets due to their family responsibilities and especially their lack of collateral.

Exercises and Questions for Discussion

1. Consider the following application of John Roemer's model, discussed in this chapter. In a village economy, there are 50 women and 50 men. There are two technologies available: gathering technology (GT) and farming technology (FT). These technologies produce according to the following rules:

GT: 0 pound corn + 4 days' labor → 1 pound corn

FT: 1 pound corn + 2 days' labor → 2 pounds corn gross (or 1 pound corn net)

The production period is 1 week. Corn used as seed corn in FT is tied up for 1 week and is replaced by the end of the week. The subsistence requirement for each person is 1 pound of corn per week. People work for the minimum amount of time necessary to generate their subsistence (and then consume the remaining time as leisure). There is a total stock of 50 pounds of corn in this village. Suppose that the corn is distributed in an egalitarian manner.

(a) How long will each person work per week in this village?
(b) Define *socially necessary labor time*. What is its magnitude for this village?

Now suppose that the initial stock of corn is distributed in an unequal manner: 10 men own all of the corn in the village, with each owning 5 pounds of corn.

(c) How many days per week will each landlord work? How about each worker? How much will each worker be paid in the event that he or he is hired by a landlord? Explain your reasoning.
(d) In what sense is there "exploitation" in the outcome? Are women exploited more, on average, than men? Why or why not?
(e) What does this exercise suggest to you about the relationship between the distribution of wealth and the exploitation of women?

2. Suppose that, in a society of 100 adults, there are equal numbers of women and men. Some of these people have the opportunity to become entrepreneurs who run firms, and the rest have to earn their livings as workers. The number of workers demanded by a single entrepreneur, l^d, depends on the wage rate, w, of a worker in the following manner: $l^d = 10 - w$. Assume that the labor supply function is vertical at the number of workers available. This wage rate is determined competitively as the value at which labor supply equals labor demand. Suppose that we arrange all the women in the order of increasing wealth and label them woman 1, woman 2, . . . , woman 50 (and likewise the men). The distribution of wealth (measured in thousands of dollars) in this society is as follows:

Women: 1–20 have no wealth; 21–40 have $10 each; 41–50 have $30 each.

Men: 1–10 have no wealth; 11–30 have $10 each; 31–40 have $20 each; and 41–50 have $50 each.

To become an entrepreneur, a person requires $40 of wealth.

(a) Draw separate bar graphs for women and men showing their wealth distributions. How many entrepreneurs will there be in the society?

(b) What is the total demand for labor, L^d, from all the entrepreneurs (in terms of w)? What will the equilibrium wage be? How much profit will each entrepreneur make? (*Hint*: The area of a triangle is one-half the base times the height.)

(c) If the wealth distributions of women are identical to the distributions for men given above, how many entrepreneurs will there be? Redo part b above for this case.

(d) What do your answers in parts b and c tell you about the relationship between the distribution of wealth and the well-being of workers?

(e) On the basis of your answers to the above, comment on the long-term prospects for the average woman and the average man in a society described by the original wealth distribution given above.

3. Suppose that a project requires an investment of $200,000 that cannot be recovered once invested. A potential entrepreneur approaches a bank for a loan. The bank has full information about the entrepreneur's utility function (which is consumption less effort) and about the details of the project. The bank agrees to lend the money at an interest rate of 10% provided that the borrower supplies the necessary collateral. The project, if successful, will yield revenues of $480,000. However, for the enterprise to succeed and generate these revenues, a minimum effort worth $100,000 is required from the entrepreneur; anything less and the project will fail to generate any revenues. Suppose that the potential entrepreneur has the option of absconding with the borrowed money instead of investing it in the proposed project.

(a) What is the minimum collateral the bank will require of the borrower in order to lend to her?

(b) Suppose that the borrower has access to no other bank; should she require loans in the future she will be forced to return to the same bank, and the bank manager knows this. Is it conceivable that the bank will lend to this borrower even if she does not have quite the required collateral you computed in part a? Why or why not?

(c) Suppose that the borrower is a housewife who did mostly unpaid housework in the past and so she does not have the requisite collateral. The bank manager, inspired by Muhammad Yunus of the Grameen Bank, says to her, "We'll lend you the money without collateral. But you have to repay the money with interest in 3 months. Otherwise, we will not lend to your next-door neighbor in the future." Could this scheme work? Explain why or why not. How would the outcome depend on whether the scheme was implemented in a village in Bangladesh or in New York City?

4. Suppose that there are two projects in which potential entrepreneurs would like to invest using money borrowed from a bank. (Assume that they can offer no collateral to the bank.) Each of the projects requires an investment of $1,000 that cannot be recovered once invested. Project A will return revenues of $1,200 with certainty. Project B will return either $0 or $2,400 with equal probability. No effort on the part of the entrepreneur is required for either project. The bank knows that Project A is available to only half the entrepreneurs and Project B to only the other half. However, the bank has no information about which project any specific entrepreneur has access to. The opportunity cost to the bank of lending money is 10%, and it operates in a competitive environment. Assume that borrowers and banks are risk neutral.

(a) Verify that the expected rate of return on the two projects is the same. What is that rate?

(b) If the bank knows for sure that an entrepreneur will invest the money in Project A, what interest rate do you think the bank should charge? If the bank knows for sure that an entrepreneur will invest the money in Project B, what interest rate do you think the bank should charge? Explain the reason for the difference in interest rates (if any).

(c) The bank, not knowing in which project specific entrepreneurs will invest, chooses to charge all of them the average of the two rates of interest computed in part b above. Do you see a problem with this? If so, what is it?

(d) In what sense will the credit market be "adversely selecting" between the entrepreneurs in part c above?

(e) Explain how asking for collateral may resolve, at least partly, this problem of adverse selection.

5. What reasons can you offer to suggest why credit markets put women at a disadvantage because of incentive and asymmetric information problems? How do these relate to the gendered distribution of wealth in a society, and why are women in developing countries more handicapped by these than are those in rich countries?

6. If men tend to own firms that require heavy equipment financed by borrowing and women tend to own firms that are more labor intensive, explain why it might appear that banks require higher collateral for loans given to women than to men. Does this suggest discrimination by sex in the credit market?

7. Do you think there might be a taste for discrimination against women in the credit market? Why or why not?

CHAPTER SIX

What Are the Effects of Globalization on Women?

I. Introduction

In the past few decades, one of the hallmarks of changes in economies worldwide has been the increasing extent to which they have been integrating with the rest of the world. Hardly any economies operate in isolation any more. Whether democratic countries like India, which sought for decades to shape its own destiny by pursuing a policy of closing itself off from the rest of the world, or communist countries like China, which allocated resources through central planning, most countries have come to integrate with the world economy through a process commonly referred to as globalization.

Globalization confers many benefits on countries that participate in it. Incomes increase faster, better technologies become available, and there is increased exposure to a variety of goods, world-views, and cultures. The importance of education is brought home, notions of human rights are disseminated and become universalized, and world opinion is brought to bear on human rights violations. There are many aspects to the phenomenon of globalization.

But globalization is not without its detractors. Violent protests against the governments of rich and poor countries speak to the mixed feelings of many people about the phenomenon. An economy integrated with the rest of the world is exposed to certain dangers. For example, a financial crisis that originates in one country may set back the economy of another country that is halfway around the world. Also of great concern is the fact that globalization generates winners and losers in a country. In particular, trade can increase poverty in poor countries. It is possible that the benefits of increased trade accrue to those who are already rich while the poor become worse off, thereby exacerbating an already unpalatable degree of inequality.[1]

In this chapter we shall inquire into how globalization has affected the economic lives of women relative to men. In Chapter 4 we saw that one route through which this may happen is by reducing discrimination against women when employers engage their taste for discrimination in industries that are not perfectly competitive. Exposing these industries to greater competition via international trade, we have seen, tends to reduce the gender gap in wages. However, there are additional effects of trade. For one, trade changes the prices of inputs such as labor, land, and skills in a manner that depends on a country's comparative advantage. If women and men have different skills or own different amounts of assets, international trade can change their relative incomes. Thus greater trade liberalization by a country need not have effects that are gender neutral. In this chapter we shall examine how the nature of the goods traded and the ownership of productive assets determine whether women are better or worse off relative to men due to trade.

Another aspect of globalization that has important consequences for women is foreign direct investment, whereby multinational firms open up subsidiaries in foreign countries for various reasons. Existing evidence strongly suggests that women can greatly benefit from the presence of multinational companies, especially in poor countries. If women have limited employment opportunities in these economies and so have low wages, they are particularly attractive to multinationals. By offering them employment, multinationals can substantially raise the standard of living of their female employees.

If globalization increases the amount of income in the hands of women, they and their families will clearly be better off as a result. Furthermore, the increase in their income will increase their bargaining power with their spouses and thereby increase their say within their households. As we have seen, one of the consequences is that children are likely to receive more nutritious food. They are also likely to receive more schooling. In addition, greater participation in economic activities outside the home will likely allow women to have a greater voice in the public arena. It is conceivable, therefore, that globalization will work to the detriment of patriarchy. We shall inquire into this possibility in this chapter.

That globalization cannot have been an unalloyed boon to all women can be seen from the visible increase in trafficking in women (and children) across national borders for prostitution. This horrifying development has arisen because the demand for sexual services in the rich countries has

---

[1] For a nice survey of the evidence on this, see Harrison, A. (2007), "Globalization and Poverty: An Introduction," in *Globalization and Poverty*, ed. A. Harrison, University of Chicago Press, Chicago, Chap. 1.

attracted organized crime to provide a supply from poorer countries. In this chapter we shall examine the motivation of transnational trafficking. In particular, we shall examine the evidence on whether the legalization of prostitution in destination countries tempers or exacerbates transnational trafficking.

One of the puzzling things about trade liberalization is that there is a gender gap in its perceived desirability; women are *more* in favor of protecting the domestic economy from foreign competition than men. What is more, this gender gap seems to be more prevalent in the rich countries than in the poor. We shall examine in this chapter what economic factors impinge on an individual's support for trade and discuss studies that identify this gender gap.

II. Advantages of Globalization

Trade

When a country operates as a closed economy, it has to produce by itself (in the exact amounts) all the goods and services its residents consume. It may have to produce goods that it is inefficient in producing if its consumers demand them, and these goods will cause the country to use more resources than are used by other countries that are adept at producing them. Furthermore, the country may produce the goods that it can produce efficiently only in limited amounts, because the country's demand for these goods may be limited.

Now suppose that the country opens up its borders to engage in free trade with other nations. The country can now specialize in producing the goods that it is good at producing and sell them to other countries. In other words, what it produces is no longer restricted by domestic demand. And the goods it can produce only inefficiently it can now import from other countries that are better at producing these goods. By enabling a country to concentrate its resources in producing goods it can produce efficiently (that is, specialize), international trade benefits a country. This, in simple terms, is the argument of gains from trade made possible by specialization, an argument first clarified by the classical economist David Ricardo.[2]

The argument is illustrated in Figure 6.1 for a country that produces only two goods, say food and cloth. The figure displays XY as the production possibility frontier (PPF)—the combinations of food and cloth that a country can produce if it devotes all its resources to producing these goods. The country can produce all combinations of food and cloth on XY or within OXY (if it leaves some resources unused) but not outside. Suppose that all citizens of the country have identical preferences and hence identical indifference curves. Examples of these curves in the figure are DE and FG. If the

[2] Ricardo, D. (1817), *Principles of Political Economy and Taxation*, John Murray, London.

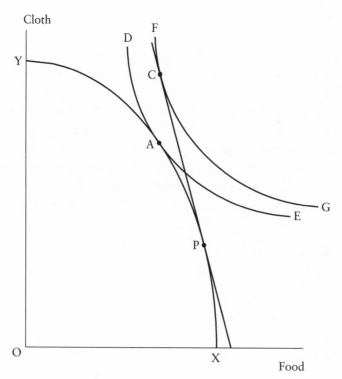

FIGURE 6.1 The benefits of specialization in international trade

country does not trade with other countries (that is, if it chooses autarky, or complete economic independence), its consumption of food and cloth must equal the respective outputs of those goods because neither good is imported or exported. The country will produce the combination of food and cloth denoted by point A in the figure. No other combination on or within the PPF will afford a higher utility to the typical consumer.

Now suppose that the country engages in free trade. If its economy is small compared to the rest of the world's, it will take the prices of food and cloth as set in world markets. Suppose that the ratio of prices is given by the slope of the line CP in Figure 6.1. This slope tells us how much cloth 1 unit of food can be exchanged for in the world market. If food is expensive relative to cloth, a great deal of cloth has to be surrendered to obtain 1 unit of food, and the slope of line CP will be steep. On the other hand, if food is cheap relative to cloth, little cloth will have to be given up to obtain 1 unit of food, and the slope of line CP will be shallow. The slope of CP is given by the ratio of the price of food to that of cloth in the international market.

At the price ratio indicated in the figure, the country is best off producing at point P (thereby maximizing its income) but consuming at point C, because this maximizes the utility of the typical consumer. When the country engages in trade with other countries, its consumption of a good need not match its production of that good. Notice that the consumption basket at C is on a higher indifference curve than the autarky basket at A. Trade makes the country better off. In the absence of trade, not only production but also consumption must lie on the PPF. What trade does is remove the constraint that consumption, too, must lie on the PPF. As can be seen from the figure, the country can produce what it is better at producing at world prices and trade in order to achieve a more satisfactory consumption basket. In the figure, the amount of food consumed at point C is less than that produced at point P, whereas the reverse is true for cloth. In other words, the country exports food and imports cloth.

Therefore, when a country embarks on trade its pattern of production changes. It produces more of some goods and less of others. Because production requires various inputs ("factors"), the demands of producers for these factors will also change as a result of trade. These, in turn, will change the prices of these inputs and, hence, the income that accrues to the owners of these inputs. Factors that experience an increase in demand will now fetch higher prices than before, whereas factors experiencing a fall in demand will fetch lower prices. Can we predict which factors will experience an increase in demand and which will see a fall? The Heckscher–Ohlin theory provides an answer to this question.[3]

To understand this theory, consider two countries (say, India and Australia) in isolation from the rest of the world. Suppose that they both produce two goods (food and cloth, as above) using two factors (labor and land). Assume that both countries have access to the same production technologies and that the consumers of both countries have identical preferences for the two goods. Suppose, however, that labor is abundant relative to land in India, whereas land is abundant relative to labor in Australia. If both countries are autarkic (that is, they do not trade), labor will be relatively cheap in India, whereas land will be relatively cheap in Australia.

Now suppose that India and Australia embark on free trade. What will each country export to the other? Suppose, as is reasonable, that food production is intensive in the use of land compared to labor, whereas cloth is relatively intensive in the use of labor compared to land. In autarky, food will be cheaper in Australia because this good requires land more intensively than labor and Australia has a greater abundance of land than India. Likewise, in autarky, cloth will be cheaper in India because this good requires labor more intensively than land and India has a greater abundance of labor than Australia. So when trade opens up, Indian textile producers will find it profitable to export cloth to Australia and Australian farmers will find it beneficial to export food to India. In other words, India will have a "comparative advantage" in cloth production and Australia in food production.

[3] Heckscher, E. F., and B. Ohlin (1991), *Heckscher–Ohlin Trade Theory*, trans. and ed. H. Flam and M. J. Flanders, MIT Press, Cambridge, MA.

The logic outlined above suggests that Australia will produce the food sufficient for all its own needs and some for the needs of India, too. India, on the other hand, will produce all of the cloth it needs and some of Australia's requirement, too. When the two countries move from autarky to trade, Australia will see an increase in the demand for its food and a decrease in the demand for its cloth. Because food production is intensive in the use of land and cloth production is intensive in the use of labor, in Australia the demand for land will increase and the demand for labor decrease. Thus in Australia the price of land (or, more accurately, the rental rate per acre of land) will rise and the price of labor (the wage rate) will decline. India, on the other hand, will see an increase in the demand for its cloth and a decrease in the demand for its food. Therefore, in India the demand for labor will rise and that for land will fall. As a result, the wage rate in India will rise and the land rental rate will fall.

Thus we arrive at some essential insights in this two-country, two-good, two-factor scenario: (i) trade will increase the price of the factor that a country has a relative abundance of and lower the price of the factor that it has a relative scarcity of. This is an illustration of a well-known theoretical result in trade theory called the Stolper–Samuelson theorem.[4] (ii) The good that intensively uses the relatively abundant factor will be exported, and the good that intensively uses the factor that is relatively scarce will be imported. Thus those who own the factor that is abundant in a country will gain from trade, and those who own the factor that is scarce will lose.

The two factors chosen in the discussion above were labor and land. However, they need not be restricted to these. If one country is developed and the other is developing, the factors relevant for discussion could well be skilled labor and unskilled labor. Developing countries have an abundance of unskilled labor and developed countries an abundance of skilled labor. The Heckscher–Ohlin theory predicts that trade between the two countries will raise the wage rate of skilled labor and lower that of unskilled labor in the developed country. In the developing country, on the other hand, trade will raise the wage rate of unskilled labor and lower that of skilled labor.

If in a developing country unskilled workers are in abundance and women are over-represented among the unskilled workers and men among the skilled, according to the Heckscher–Ohlin theory women will see an increase in their wage and men a decrease with trade. In other words, the gender wage gap should decline with increased exposure to international trade in the developing country. In a developed country with an abundance of skilled workers, if women are over-represented among the unskilled workers and men among the skilled, the gender gap will increase with greater exposure to international trade.

---

[4] Stolper, W. F., and P. A. Samuelson (1941), "Protection and Real Wages," *Review of Economic Studies* 9, pp. 58–73.

Foreign Direct Investment

There is another important manner in which globalization benefits a country. Foreign firms may invest in the country, building factories, importing equipment, and so on, which will enable the country to export. This is referred to as foreign direct investment (FDI). What benefit does a country derive from FDI? There are several.

First, one of the main reasons for firms in developed countries to engage in FDI, especially in developing countries, is the availability of cheap labor. International competition puts pressure on firms to minimize costs. When a country undergoes economic development, its workers' wage rate increases. Consequently, the phenomenon that raises workers' standards of living (namely, economic development) also tends to make the country's industries uncompetitive. To remain competitive, these firms look to relocate production in regions where the wage rates are low. Multinational companies from rich countries undertake research and development in their own countries to come up with new technologies. This increases the demand for skilled labor in their countries. They then tend to undertake production activities in poorer countries where wages are lower. This reduces manufacturing employment in the rich countries and increases the demand for unskilled labor in the developing countries, thereby increasing the wage rates in the latter.

If foreign countries impose stiff tariffs on imported goods, multinationals are at a disadvantage because their goods will be priced higher for consumers in these countries than will the products of domestic firms. Multinationals then have an incentive to engage in FDI for reasons that have little to do with the use of cheap labor. They may build production facilities in those countries in order to jump the "tariff wall"; that is, by producing the goods in these countries they avoid the tariffs that need to be paid on imported goods. In any event, this motive for FDI also increases the demand for labor in foreign countries and raises the wages there.

Second, when a firm from a developed country builds a factory in a poor country, it brings in new technology that increases the productivity of workers. It also imparts skills (human capital) to these workers and reduces the gap in the skills between workers in rich countries and those in poor countries. There is evidence indicating, for example, that there is a positive relationship between the upgrading of skills in countries and the presence of firms affiliated with U.S. multinationals. This relationship is even stronger in developing countries.[5] We shall discuss the avenues through which this works in a later section of this chapter.

[5] See Slaughter, M. J. (2002), "Does Inward Foreign Direct Investment Contribute to Skill Upgrading in Developing Countries?," Center for Economic Policy Analysis Working Paper 2002-08, New School University, New York.

Third, FDI may help the transfer of technologies to the domestic firms of developing countries. The subsidiaries of multinationals will certainly use the technologies of the parent companies. But we expect that even domestic firms, when forced to compete with multinationals locating in their country, will find it necessary to upgrade their technologies through licensing arrangements. These are arrangements whereby firms in developing countries pay for "leasing" a technology for a certain fee (the licensing fee). In this case, even firms that are not subsidiaries of multinationals are forced to upgrade their technologies because of FDI.

Fourth, FDI is likely to encourage entrepreneurship. One of the main reasons that producers in developing countries cannot export is not lack of ability but lack of knowledge of what needs to be done. In particular, they are not aware of the stringent standards of quality control, punctuality in delivery, and so on that are crucial to success in world markets. In providing this knowledge, FDI may play an important role. Potential entrepreneurs can acquire firsthand knowledge of these international requirements by working in a foreign firm for a while. This enables them to then start their own firms.

III. Effects of International Trade and Foreign Direct Investment on Women

We now address the question of how globalization has affected women. We have noted that in the developed countries, which have a greater abundance of skilled as opposed to unskilled workers, skilled workers are made better off and unskilled workers worse off when there is more exposure to foreign trade. In developing countries, which tend to have a greater abundance of unskilled labor, the opposite is true. But are the genders affected differently? We might expect the answer to be in the affirmative because women and men have different skills and different constraints on their time. For instance, women are more likely to be responsible for children and so are less likely to have much flexibility with regard to their jobs when their children are young.

It is useful to mention one extreme example to begin with. In Bangladesh, globalization has resulted in a substantial garment sector. Employment in this sector has increased greatly in the past three decades, and most of the people employed in this sector are women. Bangladeshi society is highly patriarchal, and women have had relatively little opportunity to participate in the labor force. The practices of female seclusion and of veiling one's face (*burqa*) have drastically curtailed the opportunity for women to work in the labor market. The resulting low wages of women gave the industry a competitive advantage with trade liberalization. The expansion of the garment sector afforded women in Bangladesh the opportunity to participate in the labor market on a scale not previously witnessed. One study based on a sample of 1,322 women surveyed in 2001 found that women working in the garment export industry were economically much better off than women who worked elsewhere in the domestic economy.[6] And among these women, those who worked in the export-processing zones, where the output was meant only for foreign markets, were the best off. The dimensions along which the comparison was made were considerations such as wages, working conditions, maternity leaves, and transportation facilities. If one can make predictions from a relatively small sample, this study suggests that globalization has helped Bangladeshi women.

Marzia Fontana (2009) has pointed out that, as far as employment is concerned, women in East Asia have fared better under globalization than women in Africa.[7] Pursuing an explanation for this is quite revealing, because it brings out how the distribution of asset ownership and the nature of the export goods affect women when a country embarks on international trade. Much of the reason for the difference in outcomes for women in East Asia and Africa has to do with the fact that in East Asia globalization has resulted in the export of labor-intensive goods, whereas in Africa the exports have largely been primary goods. Why does that make a difference? Because trade changes the demands for various inputs into production, as we have seen. The change in the well-being of women depends on whether the resources they own experience an increase or a decrease in demand. The ownership of land is highly skewed in favor of men in African and in most developing countries (as we saw in the previous chapter); the resource that women most commonly own is their labor. If trade raises the demand for land, women do not have much to gain and, in fact, have something to lose. If, on the other hand, trade raises the demand for labor, women can benefit.

Which input experiences an increase in demand when trade opens up depends on the comparative advantage of a country. East Asian countries have a comparative advantage in labor-intensive goods, whereas most African countries have a comparative advantage in primary goods (which are intensive in land and other natural resources). The logic of the effects of globalization on women can be seen by adapting a model constructed by Mukesh Eswaran and Ashok Kotwal (1992).[8] Consider an economy with two sectors, grain and textiles. Grain stands as a proxy for all primary goods and textiles for all industrial goods. The difference between them is that grain requires unskilled labor as well as land, whereas textiles require only unskilled labor. Because the total amount of land in most developing countries is fixed, in the production of grain labor will face diminishing returns: every additional unit

[6] Kabeer, N., and S. Mahmud (2004), "Globalization, Gender, and Poverty: Bangladeshi Women Workers in Export and Local Markets," *Journal of International Development* 16, pp. 93–109.

[7] Fontana, M. (2009), "The Gender Effects of Trade Liberalization in Developing Countries," in *Gender Aspects of the Trade and Poverty Nexus: A Macro-Micro Approach*, ed. M. Bussolo et al., Palgrave Macmillan, World Bank, Washington, DC.

[8] Eswaran, M., and A. Kotwal (1992), "Export Led Development: Primary vs. Industrial Exports," *Journal of Development Economics* 41, pp. 163–172.

of labor applied will increase the output of grain by less than the previous unit. In other words, the marginal product of labor in grain production will diminish with increased labor use.

The worth of the marginal unit of labor (the value of the marginal product of labor, or VMPL) in agriculture is given by the marginal product multiplied by the price of grain (assumed to be given). Similarly, the VMPL in industry is given by the marginal product multiplied by the price of textiles. In a competitive labor market, the wage rate will be equal to the value of its marginal product. If the wage rate is lower than the value of the marginal product, say in the grain sector, producers will gain by increasing employment and hence output. The greater employment of labor will lower its marginal product. This process will continue until the VMPL is exactly equal to the going wage rate. (Likewise, the rental rate on land will be equal to the value of the marginal product of the land.) Because workers can move between the grain and textiles sectors, if there is a difference in the wage rates of the two sectors, the sector with higher wage rate will attract workers. The flow of labor into one sector and out of the other will ultimately equalize the wage rates in the two sectors.

Suppose that, when a country moves from autarky to international trade, it has a comparative advantage in textiles. In that case, the country will export textiles and import grain. So when it embarks on trade, the textiles sector will expand and the grain sector will contract. The expanding textiles sector will absorb labor from the grain sector. Because the fewer workers left in agriculture are working the same amount of land as before, the marginal product of labor will increase and, hence, so will the wage rate. Suppose that the wage rate increases by 15%. Because women gain their income mostly from labor, they will definitely benefit when the country embarks on international trade. If they work the same number of hours as before, their incomes will increase by 15%.

What will happen to the well-being of men? Their labor income, too, will increase by 15% if they work the same number of hours as before. However, labor income is only part of their income—they also receive income from the ownership of land. When the grain sector shrinks, less labor will be working on land and so the value of the marginal product of land will decline. Hence the rental rate for land will decrease. Suppose that this decline is 10%. Men will see their income from labor increase by 15% but their income from land decrease by 10%. So the percentage increase in their *total* income will be less than 15%. Women, on the other hand, will see a 15% increase in their total income. So women will benefit *proportionately more* than men if the country exports labor-intensive goods.

How women are affected by trade, we see, depends very much on how the use of resources changes with trade. The economic intuition for this important mechanism is better seen diagrammatically. To pursue this, let us set the

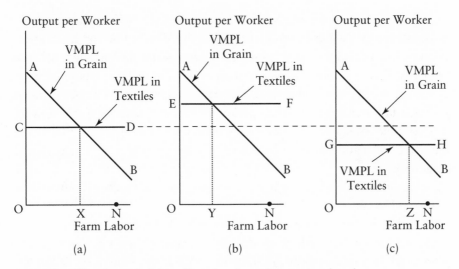

FIGURE 6.2 The change in labor allocation due to international trade

price of grain at 1. The price of textiles will then be its price relative to that of grain. If this price is 4, for example, it means that 4 units of grain are needed in exchange for 1 unit of textiles. In this way, all prices can be expressed in terms of the number of units of grain they will fetch in exchange.

We have seen that the demand for labor in a sector, agriculture or industry, is given by the VMPL in that sector. Now consult Figure 6.2, which has three panels. On the horizontal axis we have the amount of labor employed in the agricultural (farm) sector to produce grain, and on the vertical axis we have the value of the marginal product of a worker. The distance ON along the horizontal axis represents the total amount of labor in the economy. Obviously, farm employment cannot exceed ON.

Consider first panel a, which treats the case in which the country does not trade with any other (autarky). The VMPL in agriculture is represented by the line AB, and it is downward sloping because agriculture has diminishing returns to labor. The demand for labor from the industrial sector is shown by the horizontal line CD. It is horizontal because there are constant returns to labor in the textiles sector. If for some allocation of labor between the grain and textiles sectors the vertical distances to the two lines are not the same, that allocation cannot be in equilibrium. That is because what labor is being paid in one sector (the value of its marginal product) is lower than that in the other sector, so labor will flow from the former to the latter. Thus the equilibrium allocation of farm labor in autarky will be given by OX and the amount of labor in the textiles sector by XN. The equilibrium wage rate in autarky will be the common value of the marginal product, which is OC.

Now suppose that the country opens itself up to free trade with the world and the world price of textiles is higher than the autarky price. (Remember, the price of grain remains at 1 because all other prices are being measured in terms of grain.) This means that the country will find it has a comparative advantage in textile production, and the VMPL line for textile production will shift up. This is shown as the horizontal line EF in panel b of Figure 6.2. We see that the equilibrium allocation of farm labor will now be lower, at OY; some labor from the agricultural sector has been drawn into the industrial sector. The employment in the textiles sector will be YN, and the wage rate of labor will now be OE. Thus specialization in the labor-intensive good (textiles), as in East Asian countries, will increase the wage rate of labor. (The withdrawal of labor from agriculture will lower the rental rate on land, as we have discussed, and the landlords will receive less rental income.)

In the above argument it was assumed that, after the country embarks on trade, women and men will work the same number of hours as before. However, a person's labor supply generally responds to the wage rate. When the wage rate increases, the opportunity cost of leisure is higher than before, and people will usually tend to work more hours. (This is certainly true in developing countries.) Thus, if the wage rate increases by 15%, women's income will increase by more than 15%. The same thing will be true of the labor component of men's income. Nevertheless, it will still be true that women's income will increase by a higher percentage than men's because men's income from land will decline. So when the country exports labor-intensive goods, women's income increases for two reasons: their wage rate rises, and they work more hours. Furthermore, in relative terms, women gain more than men.

What will happen if, on the other hand, the country has a comparative advantage in grain (and a comparative disadvantage in textiles)? In this instance, the grain sector will expand by absorbing labor from the textiles sector. The extra grain produced will be exported, and the shortfall of textiles will be imported. The increase in labor working the same amount of land in the agricultural sector will lower the marginal product of labor, and the wage rate will fall. Suppose that the decline is 10%. If women work the same number of hours as before, their income will fall by 10%. What will happen to the income of men? The labor component of their income, too, will fall by 10%, assuming a fixed number of work hours. But their income from land will increase. This is because the same amount of land will now be worked by more labor, which will increase the marginal product of the land and, hence, its rental rate. Suppose that the income from land increases by 20%. If the country has a comparative advantage in grain when it embarks on trade, women will see a 10% decline in their income, whereas men will see an increase in their total income (because of the land income component).[9]

---

[9] The increase in land income can be shown to exceed the decline in labor income, so men's total income must increase.

Now consult Figure 6.2 again. If the country has a comparative advantage in grain and a comparative disadvantage in textiles, it means that the world price of textiles is lower than the country's autarky price of textiles. In this case, the VMPL in textiles will decline in the country after it embarks on free trade. The VMPL in this sector will shift down; this is shown as the line GH in panel c of the figure. We see that the equilibrium allocation of farm labor will now be OZ, which is larger than in autarky, and the amount of labor in textile production will be the smaller amount ZN. The equilibrium wage rate will be OG, which is lower than it was in autarky. (The infusion of labor into agriculture will raise the rental rate on land, and the landlords will receive greater rental incomes.)

Because labor supply responds to the wage rate, a decline in the wage rate will induce women and men to work fewer hours. So the decline in their labor income will actually be greater than the 10% assumed above. Our conclusion, however, remains intact: if the country specializes in exporting primary goods, women will see a decline in their income and also experience a decline relative to men.

International trade, therefore, can have very different effects on women and men. Women in a developing country are more likely to benefit if the country exports labor-intensive goods and to be hurt if it exports primary goods. The difference arises because of differences in the ownership of assets: in developing countries, important assets such as land tend to be owned by men. This disparity, however, is far less pronounced in developed countries. It must be kept in mind that when international trade changes the relative incomes of men and women, the effects go beyond that. The reason is that incomes earned determine bargaining power within households. So a relative loss of income for women translates into a loss of status and, therefore, reduced autonomy in the allocation of resources within their households.

I should note that we have assumed that both agriculture and industry use only unskilled labor. In reality, industry offers more scope for the employment of skilled labor. In terms of skills, there is an asymmetry between women and men: women tend to be less skilled than men. This is true not just in developing countries but also in developed countries. Part of the reason is that skills are acquired through work experience and traditionally women have tended to work less than men. Also, because women have tended to work less in the labor market (for reasons related to raising a family), it has been rational for them to invest less in human capital. If a country has a comparative advantage in industrial goods when trade opens up, the demand for skilled labor will increase. If women are predominantly unskilled, they may not see a huge increase in the demand for their relatively unskilled labor. In this case, their *relative* income will decline even when the country exports labor-intensive goods that intensively use skilled labor.

Adrian Wood (1991) has found that, from the early 1960s through the mid-1980s, increased exports of manufactures to developed countries were associated with a higher demand for female labor in developing countries.[10] This shows up as an increase in "female intensity" (defined as the number of females per every 100 males employed) in the manufacturing sectors of developing countries. If developed countries import more from developing countries, one might expect that the manufacturing sectors of the former will shrink and, as a result, that female intensity will decline in the developed countries. However, Wood found that this is not the case: trade with developing countries does not seem to have lowered the demand for female labor in the developed countries. In other words, women in developing countries have not gained at the expense of women in the developed countries. There are many possible reasons for this. For one, increases in demand for female labor unrelated to trade may have compensated for the decline in demand due to trade. Or perhaps women are better able than men to find alternative employment because, having less work experience on average, they have fewer skills that are specific to particular industries.

Remco Oostendorp (2009) examined the effect of trade on the wage difference ("gap") between the genders over the period 1983–99 using a survey done by the International Labor Organization.[11] This survey contained information on the gender wage gap for 161 narrowly defined occupations in more than 80 countries. The study used the gender wage difference expressed as a proportion of the men's wages as a measure of the occupational gender wage gap. Because the occupations were narrowly defined, it can be assumed that they required similar human capital for men and women in each occupation. Therefore, wage differences by gender can be taken to have been due to discrimination. The gender gap, surprisingly, was greater in the richer countries. The extent of a country's globalization with respect to trade is measured by its volume of trade (the sum of the values of its exports and its imports) expressed as a proportion of its gross domestic product (GDP); the extent of its globalization with respect to FDI is taken to be its net FDI inflow expressed as a proportion of its GDP.[12]

Oostendorp found that trade reduces the size of the occupational gender gap. This is in line with Becker's theory: more exposure to international trade reduces the scope for firms to indulge in a taste for discrimination against women. Recall that this is also what Sandra Black and Elizabeth Brainerd (2004) found for the United States in their study that we discussed

---

[10] Wood, A. (1991), "North–South Trade and Female Labor in Manufacturing: An Asymmetry," *Journal of Development Studies* 27, pp. 168–189.

[11] Oostendorp, R. H. (2009), "Globalization and the Gender Wage Gap," *World Bank Economic Review* 23, pp. 141–161.

[12] Net FDI inflow is the FDI in the country by foreign countries net of the country's FDI in foreign countries.

in Chapter 4. However, trade may impinge differently on different occupations, which may require different levels of human capital, which in turn may differ by gender. Furthermore, because the people living in rich and poor countries have different amounts of human capital, these effects may differ across them. If trade increases the demand for women's labor relative to men's, one would expect the gender wage gap to decline in low-skilled occupations in poor countries and to decline in high-skilled occupations in rich countries.

Oostendorp found that trade and FDI decrease the gender wage gap in low-skilled occupations in poor countries (as expected). They also decrease the gender wage gap in the high-skilled occupations of rich countries (as expected) but not in those of poor countries. The latter result is paradoxical, because in poor countries industries using high-skilled labor should contract and the decline in demand for this factor should reduce the gender wage gap. In fact, FDI seems to actually increase the gender wage gap in the high-skilled occupations of poor countries. It is conceivable that this is because even within occupational categories there are differences in the human capital levels of men and women (with higher levels for men). If multinationals place a premium on human capital, they may bid up the wages of skilled men relative to those of skilled women.

An important factor that impinges on the effect of FDI on the gender wage gap has not been discussed so far. This is seen in a comparison of the trends in the gender wage gaps in two of the original "Asian Tigers," Taiwan and South Korea. The growth performance of these two countries since the early 1960s has been spectacular. Until about the early 1980s, their export sectors employed more women—especially in sectors such as textiles, clothing, and electronics. From the mid-1980s to the early 1990s, however, the trends in the gender wage gaps in the two countries showed a sharp contrast: in South Korea, the wage gap declined, that is, the disparity between female and male wages declined. In Taiwan, however, it increased. This difference in the two countries was due to the difference in the effects of FDI.

Both countries have industrialized since the late 1950s through active government intervention that has promoted exports. In the 1970s, however, they started liberalizing with regard to FDI—Taiwan more than South Korea. In Taiwan, much of the FDI was by foreign firms, but domestic firms also undertook considerable outward FDI, especially in China, in the kind of labor-intensive industries that employed women in Taiwan. South Korea, however, placed greater restrictions on the movement of capital. As a result of this difference in policy toward FDI, capital could move offshore much more easily from Taiwan than from South Korea. There is evidence that the greater freedom of capital to move out of Taiwan undermined the bargaining power of labor in these labor-intensive industries: wage demands could be countered by the threat of moving offshore.[13] The erosion of the bargaining power of labor in the industries employing women accounts for the difference in the trends of the gender wage gaps in Taiwan and South Korea. In its effect on gender wage gaps, we see, FDI can cut both ways.

IV. Globalization and Investment in Human Capital: Lessons from India

There are some very interesting lessons to be learned on gender effects from the relatively recent Indian experience with liberalization and globalization. From the time it achieved independence from British rule in 1947 until 1991, India largely followed a closed economy model. The emphasis was on self-sufficiency and egalitarianism (called Fabian socialism) within a capitalist framework and a democratic country. The economy was highly regulated. This "inward-looking" model of economic development failed quite badly; it was responsible for countless inefficiencies, lackluster growth, and corruption. After a serious financial crisis in 1991, however, the country was forced to liberalize by drastically reducing its tariffs across the board in numerous industries. Furthermore, the country became open to FDI. The recent nature of its globalization, its large population, and its having English as one of the two national languages make it one of the most studied developing countries. Consequently, India serves as an instructive case study of the effects of globalization.

One of the benefits of globalization is that it can induce investment in women's education and health (human capital) even in patriarchal societies in which parents tend to invest more in boys than in girls. In poor countries, parents rely on sons for their retirement; the daughters are married off and become part of their husbands' families. So when their children are young, parents tend to spend their limited funds on the education of their sons. But when multinationals specifically offer young women better employment opportunities, parents may increase their human capital investment in daughters, too. This is seen in an interesting study conducted by Emily Oster and Bryce Steinberg (2013) in three southern states of India.[14] Since the 1990s, rapid advances in telecommunications have made it possible for foreign companies (mostly American) to employ young English-speaking workers in "call centers" in India.[15] The workers are paid well by Indian standards. Oster and

---

[13] Seguino, S. (2000), "The Effects of Structural Change and Economic Liberalization on Gender Wage Differentials in South Korea and Taiwan," *Cambridge Journal of Economics* 24, pp. 437–459.

[14] Oster, E., and B. M. Steinberg (2013), "Do IT Service Centers Promote School Enrollment?: Evidence from India," *Journal of Development Economics* 104, pp. 123–135.

[15] Call centers receive calls from and make calls to clients of multinational companies from all over the world. The calls are routed to these centers in developing countries in which the multinationals recruit and train employees to respond to the concerns and inquiries of clients. India has many such call centers because educated Indians are fairly knowledgeable of English.

Steinberg examined whether the introduction of these so-called information technology enabled service (ITES) centers has had any causal impact on primary school enrollment. (Not all ITES centers are necessarily call centers, however.) They found that the ITES centers did indeed increase the enrollment, especially in English-language schools, of children of both genders, but the effect was highly localized geographically. The authors' interpretation is that the ITES centers increased enrollment by disseminating information regarding employment opportunities.

Robert Jensen (2012) has conducted a study that provides a somewhat more direct test of whether the increase in the returns to human capital made possible for women by globalization has resulted in an increase in their human capital investment.[16] It is not obvious that higher returns will automatically induce greater investment when there are cultural norms such as a preference for sons that militate against such a response. Also, the findings of Oster and Steinberg alluded to above may have other explanations. For example, if globalization increases the income of women who are mothers, their bargaining power within their households will increase. If they are less biased than their husbands against investing in daughters, more female children may be enrolled in school as a consequence. But this mechanism leading to greater enrollment of female children will have more to do with mothers' bargaining power than with higher returns to human capital. To isolate the correct mechanism, Jensen performed a three-year experiment in northern India. He had recruiters disseminate information about call center jobs in randomly chosen villages, where training for interviews and related matters was freely given to young girls, clearly emphasizing that knowledge of English and familiarity with computers were required for these jobs. The recruiters offered no jobs; they only dispensed information and facilitated preparation for the competition for jobs. Over the three-year period, Jensen found significant increases in girls' enrollment in English-language schools and in their health, as measured by the body mass index.[17] No such effect was detected for boys, either positive or negative.

The finding of Jensen is important because it reveals that increases in the returns to human capital made possible by globalization do elicit a response that undermines cultural norms that work against human capital investment in girls. Furthermore, it is noteworthy that this investment in girls did not come at the expense of boys; parents appear to have cut back other expenditures to increase their total investment in children's human capital. Gauri

---

[16] Jensen, R. T. (2012), "Do Labor Market Opportunities Affect Young Women's Work and Family Decisions?: Experimental Evidence from India," *Quarterly Journal of Economics* 127, pp. 753–792.

[17] The body mass index is a person's weight expressed in kilograms divided by the square of height expressed in meters. It is a measure that is widely used to assess deviation from the healthy norm in the directions of undernourishment or obesity.

Shastry (2012) has shown that, throughout India, globalization has elicited a greater increase in schooling in those areas of the country in which the linguistic history was more conducive to the learning of English.[18] Although she did not inquire into the gender aspect of this phenomenon, her work reveals that within a given country the benefits of globalization may materialize differently in different regions depending on how well equipped they are to reap the rewards of human capital.

The encouraging empirical findings discussed above should be kept in perspective, however. Globalization has many effects, and an increase in the returns to education is only one of these. When tariff protection is removed to liberalize trade, the proportion of people in poverty in a country or region could well increase. This is because people working in highly protected industries might lose their livelihoods in the face of competition. If sending children to school is expensive (because of fees, the costs of books and uniforms, and so on), the schooling of many children may be discontinued. In fact, this is precisely what was found in a study by Eric Edmonds, Nina Pavcnik, and Petia Topalova (2010) of the numerous districts in India over the period 1987–2000.[19] Although the tariff reduction for any given industry following the 1991 liberalization was the same across all of India, the effect of the reduction was felt differently across the various districts even within each state. This is because different districts concentrated on producing different goods, so the tariff reduction for a given good had different relevance to different districts. For example, the tariff reduction in the industry with the most employment in a district had the greatest effect on the district. As a result, the tariff reductions effectively faced by different districts were not the same.

Edmonds et al. examined how this variation in tariff reduction at the level of districts produced different effects on the schooling of children. In the 1990s, schooling increased all across the country for various reasons. The authors found, however, that the districts that faced the greatest reductions in tariffs experienced the slowest increases in schooling. That is, relative to the national trend in schooling, the districts with the greatest tariff reductions saw a decline in schooling. Furthermore, this response was highly gendered: the decline was almost twice as great for girls as for boys. The authors rule out the possibility that this may have been due to a decline in the returns to human capital; in fact, these returns increased. They also rule out the possibility that the schooling decline occurred because the families that fell into poverty as a result of trade liberalization wanted income from child labor. The mechanism the authors support is quite simple: families that fell into poverty withdrew their

---

[18] Shastry, G. K. (2012), "Human Capital Response to Globalization: Education and Information Technology in India," *Journal of Human Resources* 47, pp. 287–330.

[19] Edmonds, E. V., N. Pavcnik, and P. Topalova (2010), "Trade Adjustment and Human Capital Investments: Evidence from Indian Tariff Reform," *American Economic Journal: Applied Economics* 2, pp. 42–75.

children from schools because schooling was quite costly to them. In a separate study of India during the same period, Petia Topalova (2007) found that in rural areas, districts that faced the average tariff reduction during liberalization experienced significantly less decline in poverty relative to districts that faced no tariff reduction.[20]

What are we to take away from the experience of India discussed above? First, the schooling of children in developing countries does indeed respond to higher returns to human capital. Second, if these returns are substantial, they can overcome cultural norms that undervalue the education of girls. Third, the higher return to human capital is only one effect of globalization. If trade liberalization reduces the incomes of those who are already poor, these people might respond (at least in the short run) by withdrawing their children from school. Trade often does increase the poverty level in poor countries. Pinelopi Goldberg and Nina Pavcnik (2007) found similar effects of trade reforms in the 1980s and early 1990s on urban poverty in Colombia.[21] Unless governments have in place policies that facilitate the re-employment of those who have lost their jobs as a result of declining tariff protection, poverty can increase. And this, as we have seen, can have gendered effects on the education of children.

V. Globalization and Patriarchy

An interesting and important question to ask is this: what effect has globalization had on the institution of patriarchy? If patriarchy arises because women's bargaining power relative to men is low, it would appear that anything that improves women's status in these terms would work toward undermining patriarchy.

Opponents of globalization frequently argue that multinational firms, a visible accompaniment of globalization, exploit women in developing countries by paying them a pittance. As a result, so the argument goes, women are exploited at work outside their homes, and they are exploited within their homes by the patriarchs. Linda Lim (1983) has offered a compelling critique of this position.[22] Proponents of the view that globalization results in the exploitation of women forget to ask themselves a crucial question: what is the opportunity

---

[20] Topalova, P. (2007), "Trade Liberalization, Poverty, and Inequality: Evidence from Indian Districts," in *Globalization and Poverty*, ed. A. Harrison, University of Chicago Press, Chicago, Chap. 7. No link between tariff reduction and poverty may exist for urban areas because the poor are usually concentrated in rural areas. See, for the example of Colombia, Goldberg, P. K., and N. Pavcnik (2007), "The Effects of the Colombia Trade Liberalization on Urban Poverty," in the same volume, Chap. 6.

[21] Cited in the previous footnote.

[22] Lim, L.Y.C. (1983), "Capitalism, Imperialism, and Patriarchy: The Dilemma of Third World Women Workers in Multinational Factories," in *Women, Men, and the International Division of Labor*, ed. J. Nash and M.P.F. Kelly, State University of New York Press, Albany.

cost of those who are employed by multinationals? If they are paid a pittance (by the standards of developed countries), it is because what women can earn in their next-best alternative is a pittance. In fact, it is precisely inexpensive labor that gives a comparative advantage to developing countries in labor-intensive products. If multinationals were forced to pay developed-country wages, they would have little incentive to locate in poor countries. This is also the argument made by Paul Krugman (1997).[23] By providing alternative sources of employment to those with few such opportunities, multinationals reduce the burden on land and raise the land-to-labor ratio in agriculture. As we saw in Section IV, this increases the wages of all workers.

In fact, it is typically the case that multinationals pay women more than what they would earn elsewhere in the economy. There are several reasons for this. One is that, by paying workers an "efficiency wage"—a wage above the market wage—firms reduce shirking by workers on the job by giving them a stake in keeping their lucrative jobs. Another reason is that, by paying their workers more than what they can earn elsewhere, firms can prevent workers from forming unions. Whatever the reason, it is the case that women working for multinationals in poor countries are better off than women who do not. This is also the opinion of the women themselves. Gillian Foo and Linda Lim (1989) report the gist of interviews with a sample of such Malaysian women.[24] These women offered many reasons that they preferred to work when employment was available, among which were that it increased their autonomy and enabled them to compensate their parents for the parents' expenditures on them.

If the people who work in multinationals themselves feel that they are better off by doing so, why is it that critics of globalization in rich countries argue that they are being exploited? In particular, Krugman asks why the critics ignore the millions who work for a pittance in poor countries but get exercised over those who work for a pittance in multinational firms. His answer is that it is perhaps because multinationals (such as Nike) import the output back into rich countries and consumers in the West feel "unclean" for using these products. Thus much of the criticism appears to be based on a self-righteousness that is not warranted because it ignores the greater number of workers who are paid just as poorly but are not employed by multinationals.

But let us return to the effect on patriarchy of women in developing countries working for multinationals. Is it conceivable that the patriarchs can make these women worse off for doing so? A patriarch could be a husband or,

---

[23] Krugman, P. (1997), "In Praise of Cheap Labor," *Slate*, March 27.

[24] Foo, G.H.C., and L.Y.C. Lim (1989), "Poverty, Ideology, and Women Export Factory Workers in South-East Asia," in *Women, Poverty, and Ideology in Asia*, ed. H. Afshar and B. Agarwal, Macmillan, Houndmills, UK.

perhaps, the father of the husband if the family lives with the man's parents. When a woman switches from not working outside the home or from working in a domestic firm to working in a multinational, she earns at least as much money as before and most likely more. (If not, why would she switch?) Even if her bargaining power within her household remains unchanged, she is likely to be better off, as will the rest of the family. This is because the family income is now higher and everybody will likely be able to consume more of the goods they prefer. For the woman to become worse off, her bargaining power will have to become substantially *lower* than it was before. This is very unlikely to happen when she is earning a higher income. She may certainly confront opposition from the patriarch because his status is being undermined. But he has a difficult trade-off to make: on the one hand, the family income is higher (which makes him better off), and, on the other, the woman's contribution to the family income is now higher (which makes him worse off). The patriarch may try to counteract the perceived decline in his status by exercising greater control over the woman. However, this is unlikely to fully offset the benefit to her of her greater financial contribution and independence. The empirical evidence that we reviewed in Chapter 3 firmly demonstrates that a woman's bargaining power increases, not decreases, when she earns more. So we can conclude that, although patriarchy may dilute the benefits to women of their higher income, it is very unlikely to make them worse off. Rather, it is patriarchy that is likely to be weakened.

We might expect, however, that the greater the impediments women face in responding to the new opportunities offered by globalization, the fewer will be the benefits they receive. In the developed countries, the more advantaged women may be expected to reap greater benefits because of their education, social networks, and so on. This is not necessarily so in developing countries, because women in the higher socioeconomic groups often have greater restrictions placed on their mobility. For example, in India the actions of women in the higher castes (who also tend to be more educated than those in lower castes) are scrutinized more closely by their households than those of other women, and their movements are more circumscribed. In such scenarios, paradoxically, the more disadvantaged women may benefit more from new opportunities.

Nancy Luke and Kaivan Munshi (2011) did a case study that confirms the above in a scenario analogous to that of globalization.[25] They studied the labor forces on some tea plantations in southern India. These plantations are located in mountainous regions, but they recruit permanent labor from the plains in the state of Tamil Nadu. The plantation workers retain ties with their ancestral homes on the plains in several ways: by marriage, by sending their children

[25] Luke, N., and K. Munshi (2011), "Women as Agents of Change: Female Income and Mobility in India," *Journal of Development Economics* 94, pp. 1–17.

back home for their studies, and by ultimately returning to the land in retirement. Around 90% of the workers hail from a few disadvantaged castes, but two-thirds of the workers are from the most disadvantaged. The ancestors of the latter were slaves until slavery was abolished in India by the British in the 1840s. Social ties between members of the same caste in India are usually pretty strong because they rely on each other for insurance purposes.[26] For example, the wife of a farmer who has fallen seriously ill may be able to rely on support from fellow caste members in her neighborhood with the understanding that their help will be reciprocated in the future. For the slave subcastes, however, these ties have traditionally not been very strong because the subcaste members have been geographically spread out and have had less communication between them than members of other castes.

Work on the tea plantations offers women from these disadvantaged groups a welcome opportunity for employment. The wages received by all castes are the same, and women from the former slave subcastes receive considerable respect. Luke and Munshi conjecture that, because this so, the women in these subcastes are more reluctant to retain ties with their ancestral homes for the reason that the costs of maintaining these ties fall disproportionately on them. If this conjecture is correct, it should be seen in less frequent marital alliances between their children and caste members on their ancestral land, in greater reluctance to send their children back to their ancestral land for schooling, and in educating their children to higher levels (making it less likely that they will return to their ancestral homes). This is precisely what Luke and Munshi find. And the effect is stronger in the former slave subcastes than in the other subcastes. So the most disadvantaged women have weaker impediments to overcome in embracing new opportunities. In the same manner, globalization may have an equalizing effect in a society because women in the most disadvantaged segments of the population may reap the highest benefits.

The discussion and evidence presented in this section suggest that globalization tends to undermine the institution of patriarchy. By increasing employment opportunities for women, it increases their bargaining power relative to men and levels the playing field somewhat.

VI. A Downside of Globalization: Increased Trafficking of Women

Lest we become too complacent about the beneficial effects of globalization on women, we shall now discuss one of the downsides of globalization. In the past few decades, just as national borders have been becoming more open

---

[26] See, for example, Munshi, K., and M. Rosenzweig (2009), "Why Is Mobility in India so Low?: Social Insurance, Inequality, and Growth," NBER Working Paper 14850, National Bureau of Economic Research, Cambridge, MA.

to foreign capital and foreign labor, there has been an astounding increase in the trafficking of women (and children).[27] This phenomenon is quite different from human smuggling. In the latter case, a smuggler illegally transports migrants without immigration papers across national borders for a certain sum of money. Once they have been transported, the illegal immigrants are left to themselves and survive as best they can by staying below the radar, as it were. In the case of human trafficking, however, there is a coercive element. Those who have been trafficked do not own their own persons. In fact, the very purpose of traffickers is to exploit the labor of their victims for profit. Trafficking reduces human beings to mere objects and commodities.

As reported by David Hodge and Cynthia Lietz (2007), from 0.6 to 0.8 million people are trafficked across countries annually for various purposes.[28] However, trafficking also occurs within countries, and when the people trafficked intranationally are included, the number of trafficked people ranges from 2 to 4 million per year. Around 80% of these are women (and girls), and most of them are trafficked for purposes of prostitution under conditions that are slavelike. In transnational trafficking (the focus of this section), the destination countries are rich: the United States, Japan, and Western European countries. The source countries are typically poor: those in Asia, Africa, the former Soviet Union, Eastern Europe, and Latin America. Transnational trafficking is largely done by organized crime groups. Next to the sale of drugs and weapons, this kind of trafficking ranks as the third-largest growth industry for organized crime. The victims are recruited in various ways, ranging from deception and fraud to purchase and kidnapping. After they have transported the victims to the destination countries, the traffickers confiscate their passports and put them to work mostly in prostitution under the threat of violence—to them or their families back home.[29] The profits are mostly siphoned off by the traffickers.

Organized crime is attracted to trafficking in women because prostitution (alternatively referred to as sex work) is a lucrative activity.[30] Before we proceed, therefore, it is important to understand why sex work is so lucrative. As Lena Edlund and Evelyn Korn (2002) point out, because prostitution (which they define as the offering of sex for nonreproductive purposes) is a relatively

---

[27] There is also trafficking of men, but men and children constitute a small fraction of the women who are trafficked.

[28] Hodge, D. R., and C. A. Lietz (2007), "The International Sexual Trafficking of Women and Children: A Review of the Literature," *Affilia* 22, pp. 163–174. The numbers and stylized facts in this paragraph are drawn from this useful review.

[29] Hodge and Leitz (2007) suggest that 70% of the trafficked women are forced into prostitution.

[30] For some evidence on this, see Ford, K.-A. (1998), "Evaluating Prostitution as a Human Service Occupation," in *Prostitution: On Whores, Hustlers, and Johns,* ed. J. E. Elias et al., Prometheus Books, Amherst, New York.

unskilled activity, it is puzzling that the returns should be so high.[31] They offer the view that marriage (which provides sex for reproductive and non-reproductive purposes) is the most relevant alternative to prostitution and that the two are more or less mutually exclusive. Because going into prostitution virtually rules out the possibility of marriage, women who do so have to be compensated for the lost opportunity. But then why is marriage so lucrative for women? Edlund and Korn reason as follows. Until very recently, when DNA testing became available, only maternity was certain; paternity was not. Maternity is easily verifiable because the birth of a child can be observed by others and motherhood certified. However, if the woman has been in a nonmonogamous relationship, the identity of the biological father is never certain. Edlund and Korn posit that men are willing to concede a great deal of income to their wives for assurance of paternity in the eyes of society. Thus marriage is lucrative for women. Through marriage, women share their claim to the parenthood of their children with their husbands. Thus the high price received by sex workers on average relative to unskilled workers is a *compensating differential,* a concept we encountered in Chapter 4: women in sex work have to be compensated for the forgone opportunity of marriage, which to them is relatively lucrative.

In light of the above, we can understand why trafficking women for sexual exploitation is attractive to those in organized crime. If middlemen between sex workers and the ultimate clients can appropriate the substantial compensating differential, it is very profitable for the traffickers. But this can and does happen even in closed economies. Why has transnational trafficking increased with globalization? As we have seen, globalization integrates world markets so that the demand for goods and services in one country can be satisfied by imports. In this case, the demand for prostitutes in rich countries can be satisfied to a considerable extent by trafficked women from poor countries. The flow of traffic is from poor to rich countries because the compensating differential (which determines the price of sex work) is much higher in rich countries. Traffickers can garner even higher profits with women trafficked from the developing world than they can by trafficking women from the same country because the poor are more easily enticed by false promises of the good life.

If prostitution is illegal in a country (as it is in many), it does not of course mean that the activity will be absent. Because enforcement is costly to the state and there is always a demand for it, prostitution cannot be completely eliminated. There will always be women who take the risk of illegally engaging in the activity, and pimps and traffickers will exploit many of these women by running illegal brothels. But because illegality raises the cost of

---

[31] Edlund, L., and E. Korn (2002), "A Theory of Prostitution," *Journal of Political Economy* 110, pp. 181–214.

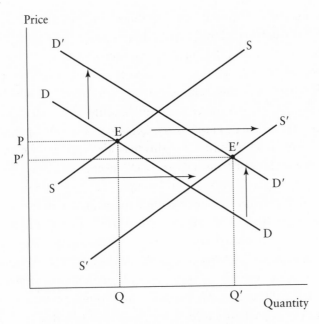

FIGURE 6.3 The effects of legalizing prostitution

providing the service and reduces its supply, the price that clients have to pay in market equilibrium will also have to be higher. If prostitution is made legal, the price of sexual services in the market might fall. One advantage of making prostitution legal is that the state can ensure that sex workers receive routine health checkups so that their health can be better monitored and sexually transmitted diseases can be controlled. Also, if some clients are violent and assault sex workers, the latter may have recourse to police protection. (They have little protection if sex work is illegal.) Furthermore, if some women prefer to engage in sex work (as opposed to being compelled into it by either pimps or traffickers), legalizing the activity does not marginalize them.

We may diagrammatically illustrate how various factors influence the price and quantity of sexual services transacted in the market. Consult Figure 6.3, in which the quantity of sexual services transacted in the market is represented along the horizontal axis and the price per unit of service along the vertical. Suppose that the economy is closed and that, initially, prostitution is deemed illegal. Despite its illegality, there will be a demand for sexual services in the underground market; the demand curve is shown in the figure as DD. It is downward sloping because presumably more services will be demanded when the price in the underground market is lower. The supply curve is shown as SS. It is upward sloping because, as more and more services are required, women with higher and higher opportunity costs will have to enter the market, and they will do this only if the price is higher. Likewise, owners of brothels will find it increasingly difficult to recruit greater supplies of women and, therefore, will require increasingly higher prices to do so. The illegal prostitution market will be in equilibrium at point E, where the quantities of services demanded and supplied are equal. The figure indicates the equilibrium price as P and the quantity transacted as Q.

Now suppose that the country legalizes prostitution but the economy is still closed. Clients wanting commercial sex who were previously afraid of being apprehended by the police may now manifest their demand. Furthermore, government regulation of sex workers may be seen by potential clients as making commercial sex safer, and this may also increase the demand. The demand curve shifts out from DD to D'D'; at each quantity, the price clients are willing to pay increases. On the supply side, women who want to be sex workers but were previously unwilling to engage in an illegal activity or to risk being apprehended by the police may now opt to become sex workers. The supply curve shifts from SS to S'S' in the figure. The legal market for prostitution clears at E'. Because both the demand and the supply curves have moved out, one thing is clear: in the legal market more transactions will occur than in the illegal one. Although the equilibrium price in the legal market, P', is shown in the figure to be lower, this need not always be the case: it depends on how much demand shifts relative to supply. For example, if the demand curve shifts out a lot but the supply curve does so only barely, the equilibrium price might well go up when prostitution becomes legal.

If the country's economy is integrated into the world market (due to globalization), the domestic prostitution market may attract trafficking. The market price of sexual services will be higher in the developed world than in developing countries because of the former's greater purchasing power. The higher the equilibrium price in a country, the greater the profit incentive for traffickers to bring women for sexual exploitation from countries where the price is lower. Thus the flow of trafficked women is invariably from poor to rich countries. Of course, because the supply increases if there is trafficking, the equilibrium price in the presence of globalization will be lower than the price P' shown in Figure 6.3.

Prostitution is an activity that invites diverse opinions. Many people have strongly held religious beliefs that prostitution is unacceptable. Many nonreligious people, too, believe that prostitution is immoral. Feminists are divided in their views on the legitimacy of prostitution.[32] On the one hand, some feminists claim that prostitution is an expression of male domination and is a form of violence against women. Their position is that prostitution should be abolished for this reason. Other feminists argue that women should have the freedom to choose their occupation and that prostitution (sex work) is a legitimate activity. In their view, making prostitution illegal

---

[32] For a good discussion of these views, see Outshoorn, J. (2005), "The Political Debates on Prostitution and Trafficking of Women," *Social Politics: International Studies in Gender, State, and Society* 12, pp. 141–155.

deprives some women of their chosen means of livelihood. They contend that it is not prostitution itself but rather the coercive and exploitative nature of trafficking that is unacceptable because it forces women into prostitution against their will.

Whatever the position one may adopt regarding the moral legitimacy of prostitution, however, we can address an important question via economics: does the legalization of prostitution increase or decrease trafficking in women? This is an issue because national governments might seek to legalize prostitution so that sex workers will register with them and the state can monitor their health, prevent the spread of sexually transmitted diseases, and so on. By making sex work legal, the government is opening up lines of communication with sex workers instead of hounding them for illegal activity and thus providing them greater protection from pimps and traffickers. From an economic standpoint, it might appear at first blush that if legalization drastically lowers the price of a product, organized crime will have less incentive to participate in the market. To cite a well-known example, the prohibition of alcohol in the United States in the 1920s increased the price of alcohol in the black market because supply was restricted. This led to the entry of organized crime into the black market for bootlegged alcohol—an unintended consequence that was very unpalatable and destructive to American society. (The same has been true in cases of the prohibition of various drugs.[33]) The repeal of prohibition in 1933 reduced the profits from alcohol to these organizations, which then sought their illegal profits elsewhere. One might be tempted to apply the same logic here to claim that the legalization of prostitution would reduce trafficking in women. However, as we have noted above, the effect of legalization on prices is ambiguous. Furthermore, legalizing prostitution might drastically lower the costs of trafficking operations because the traffickers will be able to evade scrutiny by passing off their activities as legal. The net effect on trafficking of the legalization of prostitution is theoretically ambiguous and so needs to be ascertained empirically.

Recently there have been some attempts to empirically discern this effect. One such endeavor was that of Niklas Jakobsson and Andreas Kotsadam (2013).[34] These researchers used data on European countries over the period 1996–2003 to assess the matter. Because not all countries have the same laws regarding prostitution, they were able to identify differences in the effects of legislation. They distinguish among three types of legal stances: (i) the buying and selling of sexual services are illegal; (ii) the buying and selling of sexual services are legal, but procuring these services is not, that is, acting as

---

[33] For a nuanced economic analysis, see Miron, J. A., and J. Zwiebel (1995), "The Economic Case against Drug Prohibition," *Journal of Economic Perspectives* 9 (4), pp. 175–192.

[34] Jakobsson, N., and A. Kotsadam (2013), "The Law and Economics of International Sex Slavery: Prostitution Laws and Trafficking for Sexual Exploitation," *European Journal of Law and Economics* 35, pp. 87–107.

pimps or owning brothels is illegal; and (iii) the buying and s elling of sexual services and procuring them are all legal. Clearly i can be deemed the most severe and iii the least severe of the three kinds of legislation. Jakobsson and Kotsadam coded trafficking into a country in five categories, depending on the intensity of trafficking into the country: very low, low, medium, high, and very high. In their statistical analysis, the authors found that trafficking is greater in countries with the least severe legislation regarding prostitution. In particular, if a country goes from regime i to regime iii in its legislation, the probability that it will be ranked high or very high on the trafficking scale goes up by about 68%.

Similar findings were obtained in a study by Seo-Young Cho, Axel Dreher, and Eric Neumayer (2013).[35] They argue that the legalization of prostitution has two effects on trafficking: the scale and the substitution effects. The scale effect is simply that, when prostitution is legalized, the market for sexual services increases in size, as we have seen. Even if the proportion of trafficked women among the prostitutes is the same as before, because the scale (that is, the size) of the market is greater, there will be more trafficked women. Cho et al. argue that there is another effect: when prostitution becomes legal, clients may move away from trafficked (still illegal) foreign prostitutes toward domestic (legal) prostitutes. The latter substitution effect reduces the number of trafficked women. So the effect of legalizing prostitution on the extent of trafficking is theoretically indeterminate. To determine the net effect, the authors use data from about 150 countries over the period 1996–2003. They find that the scale effect dominates; that is, on balance, the legalization of prostitution increases the trafficking of women.

Cho et al. also present some interesting case studies. In particular, the two Scandinavian countries Sweden and Denmark offer an interesting contrast. In 1999 Sweden made illegal the purchase of sex but not the sale of it. (The difference in treatment toward buyers and sellers was intended to prevent the victimization of women; the focus of the law was to curb the demand side of the market.) In contrast, neighboring Denmark made prostitution legal in 1999 but prohibited the operation of brothels. In 2004 the number of prostitutes and the number of trafficked women were around four times greater in Denmark than in Sweden—even though the population in Sweden was about 40% higher.

The evidence to date seems to suggest that legalizing prostitution actually increases the extent of trafficking of women.[36] How does this evidence

[35] Cho, S.-Y., A. Dreher, and E. Neumayer (2013), "Does Legalized Prostitution Increase Human Trafficking?," *World Development* 41, pp. 67–82.
[36] The evidence, however, is not so clearcut in Akee, R., A. Bedi, A. K. Basu, and N. H. Chau (2010), "Transnational Trafficking, Law Enforcement, and Victim Protection: A Middleman's Perspective," unpublished manuscript, Cornell University, Ithaca, NY. But see Cho et al. (2013) for a critique of the data inadequacies and methodological problems in this work.

help address differences between the two opposing feminist views, the one that prostitution is essentially a form of male violence against women and should be abolished and the other that women who voluntarily opt to make a living through prostitution should have a right to do so? To answer this from the standpoint of economics, we have to refer to the concept of externality. An externality occurs when one person's actions have economic consequences for others that they themselves do not bear. These consequences can be in the form of benefits to others (positive externalities) or in the form of costs (negative externalities). To the extent that negative externalities are significant, individual rights may need to be curbed in the collective interest. It may be reasonable to construe the trafficking of women—which makes some women much worse off to the point of abject slavery—as an externality arising from legalized prostitution markets in which some other women get to exercise their choice. Whatever our moral views on prostitution may be, there is little doubt that the trafficking of humans is decidedly dehumanizing and should be rooted out. Accounting for externalities, if these are serious enough, might rationally lead us to limit the freedom of some women who might voluntarily opt to sell sexual services. This is what economics will suggest if the evidence on the link between the legalization of prostitution and trafficking is substantiated by future research.

It may be reasonably argued that the trafficking of women is ultimately an offshoot of patriarchy. After all, it is women who are poor, helpless, and vulnerable who fall prey to trafficking, an activity that is largely conducted by men. Globalization may be said to have provided a vent to a ruthless aspect of patriarchy. How can we square this with the position we argued for in the previous section, that globalization has largely worked to undermine patriarchy? It is perhaps useful to keep in mind the proportions of women affected. As we have seen, anywhere between 2 and 4 million women per year are victims of domestic and transnational trafficking. Although this is a large number, the beneficial economic effects of globalization discussed in the previous section are spread over several billion women. On balance, it may be fair to say that globalization has worked to the benefit of the majority of women, but certainly not all women.

VII. Are Women More Protectionist Than Men?

Before we end this chapter, we should discuss the issue of gender differences in attitudes toward trade. The opinions of ordinary citizens on whether their countries should liberalize international trade are surprisingly divergent. In fact, as Anna Mayda and Dani Rodrik (2005) point out, in a widespread survey of people whose views were canvassed in opinion polls, 60% expressed the opinions that their countries should protect domestic industries from international competition, that is, they were protectionist.[37] Furthermore, there was a definite gender bias in the opinions: women were typically more protectionist, at least in the developed countries.

Before we inquire as to why there is a gender gap in views about trade liberalization, it will be useful to review the considerations that economic theory suggest are important in influencing the views of people on this issue. If inputs can freely move across different sectors, the Stolper–Samuelson theorem discussed earlier predicts that the prices of inputs that are in more abundant supply in a country will increase upon liberalization, whereas the opposite will be the case for those of the scarce inputs. The country will have a comparative advantage in the goods that intensively use the abundant—and therefore cheap—inputs. These will flow into the sectors that are export oriented and thereby benefit from the higher demand for their use. In the twenty-first century, the input that is probably the most important is human capital (skill). As we have seen earlier, the distribution of human capital differs between rich and poor countries. Suppose that for simplicity we take education as the measure of human capital, even though work experience is also important for skill development. In the developed countries, education levels are high and so skilled labor will be deemed the abundant input and unskilled labor the scarce input. In developing countries, in contrast, it is unskilled labor that is the abundant input and skilled labor that is the scarce one.

Let us briefly recapitulate an argument reviewed in Section III in our discussion of the Heckscher–Ohlin theory. When a developed country opens itself up to international trade and its inputs can freely move across different sectors, the Stolper–Samuelson theorem predicts that the wage of skilled labor will increase and that of unskilled labor will decrease. If the country is developing, the reverse will be the case. Therefore, economic theory predicts that in the developed world individuals with high levels of human capital (a large proportion of the people) will be pro-trade. On the other hand, in the developing world individuals with high levels of human capital (a small proportion of the population) will be protectionist.

But what happens if the inputs cannot freely move across sectors, that is, if they are useful only in specific sectors? For example, in our treatment in Section III, land was an example of an input that was useful only in agriculture and had no use in industry. In this case, economic theory predicts that support for or opposition to trade will depend on whether individuals own inputs used in a sector with a comparative advantage or a comparative disadvantage. Clearly the owners will favor trade in the former case and oppose it in the latter. For example, in the discussion accompanying Figure 6.2, we

[37] Mayda, A. M., and D. Rodrik (2005), "Why Are Some People (and Countries) More Protectionist Than Others?," *European Economic Review* 49, pp. 1393–1430.

saw that the owners of land will welcome trade if the country has a comparative advantage in agriculture and oppose it if the country has a comparative disadvantage in agriculture.

Mayda and Rodrik (2005) tested such predictions about the support for trade. For this they used two sets of survey data. One set (from the International Social Survey Program, ISSP) contained information on opinions canvassed in 1995 about whether trade should be liberalized and other economic and demographic details from individuals in 23 countries. Most of these were developed countries, but one was a developing country (the Philippines). The other data set (from the World Value Survey) was drawn from 47 countries. The authors found strong confirmation for the theoretical predictions. The support expressed for trade increased with the education levels of individuals in the rich countries, but the reverse was true in the poor country (the Philippines). The results for the case in which inputs are specific to sectors were somewhat weaker but did not contradict the theory.

Mayda and Rodrik also found that there was a substantial gender gap in the support for trade. This was so even after accounting for many economic and demographic factors that may differ between women and men. There was about 7.7% more support for protectionism among women. The gender difference was first examined at length by Brian Burgoon and Michael Hiscox (2003).[38] Their analysis was based on a survey of 1,600 American adults conducted in 2003. They controlled for a host of socioeconomic variables, including skill level, occupation, industry of employment, and so on. Despite this, the authors found a large gender difference in opinions on trade liberalization: women's stances were more protectionist. Why? Trade introduces a fair amount of disruption—some industries shrink and others expand, and there is uncertainty about whether one will be laid off and, if that happens, whether another job can be found, and so on. Could it be that women are more averse to risk than men and so desire more protection? If so, women will require the government to offer assistance to those who lose their jobs due to increased trade. The authors found, however, that men and women did not differ in their opinions as to whether the government should give assistance to those who became unemployed as a result of trade. So any male–female difference in attitudes toward risk could not be the reason for the gender gap in opinions regarding trade liberalization. The gender gap, they found, survived even after they accounted for differences in ideology (liberal versus conservative views) and also religion.

Burgoon and Hiscox noticed that, in their sample, the gender gap was negligible among the less educated but was substantial among college-

[38] Burgoon, B., and M. J. Hiscox (2003), "The Mysterious Case of Female Protectionism: Gender Bias in Attitudes toward International Trade," paper presented at the Annual Meeting of the American Political Science Association, Philadelphia, PA, August 28–31.

educated individuals. Furthermore, within the group of college-educated people, the gender gap increased with age. Taking their cue from this, the authors argued that differences in exposure to economic ideas may be the answer to the puzzle of the gender gap. The idea is that those who have been exposed to economics courses are more likely to understand the benefits of trade. Among college-going students today, the authors argued, there is not much difference by gender in the students taking courses in economics. However, when they went back a few decades to the 1960s, they observed that a substantially higher proportion of men had taken economics courses. In 2003, the older people among the educated would have been those who went to college in previous decades, and fewer women than men would have taken economics. This is the explanation that Burgoon and Hiscox offered for the gender gap in the desirability of protectionism and its peculiar age dependence.

The above explanation, however, has to be taken as a tentative hypothesis that requires confirmation. As Eugene Beaulieu and Michael Napier (2008) pointed out, the size of the sample on which this hypothesis was based was a relatively small one and, in addition, was drawn from only one country (the United States).[39] To rectify these problems, Beaulieu and Napier analyzed ISSP data for 24 and 35 countries for the years 1995 and 2003, respectively. They too found that, after controlling for a host of socioeconomic variables that might be relevant, there was a substantial gender gap (8% in 1995 and 9% in 2003) in the perceived desirability of trade protection. Interestingly, they found that the gender gap was present in rich countries but *not* in poor countries, but they did not uncover a reason for this. The gender gap in opinions about trade liberalization is still a puzzle that awaits resolution.

It is conceivable that women in the developed world are more sensitive than men to gender-specific vulnerabilities (such as trafficking) and this makes them more wary of globalization. Statistical studies to date do not capture such concerns. More research is required on this issue.

VIII. Summary

This chapter was motivated by the importance of globalization in recent decades and the changes it has been bringing about in the economic lives of all people, especially women. We first summarized the logic of some well-established predictions of trade theory and went on to discuss the intuition of the Heckscher–Ohlin theory. This theory predicts that, on opening up to international trade, developing countries should see an increase in the wage for unskilled labor and a decline in that for skilled labor. According to

---

[39] Beaulieu, E., and M. Napier (2008), "Why Are Women More Protectionist Than Men?," unpublished manuscript, University of Calgary, Calgary, Alberta.

this theory, to the extent that women are more unskilled than men, the gender wage gap should decline with trade in poor countries and the opposite should happen in the developed world.

We went on to review the various reasons for which multinationals engage in FDI. We then discussed the many potential benefits of FDI for poor countries—from increasing employment to providing domestic workers with human capital. Women, in particular, should benefit from the opportunities offered by FDI.

Next we discussed the empirical evidence on how trade impinges on the well-being of women relative to men. Looking at the contrast between East Asian and African countries, we saw that much of the effect of trade depends on the distribution by gender of land ownership and on the nature of the goods exported by the countries. We saw why women become better off relative to men in developing countries that export labor-intensive goods and why they become worse off relative to men in countries that export land-intensive goods.

We then went on to survey the evidence on the effect of trade on the gender wage gap. Consistent with theoretical expectation, for unskilled workers the gender wage gap declines in poor countries. Furthermore, we saw that FDI can reduce the gender wage gap if it increases the demand for women's labor. However, it can also undermine women's bargaining power if foreign capital is very mobile and can quickly go offshore.

Using India as a case study, we reviewed evidence revealing that in the past 20 years globalization has increased the returns to human capital for women and that this has elicited an increase in schooling for girls. Thus pressure from globalization can overcome cultural norms that militate against the education of girls. However, we also saw that in regions where people fall into poverty when tariff protection is removed, girls can be withdrawn from schools.

We next considered the issue of whether globalization undermines the institution of patriarchy. We saw that, to the extent that globalization offers women employment opportunities that were previously unavailable to them, their own earned income will increase their bargaining power relative to the patriarchs within their households and will make women better off.

We also studied one scenario in which globalization has worsened matters for women: transnational trafficking. We studied the economics of this phenomenon and also examined the evidence on whether legalizing prostitution increases or decreases trafficking in women.

Finally we discussed some empirical findings on attitudes toward protectionism. In rich countries, women are more protectionist than men. This gender gap in preferences for protection is still a puzzle that awaits resolution by more research.

Exercises and Questions for Discussion

1. Consider a closed economy with two productive inputs: land and labor. All people supply labor, but only men own and supply land. The economy produces two goods: food in agriculture (which requires labor and land) and cloth in industry (which requires only labor). Consumers demand both food and cloth. Suppose that the economy, initially in autarky, embarks on free trade with the rest of the world.

(a) Explain the process through which labor will reallocate itself between the two sectors when the country has a comparative advantage in cloth production.

(b) Explain the process through which labor will reallocate itself between the two sectors when the country has comparative advantage in food production.

2. Now consider how the scenario described in Question 1 determines the relative bargaining powers of the male and female members of a couple. Women earn only labor income, whereas men earn labor income and rental income from their land (by renting out their land to cultivators). The bargaining power of women in households is determined by their threat utility, which in turn is determined by their income; the same is true for men.

(a) On opening up to international trade, suppose that a country has a comparative advantage in cloth production. How will the bargaining power of women change as a result? Explain.

(b) On opening up to international trade, suppose that the country has a comparative advantage in food production. How will the bargaining power of women change as a result? Explain.

(c) Using the logic of your explanations in a and b, can you explain why in the past five decades women in East Asia benefited from international trade but women in Africa did not?

(d) Discuss the role played by the ownership of assets (here land) in the gendered impact of international trade.

3. Consider the reasons motivating FDI and its benefits. In particular:

(a) What are the reasons that multinational companies engage in FDI?

(b) What benefits accrue to poor countries from this FDI?

(c) Are there benefits that accrue to women in particular in poor countries from FDI undertaken in their countries?

4. From the recent experience of India with globalization, what general lessons can one learn with regard to the following:

(a) The effect of globalization on the returns to human capital and the response in terms of schooling for girls.

(b) The effect of globalization on poverty and the response in terms of schooling for girls.

5. It is often argued that multinationals exploit women in developing countries by paying them a pittance compared to what they would earn in rich countries. Do you agree that women in poor countries are exploited in this manner? Explain your reasoning.

6. Can you suggest reasons that globalization has been partly responsible for the retreat of patriarchy?

7. Why has globalization increased the transnational traffic in women and children? Why is the trafficking flow from poor countries to rich ones? What is the empirical evidence on how legislation regarding prostitution in destination countries affects the extent of transnational trafficking in women?

8. Suppose that in a rich closed economy commercial sex is illegal. An underground market for commercial sex develops, and the demand for the sexual services of women is given by $q^d = 200 - 3P$, and the supply of these services is given by $q^s = 100 + P$, where P denotes the price in dollars per sexual act transacted and quantities are measured in thousands of acts.

(a) Compute the market clearing price in the illegal market and the amount of sex work transacted in this equilibrium.

(b) Now suppose that the government legalizes sex work. As a result, the demand and supply curves change to $q^d = 230 - 3P$ and $q^s = 110 + P$, respectively. Can you explain why the demand and supply might shift in this manner? Compute the new equilibrium price and quantity.

(c) Now suppose that the country integrates with the world market and allow for the possibility that the trafficking of sex workers into the country is an unfortunate accompaniment of this integration. Comparing your answers in parts a and b above, do you think the transnational trafficking of women into the country is likely to be greater when prostitution is legal in the country or when it is illegal? Why?

(d) Using this example as a springboard for discussion, elaborate on how economics can contribute to the debate on whether or not prostitution should be legal.

9. (a) Discuss the economic reasons that would influence the opinions of the owners of the inputs of production on how protectionist or liberal a country should be with regard to trade.

(b) Can you suggest some possible reasons why there is a persistent gender gap in the rich countries in the opinions with regard to protectionism?

Marriage and Fertility

CHAPTER SEVEN

How Do Women Fare in the Institution of Marriage?

I. Introduction

Of all the institutions that affect women's (and men's) well-being, marriage is surely an extremely important one. Recent studies on the factors that contribute to human happiness have identified a strong connection between being married (or cohabiting) and being happy. In this chapter we shall examine many of the observed features of this institution and seek to understand why they arise and what role gender plays. We shall take a largely economic view here, though I often present and discuss other points of view when pertinent.

Because marriage is observed in every society around the world, we tend to take the institution for granted. Though it is ubiquitous now, it was not necessarily so in our evolutionary past. So we shall seek to discover why people find it necessary to marry (or cohabit). And then, after reviewing the various beneficial consequences of marriage in contemporary societies, we shall step back to inquire into what perceived *private* benefits may motivate people to get married.

Among the causes and consequences of marriage, one is division of labor: women and men have tended to concentrate on different activities. This specialization has economic benefits that enable both partners and their children to become better off. Well-being, however, is not necessarily measured in terms of economic costs and benefits. We shall discuss a theory from evolutionary psychology in which costs and benefits can be interpreted in evolutionary terms, too. Nature cares nothing for individual well-being or happiness; what matters to natural selection is survival. An institution that promotes survival is likely to become an accepted and entrenched part of society as long as natural selection is in operation.

Even if we understand the private benefits that motivate marriage, however, we must still understand the particular form that marriage takes. One can conceive of many forms of marriage. It might occur as polygyny, in which one man has many wives; as polyandry, in which one woman has more than one husband; as monogamy, in which each person has only one spouse; or as serial monogamy, in which a person can have many spouses over a lifetime but only one spouse at a time. Historically, polygyny has been observed frequently. In fact, it is still practiced in several countries. No doubt, religion has much to do with this, but economics does, too. The institution of polyandry, however, is quite rare. In most democracies, monogamy is the norm. It is important to understand why the institution of marriage has taken on some forms and why it has gravitated to monogamy in modern times, at least in the developed countries.

The practice of paying a bride or groom price or offering a dowry often accompanies marriage. Upon marriage, if a groom or his family transfer some form of wealth to the bride's family, the payment is referred to as a *bride price*. If the bride's parents transfer some wealth to the groom or his parents, the payment is called a *groom price*. If the parents' gift is to their own daughter, it is called a *dowry*. It has been argued that a dowry may not be a payment of any kind—it may be the bride's share of her inheritance. In practice, however, the distinction between a groom price and a dowry tends to become muddied because the bride may not get to control her dowry. It is interesting to inquire why such marital practices arose. Dowries and bride prices may be things of the past in the developed countries, but in the developing world they are still widely prevalent practices. Bride prices are observed in African countries, dowries in South Asian countries, and in some regions of China one observes both. It is important to inquire how and why such practices arose in the context of marriage because they seriously impinge on the well-being of brides and grooms.

The division of labor that occurs within marriage has important consequences for the human capital acquired by women and men. Because there is a greater incentive to acquire education if one plans to participate in the labor market and more occasion to accumulate on-the-job skills when one is actually on the job, the marital division of labor has profound effects on the labor market incomes of women and men. Differences in this income become all the more important when we recognize that they impinge on the relative bargaining powers of the partners. Research has shown, however, that the ability of women to participate in market work depends on the availability of household appliances that reduce their housework. Furthermore, it has become increasingly clear in recent research that the extent to which women avail themselves of the market opportunities also depends on their sense of identity and how tethered they are to the notion that their place is in the home. An understanding of the work and human capital consequences of marriage is very important in making sense of how changes in the labor market have altered the lives of women in the past six decades in the developed countries and more recently in the urban areas of developing countries.

The effects of what happens within the household can often be expected to spill over into the marketplace. For example, a housewife who takes care of the couple's children and all of the housework enables her spouse to focus exclusively on his job. This freedom from all "distracting" activities and effort may increase his productivity on the job and fetch him higher earnings in the labor market. If this is so, married men will earn incomes that are higher than those of similarly qualified unmarried men. It would be interesting to know if this is a fact.

Although the benefits to marriage are many, it is clear that a significant proportion of marriages go sour. An extreme feature of some unhappy marriages is spousal violence. Women sometimes become trapped in physically abusive marriages. Although some abused women leave their spouses, others do not, and occasionally this choice results in their death through spousal homicide. What are the causes of domestic violence, and why don't abused women leave their violent partners? We might suspect that physical violence may be motivated by the desire to curtail women's independence through the use of physical force because men, on average, are stronger. We might also conjecture that abused women don't leave because they have few outside options. Is this empirically true? If so, what are the policy measures that governments can undertake to minimize domestic violence? These are important questions that warrant answers.

Finally, there is the important issue of marital dissolution or divorce. More and more marriages have been ending in divorce over the past several decades in the developed world. This, no doubt, is partly because women's participation in the labor market has been increasing, so they are becoming more independent. One may suspect that more marriages are also dissolved partly because of changes in divorce laws that have made it possible for a divorce to be obtained even if only one party wants it. Theoretical arguments have been put forward claiming that divorce laws should make no difference in the incidence of divorce under certain circumstances. What are these arguments, and are they empirically borne out? Furthermore, it has been argued that, on average, women's standard of living falls after divorce. Is this so? These are important questions to answer, especially because the traditional division of labor within the household puts women at a disadvantage in the labor market that they are forced to enter after a divorce.

The topics alluded to above and the questions posed constitute the focus of interest in this chapter.

II. Social and Private Benefits of Marriage

In recent decades, research has documented numerous benefits to marriage, many of them accruing at the private level to individuals. These benefits are not merely economic; they are also psychological. Furthermore, some of the benefits also accrue to society at large because individual actions often have external consequences for others. A couple's well-adjusted and educated children, for example, benefit society by being law-abiding and tax-paying adults. Children who have not been suitably socialized, on the other hand, may engage in crime as adults and become a burden to society. The existence of such positive and negative "externalities" undoubtedly is one of the reasons that almost all societies in the world highly regulate the institution of marriage through norms and laws. The idea is to ensure, as far as is possible, that the positive externalities to society are maximized and the negative minimized. Before we launch into individual motivations for embarking on marriage, it would be good to be aware of the social and psychological benefits of this institution in contemporary societies.

Less Crime

One of the effects of marriage is on crime rates. Most crimes are committed by males, and the effect of marriage on crime mostly pertains to males. If we examine the criminal records of married men and those of comparable unmarried men, we may find that the former have lower crime rates. There is an important issue pertaining to causality, however. Is it the case that getting married reduces criminal activity in men, or is it that men who are not prone to commit crimes are the types who are more likely to marry? If the men who tend to marry are less crime prone to begin with, marriage may have nothing to do with their lower levels of criminal activity. If this is the case, we cannot attribute any crime-reducing benefit to marriage.

To resolve this issue of causality (does A cause B, or does B cause A?), researchers often use data on the same individuals over long periods of time in which they have made a transition from being single to being married. (Data on many observations of the same individuals are referred to as *longitudinal data*.) So they can compare the criminal activities of the *same* persons before and after marriage, and these results will give the researchers more confidence in their findings on the effect of marriage on crime. One such study, among many, has been conducted by Robert Sampson, John Laub, and Christopher Wimer (2006), who tracked individuals over a period of 70 years.[1] These authors used a classic data set of 500 high-risk males between 17 and 32 years of age from Massachusetts, conducting interviews with 52 of them (between the ages of 17 and 70 years). They found through

---

[1] Sampson, R., J. H. Laub, and C. Wimer (2006), "Does Marriage Reduce Crime?: A Counterfactual Approach to Within-Individual Causal Effects," *Criminology* 44, pp. 465–508.

their statistical analysis that entry into marriage does indeed cause a reduction in criminal activity (to the tune of 35%). Among the reasons the authors give for this finding is that the event of marriage offers individuals with a criminal past the opportunity to make a fresh start and to create a new identity by bonding with a spouse who monitors their activities.

This benefit of marriage to men, however, depends on when the men get married. If they get married late, their criminal activities do not decline appreciably. Delphine Theobald and David Farrington (2011) examine why a previous Cambridge University study of over 400 offenders in London showed that those who married early were more likely to give up criminal activities than those who got married later.[2] One of the contributing factors was drug use: those who married late were more likely to be drug users, and drug use seems to correlate with continued criminal activity after marriage. When men marry early, they normally reduce the amount of time they spend with their peers. This is not so to the same extent, however, among men who marry late. All in all, it appears that men who marry late are more set in their ways and are less likely to change for the better; the good effects of a spouse do not materialize as much.

More generally, there is an age dependence in criminal behavior: across all societies, the frequency of criminal activity rises in adolescence and early adulthood and then declines when men are in their twenties and thirties. Satoshi Kanazawa and Mary Still (2000) offer a theory, based on the work of Martin Daly and Margo Wilson (1988) in evolutionary psychology, that bears on this and the issue of marriage.[3] The number of children that they father varies considerably across men. In our evolutionary past, men who were very successful at finding mates fathered many children, while those who were unsuccessful had few. The latter were less likely to pass on their genes and so were more likely to become evolutionarily extinct. Because they had little or nothing to lose, nature devised a strategy on their behalf; these men undertake risky activities such as stealing resources, which in turn attracts mates. It is not that these men think like this; they only feel the urge to steal, and it so happens that there is an evolutionary payoff because the resources they acquire increase their chances of finding a mate. So after puberty, men have a built-in proclivity for crime that may kick in if they have little to lose. However, as they get older they are more likely to have found a mate and have had one or more children. Now they do have a lot to lose by engaging in crime. If they are caught and punished, injured, or killed, their children are more likely to die for want of resources. So natural selection,

[2]Theobald, D., and D. P. Farrington (2011), "Why Do the Crime-Reducing Effects of Marriage Vary with Age?," *British Journal of Criminology* 51, pp. 136–158.

[3]Kanazawa, S., and M. C. Still (2000), "Why Men Commit Crimes (and Why They Desist)," *Sociological Theory* 18, pp. 434–447, and Daly, M., and M. Wilson (1988), *Homicide,* Hawthorne, Aldine de Gruyter, New York.

through trial and error, builds in a resistance to criminal activity in parents. In this way, marriage may make men more responsible—not because they necessarily make a conscious decision to be so but because nature found it expedient to hard-wire such behavior into them.

We should not push this evolutionary argument too far, however, for it suggests that crime is more likely among the poor. This implication is also consistent with standard economic theory that would suggest that the poor commit more crimes because they perceive time as having a lower opportunity cost and so the punishment for crimes (jail time) is less costly to them. An interesting study of crime in India was done by Jean Dreze and Reetika Khera (2000) and explicitly shows that this claim is certainly not true for all crimes.[4] These researchers examined how homicides in Indian districts varied with the characteristics of the districts.[5] They found that districts with a greater incidence of poverty did not exhibit higher homicide rates.

More relevant to the issue of gender, however, Dreze and Khera found that the homicide rate was higher in districts where the sex ratio (number of females to males) was lower. Why was this? A reason they offer, which is highly plausible in the context of India, has to do with patriarchy. The districts that are highly patriarchal (which tend to be in northern parts of the country) exhibit more of a culture of violence. But these are also the types of societies in which male children are preferred over female children. This preference translates through various means into a lower ratio of females to males.[6] This could account for the fact that high homicide rates and low female-to-male ratios go together. The lower sex ratios may also incite more violence for the evolutionary reasons that Kanazawa and Still (2000) suggested. A scarcity of women would make finding spouses more difficult for men, and they might resort to violence to secure mates, which might, in turn, lead to deaths. We may speculate that marriage may lower crime rates through this avenue, too, because men who have found mates will withdraw from the strife.

Less Alcohol and Drug Abuse
There is considerable evidence that marriage reduces the consumption of alcohol and drugs. Here again there is the question of causality, for it is unclear whether those who consume less alcohol and drugs are more likely to be the marrying kind. What reasons are there to suspect that the causality goes from marriage to reduced consumption of these products? As Greg Duncan, Bessie Wilkerson, and Paula England (2006) point out, one reason might be

---

[4] Dreze, J., and R. Khera (2000), "Crime, Gender, and Society in India: Insights from Homicide Data," *Population and Development Review* 26, pp. 335–352.

[5] Although data on other crimes such as rape, theft, burglary, and so on are available, the authors settled on homicide because data on these other crimes are likely to suffer from severe under-reporting.

[6] This is an issue we shall study in Chapter 8.

that marriage is viewed as an institution in which one gets to "clean up one's act."[7] Another is that, because married people typically live together, each spouse can easily monitor the activities of the other, and this may help reduce the consumption of these substances. These authors examined the issue using nationally representative longitudinal data from the United States covering the period 1979–2000. Using an 11-year window (from 5 years before the year of marriage to 5 years after), they examined whether marriage or cohabitation changed behaviors and how these changes depended on gender.

The authors found that the effect of marriage differs by gender. Men's binge drinking and marijuana consumption declined significantly with marriage. However, women's binge drinking declined but their marijuana consumption remained the same. The cigarette consumption of both sexes was not affected by marriage. Those conducting this study were careful to separate the effect of marriage from the effect of age. It is well known that the consumption of the substances in question declines with age. Because married people tend to be older, was the effect of age being mistakenly attributed to marriage? To ensure that this was not the case, the authors compared not the actual consumption levels but rather the trends in consumption before and after marriage. The effect of age was already present in the trend (lower consumption in older people). It was the difference in trends before and after marriage that captured the effect of marriage.

Better Physical and Psychological Health

Given that we have already seen that marriage helps reduce risky behavior such as engaging in alcohol binges, we might suspect that marriage might have what is called a "protective effect" on health. There is an extensive literature suggesting that marriage has health consequences: married people are in better physical and mental health.[8] Much of the literature is devoted to isolating the causality. If the married people in the sample exhibit better health than those who are not married, it may be because healthy people have self-selected into the married state because they are healthy. This is called the *selection effect*. Before we can conclude from the data that marriage confers health benefits, we have to be careful to separate the selection effect from the protection effect that we wish to isolate. One way to deal with this issue, as we have seen, is by using longitudinal data, because that affords observations on the same individuals both in and out of the married state.

In a study of the effect of marriage on longevity, Lee Lillard and Linda Waite (1995) used longitudinal American data from the period 1968–85 to

---

[7]Duncan, G. J., B. Wilkerson, and P. England (2006), "Cleaning Up Their Act: The Effects of Marriage and Cohabitation on Licit and Illicit Drug Use," *Demography* 43, pp. 691–710.

[8]This literature is nicely summarized by Wilson, C. M., and A. J. Oswald (2005), "How Does Marriage Affect Physical and Psychological Health?: A Survey of the Longitudinal Evidence," Discussion Paper 1619, Institute for the Study of Labor, Bonn.

compare married people with those in four other groups: never married, separated, divorced, and widowed.[9] They found that married individuals have a significantly lower risk of dying than unmarried ones. The decline in mortality risk in the case of women is largely because married couples have higher per capita incomes (for reasons we shall discuss later), and this affords women better nutrition, healthcare, and so on. Furthermore, the effects seem to be cumulative: the longer the duration of the marriage, the greater the benefits in terms of longevity. For men, the benefits of marriage materialize immediately and appear to be largely due to a decline in behavior that is risky to health. The study also found that the death of a spouse has different effects by gender: the risk of mortality for widowed men is much greater than that for widows.

Although there is persuasive evidence of the effect of marriage on longevity, the underlying mechanisms responsible for this effect are unclear. In a study using British longitudinal data, Jonathan Gardner and Andrew Oswald (2004) found that the beneficial effect of marriage on longevity is significant for both men and women and stronger than that of income.[10] The effect of marriage on longevity is equivalent to that of cutting out cigarette smoking for men and half that for women. However, the researchers also found that although mental stress reduces longevity, the effect of marriage on longevity is not through stress reduction; marriage has an independent effect.

In the fields of psychology, sociology, and more recently economics, there is also a substantial literature documenting the effects on psychological well-being of marriage. Married people are happier than others and are less prone to depression. One study in economics, done by David Blanchflower and Andrew Oswald (2004) on two affluent countries (the United States and the United Kingdom), offers an informative perspective on this issue.[11] The authors examined the factors that impinged on self-reported measures of happiness that were given in response to standard questions.[12] They found that, in both the United States and the United Kingdom, having more money improves a sense of well-being. Among other factors, they found that the state of marriage and that of being unemployed have the most serious effects (in opposite directions). From their estimates, being married is equivalent in effect to having an extra income of $100,000 a year. This is a substantial effect.

---

[9] Lillard, L. A., and L. J. Waite (1995), "'Til Death Do Us Part: Marital Disruption and Mortality," *American Journal of Sociology* 100, pp. 1131–1156.

[10] Gardner, J., and A. Oswald (2004), "How Is Mortality Affected by Money, Marriage, and Stress?," *Journal of Health Economics* 23, pp. 1181–1207.

[11] Blanchflower, D., and A. Oswald (2004), "Well-being Over Time in Britain and the USA," *Journal of Public Economics* 88, pp. 1359–1386.

[12] The question is this: "Taken all together, how would you say things are these days—would you say that you are very happy, pretty happy, or not too happy?"

Many of the benefits of family formation, such as those we have just seen, occur only at the level of society (because of externalities). Because family units form only if there are substantial *private* benefits, we now ask these questions: Why do people form family units? Why do they marry or cohabit? If this seems natural, we should remind ourselves that during the hunting and gathering phase of our evolution (which comprised around 99% of our time as humans), family units did not form. So what changed that made humans all over the world find it worthwhile to have marital arrangements? We discuss two viewpoints below, one from economics and the other from evolutionary psychology.

The Economic View

The reasons that economists offer to answer the question "Why marry?" are largely derived from the seminal work of Gary Becker (1981).[13] Becker developed a theory that is based on the theory of comparative advantage, which has proved quite useful in the theory of international trade. In effect, when a family unit forms (that is, when people marry), they can specialize in different activities, and this division of labor allows both parties to benefit from the arrangement. Who specializes in an activity depends on who has a comparative advantage in that activity.

Consider two activities that are important to survival and reproduction: (i) bringing in resources ("market work" in today's context) and (ii) converting resources into consumable form and raising children ("housework" for short). The former activity usually requires one to work away from the home, especially in evolutionary and historical settings, while the latter can be done at home. Consider two individuals, Anne and Brett, who are contemplating the formation of a family unit. How should they specialize? In one day, suppose that Brett can bring in 2 units of resources but can convert 1 unit into consumable form. So his opportunity cost of performing activity i is ½ and that of performing ii is 2. This is because he has to give up ½ unit of housework output to generate 1 unit of resources from the market and 2 units of market resources to generate 1 unit of housework output. In contrast, suppose that in one day Anne can bring in 1 unit of resources but is able to convert 2 units into consumable form. Her opportunity cost in i is 2 and in ii is ½. We can say that Anne has a comparative advantage in activity ii and Brett has a comparative advantage in activity i. In determining who should specialize in what, Anne and Brett would clearly see that each activity should be performed by the person with the *lower* opportunity cost (that is, each of them should perform the activity

---

[13] Becker, G. (1981), *A Treatise on the Family*, Harvard University Press, Cambridge, MA. This book is based on several papers by Becker on the subject.

in which he or she has a comparative advantage). This is because less of the alternative activity is given up as a result. They can each specialize in doing what they are relatively good at, and both can benefit when they form a family unit and share their outputs.

The above argument on specialization hinges on the assumption that Anne and Brett differ in their comparative advantage. The theory, so far, offers no prescription for a division of labor when both have identical skills; there is no role for specialization. Becker makes an important point in this context. He argues that people usually become more efficient at doing a job the longer they work at it. Put differently, the returns to an activity increase the more that people engage in it. The highest return can be garnered only when a person completely specializes in it. So even if Anne and Brett have identical skills to begin with, they can do better for themselves if they form a family unit, with each specializing in one activity and sharing the output. That way, the family unit receives the highest returns on *both* activities—which is something that is not possible if, for example, both Anne and Brett work part time in both activities. In other words, even if Anne and Brett have identical abilities to start with, there are gains to be made if each specializes in a different activity and they share the proceeds.

But how are they to decide on their activity of specialization, especially if they have identical skills to begin with? This is where even the slightest differences in abilities become relevant. Women alone give birth, and they alone lactate. So it is reasonable to claim that, at least in the early years of a child's life, women have a comparative advantage in taking care of children. What is more, while they are nursing one child, they may be able to monitor their older children, too. If this claim is accepted, then even if Anne and Brett have identical skills in bringing in resources, as in activity i, Anne's comparative advantage in ii should translate into a prescription that she should specialize in ii and Brett in i.

I should emphasize that for the above argument to be made we are not required to claim that only women can take care of young children or that men simply cannot. Such a claim would be untenable. All that is required is that women have a *comparative* advantage in activity ii, no matter how small this advantage is. But the consequences of this specialization are quite enormous. Because specialization increases the efficiency with which the specialist does the job, even if Anne and Brett were initially equally capable of market work, after specialization the disparity in their abilities could be quite great. Thus small differences can be magnified by specialization.

This, then, is the essential reason offered by economists as to why marriage occurs. Specialization, however, has its dangers: it makes women more vulnerable to breakups. If Brett wants a divorce after Anne has specialized for many years in housework and raising children, she can find herself in dire straits. To protect against this possibility, society offers women various legal measures such as giving mothers exclusive custody of children (until recently) and requiring their former husbands to pay alimony, child care expenses, and so on. In this sense, Becker claims that marriage is a contract that, if broken, requires reparation. These legal measures also make formal marriage more of a commitment for both parties than the more informal arrangement of cohabitation.

One of the important consequences of specialization is that the bargaining power of women is adversely affected. As discussed in Chapter 3, Torben Iversen and Frances Rosenbluth (2010, Chap. 2) have argued that women's bargaining power depends on the technology of production. When humans were hunters and gatherers, women contributed substantial amounts of gathered vegetables to their families' consumption. Because the livelihood of women was not dependent on men, they commanded considerable status. Because social norms reflect these relative bargaining powers, the norms that prevailed were not oppressive to women. With the Neolithic Revolution, humans gave up hunting and gathering and adopted settled agriculture. Because this required physical strength, it made women more dependent on men for survival, and the social norms in agricultural societies reflected this change to a more subservient status for women. Early industrialization, with its factory system, did not much improve women's status because married women with young children could not work in factories. In fact, it was early in the period of industrialization that the concept of a traditional household—with a wage-earning husband and a wife specializing in maintaining the household—took firm root in society's consciousness. It was only in the postindustrialization phase of development, with the rise of the service sector in which women could participate, that the bargaining power of women improved. Thus, although the short-term benefits of specialization as envisaged by Becker are undeniable, the long-run consequences are less clear. Specialization in nonmarket activities undermined the autonomy of women, and it was only when technology changed so that they could resume bringing resources into their households again that their bargaining power began to improve.

I must note that much of the logic of the economic theory of family formation discussed above applies equally to heterosexual and same-sex couples. That is not so for the theory below, which applies only to heterosexual couples.

The View from Evolutionary Psychology

Whenever an institution or practice appears all over the world and in all periods of recorded history, evolutionary psychologists seek an evolutionary explanation for it. For one thing is shared in common by all of humanity: we are all products of evolution (but certainly not *only* evolution). Marriage or family formation is a case in point. Below I present the view of evolutionary psychologists such as Martin Daly and Margo Wilson (2000).[14] This rationale for marriage revolves around two core ideas: how two parents can increase the survival chances of children and how uncertainty of paternity plays a role in social organizations.

One of the unique features of humans is that our brain sizes are large compared to the rest of our bodies. But building large-brained infants in the womb is a time-consuming process that is intensive in energy. During the nine-month gestation period, women can use help in sustaining themselves and their children (born and unborn). It seems natural that the father of the children can be counted on to provide for them. But whether he will or not depends on what he gets out of this arrangement and on the alternative uses he has for his time and other resources. What would induce the father to provide resources to his children's mother?

Half the genes a child carries are from the mother and half from the father. When a child dies, both its parents lose the representation of their genes in future generations in the form of this child and his or her future children. Such considerations are of course the last things on the minds of parents. When a child dies, the parents grieve because they are emotionally attached to the child. From an evolutionary psychologist's perspective, however, this attachment is the means that nature uses to ensure that parents take care of their children. Not that nature "thinks this"—natural selection, after all, is a mechanical process that works by trial and error. When an emotional attachment is formed, parents try to ensure their children's survival, and these very genes that promote emotional attachments to one's offspring are passed on to them. This is how natural selection works; in effect, it uses parents' love for their children to facilitate the survival of the children.

So love for one's child may be an inducement for a father to give resources to his partner. But that may not be enough, because he may not know that his partner's children are his. This is the fundamental issue of *paternity uncertainty* that we have encountered in earlier chapters. Maternity is always certain: there is no doubt as to who is the mother of a child because it is she who gave birth. But paternity is never certain; the biological father's identity is unclear if the child's mother has been openly or surreptitiously unfaithful. Why would this matter to a man? It matters because if the children are not his, he will be devoting his resources to promoting the survival of some other man's genes. His own genes will fade out of the future gene pool. It is a sad

[14] Daly, M., and M. Wilson (2000), "The Evolutionary Psychology of Marriage and Divorce," in *The Ties That Bind: Perspectives on Marriage and Cohabitation,* ed. Linda Waite, Aldine de Gruyter, New York. See also the references cited in this article, especially Wilson, M., and M. Daly (1992), "The Man Who Mistook His Wife for a Chattel," *The Adapted Mind: Evolutionary Psychology and the Generation of Culture,* ed. J. H. Barkow, L. Cosmides, and J. Tooby, Oxford University Press, New York, and Irons, W. (1983), "Human Female Reproductive Strategies," in *Social Behavior of Female Vertebrates,* ed. S. Wasser, Academic Press, New York.

irony that nature promotes the genes of men who jealously guard their partners' sexuality so that their children (whom they help survive) also carry the men's genes. By living in close proximity as a family unit with their female partners, men are better able to monitor the sexual activities of their mates. In other words, men are more assured of the paternity of the children.

This, then, is the view of family formation from evolutionary psychology. By "marrying," women receive resources that help their children survive. And men receive more assurance of their paternity of their partners' children. Although this argument appeals to natural selection, the reasoning employed here is fundamentally economic. The difference is that costs and benefits are more generally defined here than is usual in an economic context.

The underpinnings of this argument of Daly and Wilson (2000) and other evolutionary psychologists are not as far-fetched as they might appear at first blush. Men are indeed extremely concerned about their partners' sexual activities, and these have serious consequences in terms of how women's autonomy is restricted. This is also the view of feminists, who argue that men try to control women's sexuality. Even nonfeminist evolutionary psychologists agree with them, for the reason provided above (paternity assurance). In fact, the evolutionary hard-wiring of this trait is so strong that it manifests even when there are no children on the scene and paternity is not an issue.

In any event, how significant is uncertainty about paternity in the present day? Mark Bellis, Karen Hughes, Sara Hughes, and John Ashton (2005) surveyed the evidence from published works on what they call "paternal discrepancy."[15] By this term they mean that there is a discrepancy between the actual biological father of a child and the man who believes he is the father. This is usually the result of marital infidelity by the child's mother. The authors found that figures for paternal discrepancy fell within a wide range, varying from 0.8% to 30%. The median figure was 3.7%, that is, half the studies showed figures below 3.7% and the other half above this. If we adopt the median figure and round it off to 4% and assume that each family had two children, say, then roughly 1 in 12 or 13 families would have revealed a case of paternal discrepancy. This is not a small number. And this is a figure in contemporary societies, in which men who suspect they may not have fathered their wives' children have the option of having various tests performed (such as blood and DNA tests) in order to find out the truth. In our evolutionary setting hundreds of thousands of years ago, when there was little possibility of finding out, the incidence of paternal discrepancy would likely have been higher.

Furthermore, it is also well documented that women prefer men with resources, for the reason given above (survival of children). On the basis of

[15] Bellis, M., K. Hughes, S. Hughes, and J. R. Ashton (2005), "Measuring Paternal Discrepancy and Its Public Health Consequences," *Journal of Epidemiology and Community Health* 59, pp. 749–754.

surveys conducted on samples of 37 societies from 33 countries, David Buss (1989) examined various evolutionary hypotheses about the mating strategies of men and women.[16] Arguing that in the present day a preference for resources and earning power would translate into a preference for mates who exhibit ambition and industriousness, Buss looked for sex differences in such preferences. He found that in 36 of the 37 samples women more than men found it attractive for potential mates to exhibit these traits. In 23 of the 37 samples, men showed a preference for chastity in potential mates. Presumably this is because men view chastity as a cue for future marital fidelity.

Now that we have acquired some insight into why people marry, we move on to address the next puzzle about marriage, namely, the form it takes.

IV. Why Monogamy?

Anthropologists have documented the fact that 85% of the world's societies have been polygynous.[17] Before we launch into reasons that monogamy is the preferred marital arrangement in the contemporary world, it is incumbent on us to understand how and why polygyny arose in the first place. Ester Boserup (1970) was the first economist to suggest that polygyny was associated with greater agricultural labor productivity of women.[18]

With a very simple model, Becker (1981, Chap. 3) offered some provocative economic reasons for the emergence of polygyny.[19] Suppose that only men own a productive asset, say land. Consider two possible scenarios. In one, all men own the same amount of land but the number of men is smaller than the number of women. In the second, we shall assume that the numbers of men and women are equal but the distribution of land between men is inegalitarian; some men have more than others. We let the marginal product of a single woman be P_f. This can be taken as a measure of the well-being of a single woman. If the marginal product of a single man is P_m, we can expect that $P_m > P_f$ because men have an asset (land) that makes their labor more productive and women do not.

This suggests that men could benefit if they could get women to work their land. Suppose that there is no labor market and farm labor comes only from the family and, to make it worthwhile for women to marry, men offer them a "bride price." If we go along with this, the maximum bride price that a

[16] Buss, D. (1989), "Sex Differences in Human Mate Preferences: Evolutionary Hypotheses Tested in 37 Cultures," *Behavioral and Brain Sciences* 12, pp. 1–49.

[17] See White et al. (1988), "Rethinking Polygyny: Co-Wives, Codes, and Cultural Systems," *Current Anthropology* 29, pp. 529–572.

[18] Boserup, E. (1970), "The Economics of Polygamy," in *Woman's Role in Economic Development,* Earthscan Publications, London, Chap. 2.

[19] A diagrammatic elaboration of Becker's model, which we follow here somewhat, can be found in Grossbard, A. S. (1980), "The Economics of Polygamy," *Research in Population Economics* 2, pp. 321–350.

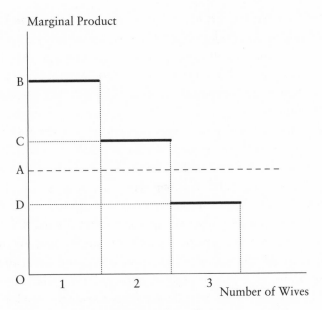

FIGURE 7.1 The marginal product of wives

man will be willing to pay is related to the woman's marginal product. Now, as more and more labor is applied to a given amount of land, this marginal product of labor declines because each worker has less land to work with. We illustrate this in Figure 7.1. Let OA denote the marginal product of a single woman (who owns no land), which we have called P_f above. For a man's first wife, the marginal product is OB; for the second, it is OC; for the third, it is OD; and so on. So the schedule shown in Figure 7.1 represents a single man's "demand for wives." Now if there are N_m males, at a bride price that is between OC and OB there will be a demand for N_m wives because each man would like to have one wife. This is because the marginal product of the first wife exceeds the bride price but that of the second wife falls short of it. At a bride price that is between OD and OC, there will be a demand for $2N_m$ wives because each man would like two wives but not a third; at a bride price just below OD, there will be a demand for $3N_m$ wives, and so on.

Now let us suppose that there are fewer men than women, that is, $N_m < N_f$, perhaps because more men than women die in wars. If monogamy is the norm enforced by the society, each man can "demand" only one wife. Clearly, there can be only N_m marriages, and $N_f - N_m$ women will remain single.[20] What will the bride price be? Even though men are willing to pay a bride price of OB for their one and only wife, the equilibrium bride price in this marriage market will be the lower value OA. This is because when $N_m < N_f$, there is an excess supply of potential wives. If some men offer a bride price in excess of

[20] All marriages are presumed to be heterosexual here.

OA, other women who expect to remain single will offer to marry for less, as long as the bride price is no less than OA. Thus competition between women who are in excess supply will drive the bride price down to OA even though men are willing to pay a bride price of up to OB. Whether they are married or single, all women will achieve the same level of well-being—as is indicated by OA in the figure.

If the society allows polygyny, what does Becker's model predict? To keep things concrete, suppose there are 100 men and 150 women in this society. If men are allowed to have more than one wife, we see that, after all the men have one wife, they will want a second wife because they will be willing to pay a bride price of OC for a second wife (their marginal product), which is more than the minimum OA that is required to fetch a wife. But not all men can get a second wife because there are only 50 "surplus women" in the marriage market. So half the men will end up getting second wives and the other will have only one wife. The bride price in the marriage market will now be OC. Why? Because if any of the 100 men offers a bride price of less than OC, other men with only one wife will bid up the bride price to OC.

We see that under monogamy the bride price is OA, whereas under polygyny the bride price is OC, which is larger than OA. Competition between men for more wives under polygyny raises the bride price. Thus Becker's model predicts that polygyny makes women better off. This is a surprising prediction and a contentious claim that has invited criticism.[21] The response to the criticism is that, if women are going to be worse off, they will not agree to marry a man who already has a wife. If choices are voluntary, when men are relatively scarce women will choose to become second wives only because this will make them better off relative to remaining single.

The rendition of Becker's model above presumes that there is no labor market. If men have assets that can be made more productive when employed with labor, why don't they just hire women to work these assets? Why do they have to get married? Presumably parents would not like unmarried daughters working with unrelated males—especially in developing countries. Also, among other things, this model ignores the fact that polygyny might encourage more patriarchal control of women and thereby undermine the status of women relative to men.

Becker's model has more to say about polygyny. Suppose that there are equal numbers of men and women ($N_m = N_f$), but the assets are distributed unevenly across the men. In this case, some men (those with more land) will be willing to pay higher bride prices than others because they will perceive the marginal product of additional women to be higher. (In terms of Figure 7.1, the marginal product schedule for additional wives will shift up for

---

[21] See, for example, the feminist critique of Bergman, B. (1996), "Becker's Theory of the Family: Preposterous Conclusions," *Challenge* 39, January–February, pp. 9–12.

these rich men relative to that for poor men.) So in this case, some men (the rich) may end up having more than one wife, while others (the poor) may not be able to find even one wife because they cannot afford the bride price that the rich are willing to pay for second or third wives. Thus, if society does not forbid polygynous marriages, polygyny can arise when the distribution of wealth among men is uneven. In other words, polygyny is likely to arise when men are in short supply relative to women but this short supply is not essential. Even when the number of men is the same as (or greater than) that of women, polygyny can arise if the distribution of wealth among the men is relatively uneven.

If some men are left without mates, a considerable amount of social unrest can arise. Because sex is a very powerful drive, desperate men can take a lot of risks to find a mate. In polygynous societies, the rich men with multiple wives are known to carefully sequester their wives to prevent possible contact with other men. And because the rich also often have political power, they can pass legislation that is very repressive in order to retain control. The male need to control the sexuality of women is certainly much greater in polygynous societies than in monogamous ones.

Despite the provocative nature of the implications of Becker's model, it must be said that the model does have predictive power. It is empirically true that polygyny is observed in regions of the world where men have been in short supply.[22] It is also the case that very skewed (uneven) distributions of wealth among men are conducive to polygyny. This was shown by Hannan Jacoby (1995) using data from Côte d'Ivoire, an African country that shows a great deal of variation in the labor productivity of women.[23] He found that wealthier men had more wives. Furthermore, men on whose farms women's labor productivity was higher had more wives—which validates Boserup's hypothesis about polygyny.

An interesting question that arises is this: if the relative scarcity of men makes polygyny more likely, does the relative scarcity of women make polyandry more likely? Common sense might suggest that the answer must be yes. There is evidence that this is so.[24] However, there are very few societies in which polyandry has been observed. Why is this? One argument from evolutionary psychology that is consistent with economic logic is based on the fact that paternity is uncertain in polyandry.[25] When multiple men are

[22] See Ember, M., C. R. Ember, and B. S. Low (2007), "Comparing Explanations of Polygyny," *Cross-Cultural Research* 41, pp. 428–440.

[23] Jacoby, H. (1995), "The Economics of Polygyny in Sub-Saharan Africa: Female Productivity and the Demand for Wives in Côte d'Ivoire," *Journal of Political Economy* 103, pp. 938–971.

[24] See Starkweather, K. E., and R. Hames (2012), "A Survey of Non-Classical Polyandry," *Human Nature* 23, pp. 149–172.

[25] See Miller, A. S., and S. Kanazawa (2007), *Why Beautiful People Have More Daughters*, Perigee (Penguin), New York, Chap. 4.

married to one woman, they do not know who are the respective biological fathers of her children. As a result, each one of the husbands will be reluctant to invest in their common wife's children, leaving it to other husbands to do what is needed. But all of the husbands will behave in this manner. This free-riding across husbands will result in underinvestment in children, and this will show up in a lower survival rate of children from polyandry. Over time, polyandry will be seen as an unviable marital arrangement and will be abandoned.[26] We see that polygyny and polyandry are not exactly symmetrical. The reason suggested may explain why, when polyandry is observed, it tends to be *fraternal* polyandry, that is, brothers marry the same woman. This is understandable because brothers share genes and they will consider each other's children less alien than will men who are genetically unrelated. In other words, free-riding in parental investment is likely to be less of a problem in polyandry that is fraternal.

We have mentioned that a large proportion of the societies in the world has been polygynous. Yet in contemporary times all developed countries are monogamous. Today polygyny is practiced mostly in African and Middle Eastern countries. Why did the economically developed world move away from polygyny? One reason might have to do with religion. Some religions (like Islam) permit multiple wives; others (like Christianity) do not.[27] One answer to the question posed above might be that in most countries in which a substantial proportion of the population either is or was Christian, laws were passed that forbade polygyny. However, this is not an entirely satisfactory answer because even countries in which Christianity is not the major religion have moved toward monogamy. Furthermore, even some countries with a substantial Islamic population (for example, Turkey) have opted for monogamy. What is the connection between economic development and monogamy?

One answer has been provided by Eric Gould, Omer Moav, and Avi Simhon (2008).[28] Their argument is that, just as inequality among males is responsible for polygyny, inequality among females results in monogamy. With economic development, labor income from human capital becomes more important than nonlabor income. Males with human capital would like to have children with human capital, and this is facilitated by wives who have human capital, too. Therefore, educated males demand wives who are also educated. But the bride price of educated wives will be higher. So males

[26]There are also other problems with polyandry. See Levine, N. E., and J. B. Silk (1997), "Why Polyandry Fails: Sources of Instability in Polyandrous Marriages," *Current Anthropology* 38, pp. 375–398.

[27]Not all Christian sects disallow polygamy, however. A prominent example is the Mormon sect, which belongs to the Church of Jesus Christ of Latter-Day Saints.

[28]Gould, E. D., O. Moav, and A. Simhon (2008), "The Mystery of Monogamy," *American Economic Review* 98, pp. 333–357.

with human capital will relinquish the possibility of having many uneducated wives in order to have one wife with human capital. Rich uneducated males (whose source of wealth is nonlabor income) will have no such preference and so will continue demanding many wives with little or no human capital. As economic development increases the income from human capital, rich males of the latter kind become relatively few and far between. In this manner, the society makes a transition to monogamy.

Anthropologists have recently suggested an alternative view as to why most societies made the transition to monogamy. In an intriguing argument, Joseph Henrich, Robert Boyd, and Peter Richerson (2012) have proposed that groups that practiced monogamy performed better on several counts pertaining to survival and economic development compared to polygynous societies.[29] As a consequence of these advantages, in cultural competition *between groups,* monogamous societies won out. In polygynous societies, as we have seen, some men without resources can be left without mates. This, the authors argue, leads them to undertake risky and violent actions—with the result that such societies have higher crime rates than do monogamous ones. Also, men with wives in polygynous societies do not withdraw from the marriage market. They devote their resources to finding more mates instead of using them for other purposes—in particular, investing in their children. In addition, greater competition between men in polygynous societies increases the demand for brides and thereby lowers the age at which women get married. Because women then have a longer period during which they can have children, this raises the fertility rate, making it more difficult for the economy to grow (see below). All these disadvantages of polygyny have made this arrangement lose out to monogamy in cultural competition.

Michele Tertilt (2005) asks whether polygyny slows down economic growth and whether banning polygyny might speed up economic development.[30] She takes her cue from the fact that in Sub-Saharan African countries, in which polygyny is quite prevalent, the fertility rates are much higher and the savings rates much lower than in countries that have monogamy. Could polygyny be responsible for the slow economic development of Sub-Saharan African countries? When polygyny is accepted by society, the rich are willing to pay a high bride price to have multiple wives. The fathers of daughters who are thus given away in marriage get to keep the bride price. Because they find having daughters a good investment, the fertility rate is high and there is less investment in physical capital—which causes economic growth. Furthermore, because the demand for wives is relatively higher in polygynous societies, girls are given

[29] Henrich, J., R. Boyd, and P. J. Richerson (2012), "The Puzzle of Monogamous Marriage," *Philosophical Transactions of the Royal Society B* 367, pp. 657–669.

[30] Tertilt, M. (2005), "Polygyny, Fertility, and Savings," *Journal of Political Economy* 113, pp. 1341–1371.

in marriage at younger ages, whereas their husbands are considerably older because they need to have accumulated enough wealth to pay the bride price. Banning polygyny reduces the demand for brides and therefore lowers the bride price (and may even convert it into a dowry that the daughters' parents have to provide). Because having daughters is no longer such a good investment, parents have fewer children, releasing resources for investment in physical capital. Using a theoretical model, Tertilt finds that banning polygyny can increase the savings rate by around 70%, which, together with a decline in fertility of around 40%, causes the GDP per person to increase by up to 170%. Polygyny most definitely lowers the pace of economic development. How women are exchanged in marriage may go a long way toward explaining the poverty in Sub-Saharan African countries.

V. Dowries

In the previous section, while discussing Becker's theory of polygyny, we got a glimpse of the role that prices could play in the institution of marriage. We are now ready to discuss the existence of another institution that is related to marriage, namely dowries. Across the world and in different time periods, we have observed the practice of paying bride prices and sometimes of offering dowries. In rare cases, they seem to coexist. Why are these marriage payments made? In this section we go into the issue of marriage payments in a little more depth.

According to Becker, the direction of the marriage payment depends on the relative worth of economic contributions to the family by the two spouses. If men contribute more, their share of the joint output of the couple will be larger, and the reverse will be true if the contribution of women is larger. But what happens if the distribution of this output does not easily respond to differences in contributions? For example, it is possible that for cultural reasons the bargaining power of wives and husbands is not determined only by their economic contributions. Or it may be the case that some purchases (say, a good house) or the output of some activities (say, housework) are by their very nature things that both spouses enjoy, irrespective of their individual contributions. In this instance, for marriage to take place those who contribute less will have to make a lump-sum payment to those who contribute more. In this case, we shall observe these lump-sum payments as bride prices in some scenarios and groom prices in others.

Maristella Botticini and Aloysius Siow (2003) have proposed a different theory of why dowries arise.[31] They observe that altruistic parents leave a son a bequest (an inheritance after the parents die) but give a daughter a

---

[31] Botticini, M., and A. Siow (2003), "Why Dowries?," *American Economic Review* 93, pp. 1385–1398.

dowry at the time that she gets married. They propose that a woman's dowry is a "premortem" (that is, before death) bequest. This arrangement especially manifests in the mostly agricultural *virilocal* families, that is, those in which women leave their natal families and move to their husbands' homes upon marriage and the sons continue working on their parents' farms. Botticini and Siow argue that the difference in timing of when daughters and sons are given a share of the parents' wealth is not an accident. This difference arises because it is intended to solve a particular economic problem that has to do with incentives.

In virilocal families, sons keep working on their parents' assets and adding value by doing so. Daughters cannot do this to the same extent because they leave home after marriage. Suppose that parents with a son and a daughter leave their wealth as bequests for both, say by splitting the amount equally. The son will receive only half the value he adds to his parents' assets because his sister will receive the other half. Anticipating the outcome that he will receive only half the benefit he generates, the son will apply less effort. In effect, this arrangement of equally splitting the inheritance at the time of death dilutes the son's incentives to work hard. By giving the daughter a dowry but no bequest, the parents can get around this problem.

A numerical example will clarify this argument. Suppose that, at the time of the daughter's marriage, the parents have wealth of $10,000. Suppose that they expect to live another 20 years and that over this period, if the son puts in a high level of effort, this amount is multiplied fourfold and becomes $40,000. If this is split two ways between the two siblings, each will receive an inheritance of $20,000. However, anticipating that his sister will get a free ride from him by receiving half the fruits of his efforts, the son will apply less effort. As a result of this lower level of effort, suppose that the parents' wealth increases from $10,000 to only $20,000 over the 20 years. When this is split in half, each sibling will end up with an inheritance of just $10,000.

In order to get around this problem, the parents can adjust the timing of when they give wealth to their two children. Suppose that they put in place an arrangement in which the daughter will receive a dowry upon marriage but no bequest and that the son will receive an inheritance. Suppose that they split the original amount of $10,000 equally and give the daughter a dowry of $5,000. The son will now put his effort into the remaining $5,000. Because he knows that he and he alone will receive the full value added by his effort, he will work hard. In the next 20 years, say, he increases his parents' remaining wealth fourfold, bringing it up to $20,000. This is the amount he will receive as an inheritance (which is twice what he would have received in the previous arrangement). This arrangement solves the problem of dilution of the son's incentives due to his sister's free ride.

Is this dowry arrangement unfair to the daughter? Not necessarily. In the above example, the parents' wealth at the time of their daughter's marriage is split evenly. One might argue that the son will ultimately receive $20,000, whereas the daughter receives only $5,000 as a dowry. True, but she receives her dowry 20 years earlier than her brother will receive his inheritance. During these 20 years, she too can apply effort to her dowry and increase it in value to $20,000. The dowry arrangement with no bequests for daughters is not inherently unfair. Under this theory of dowries, daughters tend to receive inheritances only when their parents do not have any sons.

Botticini and Siow provide evidence from early Renaissance Tuscany that is consistent with their theory. This theory proposes that dowries disappear when families stop being virilocal. As economies develop, employment opportunities elsewhere improve and sons do not necessarily work with their parents. Human capital becomes important, and parents give their inheritance to their children in the form of education rather than as dowries or bequests.

In her review of bride prices and dowries, Siwan Anderson (2007) points out that dowries are much rarer than bride prices.[32] In a well-known compilation of data on preindustrial societies, Murdock's *Ethnographic Atlas* reveals that about 4% of the nearly 1,200 societies had dowries, whereas around 66% had bride prices.[33] Comparing bride prices with dowries, Anderson identifies the former as being more or less uniform in value and as occurring in more primitive societies. Dowries, in contrast, occur in more advanced societies that show stratification (such as having a class or caste structure) and the dowries are not uniform in value. The reason she gives for these differences between bride prices and dowries is that they arise from the fact that in growing economies men have more economic opportunities available to them than women. So the incomes of men show greater variability. In a stratified society where status matters, rich parents with daughters vie for high-status grooms. The relative scarcity of such grooms means that they will be rationed among the potential brides either through a groom price that the brides' parents pay or through a dowry that their brides receive from their parents.[34]

In contemporary economies, it is not clear whether dowries improve the well-being of women. In countries like India, the giving of dowries is a huge burden on the poor. The average dowry required may be several times the annual income of the parents. This is one reason that parents view having daughters as very onerous, and it is the source of much of the discrimination against girls. In recent decades dowries occasionally have become sources of extortion in India by grooms and their families and have led to the phe-

[32] Anderson, S. (2007), "The Economics of Dowry and Brideprice," *Journal of Economic Perspectives* 21, Fall, pp. 151–174.

[33] Murdock, G. P. (1967), *Ethnographic Atlas,* University of Pittsburgh Press, Pittsburgh, PA.

[34] Anderson uses an analogous argument to explain why there has been dowry inflation in recent decades in India. See Anderson, S. (2003), "Why Dowry Payments Declined with Modernization in Europe but Are Rising in India," *Journal of Political Economy* 111, pp. 269–310.

nomenon of "bride burning" when additional payments are not forthcoming from the brides' parents.[35] The institution of the dowry worsens the lives of women whose parents cannot afford dowries, not only because of the treatment they receive at their in-laws' hands but also because of how they may be discriminated against, compared to their male siblings, in their natal homes.

Among families that can pay dowries, however, there is empirical evidence to suggest that women with larger dowries are better off in their married life. In China one observes dowries and bride prices coexisting—something that is not compatible with Becker's theory of marriage payments if one interprets a dowry as a groom price. In an interesting paper Junsen Zhang and William Chang (1999) offer a theory for this apparent discrepancy and test the effect of dowries on married women's welfare.[36] They argue that bride prices (and groom prices) help clear the marriage market in accordance with Becker's model, but dowries are premortem inheritances given to daughters. In China (as opposed to India), dowries remain under the control of the wives. Using data from Taiwan collected in 1989, the authors show that dowries, by increasing the bargaining power of married women, increase their welfare. In particular, when women receive dowries their husbands are more likely to help out with household chores. This finding is confirmed by Phillip Brown (2009) using data collected in China in 2001 on women married between 1950 and 2000.[37] He finds that women with larger dowries had greater autonomy in household purchasing decisions on women's goods, an increased likelihood of their husbands' participating in household chores, an increased proportion of time spent in leisure, and increased (self-reported) satisfaction with their lives.[38] This is fairly compelling evidence that dowries improve the welfare of married women by increasing their bargaining power.

VI. The Human Capital and Labor Market Consequences of Marriage

Now that we have discussed why marriage arises, the forms it takes, and the reasons for some of the institutions associated with marriage, we are ready to examine some of the many consequences of marriage. We saw in Section III that Becker's theory of family specialization emphasizes the implications of

[35] See Bloch, F., and V. Rao (2002), "Terror as a Bargaining Instrument: A Case Study of Dowry Violence in Rural India," *American Economic Review* 92, pp. 1029–1043.

[36] Zhang, J., and W. Chang (1999), "Dowry and Wife's Welfare: A Theoretical and Empirical Analysis," *Journal of Political Economy* 107, pp. 786–808.

[37] Brown, P. H. (2009), "Dowry and Intrahousehold Bargaining: Evidence from China," *Journal of Human Resources* 44, pp. 25–46.

[38] For somewhat analogous but suggestive evidence for India drawn from a small sample from the state of Karnataka, see Chan, W. (2011), "Marital Transfers and Welfare of Women," paper presented at the International Conference on Applied Economics, Perugia, Italy, August 25–27.

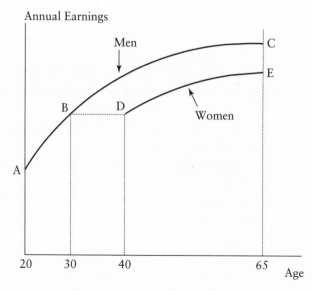

FIGURE 7.2 Earnings profiles of men and women over time

comparative advantage. Because only women can give birth and lactate and thus have a small comparative advantage in raising children (at least when the children are young), married women tend to specialize in housework and married men in market work. This is particularly so when skills increase with specialization. Once they recognize this, individuals have an incentive to consciously invest in their skills or human capital. This observation is the basis of Gary Becker's (1962) theory of human capital investment.[39] This theory simultaneously explains the trends in women's labor force participation and their investment in human capital.[40]

Before we look at the empirical side of these issues, we begin by examining the incentives to invest in human capital. This form of capital that is grafted onto human beings can come in two forms that increase a person's efficiency in work: education and work experience. Both increase work productivity. As a result, the productivity—and hence the earnings—of a worker increase with age, as shown in Figure 7.2. Suppose that an individual starts working at age 20 and continues working continuously till age 65 and then retires. The person's annual earnings (adjusted for inflation) might look like the curve ABC. These earnings increase rapidly in the beginning as human capital accumulates, and then finally the increases taper off due to diminishing returns.

[39] Becker, G. S. (1962), "Investment in Human Capital: A Theoretical Analysis," *Journal of Political Economy*, 70:5, pp. 9–49.

[40] A very readable treatment of this theory can be found in Polachek, S. W. (2006), "How the Life-Cycle Human Capital Model Explains Why the Gender Gap Has Narrowed," in *The Declining Significance of Gender?*, ed. F. D. Blau, M. C. Brinton, and D. B. Grusky, Russell Sage Foundation, New York.

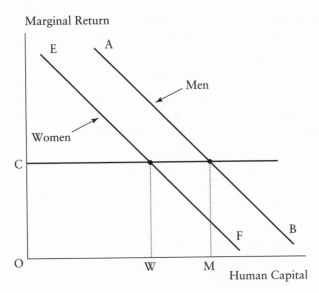

FIGURE 7.3 The optimal investment of men and women in human capital

Education typically requires that people forgo earnings because they have to be in school or college. So there is an opportunity cost to acquiring education; present income has to be sacrificed to increase future income. Work experience may lead to greater productivity as a by-product of working, in which case this form of productivity increase comes free. But much of the skill acquired on the job comes from explicitly devoting time to training—time that could have been usefully spent producing. This form of training does have an opportunity cost. In view of this, how do people make investment decisions in human capital?

Consider an individual adding to her human capital a year at a time, where a year could mean an additional year of college education or an additional year of work training. We assume that the cost of an additional year of human capital acquisition is constant and denote this marginal cost by the distance OC on the vertical axis in Figure 7.3. The amount of human capital acquired is shown along the horizontal axis. On the vertical axis we show the marginal returns to human capital, that is, the increase in future income made possible for an additional year of human capital.[41] The marginal returns usually diminish with the amount of human capital. In accordance with the law of diminishing returns, as more and more human capital is added to an individual, each additional year fetches returns less than those of the previous year. So the marginal return to human capital is shown as the downward-sloping line AB in Figure 7.3.

[41] Strictly speaking, this is the *present value* of all future income. The notion of present value is explained in the appendix to this chapter.

We now can determine how much human capital an individual will acquire through investment. As long as the (marginal) return to an additional year of human capital exceeds its marginal cost, that year of human capital should be acquired. This will continue until the marginal return is equal to the marginal cost, which will occur when the amount of human capital acquired is OM in the figure. Beyond this, the cost of present sacrifice will exceed the benefit of future returns. Thus the individual will decide to acquire OM units as the optimal amount of human capital.

How does gender play into this decision? To see this we must recognize that the marginal return to education depends on *how long* the individual expects to work. The longer a person is going to be working, the greater the length of time over which the investment in human capital will pay off and the higher the returns. Suppose that a typical male expects to work from age 20 until the age of 65 years, which means he will have a work life of 45 years. Let us say that the line AB in Figure 7.3 is drawn under the presumption of a work life of 45 years, so OM will be a man's optimal investment in human capital.

If there is specialization along the lines suggested by Becker, women will expect to work for fewer years in the market than men. In particular, women may expect to either completely withdraw from market work when their children are young or to work only part time. Suppose that a woman expects to raise 3 children and to withdraw from the labor market from age 30 till age 40 and then resume working. This means that women will effectively have fewer years of market work over which their human capital investment will earn returns. Their earnings profiles, compared to those of men, will look like the part of Figure 7.2 comprising the disjointed segments AB and DE. Because the heights of the points B and D are shown as the same, this assumes that women's human capital does not deteriorate when they are absent from the labor market—a very strong assumption. Even so, for any level of human capital the marginal returns will be lower for women than men. The marginal return for women is shown in Figure 7.3 as the line EF, which is below AB. From Figure 7.3 we see that women will undertake an optimal human capital investment in the amount OW, which is less than the men's optimum OM. If skills depreciate from lack of use when women are not working in the labor market, the earnings curve DE in Figure 7.2 will drop and the line EF in Figure 7.3 will be even farther to the left. Then the human capital that women will find it optimal to acquire will be even lower than OW in Figure 7.3.

The arguments made above have a sound empirical basis. When the earnings for the same number of hours are compared between men and women, the difference depends on marital status and on the number of children. This is shown clearly in the work of Susan Harkness and Jane Waldfogel (2003), who examine this issue in seven industrialized countries.[42] Interestingly, the earnings of single women are above 90% of those of single men in all seven countries. But when the comparison is between married women and married men, women fare poorly—this relative percentage falls within the range 60%–70%. These earnings figures are mirrored in the percentages of men and women who participate in the labor market. The percentages are around 80% for men, around 70% for married women without children, and much lower for married women with children. This makes sense because when women have children, they tend to withdraw from the labor market at least temporarily. These empirical patterns are quite consistent with the assumptions of human capital theory.

Human capital theory explains two important facts regarding women and the labor market. Taking the United States as an example of developed countries, over the past 45 years the labor market participation of women between ages 15 and 64 years increased from around 48% in 1975 to 63% in 2009.[43] At the same time, the ratio of women's earnings to men's (for full-time workers) increased from 59% to 77%.[44] Over this period many changes occurred in American society: women started having fewer children; more household gadgets became available that reduced the housework of married women (more on this below); divorce became more common; technology changed, and more work was demanded that did not require physical labor; and social norms about participating in the labor market became more liberal.[45] For all these reasons, women started participating more in the labor market.[46] As we have seen, the returns to a person's human capital depends on the extent of his or her participation in the labor market. Accordingly, the return to women's human capital increased over the twentieth century. Thus women acquired more human capital, and the ensuing increase in productivity manifested as higher wages. This reduced the gender gap in wages.

[42] Harkness, S., and J. Waldfogel (2003), "The Family Gap in Pay: Evidence from Seven Industrialized Countries," in *Worker Well-being and Public Policy*, ed. S. Polachek, JAI (an imprint of Elsevier), Amsterdam.

[43] OECD (Organisation for Economic Co-operation and Development), OECD.StatExtracts, Labor Market Statistics.

[44] Institute for Women's Policy Research (2011), "The Gender Wage Gap: 2010," *Fact Sheet*, Washington, D.C., September, Table 2.

[45] Changing social norms about working outside the home and labor market participation impinge on each other, both evolving over time through mutual feedback. See Fernandez, R. (2013), "Cultural Change as Learning: The Evolution of Female Labor Force Participation over a Century," *American Economic Review* 103, pp. 472–500.

[46] For an authoritative account of the evolution of American women's labor force participation since the beginning of the previous century, see Goldin, C. (2006), "The Quiet Revolution That Transformed Women's Employment, Education, and Family," Richard T. Ely Lecture, *AEA Papers and Proceedings* 96, pp. 1–21.

Technological breakthroughs in the domain of household gadgets were one of the important reasons for the increase in women's labor market participation in the developed world. In an interesting paper, Jeremy Greenwood, Anant Seshadri, and Mehmet Yorukoglu (2005) have persuasively argued that these gadgets have been the "engines of liberation for women."[47] Starting in the late nineteenth century, during and after the spread of electricity and piped water in the United States, a spate of innovative household appliances became available. Vacuum cleaners, washers, dryers, refrigerators, electric irons, sewing machines, flush toilets, and so on greatly reduced the time and physical energy required to do housework. As the authors point out, the mundane task of washing the clothes of a household was an unimaginable chore prior to 1900: water had to be hauled into the home and heated on a stove that ran on coal, and then the clothes had to be hand-washed on a scrub-board, wrung out, hung outside to dry, and finally ironed with a flat-iron that needed repeated stove heating. One can see how much less work was entailed when washers and dryers became available. Given the division of labor within the household, naturally it was women and their time that was most affected by innovations in household technology.[48]

The extra time that thus became available to women enabled them to work in the labor market. It is also true, as documented by Claudia Goldin (1990), that their labor force participation increased because there was an increase in the demand for women's labor in office and clerical work, and their wages rose consequently.[49] Goldin (1990, Table 5.1) shows that, between 1900 and 1980, the labor supply of married women rose from approximately 5% to 49% and the wages of women relative to men rose from 48% to 59%. Greenwood et al. argue that such a small increase in women's relative wages cannot explain the huge increase in married women's labor supply. They argue that the observed supply of women's labor would not have been so readily forthcoming had it not been for household appliances' becoming available. Using a theoretical model, they show that roughly a third of the increase in women's labor force participation in the United States over the previous century was due to household appliances.

A study by Tiago Cavalcanti and Jose Tavares (2008) has provided confirming evidence on the role of household appliances in releasing women's

---

[47] Greenwood, J., A. Seshadri, and M. Yorukoglu (2005), "Engines of Liberation," *Review of Economic Studies* 72, pp. 109–133.

[48] In the developing world, women are still stuck with the drudgery involved in washing by hand, not to mention performing other burdensome chores. We can imagine the sort of constraints this puts on the time available for leisure and other endeavors for women in poor countries.

[49] Goldin, C. (1990), *Understanding the Gender Gap: An Economic History of American Women*, Oxford University Press, New York.

labor using recent data from many countries of the OECD.[50] They find that, during the 25-year period 1975–99, the decline in the price of household appliances relative to other goods significantly increased women's labor force participation. For the United Kingdom, the authors find that around 10%–15% of the rise in women's labor force participation can be attributed to the falling prices of household gadgets. And during that same 25-year period, there was certainly less division of labor within the household than a century ago. So the effect of household appliances would have been much more pronounced earlier.

Therefore, the increase in demand for women's labor and the complementary technological breakthroughs in household appliances both led to an increase in women's labor force participation. A rational response to this increased participation is the greater acquisition of human capital, as we have seen above. Indeed, consulting Figure 1.5 from Chapter 1 we see that in recent decades women have surpassed men in acquiring college education in the United States (as they also have in the OECD countries).

There is a peculiarity in the trend of women's labor force participation in the past two decades that has attracted the attention of economists. After rising steadily for a century, the participation rate of women has leveled off since the early 1990s in the United States and also in the OECD countries. This plateau is apparent for the OECD in Figure 1.2. This is a puzzle. Why is it that, despite the fact that women's educational attainments have exceeded men's and fertility rates have sharply declined, women's participation rate in the labor market is markedly lower than men's? The gender gap in earnings shows a similar persistence. Inquiry into this puzzle has led researchers to unearth another important determinant of women's participation rate: their sense of identity. Who a person takes herself to be and the beliefs she entertains are important in shaping her identity. And this identity, in turn, dictates her behavior.[51]

Using data from the 1990s, Nicole Fortin (2005) examined how women's identity as captured by their attitudes toward gender roles are associated with their labor force participation in 25 OECD countries.[52] To identify gender roles, she focused on the agreement of female respondents with statements like "When jobs are scarce, men should have more right to a job than women" and "Being a housewife is just as fulfilling as working for pay." Fortin finds that women who agree with these statements are less likely to participate in the labor market.

[50] Cavalcanti, T. V. de V., and J. Tavares (2008), "Assessing the 'Engines of Liberation': Home Appliances and Female Labor Force Participation," *Review of Economics and Statistics* 90, pp. 81–88.

[51] For an introduction to the role of identity in economics, see Akerlof, G. A., and R. E. Kranton (2010), *Identity Economics*, Princeton University Press, Princeton, NJ.

[52] Fortin, N. (2005), "Gender Role Attitudes and the Labor-Market Outcomes of Women across OECD Countries," *Oxford Review of Economic Policy* 21, pp. 416–438.

More recently, Marianne Bertrand, Jessica Pan, and Emir Kamenica (2013) have made a fascinating study of the effect of gender identity on a fairly comprehensive list of marriage-related outcomes revolving around income differences between spouses.[53] For this the authors have used U.S. data from 1970–2000. They find revealing behavior among women in couples in which the women's potential income is equal to or greater than the men's. First of all, marital alliances between pairs in which the women earn more than the men are less likely to form. When married women have potential incomes that are greater than their husbands', the women are either likely not to enter the labor market at all or, if they do, to work less and earn much less than their potential. Likewise, divorce rates are higher among couples in which the wives earn more than the husbands. And, paradoxically, women who earn more than their husbands tend to do more housework, not less, than women who earn less than their husbands.

All these findings are consistent with entrenched notions of gender identity: the husband is supposed to be the breadwinner and earn more than the wife. If the reverse is true, it calls into question these socially constructed gender identities that are held dear, and the husband is likely to be threatened. To ease his anxiety the wife underperforms in the market and overdoes the housework, her traditional domain of activity. At first blush, it may appear that these findings contradict empirical findings in the household bargaining literature (which we studied in Chapter 3) in which women who earn more are seen to enjoy more bargaining power and do less housework. But there is no inconsistency. The study of Bertrand et al. focuses on the wife's *potential earnings,* not her actual earnings. The potential earnings are determined by the woman's education, age, and other demographic characteristics, whereas her actual earnings are determined by her actual behavior. This emphasis on potential earnings enables the authors to isolate the preferences of women, which dictate their behavior. And these preferences seem to have built into them a notion of gender identity that forces them to make concessions in order to preserve their husbands' sense of masculine identity. Thus a clear implication of such findings is that the persistent gender gap in women's labor force participation and earnings may have to do with socially constructed notions of gender identity.

As mentioned, the data used by Bertrand et al. were from the United States. If the burden of gender identity is so strong in the contemporary society of one of the most developed countries of the world, we can only imagine how much more of a burden it is in developing countries. There women still work and live under the oppressive influence of religion, culture, and patriarchy.

---

[53] Bertrand, M., J. Pan, and E. Kamenica (2013), "Gender Identity and Relative Income within Households," NBER Working Paper 19023, National Bureau of Economic Research, Cambridge, MA.

Married men earn more than unmarried men. Studies show that, after accounting for qualifications, work experience, and so on, married men earn anywhere between 10% and 40% more than their unmarried counterparts.[54] This excess is referred to as the *marriage premium*. It is interesting to inquire why there is such a premium for married men. On the one hand, there are arguments that married men benefit from the specialization that usually accompanies marriage—especially the traditional kind, in which wives take care of the housework.[55] Men are thus able to focus on their market work and their careers. This results in improved performance on their jobs, quicker promotions, higher salaries, and so on. In this view, the specialization that takes place between spouses in marriage is responsible for men's marriage premium. In other words, the causation runs from marriage to higher productivity (and therefore, earnings) for men.

However, there are other possible explanations for the marriage premium. One is that more productive men earn higher incomes, and this makes them more attractive as spouses. Therefore, men with higher earnings are more likely to be married. Here the causality goes from higher earnings to marriage. In other words, the sample of married men is more likely to also contain more productive men. If a researcher wishes to examine whether marriage increases productivity, she will want to compare *identical* men who differ *only* in marital status. But if married men were already more productive before marriage, the researcher may draw a biased conclusion by mistakenly attributing this higher productivity to marriage because the sample has selected men who were more productive to begin with. The bias that results from this problem is referred to in statistical analyses as *sample selection bias*.

Yet another view says that high productivity may not cause marriage; both may be driven by some traits that are not observable by the researcher. For example, men who are intelligent, hardworking, considerate, trustworthy, and so on would make good employees (and so earn higher incomes). But these very traits may be deemed attractive by potential wives, so such men are more likely to be married. In this scenario, both higher earnings and marital status are driven by traits about which the researcher usually doesn't have information. Here, too, one cannot attribute higher earnings to the specialization that goes on within marriage.

The question of what causes the marriage premium has generated a small body of empirical literature with differing findings. Some studies have supported the productivity argument, whereas others have supported the sample

[54] See, for example, Korenman, S., and D. Neumark (1991), "Does Marriage Really Make Men More Productive?," *Journal of Human Resources* 26, pp. 282–307.

[55] Over 100 years ago, Charlotte Perkins Gilman (1898/1994) wrote, "The labor of women in the house, certainly, enables men to produce more wealth than they otherwise could," in *Women and Economics*, Prometheus Books, Amherst, NY, p. 13.

selection argument.[56] In an interesting study, Donna Ginther and Madeline Zavodny (2001) examine the marriage premium issue in an intriguing manner.[57] Using a sample of white American males during the period 1966–80, they examined whether the marriage premium differed between men who got married the traditional way and those who entered "shotgun" marriages. The latter are marriages that began after a child was conceived. The idea here is that, although traditional marriages may be more likely to reflect sample selection because high wages might attract potential spouses, this is much less likely in the case of shotgun marriages because these are begun for a different reason. High-earning men may carefully select the women they marry, but the same is unlikely to be true regarding those with whom they have sex. If even men in shotgun marriages exhibit a marriage premium, it is likely that the premium is due to specialization within marriage rather than due to the fact that high-earning males are more likely to be married. The authors found that men in traditional marriages had a marriage premium of 16.4% over never-married men, whereas men in shotgun marriages had a marriage premium of 15.0%. They also found that the likelihood of shotgun marriages did not depend on men's earnings. The conclusion from this is that there is something about marriage itself that is responsible for men's marriage premium. More recent evidence from Britain supports this conclusion.[58]

The evidence seems to point to the fact that by specializing in home-based activities, women benefit men in their market work. To the extent that women are participating more in market work nowadays, men's marriage premium will decline if at least some of the housework needs to be done by men.

VII. Spousal Violence

So far we have discussed the reasons for marriage and the various consequences of marriage that are beneficial. But marriages also go sour, and when this happens there can clearly be adverse consequences. In this section we briefly discuss one such consequence for women, namely domestic violence. Although both women and men can be the victims of domestic violence, it is women who are preponderantly the victims of serious spousal violence. The reason is quite simple: on average, men are physically stronger.

[56] See the preceding reference as well as Nakosteen, R. A., and M. A. Zimmer (1987), "Marital Status and Earnings of Young Men: A Model with Endogenous Selection," *Journal of Human Resources* 22, pp. 248–268, and Cornwell, C. M. and P. Rupert (1997), "Unobservable Individual Effects, Marriage and the Earnings of Young Men," *Economic Inquiry* 35, pp. 285–294.

[57] Ginther, D., and M. Zavodny (2001), "Is the Male Marriage Premium Due to Selection?: The Effect of Shotgun Weddings on the Return to Marriage," *Journal of Population Economics* 14, pp. 313–328.

[58] Bardasi, E., and M. P. Taylor (2008), "Marriage and Wages: A Test of the Specialization Hypothesis," *Economica* 75, pp. 569–591.

Domestic violence occurs all over the world, but it tends to be under-reported. In the developed world, the laws against violence of this nature are enforced, but frequently the victims drop the charges either because they hope for reconciliation or because they fear future repercussions. In the developing world, domestic violence is frequently not taken seriously by the police because social norms tacitly confer on husbands the right to beat their wives. And where the law is not enforced, there will be even more reticence on the part of women to report domestic abuse for fear of retribution.

But why should men wish to inflict violence on their partners in the first place? What are the determinants of domestic violence? Feminist theory and evolutionary psychology offer similar explanations. Feminist theory attributes domestic violence to patriarchy; men wish to control the sexuality of their wives, and they use violence if necessary.[59] Evolutionary psychology traces the roots of domestic violence to the fact that men are not assured of the paternity of their wives' children.[60] In order to gain more assurance, men are inclined to inflict violence on their partners so as to ensure greater sexual fidelity. Men who do this are more successful in passing on their own genes to future generations. Thus natural selection favors the proclivity for jealousy in males and for exercising their rights to exclusive sexual access to their partners—through violence, if necessary. Actually, the feminist and evolutionary views are not that far apart. In fact, the evolutionary logic for male violence toward sexual partners may be one of the factors contributing to patriarchy.

Once the tendency to use violence in one's reproductive interests has been hard-wired by nature, this trait can be used for other purposes, too. More generally, it can be employed by males to garner resources for themselves. As William Goode (1971) has argued, men who will be the most likely to use violence to achieve their ends are those who don't have access to resources or much to offer their partners.[61] At a theoretical level, domestic violence is a bargaining weapon; it can be used by males to increase their bargaining power or, equivalently, to decrease the autonomy of their wives and increase the allocation of resources to themselves.[62]

[59] Dobash, R. E., and R. Dobash (1979), *Violence against Wives,* Free Press, New York; Yllo, K. A., and M. A. Strauss (1990), "Patriarchy and Violence against Wives: The Impact of Structural and Normative Factors," in *Physical Violence in American Families,* ed. M. A. Strauss and R. J. Gelles, Transaction Publishers, New Brunswick, NJ; and Martin, D. (1976), *Battered Wives,* Glide Publications, San Francisco.

[60] Wilson, M., and M. Daly (1993), "An Evolutionary Psychological Perspective on Male Sexual Proprietariness and Violence against Wives," *Violence and Victims* 8, pp. 271–294.

[61] Goode, W. J. (1971), "Force and Violence in the Family," *Journal of Marriage and the Family* 33, pp. 624–636.

[62] See, e.g., Rao, V. (1998), "Domestic Violence and Intra-household Resource Allocation in Rural India: An Exercise in Participatory Econometrics," in *Gender, Population, and Development,* ed. M. Krishnaraj, R. Sudarshan, and A. Sharif, Oxford University Press, Delhi.

The standard Nash bargaining model that we studied in Chapter 3 might lead us, at first blush, to the conclusion that the greater the threat utility of the husband (wife), the more (less) domestic violence the wife will face. Mukesh Eswaran and Nisha Malhotra (2011) modeled domestic violence as a means used by males to undermine their wives' autonomy and showed that neither of these claims is necessarily true.[63] On the one hand, men with higher threat utilities may already be having resources allocated according to their preferences, so domestic violence may be redundant. On the other hand, women who acquire more autonomy by owning assets or by earning labor income may face more domestic violence because their husbands try to curtail their autonomy by using violence. All we can be sure of is that women with higher threat utilities do better in marriage; this does not necessarily mean that they experience less domestic violence. The authors tested the theory using nationally representative data for 1998–99 on married women in India. In this sample, comprising more than 58,000 women, 18% had experienced violence at the hands of the husbands at least once and 11% had experienced it in the previous 12 months. Eswaran and Malhotra found that their model was in accordance with the facts. Wife-beating was indeed used by males to reduce women's autonomy. Interestingly, they also found that women who earned income by working outside their homes faced more domestic violence than women who earned incomes working at home. Why does the location of work matter? Evolutionary theory offers an explanation. Women who work outside their homes are more likely to meet unrelated males. Their husbands may perceive this as providing greater opportunities for sexual infidelity, and so it may elicit more spousal abuse.

These findings have important implications for policies designed for reducing domestic violence. Women who are battered often stay with their abusive partners because they have no other options. It is undoubtedly true that improving the outside options for women (by making income-earning opportunities available to them, for example) would benefit women. However, as we have seen, this may sometimes invite more domestic violence. So greater employment opportunities designed to empower women must be accompanied by complementary policies that reduce the possibility or the effects of increased spousal violence. Examples of such policies are harsher punishments for spousal abuse and increased support for battered women. In addition, abusive men may need to be resocialized so as to alter their behavior.[64] This seems essential because, as the evidence seems to suggest, spousal violence may have been promoted in males by evolution.

---

[63] Eswaran, M., and N. Malhotra (2011), "Domestic Violence and Women's Autonomy in Developing Countries: Theory and Evidence," *Canadian Journal of Economics* 44, pp. 1222–1263.

[64] See Bowlus, A. J., and S. Seitz (2006), "Domestic Violence, Employment, and Divorce," *International Economic Review* 47, pp. 1113–1149.

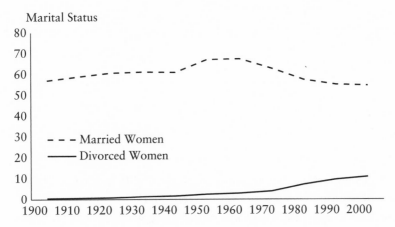

FIGURE 7.4 Trends in the proportions of married and divorced women in the United States (percent), 1900–2002

Source: U.S. Census Bureau, *The 2012 Statistical Abstract: The National Data Bank.*

VIII. Divorce and Its Economic Effects on Women

Breakups are one of the unfortunate consequences of marriage. Divorce rates have been rising rapidly in the past five decades in the developed world, Japan excepted. At the same time, marriage rates have been falling. See Figure 7.4 for the United States over the period 1900–2002. Because marriage has been one of the most important human institutions for several millennia, it is important to inquire why this is happening. Does it have anything to do with economic development? Or are more liberal laws responsible for this trend? Or is the cause the easing of social norms whereby cohabitation no longer has the stigma that it had until a few decades ago?

We have seen that the benefit of specialization and the division of labor within marriage is one of the reasons for this institution. By specializing in different activities and sharing or exchanging the outputs of these activities, both partners can make themselves better off. However, because the labor market participation of women has been steadily increasing in the developed world, there is less and less specialization within households. Consequently, there is less reason for marital alliances to form. Furthermore, we would expect cohabitation to increase and marriages to end in divorce if disagreements that previously would have been worked out are now seen as fatal to relationships. From a bargaining point of view, when women work outside of their homes their outside options improve and they no longer need to tolerate an oppressive marital situation. Also, women in the West are now having far fewer children (which itself has contributed to their greater participation in the labor market), so there is less need to stay married "for the sake of the children."

Because marriage has consequences for the formation of human capital, we would expect that divorce does, too. When divorce rates increase, women

	Wife	Husband
Married	70	100
Divorced	130	80

Couple's Total Utility Is Higher in Divorce

(a)

	Wife	Husband
Married	70	100
Divorced	80	60

Couple's Total Utility Is Higher in Marriage

(b)

FIGURE 7.5 The utilities of a wife and a husband in the married state and the divorced

entering into marriage will be wary of the possibility of divorce in the future. They will choose to keep a foot in the labor market even while they are married so that they will not be saddled with low wages in the event that they transition to a divorced state later. In other words, the possibility of divorce may induce less specialization than would have prevailed if divorce had remained rare. We see that divorce can be an effect of reduced specialization and it can also induce reduced specialization; the causation goes both ways.

Divorce Laws and the Incidence of Divorce

Divorce laws may, at first blush, be deemed an important determinant of divorce rates. Before the 1960s, divorce in developed countries required proof that one of the partners was at fault for the failed marriage. As can be expected, this caused divorces to be very contentious because neither party normally wanted to accept blame. However, the laws allowed for divorce by "mutual consent"; if both parties mutually agreed to go their separate ways, the law allowed them to do so. Beginning in the 1960s, many states in the United States moved to unilateral, no-fault divorces, which meant that if one of the partners wanted to get out of the marriage, he or she could do so irrespective of what the other wanted, without having to admit fault or blame the other spouse. What have been the consequences of this for the incidence of divorce and the well-being of people?

At a theoretical level, it has been argued that moving from divorce through mutual consent to unilateral divorce should make no difference to divorce rates. This argument, first put forward by Gary Becker, Elizabeth Landes, and Robert Michael (1977), claims that if the cost of bargaining is negligible, the divorce rates should be the same under both types of laws.[65] To see this by way of an example, suppose that the utilities of a wife and a husband in the married state are denoted by 70 and 100, respectively, and in the divorced state by 130 and 80. Consult panel a of Figure 7.5.

Suppose that these utilities are measured in the same units for both people and that these units are transferrable between the partners through some

---

[65] Becker, G. S., E. M. Landes, and R. T. Michael (1977), "An Economic Analysis of Marital Instability," *Journal of Political Economy* 85, pp. 1141–1187.

means (such as wealth). Because $130 + 80 > 70 + 100$, their total utility in the divorced state will be higher than in the married one. However, although the wife will be better off being divorced, the husband will be better off being married. How will the situation be resolved?

Suppose, first, that divorce can be obtained unilaterally under the law. In this case, the wife will ask for a divorce and get it; the husband's opinion is irrelevant. As divorced individuals, the wife's well-being will be higher by 60 and the husband's lower by 20. What happens if the law requires mutual consent? It might appear that the wife will be doomed to living in an unhappy marriage because the husband won't give his consent. However, if bargaining is costless, the outcome will be divorce in this case, too. The reason for this is that, because the couple's total utility in divorce will be higher than in marriage, the wife can compensate the husband (with wealth, say) so that he will agree to a divorce. To agree, the husband will have to be compensated by at least the amount of his loss in divorce, which is 20. After compensating him, the wife's utility in divorce will become $130 - 20 = 110 > 70$. So even after compensating her husband in order to acquire his consent, the wife will be better off with a divorce than in marriage. (In fact, the wife can more than compensate the husband and still be better off.) So even if the law requires mutual consent, a divorce will obtain. As long as the couple's total utility will be higher in divorce than in marriage, if bargaining is costless the party desiring a divorce can always compensate the reluctant party to obtain consent. If, however, bargaining is costly, some of the benefit from divorce may be lost in the squabbling (or in the hiring of lawyers, say) and there may not be enough resources left over for adequate compensation.

The above logic says that, when the couple's total utility will be higher in divorce than in marriage (and so it makes sense that the couple should divorce) and bargaining is costless, divorce will obtain whether the law requires mutual consent or not. What will happen if the couple's total utility will be lower in divorce than in marriage but the wife's utility will be higher in divorce whereas the husband's is higher in marriage? This is the scenario depicted in panel b of Figure 7.5. By mimicking the above logic, we can see that divorce will not obtain under both kinds of laws. If the law requires mutual consent, the husband will not give his consent because the wife cannot possibly compensate him enough. But if the law grants unilateral divorce, this time it is the husband who will compensate the wife to stay in the marriage. So we see that, under certain conditions, the nature of the law does not affect the marriage/divorce choice; it only determines who will compensate whom in the bargaining.[66]

---

[66] This is an application of a well-known argument called the Coase theorem, first formulated in Coase, R. H. (1960), "The Problem of Social Cost," *Journal of Law and Economics* 3, pp. 1–44.

The assumption that bargaining costs are negligible is a difficult one to accept. After all, divorce proceedings are known to be quite acrimonious, and even people who are generally mild mannered turn hostile during the emotional upheaval caused by divorce. The empirical evidence on the effect of unilateral divorce on the incidence of divorce is mixed—at least the evidence from the United States.[67] A reconciliation of these findings has been offered by Justin Wolfers (2006).[68] He finds that the move to unilateral divorce in the United States did not cause an increase in the divorce rate in the long run, but it did hasten the arrival of divorces in marriages that would have failed anyway. In short, the people's duration in the married state declined as a result of the new law. Thorsten Kneip and Gerrit Bauer (2009) find, in contrast, that in Western Europe the move to unilateral divorce permanently increased the incidence of divorce.[69]

Whether they cause a long-run shift in divorce rates or reduce the length of marriages doomed to fail anyway, unilateral divorce laws can be expected to have consequences for human capital formation. We have already seen that the expectation of divorce may induce women to undertake more market work in the early years of their marriages than they might have otherwise. This means that they will undertake less investment in marriage-specific human capital—that is, human capital that is useful in marriage but has little use elsewhere. This might mean that they will have fewer children and spend less time with their children. Furthermore, because unilateral divorce enables a person to walk away from a marriage, it might induce less sacrifice on behalf of the partner. For example, it might reduce the chances that women will work to put their husbands through medical or law school. Betsy Stevenson (2007) tested these conjectures using data from the 1970s and 1980s, comparing states of the United States that had implemented unilateral divorce laws with those that had not.[70] She examined the marriage-specific investments of couples in the first two years of marriage. She found that marriage partners in states with unilateral divorce laws are 10% less likely to support spouses through school, 8% more likely to both be in the labor force, and 6% less likely to have children. These findings are consistent with theory.

An important aspect of the change in laws from mutual consent to unilateral divorce is that it shifts bargaining power between the spouses if they have different views on their marriage. In mutual consent, this power lies

[67] See Peters, H. E. (1986), "Marriage and Divorce: Informational Constraints and Private Contracting," *American Economic Review* 76, pp. 437–454, and Allen, D. W. (1992), "Marriage and Divorce: Comment," *American Economic Review* 82, pp. 679–685.

[68] Wolfers, J. (2006), "Did Unilateral Divorce Raise Divorce Rates?: A Reconciliation and New Results," *American Economic Review* 96, pp. 1805–1820.

[69] Kneip, T., and G. Bauer (2009), "Did Unilateral Divorce Laws Raise Divorce Rates in Western Europe?," *Journal of Marriage and Family* 71, pp. 592–607.

[70] Stevenson, B. (2007), "The Impact of Divorce Laws on Marriage-Specific Capital," *Journal of Labor Economics* 25, pp. 75–94.

with the spouse who does not want a divorce, and it is this person who needs to be compensated for consent. Under unilateral divorce, the partner who wants a divorce has the bargaining power, and it is this person who needs to be compensated to remain in the marriage. We know that in Nash bargaining, the outcome of bargaining depends on the threat utilities of the two parties. If divorce defines the threat option, by changing these threat utilities the change in divorce law would also be expected to change the bargaining outcome within marriage. Betsy Stevenson and Justin Wolfers (2006) tested these implications by examining two consequences of the change in divorce law: suicide and marital violence.[71] They found that in the United States the shift to unilateral divorce significantly reduced female suicide rates, domestic violence toward women, and the homicide of wives. (They found no analogous effects on men.) By giving women caught in potentially violent marriages the option of exiting without consent, the change to unilateral divorce made them better off within marriage.

The above finding illustrates two important points. First, it shows how important it is to recognize that even though men's violent behavior toward women may have been partly promoted by evolution—as persuasively argued by Daly and Wilson (1988) and other evolutionary psychologists—it also responds to incentives and the environment. Therefore, there is no justification for the view that domestic violence is excusable because this sort of behavior has been promoted by nature. In addition, the finding shows how outside options matter in cases of domestic violence and spousal homicide. Second, the Stevenson and Wolfers finding illustrates the importance of culture. In the previous section we discussed findings of Eswaran and Malhotra from India, where the greater autonomy of women was seen to meet with more—not less—spousal violence. In India, divorce is very rare, so most women would not consider that as an option—especially in rural areas. Cultural norms are also important in deciding whether or not divorce options will be taken up even when available, and this has consequences for bargaining outcomes. The role of culture in divorce is documented in a recent study by Delia Furtado, Miriam Marcen, and Almudena Sevilla-Sanz (2013).[72] They examined the incidence of divorce among Europeans who had immigrated to the United States as children under 5 years of age. Because they grew up in the United States, they were exposed to American laws and institutions, but at home they had imbibed the cultural values of their immigrant parents. If immigrants from European countries with low divorce rates also exhibit low divorce rates when they are in the

---

[71] Stevenson, B., and J. Wolfers (2006), "Bargaining in the Shadow of the Law: Divorce Laws and Family Distress," *Quarterly Journal of Economics* 121, pp. 267–288.

[72] Furtado, D., M. Marcen, and A. Sevilla-Sanz (2013), "Does Culture Affect Divorce Decisions?: Evidence from European Immigrants in the US," *Demography* 50, pp. 1013–1038.

United States, it suggests that culture influences divorce rates. This is precisely what the authors found.

The Well-being of Divorced Women

An important question we should examine is this: what happens to the well-being of women when they divorce? It has been argued in the literature that the consequences are not good for them, that their standard of living falls drastically and the poverty level among divorced women is higher than for married women.[73] This might seem plausible because women's income-earning potential is probably not as high as that of their former husbands, especially if the women have specialized in housework. Also, custody of children has traditionally been given to women (though the trend is toward joint custody these days), which means that single mothers have more people to take care of on a limited income than do single fathers. However, the more recent literature has called some of these claims into question. The reason for the disagreement is that women whose marriages are unstable may also be women whose economic conditions are not particularly good to begin with. In other words, the sample of divorced women may contain a disproportionate number of women whose standards of living would have been low even if they had remained single. Divorced women more frequently have lower levels of human capital and are economically disadvantaged compared to their still-married counterparts.

Given that this is the case, it is important for researchers to isolate the effect of divorce from the other attributes of divorced women in order to identify the effect of divorce on standard of living. Kelly Bedard and Olivier Deschenes (2005) address this issue in a carefully executed empirical study.[74] They identify only that part of the change in the income of divorced women that is due to divorce per se, holding everything else constant. Using American data from 1980, they find that the average change in income when women divorce is positive, that is, on average women have a higher standard of living after they become divorced. The reason they cite is that divorced women tend to put more hours into the labor market and so have substantially higher labor incomes than women who are still married.

Does the above finding mean that it is incorrect to claim that poverty levels of women increase when they are divorced? No, it does not. Elizabeth Ananat and Guy Michaels (2008) compared not only the average income but the entire distribution of income of divorced and never-divorced women,

---

[73] For an overview, see Smock, P. J., W. D. Manning, and S. Gupta (1999), "The Effect of Marriage and Divorce on Women's Economic Well-Being," *American Sociological Review* 64, pp. 794–812.

[74] Bedard, K., and O. Deschenes (2005), "Sex Preferences, Marital Dissolution, and the Economic Status of Women," *Journal of Human Resources* 40, pp. 411–434.

being careful to isolate the effect of divorce only.[75] To understand their finding, imagine that the women are arranged in the order of increasing income. Now look at the effect of divorce on women who are in the bottom 10% of the income distribution, in the bottom 10%–20%, and so on, and finally in the top 10%. The authors found that, relative to the incomes of still-married women, the incomes of women in the top 40% of the income distribution actually increased with divorce, whereas those of women in the bottom 40% decreased with divorce. As a result, divorce increased the income inequality among women and also increased the poverty level among women (as measured by the proportion of women who have incomes below a prespecified poverty line). Thus, although it is true that divorce puts more women below the poverty line, it is also true that some women are better off in terms of income after divorce.

It must be noted that all these findings speak only to the issue of standard of living, which is merely one component of well-being. Assessing changes in well-being is a more difficult matter. A woman's income may fall with divorce, but on balance her well-being may nevertheless increase because she is no longer trapped in an unhappy marriage. Likewise, a man's income may be higher after divorce, but this may be offset by a decline in his physical and psychological health. Some of the evidence we reviewed in Section II suggests that this is a likely possibility in some cases.

IX. Summary

We started this chapter by noting a connection between marriage and various beneficial outcomes, especially regarding men's behavior. We saw that establishing causality is difficult, however: it is often unclear whether marriage is the cause of these beneficial outcomes.

We then examined why family units form in the first place, and we discussed two theories, one from economics and another from evolutionary psychology. The former is essentially the theory of comparative advantage applied to families. The latter argues that family units form because women benefit by receiving resources from their partners for the raising of children, whereas men receive more assurance of their paternity of their partners' children. Both theories have substantial validity, though the evidence for the latter is more circumstantial.

We next discussed Becker's theory that polygyny arises either when men are scarce relative to women or when wealth is unevenly distributed among men, and it makes women better off than monogamy. We overviewed a theory which proposed that the transition to monogamy occurs with eco-

---

[75] Ananat, E., and G. Michaels (2008), "The Effect of Marital Breakup on the Income Distribution of Women with Children," *Journal of Human Resources* 43, pp. 611–629.

nomic development, when income from human capital becomes more important than nonlabor income. Furthermore, we saw why polygyny appears to reduce the rate of growth of economic development.

We next discussed the rationale for the institutions of bride and groom prices and dowries. Becker's theory argues that whether it is a bride price or a groom price that obtains at marriage is determined by the relative economic contributions of the bride and the groom to the family. An alternative theory of dowries proposes that this practice arose as a way of giving a premortem bequest to daughters in societies in which brides joined their husbands' families after marriage while the sons continued their parents' work.

Marriage has important consequences for women's labor market participation and their acquisition of human capital. We examined how a person's investment in human capital will be determined by the extent to which she expects to participate in the labor market. We saw that, in recent decades, several factors have contributed to increasing women's participation in the labor market around the world. As a result, their investment in human capital has also increased. In studying these consequences of marriage, we also examined the role played by women's sense of identity.

We then went on to discuss one of the unpalatable features of some marriages: domestic violence. Serious spousal violence, largely perpetrated by men, is a vehicle for getting the upper hand in household bargaining. We saw that providing labor market opportunities for women caught in abusive marriages may not be enough to reduce domestic violence; it will require complementary policies like stiffer sentences for perpetrators.

Finally, we turned to the issue of divorce. We first asked whether the move toward unilateral no-fault divorce in the developed world in recent decades has increased divorce rates. We saw that in the United States, in contrast to Europe, the evidence suggests that there has been no long-run effect on incidence. We also saw that when women divorce some fall below the poverty line, but, in the developed world at least, some women also become better off. Thus, although there is an increase in the proportion of women in poverty, the average income of women upon divorce does not change by much in rich countries.

Appendix: The Concept of Present Value

This appendix formally introduces a concept that enables us to compare and add benefits (or costs) that accrue at different points in time. The essential idea is that money in hand is generally productive; it can earn interest. Therefore, money in hand is better than money to be received in the future. Adding up revenues that are received at different points in time is like adding up apples and oranges, because $1 received today is not of the same worth as $1 received tomorrow. How is one to use a common yardstick to add revenues that accrue at different points in time? The way it is done is through the concept of *present value*. In what follows, we assume that there is no inflation.[76]

Suppose that the best investment option available to a person with money is to put it in the bank and that the relevant interest rate is constant at r (when expressed as a fraction). If $100 is put into a bank today, in a year's time this will become $100 + $100 × r, that is, $100(1 + r)$. If this amount is left in the bank for another year, by the end of two years it will become $100(1 + r) + $100(1 + r) × r, that is, $100(1 + r)^2$. Carrying this exercise further, we will see that by the end of n years the amount in the bank will become $100(1 + r)^n$.

Suppose that a person is told she will receive $100 a year from now and is asked, "What is the smallest amount of money you will accept today instead of receiving $100 a year from now?" Her answer will be

(A1)
$$\frac{\$100}{1 + r}$$

because if this sum is put into a bank today it will become exactly $100 a year from now. We see that future revenues are discounted relative to the present. The amount given in (A1) is called the *present value* of $100 to be received a year from now. Likewise, the present value of $100 to be received two years from now is

(A2)
$$\frac{\$100}{(1 + r)^2}$$

In this manner, all future receipts can be reduced to present-value terms and then added. For example, suppose that a person is to receive an income of X today, Y a year from today, and Z two years from today. How much is this stream of incomes worth to the person today? The answer is given by the present value of this income stream, which is

(A3)
$$\$X + \frac{\$Y}{(1 + r)} + \frac{\$Z}{(1 + r)^2}$$

In other words, if revenues are received at different points in time we can add them after discounting them and reducing each to its present value. This ensures that we are adding apples to apples and oranges to oranges.

A similar procedure can be used when we incur costs at different points in time.

[76] Equivalently, we could say that the dollar figures used here reflect amounts after being adjusted for inflation.

Exercises and Questions for Discussion

1. Describe some of the private and social benefits that seem to go hand in hand with marriage. Discuss the fundamental issue of causality that plagues these connections and how they are resolved in empirical work.

2. This question has to do with Becker's theory of why family units form.

(a) Outline Becker's theory.

(b) Does the theory fail to explain family formation if neither partner has a comparative advantage in household or market activities?

3. Discuss the disadvantages of specialization by comparative advantage in family formation. Do these disadvantages differ by gender? Explain.

4. In the evolutionary theory of family formation, what is the specific benefit that men receive from family formation? And what benefit do women receive? What is the manner in which natural selection contrives family formation in this explanation?

5. Suppose that, in an agricultural society, all the land is owned only by men and all men own the same amount of it. There are 100 men and 100 women. The marginal product of a man on his own land is 80, that of the next person is 60, that of a third person is 40, and that of a fourth is 20. Women's marginal product in collecting wild fruit and vegetables is 30. Suppose that there is no labor market and that only family labor can be employed on a farm.

(a) How many women will be married in this society, and what will the equilibrium bride price be?

(b) Now suppose that there are 100 men and 120 women in this society. If monogamy is enforced, what will the bride price be? Are married women better off than unmarried ones?

(c) If polygyny is allowed in the scenario in part b above, how many women will be married? What will the bride price be? Explain why.

(d) In the light of your answers to b and c above, justify Becker's claim that polygyny makes women better off.

6. Discuss Tertilt's (2005) economic theory of why the developed countries have made a transition from polygyny to monogamy. What is the nature of the investment that takes place before and after the transition? Why?

7. Suppose that the cost of financing an additional year of education is constant at $10 (measured in thousands). The benefit (also measured in thousands of dollars) of receiving an additional year of education when one has already acquired E years of education is given by 50 + 4Y − 10 E, where Y denotes the number of years the person expects to work before retiring.

(a) If men expect to work for 30 years before retiring, how many years of education will they acquire?

(b) If women plan to work 10 years less relative to men (because they plan to withdraw from the labor force in order to raise their children), how much education will women acquire?

(c) If social norms change and families have fewer children, how will it affect the amount of education women receive?

(d) If medical progress and better nutrition enable humans to live longer and work longer, what effect will it have on the amount of education people receive? Why?

8. How does the application of Becker's human capital theory explain the phenomena in the OECD countries of (i) the increasing labor force participation of married women and (ii) the decreasing gender wage gap? Is the causation one-way, going from human capital to labor force participation and gender wage gap, or does it go both ways? Explain.

9. This question is based on the work of Bertrand, Pan, and Kamenica (2013), which we discussed in this chapter.

(a) Explain what is meant by the phrase "a sense of identity."

(b) How does a woman's identity affect her labor market participation and earnings?

(c) How does identity manifest itself in work choices when a husband and wife earn nearly the same income or the wife earns more?

(d) From these manifestations, can you suggest the relevance of the postmodern emphasis on "socially constructed notions" in this context?

10. Explain the reasoning behind the theoretical argument that going from mutual consent to unilateral divorce law does not necessarily change the divorce rate. Under what conditions would you expect this conclusion to hold? What is the empirical evidence on this issue?

11. Explain the increase in divorce rates in developed countries in terms of what happens to comparative advantage and relative bargaining powers within households as women increase their human capital and labor force participation.

CHAPTER EIGHT

Why Are Women the Causes and the Victims of Fertility Decline?

I. Introduction

One of the most important decisions that couples make in their adult lives is the decision to have children. After women have children, their lives change in many ways—and much more drastically than men's do. The presence of young children at home restricts women's choice of working outside their homes, and, even if they can exercise that option, the flexibility with which they can do so is constrained. Men's lives, too, are obviously affected by children, but their ability to work outside their homes remains relatively unrestricted. Indeed, given the patriarchal culture that pervades most of the world, it is traditionally viewed as a man's job to feed his family. Although this cultural norm is easing, especially in the developed world, it is far from obsolete. This chapter examines what determines a couple's fertility choices and the accompanying tensions within their households.

Because bargaining power within households is in substantial measure determined by the relative earnings of the household members, restrictions on outside work following the birth of children can seriously undermine the say women have in the couple's decisions. The greater the number of children women have, the longer they are kept from full participation in the labor market and the less their autonomy is likely to be. Fertility choices, then, have serious implications for the dynamics of the interactions between members of couples. In the reverse direction, because the costs of having and rearing children tend to be disproportionately borne by women, we would expect

In this chapter I have liberally borrowed from an earlier chapter of mine (with the publisher's permission): Eswaran, M. (2006), "Fertility in Developing Countries," in *Understanding Poverty*, ed. A. V. Banerjee, R. Benabou, and D. Mookherjee, Oxford University Press, New York, pp. 143–160.

fertility choices to depend on the extent of women's autonomy. In patriarchal cultures, we would expect fertility rates to be higher.

The motivation for having children is fundamentally biological. Given that, however, economic incentives impinge on fertility choices. Parents want the best for their children, of course, but not necessarily at all costs. And the costs and benefits of children are different in the developed world than in the developing world. In rich countries, the benefit that parents receive from children is essentially emotional well-being. In poor countries, by contrast, in addition to the emotional benefit parents obtain there is also a financial benefit. When parents' old age is insecure because of poverty, support from children is very important. Consequently, the sort of economic model that best captures incentives for having children depends on whether we are considering a developed country or a developing one.

We expect that economic development will impinge on the average fertility rate in a country. For if a financial motive adds to the other benefits of having children, as the financial need decreases, the desire for children will, too. All the rich countries of today have in their historical past made a transition (called the "demographic transition") from a regime of high fertility and rapid population growth to one with low fertility and modest population growth. This reduction and the attendant decrease in the would-be population facilitates economic growth by putting less pressure on other resources such as land and capital. In contrast, before the transition in fertility, rapid population growth blights the lives of a large proportion of the world's poor. Many countries still have population growth rates in excess of 2% per annum, a rate that would double the population in 35 years.[1] So what comes first, rapid economic development or the transition to lower fertility? In most cases, historically it has been the former. Because countries do not necessarily develop rapidly, in this chapter we shall also study what sorts of institutions can help curb high fertility rates in poor countries.

Encouragingly, many developing countries are now exhibiting transitions to low fertility rates. However, they are also exhibiting a most disturbing feature, namely, a distorted sex ratio at birth.[2] Can this be due to discriminatory treatment of females? Are female fetuses being aborted because parents have a preference for male children? And after birth, are female children discriminated against in terms of the allocation of nutrition so that fewer girls than boys survive to older ages? These are important questions. The net effect is captured by the concept of "missing women"—women who ought

---

[1] A rough rule of thumb is the following: if the rate of growth of a population is g% per annum, the number of years required for the population to double is $70/g$.

[2] This sex ratio is defined as the number of male children born for every 100 female children born.

to have been alive but are not. Because discrimination against females cannot be more serious than when their very lives are at stake, in this chapter we shall examine the empirical evidence on this issue.

In this chapter, then, we shall examine what determines a couple's fertility, why the fertility rate is high in many developing countries and why it declines with affluence, and why high fertility is intimately tied to the extent of female autonomy in decision making. We shall seek to understand the crucial role played by women's autonomy in bringing about fertility reductions. We shall then discuss the reasons that female children are victimized in fertility and nutritional choices in poor countries. We shall finally study the phenomenon referred to as missing women that is associated with skewed sex ratios. Before we can understand these issues in some depth, we need a simple economic model of fertility choice to focus our thinking and provide a conceptual framework for analysis.

II. Fertility Choice in Rich Countries

The standard theory of fertility, which is mainly applicable to the developed countries, assumes that children are analogous to "goods" that parents like to consume.[3] Because bearing and raising children is expensive, having more children implies that parents have to make do with less of all other goods. In other words, children have an opportunity cost—especially in terms of women's time—and this is the essential ingredient of the theory. Understanding the role of this opportunity cost (which changes with economic development) in fertility choice is important in tracking how women's bargaining power relative to that of their husbands changes over time.

Consider a couple in which, for the moment, both members have *identical* preferences over two goods: the number of children they will have (denoted by n) and all other goods (denoted by X). Later we shall drop this unitary model and consider the more realistic scenario in which the two individuals have different preferences. Suppose that the couple has an income y and that the cost of each child is c. So if the couple has n children, it has only an amount $y - cn$ available to be spent on all other goods. Assuming that the price of X is 1, the amount of this good consumed (denoted by x) will be given by $x = y - cn$. Rearranging this expression, we may write it as $x + cn = y$. This is the budget constraint that the couple faces. The amount c can be viewed as the "price" of a child. This budget constraint is shown in Figure 8.1 as the straight line AB. If the couple decides to have no chil-

---

[3]The model below ignores the important effect of culture, which impinges on fertility choices. Even women in rich countries bear the influence of the culture of their ancestry in these choices. See Fernandez, R., and A. Foligno (2006), "Fertility: The Role of Culture and Family Experience," *Journal of the European Economic Association* 4, pp. 552–561.

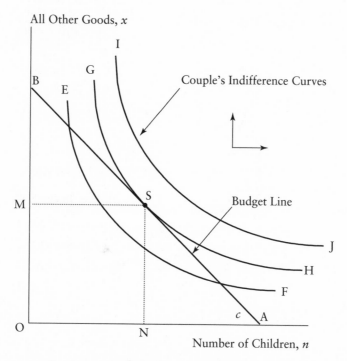

FIGURE 8.1 Determination of a couple's fertility

dren, they can consume an amount OB of all other goods. If they spend all their income on breeding children, they will be able to have OA children. In general, the couple can choose a combination of fertility (number of children) and consumption of other goods to be anywhere on or inside this line but not outside it. The intercept of the line is the couple's income, y, and the slope is the cost per child, c.

The curves EF, GH, and IJ in Figure 8.1 are typical indifference curves representing the couple's preferences. They are convex to the origin, indicating the diminishing rate at which the couple is willing to substitute one good for the other. Because more children and more other goods are both deemed better, the couple's utility is increasing in any northeasterly direction between the perpendicular lines shown with arrowheads.

In choosing their fertility, the couple will seek the combination of n and x that will generate the highest utility for them, that is, will put them on the highest indifference curve on or within AB. This point is indicated as S in the figure. The couple's optimal fertility is ON and their optimal consumption of other goods OM.

What happens to fertility when the couple becomes richer? If their income y increases, the couple's budget line will shift out in a parallel fashion to A′B′, as indicated in Figure 8.2. The new optimum for the couple is shown as S′. If children are viewed as normal goods, as they are thought to be, the couple's

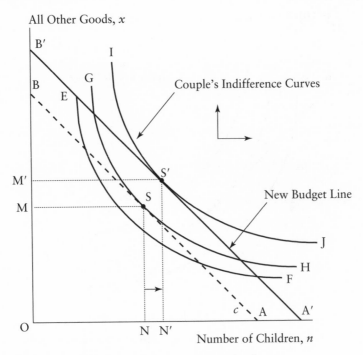

FIGURE 8.2 The effect of higher income on fertility

optimal fertility will increase from ON to ON'.[4] This is the standard *income effect,* as applied to children. In a symmetric manner, if their income declines the couple will have fewer children.

What happens if the couple's income stays constant but children become more expensive? The couple will have to give up more other goods in order to have a child. This will translate into a higher value of c (say c'' in Figure 8.3) in the budget constraint, so the slope of the budget line will become steeper. If the couple decides to have no children, however, their consumption of all other goods will stay the same as before, OB. Hence the new budget line is shown as the line A''B in Figure 8.3.

When the cost of a child increases, two effects will accompany that increase. On the one hand, there will be a *substitution effect*: the couple will substitute the relatively cheaper good for the more expensive good (children). This will tend to reduce their fertility. In addition, there will be an income effect associated with the cost increase: the couple will be relatively poorer because the cost of children has increased. As a result, the income effect will induce the couple to have fewer children (assuming that children are viewed as normal goods). The net outcome of these two reinforcing effects will be to reduce the couple's fertility from ON to ON''

[4] Recall that in consumer theory a good is defined as "normal" if more of it is demanded when the consumer's income is higher.

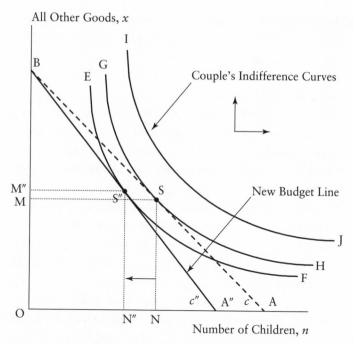

FIGURE 8.3 The effect of the cost of children on fertility

in Figure 8.3. The couple's optimal choice of children and other goods is shown as S″ in the figure.

In summary, the theory of fertility choice predicts that increases in income will increase fertility and that increases in the cost of children will decrease fertility. What evidence is there for this? I offer some interesting historical evidence from England.

As mentioned in the introduction to this chapter, all the developed countries of today have gone through a transition from high to low fertility. This transition began in England only around 1880, rather late in comparison to the timings in the other developed countries of today. The per capita income in England had been rising for nearly 100 years before that as a result of the Industrial Revolution. During this period, by the standards of the day, there was rapid population growth in England. This increase in population was consistent with the theory of fertility choice, which predicts that income increases should translate into fertility increases if children are normal goods.

Thomas Malthus also drew the link between income and fertility in his famous work of 1798, *An Essay on the Principle of Population*. He argued that in times of abundance, when income levels rise above subsistence levels, fertility rises as well. The increase in fertility reduces the wage rate and brings income back to the subsistence level. If income falls below the subsistence level, on the other hand, some people die from starvation. The decline in population raises wages, and the rest of the people are back at a subsistence-level wage.

This Malthusian theory of population is consistent with the positive income effect of wage increases on fertility. What Malthus did not allow for—and this was why his theory went woefully wrong in modern times—was that other factors might intervene that could prevent the alleged inexorable movement toward subsistence-level incomes.

The demographer John Caldwell (1980) has identified the move to universal education as having significantly hastened the transition to low fertility in the now developed countries.[5] Among other things, the laws calling for compulsory education raised the cost of children to parents and thus lowered marital fertility. The timing is uncanny. England's Education Act of 1870 started the move toward compulsory education, which then became law in 1880. As Caldwell points out, marital fertility began to decrease in England and Wales between 1871 and 1881. Other European countries saw fertility transitions that coincided with laws making education compulsory. Why should this have been so? Prior to compulsory education, the developed countries of today used child labor for their farms and factories. But once children were required to attend school, they could no longer subsidize their own existence by working, so the cost of children to parents went up. In line with the prediction of theory, when the cost of children went up, fertility went down. Myron Weiner (1991) has observed that even if there are laws banning child labor, they can really be enforced only when education is mandatory.[6] For then the authorities need peruse only school registers to identify potential child laborers.

III. Fertility Choice in Poor Countries

The standard model of fertility presented in the previous section needs to be adapted when applied to poor countries. Fertility rates tend to be *high*, not low, in poor countries. We have to first understand what motivates poor people to have many children. Policy measures that merely increase the number of family planning clinics and disburse free contraceptives, while useful, may be misguided supply-side responses to the problem. They fail to account for the reason that there is a demand for large families in the first place. Although the opinions of researchers on the effectiveness of family planning programs are not uniform, the evidence is that they are useful when the desired fertility rate has been lowered but the means to implement it are not readily available.[7] In other words, although such programs can be very effec-

[5] Caldwell, J. (1980), "Mass Education as a Determinant of the Timing of Fertility Decline," *Population and Development Review* 6, pp. 225–255.

[6] Weiner, M. (1991), *The Child and the State in India*, Princeton University Press, Princeton, NJ, Chap. 6.

[7] For a useful discussion of this debate, see, for example, Bongaarts, J. (1997), "The Role of Family Planning Programmes in Contemporary Fertility Transitions," in *The Continuing Demographic Transition*, ed. G. W. Jones, R. M. Douglas, J. C. Caldwell, and R. M. D'Souza, Clarendon Press, Oxford, UK.

tive in averting unwanted pregnancies at the onset of the demographic transition, they are not equipped to bring about a reduction in the desired number of children.

A very important source of the demand for large families in developing countries is the fact that old-age security for parents comes from children. This is particularly true in South Asia, which is a region of considerable population growth. (It comprises about a quarter of the world's population but accounts for a third of the annual increase in the world's population.) In rich countries, people set aside some of the income they earn while working for the period when they will be retired. For this they can use several financial instruments: savings accounts, ownership of bonds, shares in companies, real estate, and so on. In poor countries—especially in the rural countryside, where the bulk of the population resides—there are few financial assets available for transferring income from one's working life to one's retirement. Parents view *children* as vehicles for ensuring security in old age. Even when financial instruments are available, they are rarely deemed substitutable for children. Adult children can potentially provide security against the innumerable contingencies that can arise in old age. Eric Jensen (1990) has provided compelling evidence for the old-age security hypothesis.[8] Using Malaysian data from 1982, he examined the decisions of couples to use contraceptives. He found that old-age security concerns were very important: only couples who had satisfied their perceived old-age security needs opted for contraception.

Although security in old age may provide the motivation for having children, it does not follow that the fertility rate will be higher than what would be deemed optimal for the society. Indeed, were a benevolent social planner to have the power to impose a fertility level on each family, she would need to consult the preferences with regard to fertility of typical parents. If an imbalance is to arise between the privately optimal fertility of a typical couple and that deemed optimal for their society, there must be some mismatch between the benefits and/or costs that a social planner would account for and those that individual couples would account for. What are the sources of such a discrepancy?

An important source of socially harmful fertility behavior is the fact that although parents may altruistically consider the well-being of their children, they do not weight it equally with their own. The mechanism, which was first proposed by Philip Neher (1971), is as follows.[9] Consider a poor country in which land is communally owned and children are the only assets. An additional child imposes a cost on his parents when young. When the child

[8] Jensen, E. R. (1990), "An Econometric Analysis of the Old Age Security Motive for Childbearing," *International Economic Review* 31, pp. 953–968.

[9] Neher, P. A. (1971), "Peasants, Procreation, and Pensions," *American Economic Review* 61, pp. 380–389.

becomes an adult, he generates income in excess of his own consumption and is therefore a benefit to his parents. When the offspring reaches retirement, his consumption again exceeds his income, and now it needs to be subsidized by his children. Thus an additional child is a net cost in childhood, a net benefit in adulthood, and again a net cost in retirement. Parents incur the offspring's cost in childhood and reap a benefit in adulthood. But when their offspring again becomes a cost to society in retirement, the parents most likely will be dead. It is therefore very likely that in contemplating additional children, parents will either ignore or underestimate the cost that their offspring will impose on subsequent generations in their retirement. However, a benevolent social planner who weights future generations on a par with the present one will not. Thus parents who are not completely altruistic will *overestimate* the benefits of children relative to the costs they impose on society. As a result, their privately chosen fertility level will be too high relative to what is optimal for society.

IV. Economic Development and Fertility

Economic development, by eliminating the wedge between the private and the social net benefits of children, plays an important role in reducing fertility. With economic development come capital markets offering various financial instruments for saving. Along with these, private firms begin to offer pension plans and the government may offer social security. These greatly reduce the need for parents to use children as vehicles for transferring income from their working life to retirement. On these grounds alone, one would expect to see declining fertility with economic development.

The model presented in Section II embraces the simplifying fiction that a couple can be thought of as a single unit when it comes to fertility choices. There are at least two reasons that this is a simplification that ought to be done away with. First, children are a greater cost to women than to men. To gain a better understanding of how fertility responds to changes in economic conditions, it would be fruitful to separate out the effects on men and women. Second, the preferences of men and women as to how many children to have can be quite different.

Before we abandon the simplification of identical preferences, however, it is useful to note that the labor market wage rate and the cost of children are interrelated. Suppose that the woman's wage rate is w_f, the man's is w_m, and the time available to each for work is fixed at 1 unit. The couple's income, y, will be $(w_f + w_m)$ if both members engage in full-time market work. Much of the cost of children really comes from the time parents devote to taking care of the child. Suppose that each child requires a fixed amount of time, t, so the couple will have to curtail working in the labor market by that amount. If the woman curtails her market work, the couple will have to forgo an income of $w_f t$ for each child. Thus the cost per child, c, can be written $w_f t$. Notice that the couple's income and the cost per child both depend on the woman's wage rate.

Suppose that with economic development the wage rates increase. The couple's income will increase, but so will the cost per child. The former will tend to increase fertility (income effect) and the latter to decrease it (substitution effect), as we have seen. What will be the net effect of the wage increase? In theory, we cannot tell for sure. But economists believe that the effect of higher cost overwhelms the effect of higher incomes. It is for this reason that with economic development, fertility declines in country after country.

The wage rate that will be more relevant to fertility choice is clearly the wife's, because it is her time allocation that will be affected more strongly by the presence of young children. It is when *her* wage rate increases that we will expect to see a decline in fertility because the opportunity cost of her time will increase. She will now be giving up more by way of earnings by diverting time to children.

Oded Galor and David Weil (1996) have proposed that when the capital stock of a nation increases during the process of economic development, it impinges differently on the wages of men and women.[10] Although both engage in manual and nonmanual work, men have a relative advantage in manual work and women in nonmanual work. The productivity of a worker depends on how much capital he or she has to work with; the greater the capital stock per person, the higher the productivity of his or her labor. If the increase in the capital stock (through saving) increases the productivity of nonmanual labor more than it does that of manual labor, the wage rate of women will rise faster than that of men. Richer couples want more children, as we have seen. However, whether a couple has children and how many depend on the woman's wage rate relative to the family income, because that determines the relative cost of the woman's opting out of market work during and after pregnancy. The relative increase in the wage rate of women leads to an increase in their participation in the labor market and a decline in fertility.[11]

Given the arguments outlined above, the reader might infer that no special measures need be taken with regard to excessive population growth in developing countries if they are showing respectable economic growth. The higher cost of children in terms of income forgone and the emergence of financial instruments for the purpose of saving will automatically reduce fertility. In

[10] Galor, O., and D. N. Weil (1996), "The Gender Gap, Fertility, and Growth," *American Economic Review* 86, pp. 374–387.

[11] The ratio of the opportunity cost of the first child to the couple's income is $w_f t / [w_f (1 - t) + w_m]$, because the woman can work in the labor market for only an amount of time $(1 - t)$. It is easy to see that this ratio increases when the ratio w_f / w_m increases. When the family income goes up by, say, 10%, the opportunity cost of the child increases by more than 10%.

the words of a popular quip of the 1970s, "Economic development is the best contraceptive."

Such an inference, however, is unwarranted. The growth rates of the GDPs of many developing countries with rapidly growing populations are very low. Indeed, part of the reason that per capita GDP grows slowly is that population growth outpaces the rate at which capital accumulates through savings. Families with many children cannot save. Thus waiting for economic growth to dilute the incentives of couples to reduce their fertility by increasing the cost of children may indefinitely postpone fertility reduction.

V. The Demographic Transition

There are additional good reasons for the governments of developing countries to be more proactive with regard to population problems. A statistical relationship upon which demographers have long focused is that between the decline in a country's infant or child mortality rate and the rate of population growth.[12] As the country's child mortality rate declines, the rate of population growth also declines subsequently.

In Figure 8.4, the curve ABCD represents the death rate (say, the number of deaths, on average, per 1,000 people chosen randomly), and the curve EFGH represents the birth rate (say, the number of births, on average, per 1,000 people chosen randomly). The difference between the birth rate and the death rate, naturally, will be a measure of the rate of population growth.

Almost all countries experience long periods of time during which their birth and death rates are constant. These rates are shown as OE and OA, respectively, in Figure 8.4. The vertical distance AE measures the corresponding rate of population growth. For reasons that mostly have to do with better nutrition and advances in medical knowledge, at some point in time the death rate falls fairly steeply (from B to C) and then levels out. After a lag of a few years, the birth rate also falls steeply (from F to G) and levels out. Interestingly, the decline in the birth rate is greater than the decline in the death rate. Consequently, the rate of population growth after this "demographic transition" (as measured by the vertical distance DH) is *lower* than before the transition. This transition from high to low fertility and population growth is one of the most important events in the demographic and economic histories of societies. All the developed countries have gone through this transition.

Why does the demographic transition occur when the death rate falls? In fact, it is not hard to see that there is a causal connection between the two: all else constant, reductions in child mortality rates are responsible for

---

[12]The infant (or child) mortality rate is defined as the average number of 1,000 infants (or children) born today who will die before they are 1 year (or 5 years) old.

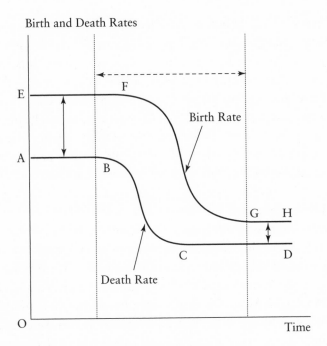

FIGURE 8.4 The demographic transition

declines in the rates of population growth. The reason for this causal connection between death rate and fertility is that the possibility of the death of children exposes parents to considerable risk. There are hardly any human attachments that are stronger than those of parents to their children. This is certainly true in developed countries, where old-age security concerns do not motivate fertility choice, but it is also true and has even greater force in developing countries, where they do. Faced with the possibility of child mortality, parents *overcompensate* for child mortality in their fertility decisions, especially when they have an old-age security motive.

To see how this happens, suppose that the number of children desired by a typical couple is 4 if all children are assured of survival. When the child mortality rate is 25%, on average 1 of the 4 children will not survive to adulthood. If the parents want to merely compensate for this expected loss, they will increase their fertility to 5, and the rate of population growth for their family will stay the same. (This is because, despite their greater fertility, on average 1 child will die and not contribute to the population.) However, quite apart from the fact that on average only 4 out of 5 children can be expected to survive, *uncertainty* is introduced by child mortality. The loss of 1 child in 4 is only an *average*; a couple can lose 0, 1, 2, 3, or all 4 children. The possibility that they may lose more than one child—and possibly all of them—invariably leads parents to overcompensate for the possible loss by increasing their fertility to more than 5. In other words, parents tend to "hoard" children to protect themselves against the contingency of being left without adequate support in their old age. The extent of the "excess" fertility will naturally depend on the child mortality rate. When this mortality rate declines, it takes some time before the new level becomes apparent to prospective parents. Sooner or later, parents perceive a reduction in the need for excess fertility, and thus the rate of population growth declines.[13]

Mark Rosenzweig and Theodore Schultz (1983), on analyzing American data for the years 1967–69, found that "the average number of children per mother would increase by one-sixth of a child if an infant mortality rate of 0.1 were anticipated."[14] This, it must be noted, is the estimated effect of increased child mortality in a highly developed country where parents do not expect their children to provide old-age security. In a developing country where parents do, one would expect the response to be even stronger.

Figure 8.5 shows the change in the fertility of a typical woman during the past five decades in various regions of the world. We see that there has been a drastic decline in average fertility in all developing regions. Nevertheless, in Sub-Saharan Africa the average fertility rate is still around 5 children per woman. We also note that the fertility rate in North America and other OECD countries has fallen below the replacement level, that is, the fertility rate that would reproduce the population in terms of size generation after generation without immigration.

VI. The Role of Child Labor in Fertility Decline

High child mortality rates in developing countries can induce high levels of fertility for an additional reason that works through the institution of child labor.[15] Although this is hardly a concern anymore in the developed countries, in a developing country the investment in a child's education depends on the child mortality rate, for two reasons. First, when the child mortality rate is low, offspring are expected to live long, so the return on their educational investment is high. Parents opt to send their children to school and thereby forgo their income from child labor. When the child mortality rate is high, however, parents do not choose this option (especially when child labor is a socially accepted institution). Second, not only does a high rate of child mortality reduce the rate of return to education, it also renders educated chil-

---

[13] For a general demonstration of how reductions in mortality rates can induce a demographic transition, see Eswaran, M. (1998), "One Explanation for the Demographic Transition in Developing Countries," *Oxford Economic Papers* 50, pp. 237–265.

[14] Rosenzweig, M. R., and T. P. Schultz (1983), "Consumer Demand and Household Production: The Relationship between Fertility and Child Mortality," *American Economic Review* 73, pp. 38–42, quote on 42.

[15] This link is examined in Eswaran, M. (2000), "Fertility, Literacy, and the Institution of Child Labour," in *Institutions, Incentives, and Economic Reforms in India,* ed. S. Kahkonen and A. Lanyi, Sage Publications, New Delhi, pp. 267–296.

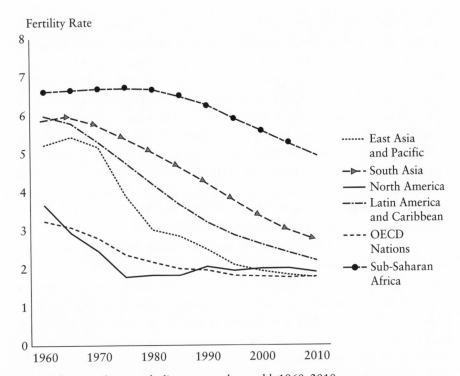

Fertility Rate

.... East Asia
and Pacific
--▶-- South Asia
—— North America
—·—· Latin America
and Caribbean
---- OECD
Nations
--●-- Sub-Saharan
Africa

FIGURE 8.5 Fertility rate declines across the world, 1960–2010

Sources: World Bank, Gender Statistics: (1) United Nations Population Division, *World Population Prospects;* (2) United Nations Statistical Division, *Population and Vital Statistics Report* (various years); (3) various national statistical offices, census reports and other statistical publications; (4) Eurostat, *Demographic Statistics;* (5) Secretariat of the Pacific Community, *Statistics and Demography Programme;* and (6) U.S. Census Bureau, *International Database.*

dren more risky "assets" than uneducated ones. For both of these reasons, people who are poor prefer to put their children to work: among the poor, child labor is promoted by high child mortality rates. In such a scenario, the poor will not educate their children even if credit is made available to them.[16] The rich, on the other hand, do not need the income from child labor, and besides, they can reduce child mortality by expending resources privately on healthcare. In effect, high child mortality rates encourage high fertility rates among the poor, and, when child labor laws are either nonexistent or unenforceable, they also increase the incidence of child labor.

Thus reductions in child mortality, apart from directly lowering fertility, have the additional salutary effect of reducing child labor and increasing the

---

[16] There is evidence from India that, holding income constant, an increase in the number of school-age children in a family increases the probability that the children will work. Furthermore, when children's survival rate in a village increases, so does the probability that they will be engaged in full-time study. See Cigno, A., and F. C. Rosati (2001), "Why Do Indian Children Work, and Is It Bad for Them?," working paper, Faculty of Political Science, University of Florence, Italy.

skill level of the labor force of the next generation. Furthermore, because educated parents tend to educate their children, improvements in the health of one generation of children can permanently increase the skill level of the labor force and move the economy out of poverty. And affluence, as we have seen, brings about an independent reduction in fertility rates if the opportunity costs of parents' time increase and also if child mortality can be reduced by accessing healthcare services. When children become expensive—because child labor income is lost to parents and instead parents need to incur educational expenditures—couples naturally have fewer children. Parents opt for "quality" rather than "quantity" with regard to their children. In most of today's developed countries, the introduction of compulsory education for children was accompanied by a decline in fertility for this reason.

Strictly speaking, the argument made above refers to children who have successfully lived through childhood but die as adults (when they would have been of use to parents for old-age security). In developing countries, we would expect the probability of death of young adults to be high when the mortality rates of children are high—because the predominant reason for both is the prevalence of infectious diseases. In India, for example, over the period 1970–83 around one in three children who lived long enough to be able to receive schooling died before providing old-age security for his parents for the entire length of their retirement.[17]

VII. The Importance of Female Autonomy in Fertility Choice

We now drop the assumption that both members of a couple have identical preferences with regard to fertility choices. Female autonomy (that is, women's independence in decision making) is an important factor determining fertility and child mortality. As before, we interpret female autonomy as women's bargaining power within their households. In Chapter 3 we saw that having higher threat utilities gives married women greater bargaining power with respect to their husbands. The first scholars to recognize the importance of female autonomy in relation to demography were Tim Dyson and Mick Moore (1983) in the context of Indian states.[18] They argued that kinship arrangements (that is, family relationships through marriage) are important in the determination of women's bargaining power. There are considerable differences in the demographics of the northern and southern states of India. The northern states are characterized by low levels of female autonomy because of kinship arrangements that minimize the support married

[17] See Eswaran, M. (2002), "The Empowerment of Women, Fertility, and Child Mortality: Towards a Theoretical Analysis," *Journal of Population Economics* 15, pp. 433–454.

[18] Dyson, T., and M. Moore (1983), "On Kinship Structure, Female Autonomy, and Demographic Behavior in India," *Population and Development Review* 9, pp. 35–60.

women receive. These states display high fertility and child mortality rates. Women in these states typically marry relative strangers from other villages, and after marriage they retain almost no ties with their natal families. They have low threat utilities and hence little bargaining power in their households. In the southern states, women have considerable autonomy: marriages tend to occur within villages, to grooms who are not relative strangers, and the women maintain considerable contact with their natal families after marriage. Their higher threat utilities give them considerable bargaining power. These southern states display lower fertility and child mortality rates than the northern states.

Even in developed countries, the relative bargaining power in couples is tilted in favor of males; in developing countries, the disparity is far greater. This asymmetry has many reasons. Males are more likely to work in the labor force, and even if wives earn incomes, their husbands' incomes are likely to be higher. As we saw in Chapter 5, ownership of property—in particular, land—is usually vested in males. Therefore, any credit that may be made available (upon the provision of collateral) to households is accessible only to the males. Added to these factors is the considerable weight of religious, cultural, and social norms that put women in a weak bargaining position relative to men. As we have seen above, kinship systems are important cultural and social determinants of female autonomy.

The relative bargaining powers of males and females have considerable influence over a couple's fertility and resource allocation within their household. Parents have some discretion over the amount of money they choose to spend on a child's nutrition and healthcare. Child mortality rates depend, to a significant degree, on the amount of this discretionary spending. These rates are observed to be much lower when mothers exercise control over household resources. As we saw in Chapter 3, empirical research has sought to identify how a household's expenditures on various goods vary with the identity of the income earner. Recall from that chapter that Hoddinott and Haddad (1995) found that, in Côte d'Ivoire, an increase in the wife's share of cash income significantly increases the shares of expenditures on food and reduces those on alcohol and cigarettes. Also recall that Thomas (1990) found that in Brazil unearned income accruing to the mother has a far greater effect on the family's health than that accruing to the father. In fact, the effect on child survival probabilities of an additional dollar is 20 times greater in the former case.

There is a simple economic reason that mothers devote more resources to the nutrition and healthcare of children.[19] For a couple with a limited amount of resources, there is a trade-off between the number of children

[19]The arguments made in this and the following two paragraphs are drawn from Eswaran, M. (2002), cited earlier.

they can have and the health of these children. If the resources are spread out over many children, naturally each child will receive less nutrition and healthcare attention. As a result, the child mortality rate will be higher than if the couple has only a few children. Because mothers bear a greater proportion of the costs of children, they prefer to have few children and ensure their survival by devoting resources to them. Fathers, on the other hand, prefer to have many children and to devote little by way of resources to each of them. This is because children take up much more of their mothers' time than their fathers'. Fathers and mothers, in other words, have different preferences regarding how many children to have and how much by way of resources should be devoted to the healthcare of these children. As bargaining power shifts in favor of mothers, couples will have fewer but healthier children. This is what happens in families in which the mothers have greater threat utilities. Empowering women is good for children.

There is an additional benefit to society that accrues from the empowerment of women. As we saw in the previous section, the lower the child mortality rate, the lower the risk and the higher the expected return from the education of children. This elicits more resources for the education of children. Thus, an increase in the relative bargaining power of mothers results not only in fewer and healthier children but also in a better-educated labor force. These benefits with regard to fertility alone render the empowerment of women an important influence on the speed of the demographic transition.

Whenever those who make the decisions share in the benefits but do not bear a commensurate share of the costs, the decisions are unlikely to be optimal from society's point of view. The reason is that the decisions will be based on the decision maker's share of the costs and benefits and not on the total costs and benefits. As a result, there is likely to be a mismatch between the total costs and the benefits of those decisions. Because in patriarchal societies males have decision-making power in excess—often vastly in excess—of the burden of the consequences of their decisions, the decisions pertaining to fertility and expenditures on the nutrition and healthcare of children are unlikely to be optimal from the social point of view. A move toward fewer and healthier children as a result of greater female autonomy, therefore, would also be in line with what would be optimal from the point of view of society at large.

VIII. Why Females Are Victims of Fertility Decline

A significant aspect of fertility in South and East Asia is the desired sex composition of a family's children: there is a strong preference for male children. Economically and culturally, males are deemed to be of greater value than females. In South Asia, old-age security is expected only from male children. Female children, in contrast, are often seen as economic burdens because they have to be married off, with dowries that are worth several years' income of their parents. In East Asia, old-age security may not be the most important reason for this son preference. Sons are valued more than daughters because, culturally, sons apparently enhance the emotional and spiritual goals of their parents, and they also perpetuate the family name.

Preference for children of a particular sex tends to increase fertility. To see this, suppose that every couple's primary desire is to have two male children (as opposed to two children of any sex). Couples whose first two children happen to be males will not have more children. Couples with one or two female children will continue to reproduce. This will naturally increase the average fertility rate relative to that of a population of couples who desire two children but have no gender preference.

One way to examine parents' preference for children of one sex is by looking at what is referred to as the *sex ratio*. This is the ratio of the number of males per 100 females. If this ratio is 110, for example, it means that for every 100 women there are 10 extra males. The sex ratio can be computed for any age group or for any segment of the population. Usually this is done at the population level and at birth. At the level of the population, this ratio is simply the ratio of all the males in the population to all the females in the population, multiplied by 100. For most developed countries, where there is no strong preference for children of one sex, this ratio is less than 100. For example, in the year 2011 the population sex ratio was 96.9 for the United Kingdom, 96.7 for the United States, and 95.9 for Canada.[20] The reason there are more women than men in the populations of these countries is that women typically outlive men. The sex ratio of the population at large in developing countries, however, is higher than 100; in the year 2011, for example, it was 105.2 for China and 107.3 for India. One important reason for distorted sex ratios is that women face various forms of discrimination that increases their death rates at every age level. In Asia, there are about 105 males for every 100 females.

The sex ratio at birth is the number of male children born for every 100 female children born. Because male children die slightly more frequently than female children in the first year of their lives, evolutionary forces have led nature to compensate for this by making the sex ratio at birth slightly larger than 100. As a result, even in developed countries with no discernible preference for children of a given sex, the sex ratio at birth is around 106. But this male advantage is quickly lost in the first year.

There is a disturbing trend in the sex ratio at birth in many developing countries: this ratio is often highly biased against girls. (Consult again Table 1.3 of Chapter 1 to review sex ratios at birth by region.) This is par-

---

[20]These figures and those for China and India (below) in this paragraph are from the *UN Demographic Yearbook 2011* and China's National Bureau of Statistics.

ticularly true in South Asia (essentially in India) and East Asia (China, Taiwan, and Korea). The immediate reason for this skewed sex ratio at birth is thought to be sex-selective abortion—female fetuses detected by amniocentesis and ultrasound techniques are often aborted—or, in some countries, female infanticide. The numbers are alarming: in 2011 this ratio was 118 in China and 108 in India.

As a result of a strong parental preference for male children, girls often do not receive the same medical attention to alleviate illnesses as boys. In India, for example, in the event of an illness boys, on average, are more likely to be taken to a doctor than girls. Discrimination against females results, as noted earlier, in a distorted sex ratio not just at birth but also at more advanced ages.

In cultures with a strong preference for sons, one would also expect that discrimination against female children would increase in the birth order of the daughters. There would be greater discrimination against the second daughter than against the first, greater against the third daughter than against the second, and so on. As a couple felt burdened with more and more children of the less desired or undesired sex, the more they would discriminate against these children. This is indeed observed.[21]

There are reasons that fertility decline may exacerbate discrimination against female infants and children. Suppose that the autonomy of adult women and/or the cost of their time increases because of better employment opportunities. This will lead, as we have seen, to a reduction in fertility. However, if cultural biases persist, it may be the case that old-age security will still be expected from only male children. Parents with only two children, say, may perceive that they cannot afford to have even one female child. Thus discrimination against female children may increase. Monica Das Gupta (1987) found that in the district of Ludhiana in Punjab, India, the education of women reduced child mortality rates but increased the disparity between the mortality rates of female children of high birth order and the remaining children.[22] The education of all children—and females in particular—may alleviate this problem over time, but it will not necessarily eliminate it by making it possible for daughters, too, to provide old-age security. To the extent that cultural values dictate which institutions (such as old-age security) promote one's self-interest, education may prove ineffective—except when it manages to dislodge cultural norms.

In Chapter 3 we discussed how beliefs are passed on through a culture and acquire a life of their own even when the environment changes. Beliefs

---

[21] For select states in India, see Das Gupta, M., and P. N. Mari Bhat (1997), "Fertility Decline and Increased Manifestation of Sex Bias in India," *Population Studies* 51, pp. 307–315. For data on China, see Hull, T. H. (1990), "Recent Trends in Sex Ratios at Birth in China," *Population and Development Review* 16, pp. 63–83.

[22] Das Gupta, M. (1987), "Selective Discrimination against Female Children in Rural Punjab, India," *Population and Development Review* 13, pp. 77–100.

become durable through the vehicle of culture. The preference for sons offers another example of this. In some cultures such a preference may have some rationale based on economics (such as old-age support). Nevertheless, even when the underlying rationale is no longer relevant, a preference for sons may persist. This is best seen by looking at the behavior of immigrants to the developed countries.

Sylvie Dubuc and David Coleman (2007) compared the sex ratios at birth of children of India-born mothers in England and Wales with those of children of native-born mothers for the period 1969–2005.[23] They found that although the sex ratios at birth of the children of native-born mothers showed a slight downward trend over this period, the sex ratios of children born to India-born mothers showed the opposite trend. This latter trend emulated that in India over the same period. Mothers were clearly transporting their preference for sons from their home country to their adopted country even though the latter's economic and social environments were very different from those of India. The conclusion the authors draw is that India-born mothers were using sex-selective abortion to choose the sex of especially higher-birth-order children.

Douglas Almond and Lena Edlund (2008) found similarly distorted sex ratios at birth of children born in the United States to parents of Asian origin.[24] Using the U.S. census for 2000, they examined these ratios for children born to Chinese, Koreans, and East Indians. The patterns they found mimicked those in the corresponding Asian countries. The sex ratios at birth were particularly distorted for children of higher birth order. For example, for the third child, boys outnumbered girls by 50%. This suggests that parents of Asian origin in the United States tolerate having girls as long as they are of low birth order but become increasing desperate for boys in higher-order births and so go in for sex selection.

Similar findings have been obtained for South and East Asians in Canada by Douglas Almond, Lena Edlund, and Kevin Milligan (2013).[25] They find that for first-generation immigrants in Canada the sex ratio at birth is higher than normal for third-order births and that these parents are more willing than second-generation immigrants to try for a third child. The highest sex ratios were found among the Sikhs. An interesting finding of the study is that among the South and East Asian immigrants who are Christian and Muslim, there is no distortion in the sex ratio (though they may be more willing to

[23] Dubuc, S., and D. Coleman (2007), "An Increase in the Sex Ratio of Births to India-Born Mothers in England and Wales: Evidence for Sex-Selective Abortion," *Population and Development Review* 33, pp. 383–400.

[24] Almond, D., and L. Edlund (2008), "Son-Biased Sex Ratios in the 2000 United States Census," *Proceedings of the National Academy of Sciences* 105, pp. 5681–5682.

[25] Almond, D., L. Edlund, and K. Milligan (2013), "Son Preference and the Persistence of Culture: Evidence from South and East Asian Immigrants to Canada," *Population and Development Review* 39, pp. 75–95.

satisfy their preference for sons by having more children). The reason for the absence of distortion in the sex ratio is most likely that both Christianity and Islam ban sex selection.

Many countries have high fertility rates, as we noted in the introduction to this chapter. The argument outlined above suggests that the serious problems of high fertility rates and the changing sex composition of families are separate issues. The solution to the former may exacerbate the latter, and this claim is supported by recent data. High fertility rates are due to the low value placed on the time of women, their low levels of autonomy, and the fact that old-age security is provided by children. The problem of the skewed sex composition of families is due to parents' perception that male children more than female children provide security of various kinds. Because males and females are not culturally assessed to have such different values in Africa, despite their poverty African countries display sex ratios at birth that are remarkably free of the bias observed in South and East Asia.

In a comparison across China, South Korea, and the northwestern states of India, Monica M. Das Gupta, Jiang Zhenghua, Li Bohua, Xie Zhenming, Woojin Chung, and Bae Hwa-Ok (2003) have argued that the high sex ratios in all three countries are largely due to the patriarchal structure of their societies.[26] Their argument is that in these societies assets pass across generations only through male children (patrilineally), and this makes it difficult for women to sustain themselves without being attached to men. Furthermore, the practice whereby women move from their natal families to their husbands' homes (patrilocality) reinforces this handicap. What separates these three societies from others in which sex ratios are not distorted is the rigidity with which patriarchal norms are enforced in the former. In Europe, Das Gupta et al. argue, the rules of inheritance historically were more lax: if there was no male heir, for example, daughters could inherit land.

It is important to note, however, that cultural values in the preference for sons do respond to economic incentives. In an interesting paper using data from China, Nancy Qian (2008) has shown that sex ratios are more balanced in regions where women's economic contributions are greater.[27] The difficulty with establishing this causality from women's earnings to sex ratios comes from the fact that women in such regions may already have higher status for other reasons, and it may be this higher status that is responsible for their higher earnings. To get around this problem, Qian uses the fact that some of the post-Mao reforms in China (after 1978) favored growing tea in some regions and orchards in others. Women have a comparative advantage

---

[26] Das Gupta, M., J. Zhenghua, L. Bohua, X. Zhenming, W. Chung, and B. Hwa-Ok (2003), "Why Is Son Preference So Persistent in East and South Asia?: A Cross-Country Study of China, India, and the Republic of Korea," *Journal of Development Studies* 40:2, pp. 153–187.

[27] Qian, N. (2008), "Missing Women and the Price of Tea in China: The Effect of Sex-Specific Earnings on Sex Imbalance," *Quarterly Journal of Economics* 123, pp. 1251–1285.

in tea production, whereas men have the advantage in orchards. As a result, tea-growing regions have seen a greater increase in women's earnings than regions with orchards. Qian compares the imbalance in the sex ratios among cohorts born before and after these reforms. In this manner she isolates the effects of increases in female and male incomes.

Qian finds that in the rural areas of China, in the early 1980s a 10% increase in female incomes, holding male incomes constant, increased the proportion of surviving girls by 1 percentage point. Furthermore, it also increased the education of girls and boys by around half a year. On the other hand, an increase in male incomes reduced the survival and educational attainment of girls but left the attainment of boys unchanged. An increase in total household incomes had no effect on either survival rates or educational attainment. What mattered were changes in the *relative* incomes of males and females. This is very strong evidence suggesting that economic factors are important contributors to skewed sex ratios. The large number of missing women in China is likely significantly affected by the gender wage gap. These results also suggest that cultural preferences can be countered by appropriate economic reforms that alter incentives.

Distorted sex ratios at birth can have serious social consequences in the long term. Over decades, an increasing gap between the numbers of males and females of marriageable age causes a serious shortage of brides. Because most cultures are averse to polyandry, this condemns a significant proportion of marriageable men to remain without mates. This, in turn, will certainly generate intense competition between males for mates. There will likely be escalating violence between males and an increase in forced abductions of marriageable females.

Lena Edlund, Hongbin Li, Junjian Yi, and Junsen Zhang (2013) have examined the relationship between sex ratios and crime rates in China.[28] The country has experienced substantial rates of increase in crime in recent decades. Edlund et al. seek an explanation along the lines suggested by the evolutionary biologist Trivers (1972), whose argument we first encountered in Chapter 2. This argument is that evolution has hard-wired men with few prospects of finding mates to engage in risky behavior, for if they don't, their genes are doomed to extinction. Edlund et al. look at the relationship between the sex ratios of 16- to 25-year-olds at the level of provinces and the rates of violent and property-related crimes. They find, using information on sex ratios from China's 2000 census, that about a seventh of the recent increase in China's crime rates can be attributed to distorted sex ratios that result in "surplus men."

Over the long haul, one might expect that the scarcity of females will increase the value of brides in societies with currently high sex ratios. Dowries

[28] Edlund, L., H. Li, J. Yi, and J. Zhang (2013), "Sex Ratios and Crime: Evidence from China," *Review of Economics and Statistics* 95, pp. 1520–1534.

that brides' families have to pay may even give way to bride prices, that is, grooms and their families may have to pay the brides' families. Parents may look more favorably on female children, and the sex ratio at birth will begin to fall. The imbalance in the sex ratio will ultimately sort itself out, though with considerable upheaval in the intervening decades.

Is there reason to believe that this upbeat but speculative scenario will actually transpire? South Korea appears to offer some evidence in the affirmative. This evidence has been provided by Woojin Chung and Monica Das Gupta (2007).[29] South Korea has been a patriarchal society with a strong preference for sons since the late fourteenth century. Female infanticide was the means used to control the sex ratio at birth prior to the appearance of sex-selective abortion technologies in the 1980s. The sex ratio at birth peaked in the country at around 115 in the mid-1990s. Remarkably, this ratio started declining fairly steeply after that, and in 2005 the sex ratio was around 108 (still way above normal). Chung and Das Gupta showed that between 1991 and 2003, the proportion of women who stated that they "must have a son" declined by half. The authors interpret this as a change in the preference for sons. (There is always the possibility that parents still have a preference for sons but are forced to accept daughters because sons may not find brides.) The authors argue that much of this purported change in preferences is due to changing social norms. They believe that this reversal in the trend in sex ratios and the change in preferences offer hope to other countries, like China and India, with currently high sex ratios.[30]

IX. "Missing Women"

If the sex ratio in a country is higher than normal, that means that there are more men relative to women than normal. In other words, women who ought to exist do not; some women are "missing," either because they were never born or because they died prematurely. Amartya Sen (1990, 1992) and Ansley Coale (1991) undertook an exercise in which they calculated the number of women missing as a result of distorted sex ratios.[31] If we make an assumption about what the sex ratio ought to be, we can readily obtain an estimate

[29] Chung, W., and M. Das Gupta (2007), "The Decline of Son Preference in South Korea: The Role of Development and Public Policy," *Population and Development Review* 33, pp. 757–783.

[30] For a less optimistic view on South Korea's sex ratio and son preference, see Edlund, L., and C. Lee (2013), "Son Preference, Sex Selection, and Economic Development: The Case of South Korea," NBER Working Paper 18679, National Bureau of Economic Research, Cambridge, MA.

[31] Sen, A. K. (1990), "More Than 100 Women Are Missing," *New York Review of Books* 37, December 20; Sen, A. K. (1992), "Missing Women," *British Medical Journal* 304, pp. 587–588; and Coale, A. J. (1991), "Excess Female Mortality and the Balance of the Sexes in the Population: An Estimate of the Number of 'Missing Females,'" *Population and Development Review* 17, pp. 517–523.

of the number of missing women. For example, suppose that we assume that the sex ratio should be 100 for a country, but in reality the sex ratio is much higher, 110. If there are 200 million males in the country, the actual sex ratio in the population tells us that the number of females the country actually has is 200 × 100/110 = 181.8 million. If the sex ratio had been 100, the number of females in the country would have been 200 × 100/100 = 200 million. Thus the number of missing women in the country is 200.0 million – 181.8 million = 18.2 million. Making different assumptions about what the sex ratio ought to be, Sen and Coale came up with different estimates. Sen computed the total number of missing women in the world to be in excess of 100 million, whereas Coale computed this number more conservatively at around 60 million in select areas of the world. Most of the women in Coale's estimate are missing from China (29.1 million) and India (22.8 million).

Whether we consider Sen's estimate or Coale's, the numbers show the colossal magnitude of the effects of what is almost surely discrimination against females. This could be due to a strong preference for sons, which parents could have implemented with greater ease in the past two decades. Technologies such as ultrasound and amniocentesis can ascertain the sex of a fetus at early stages, and parents with a strong preference for sons can opt for abortion if the child is of the "wrong" sex. This can tilt the sex ratio at birth in favor of boys, and this naturally will result in higher sex ratios at more advanced ages. Furthermore, even if female children are not desired but are born, there is scope for discrimination against them in terms of food and nutrition and also the healthcare funding devoted to them. This, too, will increase the sex ratios because more girls than boys will die of illness and malnutrition. Viewed in this way, the number of missing women is an indictment of parents' discriminatory behavior in a matter so fundamental as life and death.

The cultural preference for sons even shows up in the amount of time for which mothers breast-feed their children, as shown in a study by Seema Jayachandran and Ilyana Kuziemko (2011).[32] Breast-feeding is known to inhibit ovulation and so, naturally, reduces the probability of conceiving again. Mothers who want more children and so wish to become pregnant again will wean their babies earlier. In the presence of a strong preference for sons, mothers will be in less of a hurry to wean a son than a daughter. Of course the decision as to when to wean a child will depend not only on the sex of the present child but also on the number and sex composition of the child's siblings. Nevertheless, one would expect that in areas with a preference for sons a female child would be likely to be weaned earlier than a male child. Using three sets of data from India collected between 1992 and 2005, the authors find strong evidence

---

[32] Jayachandran, S., and I. Kuziemko (2011), "Why Do Mothers Breastfeed Girls Less Than Boys?: Evidence and Implications for Child Health in India," *Quarterly Journal of Economics* 126, pp. 1485–1538.

that this is indeed the case. The fact that girls are weaned sooner than boys has serious implications for the subsequent health of girls. Jayachandran and Kuziemko estimate that this discriminating practice with regard to breast-feeding could explain about 9% of the missing girls in India.

Siwan Anderson and Debraj Ray (2010) examined the ages at which women go missing and also the diseases to which they succumb.[33] They found that, contrary to what had hitherto been believed, missing women are not largely accounted for by sex-selective abortion. The majority of women who "go missing" in fact die prematurely in adult life, mostly due to cardiovascular diseases in India and China and to HIV/AIDS in Sub-Saharan Africa. Maternal mortality also contributes to the toll of missing women in India and Sub-Saharan Africa. The proportion of missing women due to sex-selective abortion is around 0% in Sub-Saharan Africa, 11% in India, and between 35% and 45% in China (where a one-child policy was implemented in 1979). The relatively normal sex ratio at birth in Africa had led previous researchers to believe that the problem of missing women was not serious in that region of the world. Anderson and Ray have shown that this is not so: in Sub-Saharan Africa, too, this is a very serious problem. In more recent work, the authors have shown that even in India, the distorted sex ratio at birth accounts for only 12% of its missing women.[34]

X. Summary

We started this chapter with a model of fertility choice that is relevant to rich countries. The predictions of the model are broadly consistent with the English demographic experience after the Industrial Revolution. A model more appropriate to poor countries showed that fertility rates in these countries are higher than socially optimal. Economic development alleviates this problem of excess fertility to some extent as financial instruments evolve, reducing the need for children to provide old-age support.

We also learned that an important ingredient of the demographic transition from high to low fertility rates is a reduction in child mortality. Government expenditure devoted to delivering healthcare to the poor is an important weapon for lowering fertility rates. We saw why women play a crucial role in the transition to lower fertility levels. They prefer to have fewer children but to spend more on their nutrition and healthcare than men do. When economic development tilts the bargaining power in women's favor, couples have fewer children.

---

[33] Anderson, S., and D. Ray (2010), "Missing Women: Age and Disease," *Review of Economic Studies* 77, pp. 1262–1300.

[34] Anderson, S., and D. Ray (2012), "The Age Distribution of Missing Women in India," *Economic and Political Weekly*, December 1, pp. 87–95.

Fertility decline in many developing countries in recent decades has been accompanied by increasing sex ratios at birth. We saw that this is one factor contributing to the number of "missing women" in these economies. Economic development may alleviate this problem but is unlikely to solve it by itself in a reasonable amount of time.

Exercises and Questions for Discussion

1. Outline a model of a theory of fertility appropriate for couples in rich countries. Explain how (a) an increase in a couple's income and (b) an increase in the cost of children affect the demand for children. In b, do the income and substitution effects work in the same or opposite directions? Explain.

2. How does the above model explain the facts associated with the demographic behavior of England after the Industrial Revolution? What effect did child labor have on English fertility? What role did compulsory education play in reducing English fertility? Why?

3. Explain why the fertility rates in poor countries today are high rather than low, contrary to what might be expected from a theory of fertility that views children as "consumer goods." Outline a more appropriate model for these countries. Why might economic development be expected to lead to lower fertility when children offer parents security in old age?

4. In the model of Galor and Weil (1996), what are the income and substitution effects on fertility associated with economic development? Why does fertility decline despite the increased income brought about by economic development?

5. The reduction in child mortality rates plays a crucial role in the demographic transition of countries. Explain why. What policy measures does this fact suggest for countries with high rates of population growth?

6. Why is it important to drop the "unitary" model of the household in favor of a bargaining model to understand fertility choice? Outline how culture and the kinship arrangements of marriage determine the bargaining outcome regarding fertility, and explain the mechanism through which they operate.

7. Why does a preference for sons tend to increase family sizes in poor countries? Discuss the various reasons why the sex ratios of young children (say under the age of 5) in South Asian and East Asian countries tend to be skewed in favor of boys.

8. What is the tragedy of "missing women," and what are its economic causes? What possible economic solutions are there to alleviate this serious problem?

9. In Country X, there are 300 million men and 268 million women.

(a) Compute the sex ratio for this population.
(b) If the correct sex ratio (that is, the sex ratio for a society free from bias against women) is deemed to be 96, compute the number of missing women in Country X.
(c) What would be some of the long-run consequences of a biased sex ratio of the sort obtained for Country X here?

10. Suppose that a country has an entrenched institution of dowries and also has a strong preference for sons. Explain what will happen to the dowry price in the long run when the sex ratio is distorted in favor of males.

CHAPTER NINE

How Do Women Benefit from Improved Access to Birth Control?

I. Introduction

This chapter deals with the question of how access to birth control technologies has affected, and still affects, the lives of women. In particular, we shall focus on two modern forms of contraception: the oral contraceptive ("the pill") and abortion. The magnitudes of the effects of these technologies vary widely depending on whether the women are from poor countries or rich ones. The evidence suggests that the majority of women in poor countries benefit immensely from access to birth control, and in very stark terms—maternal mortality (the death of women due to pregnancy, childbirth, and related matters) decreases as their access to birth control technologies increases. In rich countries, too, most of the women benefit from these technologies, though there may be a small minority of women who are hurt by them. By and large, modern birth control technologies have given women a considerable degree of control over their own bodies. It is the purpose of this chapter to examine the economic forces that shape the profound effects on women through these important advances in birth control technology.

Though birth control is an ancient practice, its introduction in modern forms has been hesitant and checkered. Part of the reason is that birth control goes counter to the teachings of many major religions.[1] Following a push for modern contraception by the American activist Margaret Sanger, pharmaceutical research led by George Pincus finally led to an oral contraceptive that was approved by the U.S. Food and Drug Administration in 1960. After its introduction, the pill was adopted fairly rapidly by women in America and

---

[1] For a review of the positions of the major religions on birth control, see Srikanthan, A., and R. L. Reid (2009), "Religious and Cultural Influences on Contraception," *Journal of Obstetrics and Gynaecology Canada*, February, pp. 129–137.

then in other parts of the world. Many birth control techniques were available prior to the pill, to be sure.[2] Apart from using these technologies, women prevented pregnancy through such practices as the rhythm method and the withdrawal method. But none of these techniques was anywhere near foolproof; sex always carried a nontrivial risk of pregnancy. Besides, they were not always convenient.

The pill was the first technology that gave near-perfect assurance that conception could be avoided (when used regularly). Besides being safe, it was very convenient—it could be taken at a time other than when a couple was being intimate. And, most importantly, it gave women complete control of the decision whether to get pregnant and, if so, when; birth control required neither their partners' approval nor their cooperation. These two advantages conferred on women by the oral contraceptive had a huge impact on the careers that women opted for. For all these reasons, the pill is still widely used in the developed countries.

In the developing countries, the pill was initially too expensive for women to use. This is one of the reasons that the pill never really caught on in the two most populous developing countries, China and India. Nevertheless, it is now widely in use in other developing countries. Across the world, some 8% of all married women use the pill. It ranks third in contraceptive usage, behind female sterilization (19%) and the IUD (13%).[3]

Apart from preventing conception, the pill has been shown to have various health benefits. For example, it prevents anemia (iron deficiency, which makes women weak and listless) and reduces menstrual bleeding, the intensity of premenstrual syndromes, and the chances of developing certain types of cancers.[4]

Abortion has been around for millennia. Most societies with any sort of recorded history seem to have practiced abortion and often even infanticide. In recent times, abortion has become a very charged and contentious issue. Part of the reason is that people in some religious traditions have strong opposition to abortion, though not all people who oppose abortion are necessarily religious. At the turn of the twentieth century, abortion was made illegal in most developed countries. It was gradually made legal again in the past century for various reasons, mostly having to do with safeguarding the lives of pregnant women with medical complications.

The United Kingdom made abortion legal in 1967. In 1970, some states in the United States started making abortion legal; *Roe v. Wade,* a landmark

---

[2] For example, there was the IUD (intrauterine device, comprising a copper wire that is inserted into the uterus to neutralize sperm by altering its chemistry), the diaphragm (a latex cap inserted over the cervix to prevent sperm from getting through), vaginal sponges that form barriers to prevent sperm from fertilizing eggs, the condom, sterilization, and so on.

[3] "Oral Contraceptives—An Update," *Population Reports,* Series A, Number 9, 2000.

[4] Ibid.

ruling by the Supreme Court, made abortion legal in all states in 1973. Today most developed countries have fairly liberal abortion laws that allow women to have abortions not just for health reasons but also for socioeconomic ones. Women in developing countries, with some exceptions, live under abortion laws that are more restrictive. Nevertheless, it is true that the prevalence of abortion is not greatly dependent on whether it is legal. If it is illegal, women have abortions performed illegally, often under highly unhygienic conditions and by unqualified people. And this increases the number of women who die from complications resulting from bungled abortions.

Whether access to birth control induces the demographic transition that we studied in the previous chapter is unclear. For such a transition to occur, a desire for fewer children has to materialize first. Once the desire for smaller families is present, modern contraceptives can help, but even that would not necessarily be their main benefit. This chapter examines the various ways in which access to modern birth control technology has changed the lives of women.

II. Access to Birth Control and the Well-being of Women in Poor Countries

In developing countries, concrete and compelling measures are available that capture the effect of birth control on women's well-being: the improvement in their chances of survival and in their health when they can control their reproductive lives. In particular, maternal mortality declines quite drastically with access to birth control. In the developed countries, maternal mortality is rarely discussed with regard to family planning because, relatively speaking, maternal mortality is not a widely prevalent phenomenon. In the poorest countries, however, maternal mortality is a much more serious problem.

A large proportion of pregnancies the world over are unplanned. Nevertheless, many women who are surprised by pregnancy reconcile themselves to it and, ultimately, want the child. But many do not. There are several reasons they articulate for not wanting another child. It is possible that the family is quite poor and cannot spare the resources needed for another child. Or another child might prevent the mother from going to work for some time and the family will lose out on much-needed income. Another possibility is that the mother has had a child as recently as a year earlier and having an additional one will severely damage her health. The mother may be very young, and childbirth may strain her body too much. In some cases, she may even die. Another scenario is that the woman may be unmarried and cultural pressures put a huge stigma on her bearing children out of wedlock. In some cultures, if an unmarried woman becomes pregnant her own family members (brothers, for example) might kill her to protect the "family honor"—even if the girl was raped. There are many reasons that women do not want to carry a pregnancy to term.

When a child is not wanted, taking measures to prevent pregnancy may be the most sensible thing to do. Avoiding pregnancy, however, is not always easy. This requires access to contraceptives, and in many parts of the developing world women do not have access. It has been estimated that in 2003 around 17% of all married women had an "unmet need" for contraceptives—they could not gain access to the contraceptives they wanted. This figure varies considerably across various regions of the world; in some countries, the figure is higher than 30%, and in a few it approaches 40%.[5] Unmarried women have much less access than married women. Even when women do have access, sometimes the contraceptives fail and the women end up conceiving anyway.

Pregnancy and childbirth are dangerous to women. Many complications are associated with them, and these can result in serious damage to their health and may even result in death. How do we measure the extent of this damage? One commonly used measure of the burden of disease and death is a measure expressed in terms of time and is called the DALY (which stands for disability-adjusted life years).[6] This measure attempts to quantify the number of years of life lost due to premature death or to disability caused by a disease or health condition. A healthy woman who succumbs to maternal mortality 40 years before her expected age of death would contribute 40 years to the DALY. But what happens if childbirth does not kill her but leaves her disabled? If the disability is deemed by society to be such that a year with the disability is equivalent to losing a quarter year of life, if the woman lives for 40 years with the disability she is deemed to have lost 0.25×40 years = 10 years of life. So the burden of the disability will count as 10 DALYs.

In Latin America and the Caribbean, the percentage of DALYs lost due to unwanted pregnancies is 30% of the total disease burden of women; in South Asia, the figure is 20%.[7] One can see that in developing countries, the health problems associated with pregnancy constitute a substantial portion of the overall burden of disease confronting women. Therefore, anything that impinges on their reproductive lives is likely to have very serious consequences for them.

Let us consider the pregnancy-related deaths of women. Consult Table 9.1, in which the broad geographical regions are arranged in declining order of total maternal deaths. In 2010 there were 287,000 maternal deaths the world

---

[5] Levine, R., et al. (2006), "Contraception," in *Disease Control Priorities in Developing Countries,* Chap. 57, pp. 1075–1090, Table 57.1.

[6] This measure was first introduced in Murray, C. J., and A. D. Lopez (1996), *The Global Burden of Disease: A Comprehensive Assessment of Mortality and Disability from Diseases, Injuries, and Risk Factors in 1990 and Projected to 2020,* Harvard School of Public Health, Cambridge, MA.

[7] Murray and Lopez (1996), Table 57.2.

TABLE 9.1 The number of maternal deaths and lifetime risk, 2010

Region	Number of maternal deaths	Lifetime risk of maternal death: 1 in
World	287,000	180
Developing regions	284,000	150
Sub-Saharan Africa	162,000	39
South Asia	83,000	160
South Asia excluding India	28,000	140
South East Asia	17,000	290
Latin America and Caribbean	8,800	520
Latin America	7,400	580
Caribbean	1,400	220
East Asia	6,400	1,700
East Asia excluding China	400	1,500
West Asia	3,500	430
North Africa	2,800	470
Caucasus and Central Asia	750	850
Oceania	510	130
Developed regions	2,200	3,800

Source: World Health Organization (2012), *Trends in Maternal Mortality: 1990–2010*, Geneva, with permission.

over. The bulk of these deaths were accounted for by Sub-Saharan Africa (56.4%) and South Asia (28.9%). India itself accounted for 19.2% of the world's maternal deaths; China, in contrast, accounted for only 2.1%. All the developed regions of the world contributed negligibly (0.7%) to the total.

The greater the number of children a woman has, the higher the chance that she will succumb to maternal mortality at some point in her life. This probability is presented for the various regions of the world in the last column of Table 9.1. This probability is the highest in Sub-Saharan Africa (2.5%) and the lowest (0.026%) in the developed regions of the world, which is about 100 times smaller than the maximum.

We see that pregnancies take a huge toll on the lives of women, especially in developing countries. Furthermore, for every maternal death there are many women who survive childbirth but develop serious complications that undermine their health. Hemorrhages, ruptures of the uterus, inflammation of the pelvic region, urinary infections, and incontinence are some of these health problems.

The mother's age, health, and economic circumstances also impinge on a newly born infant's chances of survival. Children of mothers less than 20 years of age have higher chances of dying than children born to older women because younger mothers are unable to care for their children properly. The chance of a child's dying depends on the birth spacing, that is, the time that elapses between each of the mother's children. The longer the birth spacing, the lower the chance of a child's dying as an infant. This is because short birth spacing leads to malnutrition of the child. The optimal birth spacing seems to be between 3 and 6 years.[8] Women's ability to space their births naturally depends on the availability of contraceptives and family planning services.

What happens if, despite the many reasons for not wanting another child, a woman finds herself pregnant? If conception is unintended and the child is *unwanted*, women are likely to resort to abortion. In 2008 there were 208 million pregnancies worldwide.[9] Of these, 59% were intended and 41% unintended. Of the unintended pregnancies (86 million), 41 million (48%) resulted in abortions, 33 million in unplanned births, and the rest were miscarriages. Nearly half of all unintended pregnancies worldwide, in other words, result in abortions.

Access to safe abortions varies across the globe. This access depends on many things: whether abortion is legal, how wealthy the country is, how wealthy the woman is, whether the government devotes resources to providing family planning services, and so on. When safe abortions are unavailable, women desperate not to have additional children opt for abortions under unsafe conditions—with practitioners who are unqualified, under unsanitary conditions, and without the support of medical interventions in the event that there are complications stemming from bungled procedures. When they are legal, abortions are generally safe.

If abortions are unsafe, a high proportion may result in the deaths of the mothers. Table 9.2 offers some numbers that put this problem in perspective. In 2008 some 21.6 million unsafe abortions were performed in the world, of which 47,000 resulted in the mothers' dying. Maternal deaths in childbirth occur for many reasons: hemorrhages, sepsis, obstructions in the labor, and so on. Of the maternal deaths due to all causes in 2008, unsafe abortions accounted for an average of 13% worldwide.

The breakdowns in Table 9.2 by rich and poor countries and by region are revealing. The incidence of unsafe abortions in Column 2 relative to the world is very low in rich countries (1.7%); the poor countries carry the rest of the burden (98.3%). Not only are the numbers of maternal deaths far lower in the rich countries, as we saw in Column 2 of Table 9.1, even the propor-

[8] Rutstein, S. O. (2005), "The Effect of Preceding Birth Intervals of Neonatal, Infant, and Under-Five Years Mortality and Nutritional Status in Developing Countries: Evidence from the Demographic and the Health Surveys," *International Journal of Gynecology and Obstetrics* 89, pp. S7–S24.

[9] The figures in this paragraph are drawn from Singh, S., G. Sedgh, and R. Hussain (2010), "Unintended Pregnancy: Worldwide Levels, Trends, and Outcomes," *Studies in Family Planning* 41, pp. 241–250.

TABLE 9.2 Unsafe abortions and the resulting maternal deaths, 2008

Region	Number of unsafe abortions (thousands)	Number of maternal deaths due to unsafe abortions	Percent of all maternal deaths	Unsafe abortion deaths per 100,000 live births
World	21,600	47,000	13	40
Developed countries	360	90	4	3
Developing countries	21,200	47,000	13	50
Africa	6,190	29,000	14	80
Asia[a]	10,780	17,000	12	30
Europe	360	90	8	3
Latin America and Caribbean	4,230	1,100	12	10
North America	b	b	b	b
Oceania[a]	18	100	12	30

Source: Compiled from Tables 5 and 6 of World Health Organization (2011), *Unsafe Abortion: Global and Regional Estimates of the Incidence of Unsafe Abortion and Associated Mortality in 2008,* Geneva, with permission.

[a] Japan, Australia, and New Zealand have been excluded from regional estimates and are included in the total for developed countries.

[b] Incidence is negligible.

tion of maternal deaths due to unsafe abortions is much lower (Table 9.2, Column 4). The regional incidence shows that Africa and Asia have the largest number of unsafe abortions (Table 9.2, Column 2). These two continents account for most of the world's maternal deaths (Table 9.1) and also for most of the maternal deaths due to unsafe abortions (Table 9.2).

The maternal mortality rates from abortions in underserved areas around the world, as revealed by Table 9.2, are very sobering. As can be seen from the last column of this table, out of 100,000 live births in 2008, the incidence of maternal mortality from unsafe abortions was 80 in Africa, 30 in Asia, 10 in Latin America and the Caribbean, 3 in Europe, and negligible in North America. The disparities between North America or Europe and Africa or Asia are staggering. These disparities are compounded, of course, by the fact that many more abortions are performed in poor countries than in rich ones. For both these reasons, the number of women who die from unsafe abortions is much higher in the developing world. If abortions are so unsafe in poor countries, why do women opt for them? Economic desperation is one of the main reasons—they simply cannot afford to have another child at the time. Another reason is that women, in particular unmarried women, wish to keep their sexual activity from becoming public knowledge in view of the often dire social consequences.[10]

It must be noted that childbirth is dangerous, too—even more than abortion, actually. The chance of maternal death from childbirth is higher than that from abortion. The maternal mortality rate in childbirth is 16 per 100,000 live births in the developed world, 240 in the developing world (that is, 15 times larger), 500 in Africa, 220 in South Asia, and 72 in Latin America.[11] Comparing these figures with those in the previous paragraph we see that, from the point of view of maternal death, childbirth is more dangerous everywhere in the world than abortion.

Why is childbirth so dangerous to women? Humans are unique in having very large brain sizes relative to the rest of their bodies. Because the heads of human infants are unusually large, their passage through the birth canal is very risky for the babies and for their mothers compared to other species. This is especially so because, to facilitate walking on two legs, evolutionary changes were warranted in the birth canal that require a baby to twist and turn as it passes through. This is also the reason that, among all the primates, human mothers alone usually require assistance during childbirth.[12]

The chance of a woman's dying in childbirth is age dependent; it is higher if she is an adolescent or older than 35 years than if she is in any of the intervening age groups. Furthermore, as mentioned before, the more frequently she has given birth (the shorter the birth spacing), the higher are the chances of her death in childbirth. This means that maternal mortality, especially in poor countries, can be greatly reduced if unwanted pregnancies are avoided or, if conception has occurred, women are given access to abortion.

The proportion of unsafe abortions performed depends, among other things, on whether abortion is legal. When it is legal, qualified personnel can perform abortions with no fear of prosecution by the state. These procedures will be done under sanitary conditions, for if complications (or even death) arise from physician incompetence or negligence, there is legal recourse for the women (or their families). As noted, when abortion is not legal, the procedures are performed in back alleys, under unsanitary conditions and by unqualified people. As Table 9.2 makes clear, many women die in developing countries because safe abortions are unavailable. If abortions were legalized, these would be performed under safer conditions.

The choice between the possibility of death in childbirth and death in an abortion is a tragic choice for any woman to have to make. This choice, how-

---

[10] This is also true in the developed world. See, for example, Torres, A., and J. D. Forrest (1988), "Why Do Women Have Abortions?," *Family Planning Perspectives* 20, pp. 169–176.

[11] From Table 2 in World Health Organization (2012), *Trends in Maternal Mortality in 1990–2010*, Geneva.

[12] See Rosenberg, K. R., and W. R. Trevathan (2002), "The Evolution of Human Birth," *Scientific American* 285, June, pp. 60–65.

ever, is much direr in poor countries because the chances of death in either option are so much higher. The last column of Table 9.1 shows the risk that a typical woman in a given geographical area will succumb to maternal death sometime during her life. This, of course, depends on the number of children the woman has and on where she resides. The chance of dying due to a maternal condition sometime during her life is 1 in 3,800 in the developed world and 1 in 150 in the developing world—roughly 25 times higher. It is clear that improving women's access to contraceptives and family planning services in developing countries would greatly enhance the quality of their lives.

III. The Effects of Oral Contraceptives on Women's Careers in Rich Countries

We now turn to a consideration of how birth control, in particular the pill, impinges on the lives of women in rich countries. Claudia Goldin and Lawrence Katz (2002), whose research I now draw on, examined how the pill affected women's decisions about marriage and their careers.[13] In the United States, after the pill was introduced in 1960, its use spread quickly among married women. Soon after, single women started using it. However, because many states had laws that prohibited its prescription to minors (who were defined as those under 18 or 21 years of age, depending on the state), adoption of the pill by single women was delayed. The use of the pill among married women peaked about half a decade before its use by unmarried women started spreading. It was only after the age of majority was lowered that universities started making family planning services available to their students.

Goldin and Katz argue that there were two ways, which they call "direct" and "indirect," in which the pill affected the lives of career women. The direct effect came from the fact that the pill reduced the cost of physical intimacy. Before the pill became available, sexual intimacy led to pregnancy with a high probability. People had to either abstain from sex (which was a cost) or take their chances. In the latter case, there were huge costs in the event of pregnancy. The possibility of unwanted pregnancy was an impediment to women in choosing careers—especially ones that required several years of investment (medical school, law school, and so on). So most women married early (as did men). Women who decided to pursue careers and to postpone marriage were faced with another cost, this one indirect: because most of the men in their age group were already married, the selection of men available to these career women when they were ready to marry was restricted.

It is easy to see how the pill impinged on the marriage and career decisions of women. Suppose that we rank all women in the order of the income that they can potentially earn over their lives if they undertake investments com-

---

[13] Goldin, C., and L. Katz (2002), "The Power of the Pill: Oral Contraceptives and Women's Career and Marriage Decisions," *Journal of Political Economy* 110, pp. 730–770.

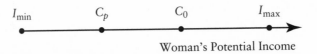

FIGURE 9.1 The direct effect of the pill on women's marriage and career decisions

mensurate with their abilities.[14] Let I_{min} denote the lowest possible income on this scale and I_{max} the highest. In other words, I_{max} represents the potential income that the most able women can earn if they undertake the needed investment. Suppose that C_0 is the cost of delaying marriage in the absence of the pill.[15] An important component of this cost will be the forgoing of physical intimacy, because that will result in pregnancy with a high probability. Suppose, further, that C_p is the cost of postponing marriage when the pill is available. Clearly we will expect that C_p will be less than C_0 because the pill makes it possible for women to engage in sex with little fear of becoming pregnant. Figure 9.1 shows the quantities I_{min}, I_{max}, C_0, and C_p on a line representing the potential incomes of all women.

In the absence of the pill, all women to the left of C_0 in Figure 9.1 will not postpone marriage. This is because the income they can hope to earn by undertaking the necessary investment will be less than the cost of postponing marriage. These women will marry early and forgo their careers. Only those women who expect to earn more than C_0 will opt for careers.

When the pill becomes available, only women who will earn less than C_p will marry early and abandon the possibility of a career. All women who can earn more than C_p will postpone marriage and choose to have careers. Of these, the women who can earn more than C_0 would have opted for careers anyway even without the pill. However, now there are more women—those who will earn incomes between C_p and C_0—who will also choose to have careers now that the pill has become available. By lowering the cost to women of postponing marriage, the pill has opened up the possibility of having careers without abandoning the possibility of enjoying physical intimacy. This is the direct effect of the pill on women's marriage and career choices.

The indirect effect of the pill, Goldin and Katz argue, stems from the fact that because more women, and therefore more men, are postponing marriage, those women who opt for careers have more men to choose from when they are ready to marry. It is still the case that there are as many men as women who marry (one man for every woman), but there is now scope for

---

[14] Because we need to add the incomes in different years, we assume that the term *income* here really refers to the present value of the lifetime income.

[15] Once again, we need to sum the costs that may last for several years, so we interpret the term *cost* here as present-value cost. We presume that we can convert utility to dollars to keep the exposition simple.

better matching because there are more of each sex available for marriage. This could conceivably induce even more women to opt for careers, secure in the knowledge that their choice of marriage partner will not be severely limited later on—as it would have been when the pill was unavailable.

The simple model presented above offers several predictions. First, a higher proportion of all women should have gone on to have careers when the pill was introduced. Second, because more women opted for the investment needed to pursue careers, the average ages at first marriage and at first birth should have increased after the introduction of the pill. This is because women who opted to go to college to pursue careers tended to delay marriage. Third, there should have been a decline in the average ability of women who entered the labor market. Prior to the introduction of the pill, only relatively high-ability women (those who could earn more than C_0) entered the labor market. The pill made it possible for women who could earn incomes between C_p and C_0 to also participate in the labor market. Because lower-ability women were added to the labor force, the average ability of working women should have fallen. Participation in the labor market should have become less exclusive. Fourth, because both members of more couples had careers, there should have been less division of labor inside the home.

What evidence do Goldin and Katz offer for their claim that the pill facilitated the entry of women into professions that required considerable investment? They look at the enrollment over time of women in law and medical schools, because these professional degrees require considerable commitments of time. They found that these enrollment rates (as a proportion of all students enrolled in B.A. degrees) sharply increased around 1970—coinciding with the timing of when the pill was becoming available to single women. Although there may have been other reasons for this precipitous increase, the uncanny timing that made it coincide with the widespread diffusion of the pill among women of college-going age lends plausibility to the claim that the pill was responsible for the sizable increase in female enrollment. Even when the female enrollment rates were expressed as ratios of male enrollment rates in these professional schools, Goldin and Katz found similar sharp increases. This was not because higher proportions of female applicants were being admitted into these programs; it was because more women were applying.

Was it the case that the pill reduced the fertility of American women and thus enabled them to do more paid work over their careers? Or was it the case that the pill enabled them to adjust not their fertility but the *timing* of their children so as to facilitate investment in their human capital and then in labor market participation? Martha Bailey (2006) has answered these questions.[16]

---

[16] Bailey, M. J. (2006), "More Power to the Pill: The Impact of Contraceptive Freedom on Women's Life Cycle Labor Supply," *Quarterly Journal of Economics* 121, pp. 289–320.

The fertility rate in the United States had been declining for many years, well before the pill was invented. (In the decade before its introduction, however, fertility was increasing. This was the "baby boom" after the end of World War II, when new families were being rapidly formed after the soldiers returned home.) Women's participation in the labor force increased for many reasons, as Bailey observes: the women's liberation movement was in full swing, and in the mid-1960s antidiscrimination laws were put in place. Bailey finds that early childbearing declined from 1960 until 1976, by which time all women in the United States who were 18 years of age had legal access to the pill. The largest decline was seen among 18- or 19-year-olds. In sharp contrast, Bailey finds that first births to 15- to 17-year-olds hardly saw a decline. This is precisely what would have been expected, because these women did not have access to the pill even after the age of majority was lowered to 18 years.

American women born before 1940 tended to withdraw from the labor force when they were having children and raising a family. Once they had achieved their desired level of fertility and the children were old enough, these women re-entered the labor market. Consequently, their labor force participation over their careers was "M-shaped." For women who were born after 1955 (and who thus had early access to the pill), this M-shaped pattern was not present and their participation rate was considerably higher. The fact that this change in labor market behavior occurred during the same period (1960–76) that pill use was diffused among young women is quite suggestive of the role of the pill.

The age of majority was reduced to 18 years at different times in the different states. Therefore, not all American women had legal access to the pill at the same time. Using this fact, Bailey is able to compare the behavior of women who had early access to the pill (that is, before reaching the age of 22 years) to that of women who did not. She estimates that early access to the pill lowered the chance that a woman would have her first birth before she was 22 years of age by 14%.

What effect did the pill have on total fertility, that is, the total number of children a woman had after she had completed her childbearing? Bailey finds that early access to the pill had *no effect* on the total number of children a woman had. So the pill reduced the chances of early pregnancy but left unchanged the target number of children for women who used the pill. The lower probability of conception in their early years enabled women to undertake the investment needed to pursue careers. What the pill did, therefore, was to give women a relatively costless means of *delaying the timing* of their children so as to increase their labor market participation in their late twenties and early thirties relative to women who did not have early access. Another finding of Bailey further supports this claim. Women who had early access to the pill but opted not to delay childbearing did not increase their labor force participation compared to women who did not have early access.

IV. Birth Control and Out-of-Wedlock Births in Rich Countries

In the United States, starting in the early 1960s the proportion of children born out of wedlock has been increasing. This proportion, which was only around 11% in 1970, increased to around 36% by 2004. For whites it went from around 6% to 30% and for blacks from 38% to 69%.[17] Marriage rates among both white and black women declined substantially over the period. Furthermore, the number of shotgun marriages as a proportion of the total number of marriages declined dramatically.[18] As a result, the proportion of children born out of wedlock increased drastically. George Akerlof, Janet Yellen, and Michael Katz (hereafter A-Y-K) have proposed that there is a link between access to birth control (the pill and abortion) and the proportion of children born out of wedlock.[19]

The A-Y-K argument hinges on what a woman can reasonably ask of a man in order for her to engage in sexual intimacy. This depends on their relative bargaining power. Suppose, for the sake of argument, that no form of birth control was available before the pill and the legalization of abortion. Before these forms of birth control became available, a woman could reasonably ask a man if he would marry her in the event that sexual intimacy between them led to pregnancy. Because all women would have wanted such a commitment, men would have been inclined to give such an assurance. In this scenario, one would have observed that most children were born within wedlock, even if a substantial number of marriages were of the shotgun variety.

The availability of the pill and of abortion changed the commitments that could be asked of men with the expectation that they would be given. We have seen that the pill gave far more assurance of birth control than previous technologies. These innovations gave most women the freedom to unilaterally ensure that they do not become pregnant and, if they do by accident, they have recourse to abortion. Suppose that most of the women embraced these innovations. These women would not have needed to ask men to commit to marriage in the event of pregnancy. The women who did ask would likely not have received such a commitment because men could seek liaisons

[17] Table 10, U.S. Department of Health and Human Services (2006), *Health, United States, 2006*, Washington, DC.

[18] The term *shotgun marriage* refers to a marriage that begins after a child has been conceived. In bygone days, the pregnant girl's father approached the father of the child with a shotgun and persuaded him to marry his daughter!

[19] Akerlof, G. A., J. L. Yellen, and M. L. Katz (1996), "An Analysis of Out-of-Wedlock Childbearing in the United States," *Quarterly Journal of Economics* 111, pp. 277–317.

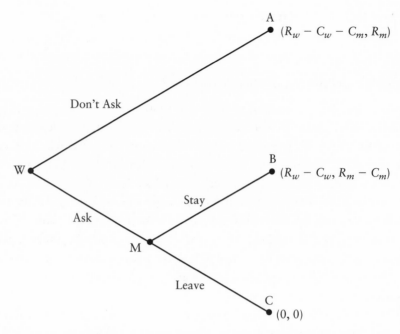

A

$(R_w - C_w - C_m, R_m)$

Don't Ask

W

B

$(R_w - C_w, R_m - C_m)$

Stay

Ask

M

Leave

C

$(0, 0)$

FIGURE 9.2 Determination of whether a shotgun marriage will obtain

with other women who had no need to ask. Thus most women who did not want children right away and perhaps wanted to pursue careers would have adopted the new technology and sought no commitment from their male partners. The few women who did not adopt the new technology—either because their religion forbade them or because they wanted children—would have been unable to receive commitments of marriage from men in the event of pregnancy. These women would have ended up having children outside wedlock. Had the pill or access to abortion been unavailable, these women would have had shotgun marriages. Consequently, the proportion of children born out of wedlock would have increased when birth control technology became available.

A simplified version of the model presented by A-Y-K that makes the above argument precise is sketched in Figure 9.2 with the help of a game tree. Suppose that the benefit ("reward") in terms of the utility that women and men receive from having a sexual relationship is denoted by R_w and R_m, respectively. Furthermore, let C_w and C_m, respectively, be the cost in terms of utility that women and men have to bear to have premarital sex. The burden of pregnancy and of raising a child will constitute the bulk of this cost. If the man refuses to commit and the woman bears his burden also, the cost of pregnancy to the woman is $(C_w + C_m)$. The net utility a person receives is the difference between his or her benefit and cost.

In Figure 9.2, before engaging in a sexual relationship the woman (denoted by W) has the option of asking for a commitment of marriage in the event of pregnancy. If she does not ask, none is given. When pregnancy occurs, the woman bears the full cost $(C_w + C_m)$ and her net utility is $(R_w - C_w - C_m)$, whereas that of the man is R_m. This explains the pair of utility entries next to point A in the figure. The first entry is the woman's net utility, and the second is the man's. If the woman asks the man for a commitment, however, he has to decide whether to give one. We will assume, as do A-Y-K, that a commitment once given is honored. If the man (denoted by M in the figure) refuses, the two people go their separate ways and each has a utility of 0, as indicated by the pair of entries beside point C in the figure. On the other hand, if the man does give a commitment, the two people will have a relationship. The woman receives a net utility of $(R_w - C_w)$ and the man $(R_m - C_m)$. These are the utility entries next to point B in the figure.

What outcome do we expect to obtain? Will the woman ask for a commitment? If so, is it in the interest of the man to give one? Will there be a shotgun marriage? Will any children be born out of wedlock? The answers to these questions depend on the sizes of the various benefits and costs.

First consider a world in which there is no access to birth control. Suppose, further, that all the men are of one kind, that is, their benefits and costs are identical. Women, on the other hand, are of two kinds: those for whom pregnancy has a high cost (say, C_1) and those for whom it has a low cost (say, C_2). We shall refer to these women as Type 1 and Type 2, respectively. Perhaps Type 1 women are those with career goals or those with high psychic costs if they have children out of wedlock, whereas Type 2 women are those who are very fond of children or have strong religious beliefs that would make them opposed to using contraception or having an abortion. Type 1 women are unlikely to engage in premarital sex unless they are given a commitment.

To facilitate understanding, suppose that the benefits and costs take on the following values: $R_w = R_m = 100$; $C_1 = 70$; $C_2 = 20$; $C_- = 50$. If a Type 1 woman engages in premarital sex without a commitment from her partner, she will receive a net utility of $100 - 70 - 50 = -20$. This is less than the utility of 0 that she will receive in the absence of any relationship. Therefore, a Type 1 woman will refuse to engage in premarital sex without a commitment of marriage in the event of pregnancy. If she receives a commitment from her partner, she will obtain a utility of $100 - 70 = 30$, that is, she will be better off than if she were not having a relationship. Therefore, Type 1 women will engage in premarital sex with a commitment from their partners (but not without one).

What about Type 2 women? If a Type 2 woman engages in premarital sex with a commitment from her partner, she will receive a net utility of $100 - 20 = 80$. This is greater than the utility of 0 that she will receive in the absence of any relationship. Therefore, a Type 2 woman will certainly be willing to engage in premarital sex with a commitment of marriage in the event of pregnancy. If she does not receive such a commitment, however, her net utility will be $100 - 20 - 50 = 30$. Even this is higher than her utility in the absence of a relationship (which will be 0). Therefore, Type 2 women will be willing to engage in premarital sex *even without* a commitment from their partners. Nevertheless, it is clearly in their interest to ask for a commitment.

Will women ask for commitments from their partners, and will men give these commitments? The answer to that depends on the proportion of Type 1 and Type 2 women there are in the population. Suppose that most of the women in the population are of the high-cost (Type 1) variety. This could be because most of the women are career oriented or because societal norms and the stigma associated with having out-of-wedlock children make the burden of children very onerous for single mothers. In this case, most of the women in the population will ask for commitments of marriage in the event of pregnancy. Type 2 women, who are willing to engage in premarital sex even without commitments, will also find it in their interest to ask for such commitments. This is because they will be better off with such commitments than without. If most of the women in the population refuse to engage in sex without a commitment, men have no option but to give such commitments. Not only Type 1 women but also Type 2 women will ask for and receive commitments. The outcome we will observe will be one in which there is premarital sex but shotgun marriages will be the norm.

We can now consider what happens to the outcome when easy access to birth control becomes available. In this scenario, Type 1 women (who do not wish to have children in the near future) will willingly practice birth control. If, despite being on the pill, they happen to get pregnant, they can have recourse to legal abortion. These women do not need to ask men for a commitment. Because they do not, neither can Type 2 women, for men who are asked for commitments will generally not give them. In the new outcome, no commitments will be asked and none will be given.

The net utility of men will now be R_m as opposed to that $(R_m - C_m)$ they received in the scenario before birth control became available. Hence all men will be better off. Type 1 women will now receive a net utility of R_w as opposed to $(R_w - C_1)$ in the scenario before birth control became available. These women are clearly better off now. Type 2 women will now receive a net utility of $(R_w - C_2 - C_m)$ as opposed to that of $(R_w - C_2)$ that they received before birth control became available. These women will be worse off. These women will lose out because they refuse to adopt a new technology and, when they have children, they end up bearing the man's share of the cost also.

This theory of Akerlof, Yellen, and Katz also explains why, following the innovation in birth control, the proportion of children born out of wedlock increased in the United States. Type 2 women, who previously could ask for and receive commitments of marriage, were unable to do so afterward. These women were forced to have children out of wedlock. Because these children were born to women who *wanted* them, they were less likely to be put up for adoption. These women brought up their children by themselves. Naturally, the proportion of children being brought up in single-parent families rose. Furthermore, because there was only one income in the family, the proportion of children in poverty increased.

This theory has some bearing on what has been called the "feminization of poverty." This term means that women are more likely than men to be in poverty. Most single-parent families are female headed. Because women's incomes are on average lower than men's, it is clear that out-of-wedlock childbirth will lead to more women than men being in poverty.[20]

V. Birth Control and the Well-being of Women in Rich Countries

The Case of the United States

Until the early 1970s, most states in the United States had laws that made abortion illegal. Only a handful of states were exceptions. In the early 1970s, Norma McCorvey, using the pseudonym Jane Roe, sued the U.S. district attorney in Texas, Henry Wade, for the right to have an abortion. Roe was a single mother with limited means to raise a child. The *Roe v. Wade* case ultimately ended up in the Supreme Court. In a landmark ruling in 1973, the Court delivered the surprising verdict that laws prohibiting abortion violated women's legal right to privacy, which is guaranteed by the U.S. Constitution. In the first trimester of pregnancy, the Supreme Court ruled, women had an unrestricted right to abortion. In the second trimester, concerns regarding the health repercussions of abortion for pregnant women gave the state some right to intervene. In the third trimester (when a fetus is around 24 weeks old and becomes "viable" outside the womb), the state had the right to protect the life of the fetus by denying abortion. However, in this case, too, if the pregnancy was deemed a threat to the pregnant woman's health, she had the right to an abortion.

In one stroke, the *Roe v. Wade* verdict made abortion legal everywhere across the United States. Opinions on the ruling across the country were highly polarized. Some groups were strongly opposed to it on religious and ideological grounds. Others heralded the Supreme Court's ruling as a huge step forward in women's rights. Despite some amendments in the law in subsequent rulings, however, the essential aspect of the *Roe v. Wade* verdict still stands today.

How did *Roe v. Wade* affect women's autonomy and well-being? The availability of abortion enables a married woman to control the timing of her fertility. Termination of a relationship in the event of serious disagree-

---

[20] In 2006, 12.3% of people in the United States were below the poverty line, whereas the proportion was 30.5% for people in female-headed households. For a four-person family, for example, the threshold below which all members of the family are deemed to be in poverty was $20,614 in 2006. Source: U.S. Census Bureau.

ment between spouses is usually easier if there are no children involved. If there are children, both partners are wary of breaking up a marriage because it might reduce the well-being of their children. Furthermore, by exercising her option to have an abortion in the event she has an unwanted pregnancy, the woman can retain her outside options of working and earning an independent income. The right to have an abortion, therefore, would be expected to have altered the threat utility of married women. According to the Nash bargaining model that we discussed in Chapter 3, this should have increased women's bargaining power within the household.

Greater bargaining power within the household has many implications. The spouse with greater bargaining power has greater influence on how resources within the household should be allocated. As we saw in Chapter 3, preferences do differ across husbands and wives. Household expenditures will tilt in favor of women's preferences when bargaining power changes in their favor. For example, we have already encountered evidence that if women are more empowered, more of the household income may be spent on women's clothes or on hiring maids and less on cigarettes and alcohol. Among the resources that can be allocated to various ends, the labor of the married couple is an important one. Partners with lower bargaining power work more (and consume less leisure) than they would if they were making the decisions by themselves. An increase in their bargaining power leads to a reduction in their supply of labor and an increase in that of their partners.

One way to understand this is by working through the logic of the Nash bargaining model. When a wife's threat utility increases, the outcome of the bargaining scenario will have to deliver her a higher utility and, if nothing else changes, a lower utility to her husband. Now each person's utility is determined by the consumption of various goods and leisure. The increase in the wife's utility, then, will come from an increase in her consumption of goods as well as her consumption of leisure. Therefore, her labor supplied in the new bargaining outcome will be lower than before. The decline in the husband's utility, likewise, will come partly at the expense of the amount of goods he consumes and partly his leisure. In other words, the labor he supplies will increase.

A somewhat less rigorous but possibly more intuitive way to understand this is as follows. A part of the husband's labor income may be thought of as the wife's nonlabor income because she gets to spend some of it in the joint decision making of the household. (Likewise, a part of the wife's labor income may be construed as the husband's nonlabor income.) An increase in the wife's bargaining power due to legalized abortion will entitle her to claim a greater share of her husband's labor income than before. This is tantamount to an increase in the wife's nonlabor income. If leisure is a normal good, an increase in her nonlabor income through a positive income effect will induce the wife to reduce her labor supply. Likewise, because the husband's bargaining power is lower than before, he will receive a smaller portion of his wife's income as his nonlabor income, and this will induce him to increase his labor supply.

In short, an important ruling like *Roe v. Wade* would be expected to have had a significant impact on the well-being of married women, and this should be visible in the effects on the labor supply of couples. Has this indeed been the case? Sonia Oreffice (2007) investigated this issue using two different U.S. data sets that spanned the decade of the 1970s.[21] She considered couples who had married before the Supreme Court's decision of 1973 came into effect. As a result, she could compare the "before" and "after" scenarios in order to assess the effects of *Roe v. Wade*. She found that the legalization of abortion resulted in labor supply changes as predicted by the bargaining model. On average, the Supreme Court's ruling reduced the number of hours worked yearly by married women in the labor market by 83 and increased that of their husbands by 34.

Oreffice found that the effects of *Roe v. Wade,* however, differed across families. In couples that were Catholic or Baptist, there was no significant effect. This was to be expected, because these two Christian denominations strictly forbid abortions and so Catholic and Baptist women were unlikely to opt for abortion even after it was legalized. These women would have seen no increase in their bargaining power and so no change in their labor supply. Furthermore, no significant change in the labor supply was observed in couples who regularly used contraceptives. Again, this was to be expected because the women in these couples were unlikely to get pregnant and therefore unlikely to ever need abortions. Oreffice also found that the effect of legalizing abortion was negligible among rich women. This is because rich women would have been able to afford abortion even before it became legal across the country. For instance, they could have traveled to one of the few states that had legal abortions before *Roe v. Wade*.[22] So the ruling, when it came down in 1973, would have had no effect on them—it merely made available to other women an access to abortion that they themselves had had all along by privilege of their wealth. *Roe v. Wade* was also found to have had no effect on the labor supply of older couples. This was because access to abortion was irrelevant to couples who had already completed the reproductive period of their lives.

Remarkably, Oreffice found that *Roe v. Wade* seemed to have reduced the labor supply of even single women. Why might this have been? Single women

[21] Oreffice, S. (2007), "Did the Legalization of Abortion Increase Women's Household Bargaining Power?: Evidence from Labor Supply," *Review of Economics of the Household 5*, pp. 181–207.
[22] These five states were Alaska, California, Hawaii, New York, and Washington. Abortion was also legal in Washington, D.C., prior to *Roe v. Wade*.

who expected to be married in the future might have worked not only to support themselves but also because earning an independent income and saving some wealth conferred on them security and bargaining power in a future marriage. Legalized abortion, by increasing the bargaining power of women in their prospective marriages, would have reduced the need for them to bolster it by working harder or accumulating more wealth before marriage.[23]

The findings summarized above clearly indicate that the legalization of abortion, on average, reduced the labor supply of married women and increased that of their husbands. How do we reconcile this with other findings, like those of Goldin and Katz and of Bailey, indicating that technologies that enabled women to prevent pregnancy or to control the timing of their children enabled them to invest in their human capital and increase their labor supply? The findings of Oreffice do not contradict these. Several factors impinge on labor supply. Fertility, the timing of children, and human capital are all important factors. So is the bargaining power of women and men within marriage. Oreffice's findings isolate the effects of bargaining power that came through the legalization of abortion. Stated differently, all else constant, by improving the bargaining position of married women the legalization of abortion reduced the number of hours of market work they put in, on average, and increased that of their husbands.

It would be reasonable to think that access to abortion might be particularly beneficial to very young women. Teenage pregnancies may lead teenagers to drop out of school. The attendant loss of human capital may arguably condemn them to living in poverty subsequently. Joshua Angrist and William Evans (1999) investigated this issue using the fact that five states made abortion legal in 1970, three years before *Roe v. Wade*.[24] The authors found that, among the cohort of teenage women who were exposed to the 1970 abortion reforms, black women showed a large decline in out-of-wedlock births; the effect on such births was more modest for white women. Schooling and labor market consequences, too, were greater for black women: they saw a large increase in high school graduation rates, college enrollment, and subsequent employment. There were no perceptible effects on these among white women.

Findings additional to those above have been reported by Elizabeth Ananat, Jonathan Gruber, Phillip Levine, and Douglas Staiger (2009).[25] In particular, they found that children who were born after laws banning abortion

---

[23] An opposite effect would have been expected for single men; however, this was not detected in the data. Oreffice suggests that this might have been because future marriage considerations weighed less on the minds of single men.

[24] Angrist, J. D., and W. N. Evans (1999), "Schooling and Labor Market Consequences of the 1970 State Abortion Reforms," *Research in Labor Economics* 18, pp. 75–113.

[25] Ananat, E. O., J. Gruber, P. B. Levine, and D. Staiger (2009), "Abortion and Selection," *Review of Economics and Statistics* 91, pp. 124–136.

were repealed had better life outcomes: they were more likely to graduate from college, less likely to experience single parenthood, and also less likely to be collecting welfare. This fact suggests that the children from the pregnancies that were carried to term when abortion was available at low cost were "more wanted" by their parents, on average, than the children born when abortion wasn't available. And, importantly, this advantage of being raised in more caring families shows up even in adult outcomes.

The Case of European Countries

Silvia Pezzini (2007) examines the effect on women's welfare in European countries of various changes to women's rights between the 1960s and the 1990s.[26] This was a period with many important changes, not only because of new technologies that affected women (such as the pill) but also because of changes in laws (such as those regarding abortion, divorce, and maternity leave). These changes in technologies and laws were implemented at different times in different countries. Pezzini uses this fact to isolate the effects on women to whom these changes were relevant. The information on welfare she uses is from a countrywide survey conducted between 1975 and 1998.[27] She captures women's welfare by their answers to the question "On the whole, are you very/fairly/not very/not at all satisfied with the life you lead?" The answers are put on a four-point scale, with "very satisfied" at the top of the scale and "not at all satisfied" at the bottom.

Birth control rights can impinge positively on women's welfare in several ways: they can reduce unwanted pregnancies, lead to changes in societal norms about women participating in the labor force, and, as we have seen, facilitate greater investment in human capital and increase women's earnings. Their effects on men, however, are ambiguous. On the one hand, more income for their wives is good for married men. On the other hand, their wives' bargaining power may increase (as we have seen), and this will decrease the welfare of husbands. In order to identify the effects of abortion, say, on women's welfare, Silvia Pezzini considers the difference between the average levels of women's welfare (as measured by their answers to the survey question) *after* and *before* abortion laws were changed. This difference presumably captures the effect of the laws on women's well-being. But many other things may have also changed between the periods before and after abortion was legalized. For example, the government may have passed several other laws, too, that had consequences for women's welfare. If so, their effects would have been confounded with those of the abortion laws. How should one separate out the pure effects of the abortion laws?

---

[26] Pezzini, S. (2007), "The Effects of Women's Rights on Women's Welfare: Evidence from a Natural Experiment," *Economic Journal* 115, pp. C208–C227.

[27] This was the Eurobarometer survey that was conducted in 12 European countries.

Pezzini accomplishes this by separating out, from all other women, those who were of childbearing age; these were the women for whom abortion laws would have been relevant. Changes other than those pertaining to birth control would presumably have affected *all* women, but *only* the women of childbearing age would have been affected by the changes in abortion laws. She then compares the difference ("after" minus "before" the changes in the abortion laws) between the average welfare of women in the relevant group with the corresponding difference for all other women. If the former is larger, the changes in abortion laws improved the well-being of women in the relevant age group; if smaller, they reduced the well-being of these women. If the differences are the same, it means that women in the relevant age group were largely unaffected by the change in the abortion laws.

Pezzini finds that both forms of birth control technologies—the contraceptive pill and legalized abortion—had roughly the same *positive effect* on the life satisfaction of women in the relevant age group. In fact, the women who were exposed to the changed circumstances for the longest period registered the greatest increase in life satisfaction. How large was the effect? In studies such as these, it is invariably found that marriage or cohabitation has a hugely positive effect on life satisfaction and unemployment a hugely negative effect. The effect on women's welfare of having access to the pill, Pezzini finds, is about a third as large as the effect of marriage or cohabitation and about a third as large as the increase in life satisfaction derived from being employed (as opposed to being unemployed). This represents quite a significant improvement in well-being. A point of comparison is provided by Pezzini's finding that other changes in women's rights, such as laws assuring maternity leave to those working in firms, had no perceptible effects on their well-being.

What was the effect on men of the increased birth control rights of women? Once again, Pezzini separates out the group of men who were likely to be affected by these changes from the rest of the men. The former group comprised the men who were in the same stage of their reproductive lives as the relevant women's group. She finds that changes in the birth control rights of women had no significant effect on the relevant group of men. The opposing effects of having wives with higher earnings but also higher bargaining power seemed to offset one another.

Pezzini also investigates whether, within the relevant group of women, the effect of changed birth control rights differed by the extent of their religiosity. Women who were devout Catholics, Orthodox Greeks, Orthodox Jews, and Muslims are banned from using birth control. So more liberal abortion laws or the availability of the pill may be expected to have had no effect on the well-being of this segment of the relevant group, even if the remaining women in this group experienced increased levels of life satisfaction. Pezzini finds that Jewish and Greek Orthodox women were no better off than women outside the relevant group. Muslim women, however, exhibited lower levels of welfare. She suggests that this might be consistent with the view put forward by Akerlof, Yellen, and Katz that women who do not adopt new technologies may be hurt if most other women do. Surprisingly, however, Catholic women showed an increase in life satisfaction compared to women outside the relevant group. Pezzini suggests that this could have been because Catholic women deviated from the official Church position on the issue of birth control.

VI. Unintended Consequences of Birth Control Technologies

There have been unintended consequences of birth control. We shall discuss three such consequences in this section. One has proved harmful to women, another has had a slightly positive effect, and the third has been arguably beneficial to women and to society.

Rising Infertility in Women

The availability of birth control, we have seen, has enabled women to adjust the timing of their fertility so that they can achieve a better balance between their careers and their family lives. Women are having fewer children (for other reasons) and also postponing the age at which they have their first child. In 2009 the mean age of women at first birth was around 25 years in the United States and 30 years in the United Kingdom and Germany, having increased since 1970 by roughly 2 years in the first two countries and by 6 years in Germany.[28] The entire distribution of ages of women at first birth has shifted toward more advanced ages, with a higher percentage of women having children after 35 years of age.

Women who have children relatively late tend to be better educated and to come from better socioeconomic conditions than the rest. Nevertheless, the outcomes associated with conceiving children and successfully carrying the children to term are worse for older women.[29] As women age, they are more prone to having a higher body mass index, which reduces their chances of conception. Older women are also more prone to being afflicted with pelvic diseases, depression, cancer, and hypertension. The complications from having caesarean sections are also worse for them. Furthermore, because the partners of these women are likely to be older, the quality of their sperm is

[28] Organisation for Economic Co-operation and Development, OECD Family Database, OECD Social Policy Division, Directorate of Employment, Labour, and Social Affairs, www.oecd.org/social/family/database.

[29] Bewley, S., M. Davies, and P. Braude (2005), "Which Career First?: The Most Secure Age for Childbearing Remains 20–35," *British Medical Journal* 331, pp. 588–589. For an overview of the literature, see Carolan, M., and D. Frankowska (2011), "Advanced Maternal Age and Adverse Perinatal Outcome: A Review of the Evidence," *Midwifery* 27, pp. 793–801.

likely to be lower: children of older men are known to have higher chances of some serious illnesses.

A promising way out for older women who are having difficulties conceiving might seem to be *in vitro fertilization*. This is a clinical process in which eggs from a woman's ovaries are removed, fertilized by sperm outside her body, and then replanted in her uterus after fertilization. However, it is not certain that transplanted embryos will result in pregnancy or that the pregnancy can be carried to term. The success rate of in vitro fertilization is not encouraging. Around 70% of the women who try it do not succeed in having a live birth; of the women over age 40, some 90% do not.[30] Furthermore, there is a high probability of multiple pregnancies. Because in vitro fertilization is an expensive procedure, the cost of achieving success after repeated tries can be quite high. Despite many attempts, however, the rate of failure remains high for women over 40.

The postponement of having children until late in their reproductive cycles has resulted in a great deal of anxiety for women and, in cases of infertility, considerable grief. This chosen delay, enabled by the pill, has benefited women in many different ways. But the difficulty of infertility associated with this delay is a serious downside of access to the pill. If people could act with full knowledge, matters might be different. But because humans can rarely do so, the suffering due to the inability to conceive children later in life should be counted as one of the negative unintended effects of the pill.[31]

Decline in Child Poverty Rates

There is evidence to suggest that the availability of abortion in the United States reduced the fertility rate very slightly. Between 1970 and 1973 (when *Roe v. Wade* came into effect), the fertility rate was about 4% lower in the states with legal abortion than in the states where it was illegal. This reduction was greatest among teenagers and among women who were over the age of 35 years.[32] It is important to understand the socioeconomic characteristics of the women who opted for abortion when it became available and of the women who did not. In particular, was it rich women who primarily sought abortions, or was it mainly low-income women? The question is important because, if it was mainly the latter, it means that abortion is used as a means to cope with adverse economic conditions. Moreover, the children who were never born as a result of abortion would have been born under conditions that were disadvantageous compared to those facing the average child of the same cohort (that is, age group).

[30] See Bewley et al. (2005), cited above.

[31] For an interesting article on this aspect of the contraceptive pill, see Grigoriadis, V. (2010), "Waking Up from the Pill," *New York Magazine*, November 28.

[32] See Levine, P. B., D. Staiger, T. J. Kane, and D. J. Zimmerman (1999), "*Roe v. Wade* and American Fertility," *American Journal of Public Health* 89, pp. 199–203.

Jonathan Gruber, Phillip Levine, and Douglas Staiger (1999) answered this question.[33] By examining U.S. data from the early 1970s they found that, had the women who opted for abortion carried their fetuses to term, the children born would have been about 40%–60% more likely to have been in poverty, in single-parent families receiving welfare assistance. In other words, the women who resorted to abortion were largely those who would have had to bring up their children in disadvantageous economic conditions. If they had given birth to these children, spreading their limited resources even more thinly would have had adverse economic consequences for the women's existing children. It follows that child poverty rates would have been higher in the absence of *Roe v. Wade*.

A Decline in Crime Rates

In the United States there is evidence that abortion rights granted to women through *Roe v. Wade* led, as an unintended consequence, to a substantial decline in crime rates across the country beginning 17 years later. John Donohue and Steven Levitt (2001) first proposed this surprising hypothesis.[34] Starting in 1991, by 2001 there had been a sharp decline in crime in the United States: violent crimes and property crimes each declined by 30%. The argument that Donohue and Levitt put forward is that the missing children resulting from pregnancies not being carried to term after abortion became legal contributed to a decline in the size of the criminal population, starting some 17 years later. Furthermore, the children who would have been born had the pregnancies not been terminated were much more likely to have come from economically disadvantaged families (as we have seen above) where little parental supervision would have been exercised. The families that were least able to provide a nurturing environment for children were the ones much more likely to have opted for abortion. Had these pregnancies been carried to term, the children born, once they reached their youth, would have been more prone to crime and, therefore, would have disproportionately contributed to crime later in life. Donohue and Levitt cite evidence suggest-

[33] Gruber, J., P. B. Levine, and D. Staiger (1999), "Abortion Legalization and Child Living Circumstances: Who Is the 'Marginal Child'?," *Quarterly Journal of Economics* 114, pp. 263–291.

[34] Donohue, J. J., and S. Levitt (2001), "The Impact of Legalized Abortion on Crime," *Quarterly Journal of Economics* 116, pp. 379–420. The demonstration of this claim has not been without controversy. See Joyce, T. (2004), "Did Legalized Abortion Lower Crime?," *Journal of Human Resources* 39, pp. 1–28; Joyce, T. (2006), "Further Tests of Abortion and Crime," NBER Working Paper 10564, National Bureau of Economic Research, Cambridge, MA; Donohue, J. J., and S. D. Levitt (2004), "Further Evidence That Legalized Abortion Lowered Crime: A Reply to Joyce," *Journal of Human Resources* 39, pp. 29–49; Foote, C. L., and C. F. Goetz (2008), "The Impact of Legalized Abortion on Crime: A Comment," *Quarterly Journal of Economics* 123, pp. 407–423; and Donohue, J. J., and S. D. Levitt (2008), "Measurement Error, Legalized Abortion, and the Decline in Crime: A Response to Foote and Goetz," *Quarterly Journal of Economics* 123, pp. 425–440.

ing that 6% of any birth cohort is responsible for 50% of the crime committed by that cohort.

If this logic is correct, it must be the case that the five states in the United States where abortion became legal by 1970 (3 years before *Roe v. Wade*) should have started experiencing a decline in crime 3 years before the rest of the states. This is factually correct. Furthermore, if the argument is valid, the decline in crime in the 1990s must have come only from the cohorts of criminals who came of age around 17 or 18 years after abortion was legalized throughout the country, not from older cohorts (who were born before abortion became legal). This, too, is factually correct. Donohue and Levitt go on to provide compelling statistical evidence for their claim that the legalization of abortion in all states of the United States in 1973 was one of the primary reasons for the decline in crime in the 1990s. Thus, whatever one's position may be on moral grounds as to whether abortion ought to be legal, the evidence suggests that abortion in the United States, apart from directly improving the welfare of mothers who sought recourse to it, has had some unintended social benefits.

VII. Summary

We began our discussion of how birth control technologies impinge on the well-being of women by observing that the effects differ between women living in developing countries and those in developed ones. The effects are much more pronounced in poor countries. Easier access to birth control greatly reduces unwanted pregnancies and thus reduces maternal mortality and the number of women who die from unsafe abortions. In developed countries, modern birth control technologies have had a considerable effect on women's careers. These technologies have allowed women to undertake long-term investments in their own human capital and opt for careers that were all but ruled out for them before.

We saw that access to birth control has increased the autonomy of women. Evidence from the United States suggests that the changes in bargaining power accompanying *Roe v. Wade* were responsible for reducing the labor supply of married women relative to that of their husbands. In European countries, there is compelling evidence that access to the pill and abortion has increased the well-being of most women as measured by life satisfaction indexes.

There have been some unanticipated effects of modern birth control technologies. One is that many women in the developed world are postponing having children to a late stage in their reproductive cycle and are often plagued by problems of infertility as a result. Another unanticipated effect (and this has been documented only in the United States so far) has been that abortion has reduced crime rates in the young adult group.

1. What are some of the reasons that women in developing countries feel the need to avoid pregnancies and to terminate unwanted pregnancies? What are the dangers to these women of banning abortion?

2. In poor countries especially, women face a trade-off between maternal mortality in childbirth and mortality in abortions. What are the causes of mortality in these two scenarios? How can they be reduced?

3. How and why did the contraceptive pill enable women in developed countries to launch into careers in professions like medicine and law? What are the direct and indirect ways in which the pill benefited women, according to Goldin and Katz (2002)?

4. Consider the following simplified rendition of the article by Akerlof, Yellen, and Katz (1996). Both women and men can embark on romantic relationships (which include premarital sex), which each partner values at $R = 200$ utils (utility points). There is a possibility of pregnancy, and the expected cost of this to a woman amounts to C utils. If the man is committed to staying around and helping ("marrying") in the event of pregnancy, he incurs a cost $D = 80$ utils; if not, the woman incurs this as an additional cost. Prior to engaging in a romantic relationship, a woman has to decide whether to ask for a commitment of marriage in the event of pregnancy. If the man gives his word, assume that he keeps it. If the man declines and leaves, both people receive a net payoff of 0 (and in the next period they can try their luck again with someone else). All men are alike in this society. There are two types of women: (1) those who don't want children right away (Type 1), who have a pregnancy cost of $C = 150$ utils, and (2) those who want children right away (Type 2), who have a pregnancy cost of $C = 50$.

(a) First consider a scenario in which contraceptives and abortion are unavailable. Carefully explain why the equilibrium outcome you observe might involve "shotgun marriages," which couples enter into in the event of pregnancy. How and why does your argument depend on the proportion of Type 1 women in the society?

(b) Now suppose that the availability of contraceptives and abortion reduces the costs C and D to 0. Explain carefully how and why you might observe the equilibrium change to one in which there is a dramatic increase in the incidence of unmarried mothers.

(c) Explain how the revolution initiated by oral contraceptives and the legalization of abortion may have contributed to the "feminization of poverty" in North America.

(d) Explain why an increase in the market opportunities available to women might also induce a shift in the equilibrium to the kind observed in part b above.

5. Explain the reasons why access to abortion may have changed the bargaining power within households in favor of women. In the context of the Nash bargaining model, what does this imply about the relative labor supplies of the two members of married couples? What evidence is there to support these implications?

6. Assess the empirical evidence on how modern birth control technologies have impinged on the well-being of European women. Explain why these effects depend on the religions that women subscribe to.

7. Explain how the contraceptive pill may have facilitated the emergence of the problem of rising infertility in women of the developed world. What does this suggest to you about the trade-offs involved in long-term use of the pill?

8. What is the logic offered by Donohue and Levitt (2001) as to why legalizing abortion in the United States led to a decline in crime some 17 years later as an unintended consequence? What evidence do they offer to support this claim?

Empowering Women

CHAPTER TEN

How Did Women Gain Suffrage, and What Are Its Economic Effects?

I. Introduction

The final two chapters of this book deal with how women become empowered. Although the next chapter brings together various policies based on economic issues that we discussed earlier in the book, this chapter is dedicated to a topic that has not been dealt with at all, namely, women's suffrage or women's right to vote. One of the most empowering rights an individual can have is the right to vote. In fact, unless a person has this right she or he is not really acknowledged to be a person. There is no doubt that winning suffrage is one of the most momentous events in the lives of women and marks the beginning of the rise in their status in society. In the West, women won suffrage only in the nineteenth and twentieth centuries—long after men had this right. In developing countries, women's suffrage started materializing only in the latter half of the twentieth century.

Women received the right to vote after a long and arduous struggle. One of the earliest proponents of women's suffrage was Mary Wollstonecraft of Britain, who wrote *A Vindication of the Rights of Women* in 1792.[1] Indeed, Wollstonecraft was one of the earliest feminists. In her book she argued that unless women were given the same rights as men they would live without developing their minds, squandering their lives in emotional refinements and in attempts at making themselves subservient to the interests of men. She saw the granting of full civil rights and education for women on the same footing

---

[1] Wollstonecraft, M. (1792), *A Vindication of the Rights of Women: With Strictures on Political and Moral Subjects,* Thomas and Andrews, Boston.

as men as the way out of this slavery. Because Wollstonecraft wrote her book soon after the French Revolution of 1789, her revolutionary feminist arguments were somewhat sidelined by her commentaries on what was happening across the English Channel.

An ardent proponent of women's suffrage was the classical economist John Stuart Mill, who wrote *The Subjection of Women* in 1869.[2] Many of the ideas in this essay were drawn from an earlier one published in 1851 titled *Enfranchisement of Women*, which he acknowledged had been inspired by his wife, Harriet.[3] In the latter essay, Harriet and John Mill offer impassioned and compelling arguments as to why it is not only unjust but also irrational to deprive women of the right to vote. In 1867, as a member of Parliament in Britain, John Mill introduced a bill that would have granted the franchise to women. Although the attempt was unsuccessful, it brought serious attention to the issue through the debate it engendered. A national movement for women's suffrage materialized soon after that. In 1869 unmarried women in Britain won the right to vote in local elections. Full voting rights for all women in Britain, however, came only in 1928.

Across the Atlantic, Elizabeth Cady Stanton and Susan B. Anthony were pioneers in the struggle for women's rights in the United States. Along with Lucretia Mott, in 1848 Stanton organized the first women's rights convention in Seneca Falls, New York. In her keynote address, Stanton declared:

> We are assembled to protest against a form of government existing without the consent of the governed—to declare our right to be free as man is free, to be represented in the government which we are taxed to support, to have such disgraceful laws as give man the power to chastise and imprison his wife, to take the wages which she earns, the property which she inherits, and, in case of separation, the children of her love; laws which make her the mere dependent on his bounty.[4]

With this began the activism for women's suffrage in the United States. This culminated in 1920 with the passage of the Nineteenth Amendment to the U.S. Constitution, through which all American women received the right to vote.

The people cited above are only a minuscule fraction of those who fought for women's voting rights. Across the globe, the granting of full voting rights began in 1893 with New Zealand. The most recent country to provide such

---

[2] Mill, J. S. (1869), *The Subjection of Women*, Longmans, Green, Reader, and Dyer, London.

[3] This essay, originally published in *Westminster Review*, is reprinted in J. S. Mill (1859), *Dissertations and Discussions*, vol. 2, John Parker and Son, London. Apparently the essay was actually written by Harriet in 1851 but published under John Mill's name, according to the BBC website on history: http://www.bbc.co.uk/history/historic_figures/taylor_harriet.shtml.

[4] DuBois, E. C., ed. (1981), *Elizabeth Cady Stanton, Susan B. Anthony: Correspondence, Writings, Speeches,* Schocken Books, New York, p. 31.

rights is Saudi Arabia, which in 2011 opted to grant women the right to vote as of 2015. Women in most of the developed countries had achieved suffrage no later than 1945 (with the surprising exception of women in Switzerland, who gained it in 1971). Nearly all women in the world now have a right to vote, at least in principle.

Women obtained suffrage through peaceful means: the men who had the right to vote voluntarily extended the franchise to women. This meant that men found it in their interest to do so. Why did they? And what was the political mechanism through which women got the right to vote? What were the economic factors that were conducive to women's receiving suffrage? What determined the timing of this? These are some of the questions we address in this chapter. (In the next chapter we shall discuss the consequences of women's assuming political office.)

We then go on to examine whether women's suffrage has made any difference to governments' behavior. We might expect this to be so because in democracies political parties have to cater to the preferences of the voters in order to get elected. We shall see that in the United States, women's suffrage has increased government expenditures significantly but that the magnitude of this effect has been much less in European countries.

We shall also examine why in Western democracies there has emerged a "political gender gap," with women leaning more than men toward the left of the political spectrum. People with left-wing preferences believe that government should play a very active role in the economy and that it should provide a lot of public goods and services, even if it means that taxes are higher as a result. Right-wing people believe that government should minimize its role in the economy, restricting itself to providing essential public services (e.g., ensuring law and order, providing national defense, and so on), and therefore keep taxes low. We shall ask why women in Western democracies are more left-wing than men and what consequences follow from this. This difference in preferences is important because a greater presence of government services in the economy can translate into greater autonomy for women within their households and also outside of them.

Finally, we shall discuss how the sex composition of a family's children influences the political opinions of their parents. Recent literature has shown that parents with daughters are more left-leaning politically than parents with sons. We shall inquire why this is so, because this may be one of the important avenues through which feminism expands its sphere of political influence—which has economic consequences.

II. An Economic Motivation for Women's Suffrage

Before we discuss how women gained suffrage, we shall briefly examine the issue of why women were denied voting rights to begin with. Surprisingly, much less research has been done on this issue in economics than is warranted. Many of the reasons undoubtedly had to do, directly or indirectly, with patriarchy. In most countries, the legal codes have been strongly influenced by various religions, and all the major religions have aspects that are patriarchal. Particularly in the realm of family law—which determines laws for marriage, dissolution of marriage, ownership of assets within marriage, the rights of husbands and wives, and so on—the state appropriated the role previously played by religions.[5] There is little doubt that certain aspects of most of the major religions tend to undermine some of the rights of women. But, as the philosopher and feminist Martha Nussbaum (2000) has persuasively argued, religions also give women a sense of protection, so a blanket condemnation of religion as totally opposed to women's rights is unwarranted.[6]

Given the patriarchal bent one observes in certain aspects of religions, it is not surprising that in English common law, for example, a wife had no legal identity independent of her husband's. Within a family, the patriarch was vested with the ultimate authority and therefore spoke for the family. The view implicitly adopted by this stance of the law is that of the "unitary model" of the family, with the patriarch as head: what is good for the patriarch is good for the family. In effect, the claim is that the patriarch is a benign dictator who altruistically manages the welfare of the family in political matters.

A deeper inquiry into the matter reveals vested interests of patriarchs at work, with the backing of religious beliefs. Many of the institutions pertaining to the family are explained by such interests. In an interesting paper, Steven Cheung (1972) has argued that the Chinese joint family system in which the son stays with his parents was devised to ensure that the patriarch retains control over his son's earnings.[7] (The argument probably applies equally well to other regions as well, especially South Asia.) The daughter-in-law joined the husband's family rather than the other way around because women were deemed easier to control and therefore could be more easily prevented from running away. In this manner, even the daughter-in-law's effort was appropriated by the patriarch. Drawing on this view, Elissa Braunstein and Nancy Folbre (2001) have put forward the idea of "patriarchal property rights."[8] In effect, the patriarch provides for the subsistence of his wife and

[5] For a comprehensive treatment of this topic, see Htun, M., and L. Weldon (2011), "Sex Equality in Family Law: Historical Legacies, Feminist Activism, and Religious Power in 70 Countries," background paper for *World Development Report 2012*, World Bank, Washington, DC.

[6] Nussbaum, M. C. (2000), *Women and Human Development: The Capabilities Approach,* Cambridge University Press, Cambridge, UK, Chap. 3.

[7] Cheung, S. N. (1972), "The Enforcement of Property Rights in Children, and the Marriage Contract," *Economic Journal* 82, pp. 641–657.

[8] Braunstein, E., and N. Folbre (2001), "To Honor and Obey: Efficiency, Inequality, and Patriarchal Property Rights," *Feminist Economics* 7, pp. 25–44.

children and claims the (residual) family income that is in excess of these subsistence requirements. This is analogous to the notion that owners of capitalist firms are "residual claimants" of the income generated by the firms after all other hired inputs have been paid. This concept of patriarchal property rights is a particularly fruitful way of viewing matters when it comes to understanding how women acquired the right to vote, as we shall see in the model that follows.

Rick Geddes and Dean Lueck (2002) present a model drawn from the history of the United States of the economic reason that men acquiesced to granting women the right to vote.[9] In the United States, till the early twentieth century there prevailed an institution called *coverture*, whereby a wife was essentially her husband's slave. She could not work without his permission, and, when he gave it, her earnings belonged to him. She could not write contracts, could not own property, and therefore could not dispose of any. Why did this institution change to one of *self-ownership*, that is, one in which a woman could work without her husband's permission, claim her earnings, own assets, and dispose of them as she saw fit?

When the law of coverture was in effect, the husband would allocate his wife's time (and his own) so as to maximize his wealth. When economic opportunities opened up for her skills in the market, he would redirect their efforts in order to increase his wealth. Thus, under coverture a marriage was akin to a firm in which the husband was the owner-manager and his wife was an unpaid employee who carried out the owner's wishes.

The scenario described above presumes that the wife indeed did her husband's bidding without demurring or revolting. In reality such ownership of another human being and her efforts is costly to her husband, for no human being is a willing slave of another. In the execution of her husband's bidding, the wife always has some latitude to exercise her own will and to improve her own well-being—which, naturally, is not necessarily perfectly aligned with his. Therefore, there will always be some exercise of her own will (something that her husband might consider "shirking") that thwarts his aims. Why should she apply herself when all the benefits go to someone else? This requires the husband to monitor his wife to ensure that she does his bidding, though this can never be accomplished perfectly. Due to this diversion of time and effort on the part of both people, household wealth will not increase as rapidly with the wife's outside wage as might have been the case if she had been completely passive.

The horizontal axis of Figure 10.1 shows the wage rate that the wife's labor could fetch outside the home, and the vertical axis shows the husband's (maximized) wealth after he suitably allocates the family's time. One would

[9] Geddes, R., and D. Lueck (2002), "The Gains from Self-Ownership and the Expansion of Women's Rights," *American Economic Review* 92, pp. 1079–1092.

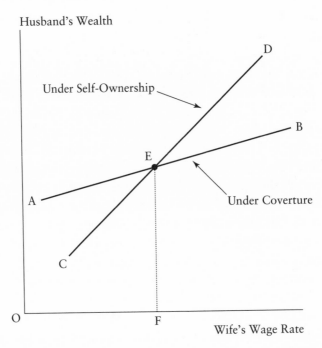

FIGURE 10.1 The choice between coverture and self-ownership

expect that, as his wife's wage rises in her market activities, the husband will direct more of her time to these. As a result, the household's wealth (which is also exclusively his under coverture) will increase with the wife's wages. This is indicated by the upward-sloping line AB.

Let us now compare the outcome under coverture with the one that will obtain in an alternative scenario in which women are equal to men under the law. What will the husband's wealth be when his wife possesses ownership of herself? In this situation, we can treat the household as a partnership in which the two partners share the household wealth. Each partner receives, let us say, half the wealth they jointly create. Under self-ownership, the wife will be more willing to apply effort in a wealth-maximizing way because she will obtain half of what she contributes. The husband's share of the family wealth is now shown by the line CD in Figure 10.1. Note that the slope of CD exceeds that of AB. This means that, when the wife's market wage rate increases, the husband's share of the wealth increases faster than under coverture. This is because the wife now has a greater incentive to apply herself appropriately because she benefits from it. The husband's incentives are diluted because he now receives only half the returns his effort generates. But this is compensated for by the fact that the time he previously spent monitoring his wife is now released for productive work.

From the husband's point of view, the disadvantage of self-ownership is that he has to share the household wealth with his wife, whereas under coverture he could appropriate it all. The advantage under self-ownership, as mentioned above, is that his wife has a greater incentive, so less time and effort on his part are required to supervise her. On balance, will the husband be better off under coverture or under self-ownership? To put it differently, when is it profitable for the male residual claimant to relinquish exclusive, patriarchal property rights to the residual income?

The answer to this question depends on the wage rate that the wife can earn in the labor market. At low wage rates, the loss to the husband from the lack of incentive under coverture for the wife is small in comparison to forfeiting half the wealth to his wife. In Figure 10.1, when the wife's wage rate is below OF, the height of AB is greater than that of CD. So the husband will prefer coverture to self-ownership. When the wife's market wage rate is high, behavior that deviates from wealth maximization under coverture becomes very costly to him and he is better off under self-ownership. When the wife's wage rate exceeds OF in the figure, the height of CD is greater than that of AB.

What the above analysis shows is that, when the wage for the wife's market work is sufficiently high, incentives become important and the husband becomes willing to *voluntarily* relinquish coverture and settle for his wife's self-ownership of her earnings. Economic development that places a premium on women's work in the labor market automatically leads to their being granted suffrage. Women become their own persons, working by their own choice, keeping their own earnings, writing contracts in their own name, managing and disposing of their own assets.

Between 1870 and 1920, many states in the United States made a transition from coverture to various aspects of self-ownership—in particular, with respect to ownership of estates and ownership of one's own earnings. Geddes and Lueck test their theory using data on states that relinquished coverture during this period. Their theory predicts that the transition to self-ownership is more likely to occur in states that are urbanized (because cities tend to have a greater degree of specialization and, therefore, place a premium on skills); have more females with schooling (because their wages tend to increase with human capital); and have higher levels of per capita wealth (because the lack of incentives under coverture is more damaging when the household is wealthy). Their findings confirm these predictions. The model above shows that the rights that women acquired to own property moved in tandem with economic development, which preceded the right to vote. This is consistent with evidence across the world.[10]

Interestingly, Geddes and Lueck also find that states that had women's organizations pushing for suffrage for longer periods of time were more

---

[10] See Doepke, M., M. Tertilt, and A. Voena (2012), "The Economics and Politics of Women's Rights," *Annual Review of Economics* 4, pp. 339–372.

likely to have abolished coverture in any given year. This shows that suffrage was not handed to American women on a platter; they fought for it. The self-interest of men was not the only reason that women won suffrage.

Raquel Fernandez (2012) has offered an interesting and more sophisticated model to explain how women acquired property rights.[11] In her view, parental concern for future generations played an important role. In a patriarchal regime, such as that of coverture described above, because only men have rights to property, fathers' bequests to daughters are appropriated by their husbands; only sons can enjoy bequests without constraint. This creates a disparity between the well-being of sons and daughters, a disparity that increases in magnitude as wealth increases or as fertility decreases (because the bequest per child is greater). When the disparity is sufficiently large, out of concern for their daughters' well-being, fathers become open to the idea of granting women property rights even though this means that they have to share their property with their wives. Thus the theory argues that economic development and a decline in fertility contribute to the transition to a regime in which women, too, can equally own property. Furthermore, the more discriminatory the older property rights regime was against women, the greater will be the disparity between the well-being of fathers' sons and daughters and the sooner will the transition to the new regime of equal rights occur. Fernandez provides supporting evidence for her theory using data from U.S. states over the period 1850–1920, when married women in America achieved such rights.

The models discussed above provide economic rationales as to what motivated the move toward women's suffrage. Even though the models may be specific to a few countries, they give us an idea of the sorts of economic considerations that are relevant to the issue. But what was the *political mechanism* by which women achieved suffrage? It is one thing to suggest economic reasons for the move to suffrage but quite another to understand the political process through which it was accomplished. We now address this issue.

III. The Political Means to Attain Suffrage

The political processes responsible for the manner in which various policies are voted for and implemented can be quite complicated. However, there is a very simple but powerful model that provides a shorthand description of how specific policies are arrived at through voting. This will suffice to help us gain some understanding of how women acquired suffrage in the developed countries. We discuss this model below and demonstrate the logic of a

[11] Fernandez, R. (2012), "Women's Rights and Development," unpublished manuscript, New York University, New York.

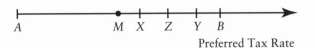

FIGURE 10.2 The distribution of desired tax rates

powerful implication called the *median voter theorem,* which is a very useful vehicle for understanding policy changes.[12]

Typically in scenarios that entail voting, the decision that is implemented is the one chosen by the majority. This is certainly how, for example, the results of elections are decided in democratic countries. So we shall assume in what follows that when voters have different preferences over which specific policy to implement, the outcome chosen is the one that receives the maximum support.

To demonstrate how the median voter theorem obtains, consider the following simple situation. Suppose that two political parties are engaging in an election and each party nominates one candidate to run for office. We shall refer to the candidates as X and Y. Let us suppose that the voters are concerned about only one issue. Say this issue is what the tax rate should be. The tax rate determines the amount of revenues the government will collect and subsequently use to provide public goods like schools, healthcare, highways, and national defense. Providing more public goods will require that the government collect more in taxes and so set a higher tax rate.

Different voters will generally have different preferences over how much they wish to receive from the government by way of public goods. Consequently, they will have different preferences over what tax rate the government should set. Suppose that we arrange the voters in the order of increasing levels of their "preferred" tax rate.[13] This is depicted in Figure 10.2. In this figure, A denotes the voter with the smallest preferred tax rate and B denotes the voter with the highest preferred tax rate. Let us assume that the rest of the voters in this society are uniformly spread out between A and B.

In Figure 10.2 we use M to denote the *median voter.* By this we mean that 50% of the voters have a desired tax rate below that of M and 50% have a desired tax rate above that of M. In other words, M is the "middle voter" in some sense.[14]

[12]This theorem was originally demonstrated in Black, D. (1948), "On the Rationale of Group Decision-Making," *Journal of Political Economy* 56, pp. 23–34.

[13]No one prefers to be taxed, of course! The "preferred" tax rate is that implied by the level of government spending on public goods that a person most prefers.

[14]The procedure for finding the median is simple. Suppose that the weights of five children (in pounds) are 40, 28, 36, 30, and 50. To find the median weight, we first arrange them in increasing order: 28, 30, 36, 40, 50. The median weight is then 36 pounds because there are two children with weights lower than this value and two with weights above. If we added a sixth child with a weight 55 pounds, there would be two "middle values": 36 and 40. The median is then taken to be the average of these, that is, 38 pounds.

The candidate of each party will choose an election platform. Because the tax rate is the only relevant issue to voters, each candidate will have to announce a tax rate that he will implement if he is elected. Suppose that candidate X chooses a tax rate to the right of the median voter's and candidate Y, at the same time, chooses one even further to the right, as indicated in the figure. Which tax rate will be implemented? That depends on who wins the election, that is, who gets the majority of the votes. To answer these questions, we need to understand how a voter will choose which candidate to cast his vote for.

Consider a voter whose preferences accidentally coincide with exactly the tax rate announced by candidate X. In other words, the voter's "location" on the political spectrum is exactly at the position X shown in Figure 10.2. Clearly he will cast his vote for candidate X because candidate Y is espousing a different tax rate that is inferior from this voter's point of view. But what about voters who are not so fortunate as to have a candidate representing precisely their position? It is reasonable to presume that voters' distaste for a policy increases with the distance of the policy from their most preferred locations. In choosing between the two candidates, then, voters will settle on the candidate whose policy is closer to their preferences. For example, the median voter M in Figure 10.2 will cast his vote for candidate X rather than candidate Y because the former is closer to his own location on the political spectrum.

The logic outlined above immediately implies that all voters whose preferred locations on the political spectrum are to the left of X will certainly vote for candidate X because he is closer to their ideal choices than candidate Y. But in fact, even some voters with preferred locations to the right of X will vote for candidate X. Consider the voters located between positions X and Y in Figure 10.2. Let Z denote the midpoint of the line segment XY. Among these voters, those to the left of Z will prefer candidate X to candidate Y because the former is closer to their preferences. Thus, all voters from A to Z will cast their votes for candidate X and all voters between Z and B will vote for candidate Y. Clearly, in this example candidate X will win the election because he will have more than 50% of the vote. The tax rate that will be implemented will be that associated with location X in the figure.

For the purpose of illustration, in the exposition above we arbitrarily chose the election platforms of the two candidates. In reality, both candidates can predict the outcome of the election if their platforms are as indicated in Figure 10.2. So, with this foreknowledge, will they in fact choose these platforms? The answer is no. This is because at least one of the candidates will have regrets about what he's announced, given what the other has announced. Candidate Y will prefer to announce a tax rate to the immediate left of candidate X and thereby win the election instead of los-

FIGURE 10.3 The equilibrium choice of election platforms

ing it. So we do not expect the election platforms displayed in Figure 10.2 to obtain.

Is there a pair of platforms such that neither candidate will have any regrets after the fact, given what his rival has chosen? If there is, we can expect that pair to obtain as the announced platforms of the two candidates for the simple reason that both of them, fully aware of the logic of the situation, will simply announce their platforms as the only rational thing to do. This pair of platforms that is free from regrets is one on which each candidate will announce the tax rate most preferred by the *median voter*. This situation is shown in Figure 10.3. (In the figure, for visual clarity the position of candidate *X* is shown to be slightly to the left of *M*, whereas that of candidate *Y* is shown to be slightly to the right.)

The reason for these choices is clear: if each candidate announces a platform at *M*, there is nothing the other can do to improve his electoral fortune. That is, neither candidate can have any regrets about his choice. This can be stated slightly differently. If candidate *X* chooses location *M*, the best thing that candidate *Y* can do is to also choose location *M*, and vice versa. These choices are the *Nash equilibrium* choices of electoral platforms.[15] We cannot predict which candidate will win the election (because each will get 50% of the vote), but we can predict one thing for sure: *the tax rate that will be implemented after the election will be that most preferred by the median voter.* This conclusion is the median voter theorem as applied to this context.

The logic of this powerful implication is quite intuitive. In an election with two rival candidates, each candidate, wishing to maximize his chances of winning the election, will identify his policy most closely with the preferences of the median voter. Thus, no matter who wins the election, it will be the median voter's choice that will be implemented. It follows, then, that even if the other voters change their preferences, as long as the median voter's preference remains unchanged, the implemented policy will remain unchanged. If the median voter's preference changes, on the other hand, the implemented policy will also change. To demonstrate the outcome of the median voter theorem, we assumed that only two parties are offering candidates for the election. If there are more than two parties, this theorem is not

---

[15] We discussed the concept of Nash equilibrium in Chapter 2.

valid. Nevertheless, we use it as an aid to thinking; it provides a simple and convenient framework that incorporates voters' preferences in the process by which policy choices are made. In this framework, to predict these choices we have to focus on the preferences of the median voter.

The median voter model has considerable empirical support. For example, it explains how the U.S. government's expenditure on its social security plan (for old-age pensions) changed between the 1940s and the 1980s. After accounting for inflation, the government's spending on this program increased threefold. It has been shown that this is explained quite well by changes in the preferences of the median voter.[16] Thus, despite its simplicity and its abstraction from many real-world complications of the electoral process, the model offers a convenient vehicle for understanding how policy changes occur. In particular, it is relevant to understanding how women acquired suffrage in democratic countries.

Ethel Jones (1991) conducted a pioneering empirical study of how economic factors impinge on women's suffrage.[17] She examined the behavior of congressmen who voted on an amendment to the U.S. Constitution to grant women suffrage in four of the eight votes in the U.S. House and Senate in the second decade of the twentieth century. She found that congressmen from states with high ratios of males to females were more likely to vote Yes on the amendment. This finding may seem surprising, but we can make sense of it through the median voter model. Congressmen from those states in which men outnumbered women would have been more in favor of granting suffrage to women because, if men's and women's opinions on some issues were very different, the median voter would have still been a man even if women could vote. In other words, control over political decisions would have remained with men, so the perceived cost of granting suffrage to women would have been less.

Another finding of Jones that is of interest (though tangential to our focus here) is that congressmen from states in which the liquor industry had a greater presence tended to vote No to the suffrage amendment. This was because the industry strongly lobbied politicians to vote against women's suffrage for fear that granting women the right to vote would lead to legislation that prohibited the sale of liquor. At the time, there were women's movements pushing for prohibition, presumably because housewives wanted to ensure that their husbands did not squander the family budgets on alcohol.[18]

---

[16] See Congleton, R. D., and W. F. Shughart (1990), "The Growth of Social Security: Electoral Push or Political Pull?," *Economic Inquiry* 28, pp. 109–132.

[17] Jones, E. B. (1991), "The Economics of Woman Suffrage," *Journal of Legal Studies* 20, pp. 423–437.

[18] Elizabeth Cady Stanton and Susan B. Anthony, in fact, were active in the women's temperance movement before they took up the fight for women's suffrage.

We are now in a position to understand how women received the right to vote. In most developed democratic countries, women acquired voting rights by peaceful means and the required legislation was passed into law when obviously only men could vote. This occurred largely between 1850 and 1930. How did this happen, and why did it happen when it did? I present below the insightful model of Graziella Bertocchi (2011).[19]

We begin with a scenario in which only men can vote. There are two differences between women and men in this model. They both have identical distributions of mental abilities, but men have more physical strength than women. Consequently, men have a comparative advantage in producing goods with physical work, but women have a comparative advantage in producing goods requiring mental work. However, in economies that are largely agricultural the demand for physical work is greater than that for mental work. In this scenario, men's income is higher than women's.

Another difference between women and men here is that women have stronger preferences for public goods (that are provided by the government). We shall discuss in the next section why this might be so, but Bertocchi argues that divorce was becoming more widespread at the turn of the twentieth century and women wanted the insurance that government provides through its various public goods. If this is true, granting voting rights to women would increase the tax rate because more revenues would have to be collected by the government in order to finance the higher level of public goods that would be demanded.

If the economy is agricultural, women do not have many opportunities to work and earn because, relative to men, they have a comparative disadvantage in physical work. If they were franchised, they would vote for a higher level of public goods, so the tax rate levied on all earning members of society would be high. Because men are earning much more than women, they will be saddled with the higher cost incurred for the public goods.

The argument can be best seen using the simple diagram in Figure 10.4. Suppose that the tax rate of the median male voter is at location M in the figure when women cannot vote. From the median voter theorem, we know that this is the tax rate that would be implemented by the government in a presumed two-party political system. If women had suffrage, they would want more public goods, so the preferences of the population would tilt toward higher taxes. Let us say that the tax rate that would prevail if women also had the right to vote is given by the location M'. Because women are poorer than men in a largely agricultural society, however, they cannot afford to pay very much by way of taxes. So in considering whether it is in

[19] Bertocchi, G. (2011), "The Enfranchisement of Women and the Welfare State," *European Economic Review* 55, pp. 535–553.

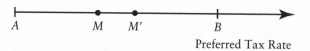

Preferred Tax Rate

FIGURE 10.4 Tax rates with and without women's franchise

their self-interest to grant suffrage to women, men will see that they will have to bear a great financial cost by way of taxes, as measured by the distance between M and M'.

However, the higher taxes that they will bear are only one side of the issue of granting women suffrage that men must consider. *Not* granting them suffrage will also have a cost for men. This may be the utility cost of seeing their mothers, sisters, wives, and daughters treated as second-class citizens by explicit discrimination under the law. This cost, as Bertocchi emphasizes, has a cultural component; the more a society's cultural norms inculcate passivity and a sense of innate inferiority in women, the lower this cost will be. Religion presumably has a great deal of influence on this cost. Let us refer to this as the "cultural cost" to men of denying voting rights to women, to distinguish this cost from the financial cost of suffrage.

In deciding whether to vote in favor of ending the male monopoly on voting, men will compare the financial cost of women's suffrage against the cultural cost of their not having suffrage. In an agricultural society, the financial cost is likely to be high because women's opportunities to earn are limited and the tax rate that will prevail in the event that women receive suffrage will be high. So men will vote not to grant women suffrage.

Things change drastically, however, when the economy industrializes. As people save from their incomes, the total amount of capital available for production increases. Then something important happens that narrows the gender gap in earnings: capital increases the productivity of labor—both physical labor and mental labor. However, it increases the productivity of mental labor by more. One thing we observe in industrial as opposed to agricultural societies is that there is no longer a premium on physical strength. In fact, with industrialization come various types of machinery that substitute for physical labor. In other words, as an economy employs more and more capital, the productivity of mental labor increases far more than that of physical labor.[20] Because women have a comparative advantage in mental labor, the gender gap between women's and men's earnings declines as the economy develops.

As women's earning power increases with economic development and industrialization, their tax contributions also increase. As a result, the *tax*

[20]This argument was first made by Galor and Weil (1996), cited in Chapter 8.

rate that would need to be levied on income earners in order to finance the level of public goods women would want if they could vote would decline. Therefore, with economic development the point M' moves to the left toward point M in Figure 10.4. Because the distance between M and M' decreases, the financial cost to men of voting for women's suffrage declines. As the gender gap in earnings continues to decline with economic development, at some point in time this financial cost to the median male voter will become lower than the cultural cost to him of denying voting rights to women. When this happens, men will voluntarily grant women suffrage.

Thus in the model of Bertocchi women obtain suffrage because economic development and industrialization increase the earnings for the kind of labor in which women have a comparative advantage. The point of transition at which suffrage becomes universal depends, therefore, on the extent to which the economy is developed. To test this prediction, Bertocchi looked at 22 countries over the period 1870–1930 and examined whether the time at which the women in a country received suffrage depended on the per capita GDP, which is a convenient proxy for the extent of the country's development. She found that this was the case: women received suffrage sooner in richer countries.

In the model, women are presumed to have a stronger preference for governmental public goods than men. If the difference in preferences is not great, men will perceive a lower financial cost to voting for female suffrage and women will attain voting rights sooner. If the male–female disparity in the desire for public goods is large, female suffrage will be considerably delayed. One reason that women rely on public goods is the prevalence of divorce. The greater the incidence of divorce, the more vulnerable women feel and the more intense is their desire for public goods. This, by the logic of the model, will delay the time at which women will obtain suffrage. Bertocchi found that, consistent with her prediction, women in countries that embraced divorce laws sooner received suffrage later.

Finally, the cultural cost of not granting suffrage is also important in the determination of when women obtain voting rights. The lower the cultural cost, the lower the financial cost will have to be in order for men to vote for women's suffrage. This cost will be low in cultures in which the dominant religion urges women to subordinate themselves to men. Bertocchi identifies Roman Catholicism as one such religion. So, Catholic women are very likely to have preferences for government spending much like those of men. Therefore, Catholicism is likely to lower both the financial cost of women's suffrage and the cultural cost. Therefore, the theoretical prediction of how Catholicism should impinge on the timing of when women will receive suffrage if people are mostly Catholic is ambiguous. Bertocchi found that in countries with a high share of Catholics, all else constant, women received suffrage later than in countries with a low share.

Another factor that may have had an important bearing on women's suffrage is not captured in Bertocchi's model: the extent of electoral competition. Before all American women received the right to vote through a constitutional amendment in 1920, several of the western states had already passed legislation for women's suffrage.[21] Soumyanetra Munshi (2010) has put forward—and has provided some evidence for—the intriguing hypothesis that stiff competition between Republicans and Democrats in the western states of the United States may have contributed to the early granting of suffrage to women in these states.[22] What might the logic have been, when presumably nothing could have been gained by catering to people who had not yet received the right to vote? Munshi's argument is that stiff electoral competition (in the sense that the distribution of seats in the legislature was quite even and so political power was tenuous) made a difference. It forced parties to take seriously the preferences of men who were open to the idea of franchising women. Because the western states were frontier states at the time, far greater numbers of men were living there than women. The younger men would have preferred a more balanced sex ratio so that they could find mates, and one way of attracting women to these states would have been by granting them suffrage. Stiff competition between Republicans and Democrats would have forced them to cater to men with such preferences, for example, in order to get a political edge on their rivals.

Did education play a causal role in women's demand for suffrage? It is possible that the causality goes both ways: from women's suffrage to women's education and also from women's education to women's suffrage. As long as only men could vote, the preferences of women could be disregarded with impunity and scarcely any public funds would have needed to be allocated for the education of women. Indeed, one of the main reasons that the pioneering feminist Mary Wollstonecraft (referred to in the chapter introduction) demanded suffrage for women was precisely that she wanted them to have the same access to education as men. She saw public funding of education as the way to accomplish this.

There is some suggestive evidence that the causality goes from women's education to their suffrage. Prior to 1920, women could vote in most of the western states of the United States, but this was not the case in the eastern and southern states. Some factors have been identified that may have been responsible for this pattern.[23] In particular, there were much higher propor-

---

[21] The first American state to grant women full suffrage was Wyoming (in 1890), three decades before women everywhere in the United States could vote.

[22] Munshi, S. (2010), "Partisan Competition and Women's Suffrage in the United States," *Historical Social Research/Historische Sozialforschung* 35, pp. 351–388.

[23] See McCammon, H. J., and K. E. Campbell (2001), "Winning the Vote in the West: The Political Successes of the Women's Suffrage Movements, 1866–1919," *Gender and Society* 15, pp. 55–82.

tions of women in college in the western states, and higher proportions were also enrolled in programs to receive professional degrees in areas such as medicine and law. Furthermore, possibly because of their greater education compared to their counterparts in the eastern and southern states, women in the western states had made greater inroads into occupations that were deemed to be men's. This may have led to greater acceptance among men of the idea that women should have the right to vote. Brayden King, Marie Cornwall, and Eric Dahlin (2005) have found that the proportion of women in nonagricultural (and therefore relatively skilled) jobs was important to the success of state-level suffrage legislation at all stages, from introduction to final passage.[24]

Although there may have been many causal factors leading to women's suffrage—especially women's organizations pushing for suffrage—education could well have been one of them. This argument for education's causal role is probably quite general and not particular to the United States. Apart from specific historical circumstances, it should be applicable to all developed countries and also to developing countries that have granted women suffrage in the past six or seven decades.

Mattias Doepke and Michelle Tertilt (2009) have proposed a novel theory as to why men chose to grant women suffrage, in which education plays a crucial role.[25] Patriarchs face a tension between two effects of granting voting rights to women. First, it increases the bargaining power of their own wives, and second, it increases the bargaining power of their daughters vis-à-vis their husbands. Although the former works against men's self-interest, the latter is aligned with it because fathers care for their daughters. Furthermore, fathers also care for their grandchildren and the education of their grandchildren. Consistent with empirical evidence, Doepke and Tertilt posit that women have a stronger influence on their children's education than their husbands. So men see an increase in their daughters' bargaining power as good for the men's grandchildren. The greater the importance of human capital in the economy, the weightier this consideration becomes.

When the economy is relatively underdeveloped, human capital considerations are not salient and men are against granting suffrage to women because they do not want to relinquish bargaining power to their wives. But when the economy develops and, in particular, technology puts a premium on human capital, considerations of their daughters' and grandchildren's well-being become increasingly important. At some point, the balance tilts in favor of men voluntarily granting women suffrage. As Doepke and Tertilt

[24] King, B., M. Cornwall, and E. C. Dahlin (2005), "Winning Woman Suffrage One Step at a Time: Social Movements and the Logic of the Legislative Process," *Social Forces* 83, pp. 1211–1234.

[25] Doepke, M., and M. Tertilt (2009), "Women's Liberation: What's in It for Men?," *Quarterly Journal of Economics* 124, pp. 1541–1591.

point out, in contrast to Bertocchi's theory, it was not women's participation in the labor market that was crucial to their achieving suffrage. Rather, it was their traditional role of being "nurturers and educators of children" that was pivotal.

V. Women and the Amount of Government Spending

Bertocchi's model in the previous section explicitly assumed that women prefer more public goods than men. Is this assumption correct? There has been considerable research on the hypothesis that the granting of suffrage to women contributes significantly to an increase in government spending. The idea is that, in democracies, those who get to vote may tilt the spending toward goods and services that are of interest to them. They can do this because political parties that hope to get elected have to cater to the preferences of voters. For example, suppose that only men who owned a sufficient amount of land could vote (as was the case in Europe and the United States before suffrage became universal). In that case we would expect that government would devote a high proportion of its expenditures to defense (for security of property) and to highways to facilitate transportation and communication so that the value of the property of the landed gentry would increase. If women could vote, they might vote for increased government expenditures on employment in the public sector, increased public provision of healthcare, and inexpensive government housing to compensate for women's lower earnings compared to men's.

It is an acknowledged fact that government spending in the United States has been increasing in recent decades. John Lott and Lawrence Kenny (1999) investigate the origin of this increase, using data on the expenditures of state governments over the period 1870–1930.[26] They find that the increase in government spending does not have a recent origin. Rather, it started in the 1920s and coincided with the time when women received suffrage. They find that women's suffrage was responsible, on average, for a 10.4% increase in the government's tax collections and a 13.5% increase in expenditures. They also find that congressmen voted more liberally in the House and Senate after the passing of female suffrage. This is what we would have expected, because elected politicians would have been accountable to female voters once the latter had voting rights.

The reason Lott and Kenny offer for women's voting preferences is that women who specialize in family-specific investments are not adequately compensated in the event of divorce, so they use the government to redistribute income from men to themselves. Divorced women who are raising chil-

---

[26] Lott, J. R., and L. W. Kenny (1999), "Did Women's Suffrage Change the Size and Scope of Government?," *Journal of Political Economy* 107, pp. 1163–1198.

dren by themselves and married women who may want to insure themselves against the future possibility of divorce would lean toward greater government involvement in the economy.

We must look at the issue of causality in attributing increases in government spending to women's suffrage. How do we know that it was the voting rights of women that caused the increase in the size of the government? Perhaps it could have been, say, a growth in liberal values that was the driving force behind both women's suffrage and the increase in government spending. To ascertain causality, Lott and Kenny use the fact that not all states granted suffrage to women at the same time. Twenty-nine states had granted female suffrage before the 1920 Nineteenth Amendment to the U.S. Constitution. Of the remaining states, 7 voted to accept the amendment and 12 had female suffrage imposed on them. If liberal values were responsible for both women's suffrage and increased government expenditures, we would expect to see that government expenditures increased in states that voluntarily adopted women's suffrage but not in states that were forced to adopt it. The take-off in government spending following the adoption of female suffrage, however, was similar in the two sets of states. Thus the increase in government spending, the authors conclude, could not have been due to something (like liberal values) that led to both female suffrage and increased spending.

An analysis along similar lines was conducted recently by T. S. Aidt, Jayasri Dutta, and Elena Loukoianova (2006) for Western European countries from the late nineteenth century to the early twentieth century.[27] These authors draw a distinction, however, between two types of franchise: the economic franchise and the female franchise. The former refers to the gradual lifting of economic criteria that people had to satisfy in order to receive voting rights, and the latter refers to women's receiving suffrage. The authors also draw a distinction between various types of government expenditure: security (defense and law and order); infrastructure (roads, transportation, and communication); collective goods (private goods supplied by the government, such as housing, healthcare, and education); and transfers (redistributive programs undertaken by the government, such as unemployment insurance and old-age pensions).

The authors analyze data from 12 countries in Western Europe: Austria, Belgium, Denmark, Finland, France, Germany, Holland, Italy, Norway, Sweden, Switzerland, and the United Kingdom. They find evidence that the extension of the economic franchise increased government spending on security and infrastructure. They also find weak evidence that the extension of the female franchise increased government spending on collective goods and redistributive programs.

---

[27]Aidt, T. S., J. Dutta, and E. Loukoianova (2006), "Democracy Comes to Europe: Franchise Extension and Fiscal Outcomes, 1830–1938," *European Economic Review* 50, pp. 249–283.

Patricia Funk and Christina Gathmann (2012) have conducted a revealing study of gender differences in preferences for government expenditures using data from Switzerland.[28] Most democracies in the world are representative, that is, voters choose representatives to make decisions on their behalf. Switzerland is one of the few countries that have a history of direct democracy, that is, the government directly solicits the opinions of voters on a large number of issues through regular ballots without going through intermediaries or representatives. Because there are typically hundreds of thousands or millions of voters on any issue, no one in a direct democracy presumes that he can individually affect the policy chosen. So voters reveal their true preferences rather than camouflaging them for strategic purposes.

Funk and Gathmann use Swiss data from such ballots from 1981 through 2003 to identify gender differences in preferences. They find significant differences. Women prefer to spend more on the environment, healthcare, unemployment insurance, and social security and less on the military and nuclear energy. Women also care more for gender equality and redistribution. Because the authors control for a host of socioeconomic variables, it cannot be argued that, for example, income differences between men and women are responsible for these manifest differences in preferences. The authors find that the total spending preferred by women is at best only modestly higher than that preferred by men; the important difference is in what they think the money should be spent on. So we may conclude that Swiss voters show important gender differences in preferences as to the composition of government spending.

The fact that the effect of female suffrage on the amount of government spending is weaker in Europe than that found in the United States by Lott and Kenny (1999) is somewhat surprising and calls for an explanation. Bertocchi's model, which we discussed in the previous section, is helpful in understanding this. There we saw that in countries where the cost to men of not granting women suffrage is low (such as those with a high share of Catholics), the political preferences of women for government services would not be very different from those of men. Granting the franchise to women, therefore, would not result in a substantial increase in government expenditures. Because many European countries have a high proportion of Catholics, one would not expect to see an increase in government spending in all countries after women received suffrage. In fact, the increase would be observed in those European countries where the proportion of the Protestant population is large, as in the United States. This argument may reconcile the findings for the United States with those for European countries.

[28] Funk, P., and C. Gathmann (2012), "Gender Gaps in Policy Preferences: Evidence from Direct Democracy," Universitat Pompeu Fabra, Barcelona, https://sites.google.com/site/patriciafelicitasfunk/.

Alberto Alesina and Paola Giuliano (2011) investigated gender differences in preferences for redistribution in the United States and many other countries.[29] For the United States, they used survey data from 1972 to 2004; for the other countries, they used intermittent data spanning the period 1981–2004. The surveys collected socioeconomic information from the respondents and solicited their opinions on government's responsibility to the poor. The authors found that women favor redistribution more than men, even after controlling for the socioeconomic status of the respondents.

All the evidence in this section points to a gender difference in preferences as to what governments ought to do.

VI. Economic Reasons for the Political Gender Gap

It is interesting and important to inquire why a political gender gap has arisen in Western European democracies. Lena Edlund, Laila Haider, and Rohini Pande (2005) have examined this issue in nine European countries: Belgium, Denmark, France, Holland, Ireland, Italy, Sweden, the United Kingdom, and West Germany.[30] They attribute the gender gap to the increasing extent of divorce and single parenthood (which they term "nonmarriage"). The state plays a role in redistributing income, and the demand for redistribution from men to women with rising nonmarriage is manifested in a difference in political preferences. The authors find that marriage aligns women's preferences with men's. Single, cohabiting, and divorced women lean much more to the left in their political views than men. Women are no more disposed than men to vote for broad-based social security benefits; the difference is that women tend to favor programs that benefit children.

Edlund, Haider, and Pande point out that unmarried parenthood is often erroneously thought to be equivalent to married parenthood. Nonmarriage contributes significantly to the political gender gap and so is a nontrivial determinant of voting patterns. Therefore, it makes a difference to the composition of public spending whether parenthood is married or unmarried. Furthermore, these differences may themselves have important consequences for the choices that parents make regarding their fertility. For if the government subsidizes the cost of children to parents, it will influence the number of children they choose to have.

Torben Iversen and Frances Rosenbluth (2006) investigate some other interesting aspects of the origin and consequences of the political gender

---

[29] Alesina, A., and P. Giuliano (2011), "Preferences for Redistribution," in *Handbook of Social Economics*, ed. A. Bisin and J. Benhabib, North Holland Press, Amsterdam, pp. 93–132.

[30] Edlund, L., L. Haider, and R. Pande (2005), "Unmarried Parenthood and Redistributive Politics," *Journal of the European Economic Association* 3, pp. 95–115.

gap.[31] Recall that in Chapter 7 we encountered Gary Becker's (1981) theory that rationalized the division of labor within the household. According to him, the comparative advantage of married women during their children's early years leads to their specialization in housework; their husbands, in contrast, specialize in market work. Iversen and Rosenbluth claim that, recognizing the possibility of divorce, women and men do not specialize to the extent suggested by Becker. Women maintain their outside options by engaging in market work even though this may not maximize their joint income with their husbands within marriage. However, women are at a disadvantage in diversifying their skills beyond those needed to run their households because they have to split their time between housework and market work.

Given that men engage in market work whether or not they are married, it makes little difference to them if the market skills they acquire are highly specific to certain firms. Women, however, find acquiring such firm-specific skills risky because they may have to withdraw from the labor market to raise a family, and therefore they will find it difficult to resume market work later because the firms will have filled their positions by then. Besides, firms may not employ them for fear that they may withdraw from the labor market to have children. Thus women tend to acquire market skills that are more general in nature. A further difficulty facing women is that even the household skills they acquire are not easily transferable to another family in the event of divorce because a large part of these skills is invested in the raising of their own children.

The government is often an employer of people with general skills—for personal and social services, for example. In other words, public service improves the outside options for women. To study this issue, Iversen and Rosenbluth examine data from about a dozen countries (mostly Western democracies, plus a few Eastern European economies making transitions from communism to capitalism and one developing country). They find that the division of labor within the household declines in favor of women as the public service provision of various goods and services within the country increases. This fact may well be responsible for some of the difference in the gender gap in political preferences: a large government presence in the economy improves women's outside options. Thus the political gender gap, through its effects on government services provided in the economy, has an influence on the relative bargaining power of women within their households. By raising the threat utilities of women, government in effect enables women to exercise greater autonomy within their households.

[31] Iversen, T., and F. Rosenbluth (2006), "The Political Economy of Gender: Explaining Cross-National Variation in the Gender Division of Labor and the Gender Voting Gap," *American Journal of Political Science* 50, pp. 1–19.

Over two decades ago, Rebecca Warner (1991) proposed the intriguing idea that parents who have daughters may become more feminist in their views than parents who have sons.[32] Working women tend to become feminists through direct experience of discrimination and harassment at work; the route of men to feminism may be more indirect. Because parents care for their children, fathers (especially) may adopt pro-feminist views if they have daughters. Warner provided some evidence for this with data drawn from the cities of Detroit in the United States and Toronto in Canada.

Rebecca Warner and Brent Steel (1999) later provided further evidence for this causal mechanism.[33] Using data from the northwestern states of Oregon and Washington in the United States, they found that parents with daughters show greater support for policies promoting gender equity than parents of sons. Interestingly, the effect of daughters is greater on fathers than on mothers. The reason is that mothers already tend to be more pro-feminist through firsthand experience; fathers are more likely to arrive at this position through concern for their daughters. An interesting implication the authors draw from their finding is that child-rearing may be a route to undermining patriarchy. Fathers of daughters will tend to eschew patriarchal values because they become cognizant of the effect of gender inequities on their daughters. Fathers of sons, on the other hand, are unlikely to be sympathetic to feminist causes. However, the latter effect is unlikely to completely offset the former because the problems confronting sons in making a success of their lives typically do not revolve around gender equity issues. On balance, therefore, there should be a net undermining of patriarchal values through child-rearing.

Andrew Oswald and Nattavudh Powdthavee (2010) have pushed this line of inquiry even further—toward establishing the relationship between the sex composition of children in a family and the actual affiliation of parents with political parties.[34] They posited that having daughters tends to make their parents more left-wing in their political preferences, whereas having sons tends to make them more right-wing. Left-wing parties typically favor redistributing income between the rich and the poor and also favor large public sectors. Right-wing parties, on the other hand, tend to be more conservative in that they want to minimize the role of the government in the economy. As a result, when left-wing parties are in power the tax rates tend to be high

---

[32] Warner, R. L. (1991), "Does the Sex of Your Children Matter?: Support for Feminism among Women and Men in the United States and Canada," *Journal of Marriage and Family* 53, pp. 1051–1056.

[33] Warner, R. L., and B. S. Steel (1999), "Child Rearing as a Mechanism for Social Change: The Relationship of Child Gender to Parents' Commitment to Gender Equity," *Gender and Society* 13, pp. 503–517.

[34] Oswald, A. J., and N. Powdthavee (2010), "Daughters and Left-Wing Voting," *Review of Economics and Statistics* 92, pp. 213–227.

because the more numerous government activities have to be funded. When right-wing parties are in power, the tax rates tend to be low because the role of the government is curtailed. People with left-wing preferences, naturally, will vote for left-wing parties, and those who have right-wing preferences will vote for right-wing parties.

This link between peoples' voting behavior and the sex composition of the children in their families is quite curious. But given what we have discussed above, this should not be surprising. Oswald and Powdthavee argue that because parents care for the well-being of their children, they internalize some of their children's preferences. And we have seen in earlier sections of this chapter that women have a stronger preference for government services than men. So parents of daughters adopt the same preferences to some extent.

The consequences of this phenomenon can be readily shown graphically. Voters recognize that more of a public good can be had at a cost, that the tax rate needed to finance it must increase. Increases in the public good raise utility, though at a diminishing rate. Consider an individual who is neither left-wing nor right-wing. In Figure 10.5a the height of the line AB shows the additional benefit in terms of utility ("marginal benefit") that she derives from the public good when the tax rate is increased by one small unit (say 1%). The line is downward sloping because as the tax rate increases, the additional amount of the public good made available offers positive but diminishing marginal utility. The individual realizes that there is a cost to increasing the tax rate: more of her income will have to be surrendered to the state. Let us denote this additional cost ("marginal cost") to her by the distance OE. The line AB, then, denotes the marginal benefit of the public good to a person whose preferences are at the center of the political spectrum, and EF denotes the marginal cost. What tax rate will she prefer? The answer is OX. If the tax rate is less than OX, her marginal benefit from increasing taxes (and hence the supply of the public good) will exceed her marginal cost, so she will want a higher tax rate. If the tax rate is greater than OX, her marginal benefit from increasing taxes (and the supply of the public good) will be less than her marginal cost, so she will want a lower tax rate. The optimal tax rate for this person is one at which the marginal benefit is exactly equal to her marginal cost, which occurs at OX.

A left-wing person derives more marginal benefit from the public good than someone at the center of the political spectrum. Perhaps this is because she feels particularly vulnerable to the possibility of divorce and feels that public service employment may make her better off in that eventuality. Or perhaps she feels that the government may provide public housing for low-income people and so she would benefit, on balance, from a higher tax rate. Whatever the reason, the marginal benefit of a left-wing person is at a position like CD in Figure 10.5a. The optimal tax rate for this left-wing person is OY, which is higher than OX.

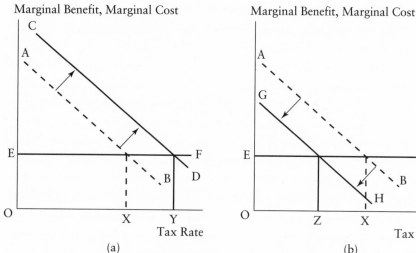

FIGURE 10.5 Illustration of optimal tax rates preferred by (a) left-wing and (b) right-wing people

A right-wing person, on the other hand, derives less marginal benefit from the public good than someone at the center of the political spectrum. Perhaps this is because he feels that he can afford to privately purchase many of the goods (education, healthcare, housing) that government provides. Whatever the reason, the marginal benefit of a right-wing person is at a position like GH in Figure 10.5b. The optimal tax rate for this left-wing person is OZ, which is lower than OX.

The upshot of the above analysis is that left-wing people tolerate a higher tax rate (OY) than a person at the center of the political spectrum (OX), whereas a right-wing person tolerates a lower tax rate (OZ). To the extent that women are more left-wing than men (for reasons elaborated in earlier sections), more women will have OY as their optimal tax rate than men, and more men will have OZ as their optimal tax rate than women. There is another reason that women may tolerate higher tax rates. They tend to earn less than men for various reasons that we have discussed in this book. So when the tax rate increases by, say, 1% the increase in the taxes paid by women is, on average, lower than that paid by men. In other words, the marginal cost associated with an increase in the tax rate is lower for women (the schedule EF is lower for women). Thus the optimal tax rate will be higher for women than for men even if they have the same political preferences.

How do daughters and sons influence the political preferences of their parents? Parents tend to embody their children's well-being as part of their own. Consider a couple with middle-of-the-spectrum political preferences before having children. They will prefer a tax rate of OX in Figure 10.5. Now suppose that the couple has two children, both daughters. The daughters are likely to have a preference for the higher tax rate OY indicated in Figure 10.5a.

Because, to some extent, the children's preferences will be grafted onto their parents' preferences, the couple's optimal tax rate will gravitate from OX toward the higher value OY—the parents will adopt the left-wing tendencies of their daughters. So in elections, this couple with two daughters, say, will vote for left-wing parties. If, instead, the couple has two sons, the couple's political preferences will become more right-wing because sons are more likely to be right-wing. The couple's optimal tax rate will now gravitate from OX toward the lower value OZ—the parents will adopt the right-wing tendencies of their sons. In elections, the couple will vote for right-wing parties.

More generally, daughters tend to make parents more left-wing than they were before they had children, and sons tend to make them more right-wing. How parents' preferences are affected if they have sons and daughters is ambiguous. Presumably they tend to lean toward the left if they have more daughters than sons and to the right if they have more sons.

By way of evidence for their theory, Oswald and Powdthavee offer an analysis of data based on interviews with British households from 1991 through 2005. The interviewees were asked which political party most closely represented their preferences, and they classified the parties as either left-leaning or right-leaning: Labour and Liberal Democrats they classified as Left and the Conservative Party as Right. The data are longitudinal, that is, the same individuals were interviewed at different points in time. This enables a more precise identification of changes in preferences following the birth of a child of a given sex. For statistical reasons, the authors focused on the effect of the sex of the first-born child only. They found that having daughters made parents more left-wing: an additional daughter made parents 2 percentage points more likely to vote for a left-wing party. The authors obtained similar findings using German data. Thus their study confirms that the sex composition of children in a family influences their parents' political preferences.

Ebonya Washington (2008) has provided evidence drawn from the United States showing that congressmen's voting on certain issues is determined by the number of female children they have parented.[35] She used data on voting in Congress on specific issues compiled by three interest groups: the National Organization of Women, the American Association of University Women, and the National Right to Life Coalition. The first two groups would be deemed liberal, the last conservative. Washington examined how, controlling for the number of children, a congressman's voting behavior on legislation in various categories differed if he parented an additional daughter as opposed to a son. She found that congressmen voted more liberally on women's issues if they parented daughters. This was particularly so if they were voting on reproductive rights. Washington speculates that this was because these rights

---

[35] Washington, E. L. (2008), "Female Socialization: How Daughters Affect Their Legislator Fathers' Voting on Women's Issues," *American Economic Review* 98, pp. 311–332.

are seen as uniquely relevant to all women—as opposed to, say, lesbian rights, which may be seen as important to only a fraction of women.

In principle it could be argued that, through the influence of their partners, marriage (including cohabitation) may itself render men more sympathetic to feminist causes. There is probably some validity to this argument.[36] However, one would expect this effect to be weaker than that operating through daughters. The reason is that, although men may potentially be exposed to feminist views through marriage, at a psychological level they are also involved in long-term bargaining with their spouses. Their self-interest makes men somewhat resistant to adopting positions that are too sympathetic to their spouses' views. In the case of daughters, however, this self-interest may be considerably attenuated because bargaining issues are less important and parental concern may make fathers less resistant.

VIII. Summary

The motivation for this chapter came from the fact that, among all the measures that empower women, one of the most important is the right to vote and to have a voice in the allocation of public resources.

We first addressed the issue of how men would have become more open to granting women suffrage. When women's earning power becomes sufficiently high, men find it in their own interest to dilute their absolute "patriarchal property rights"—to use a phrase coined by Braunstein and Folbre (2001)—and allow women to become partners in household production instead of unpaid workers in this enterprise. We then discussed the political mechanism through which this change would have manifested and introduced the median voter theorem.

We next examined a model that offered a very plausible theory of how women gained the right to vote. In this view, industrialization had much to do with women's suffrage. This model also brings home the importance of religion and divorce laws in explaining the timing of women's suffrage. We then discussed whether the education of women might have had anything to do with their obtaining suffrage.

If women have stronger preferences for public goods than men, government expenditures should have increased after women obtained suffrage. We reviewed the evidence on this. We went on to discuss the political gender gap that is observed in developed countries. Women typically invest very heavily in family and children and are vulnerable in the event of breakups. So they prefer to have a strong government presence in the economy as insurance.

---

[36] See, for example, Yamamura, E. (2010), "How Do Female Spouses' Political Interests Affect Male Spouses' Views about a Woman's Issue?," *Atlantic Economic Journal* 38, pp. 359–370.

Women invest in general—as opposed to specific—labor market skills, and the public sector employs people with general skills. Government employment opportunities also improve the bargaining power of married women within their households.

Finally, we discussed recent findings suggesting that people's political preferences in terms of which parties they vote for depends on the sex composition of the children in their families. Parents with daughters tend to affiliate with left-wing parties, and parents with sons patronize right-wing parties. This may be an avenue through which men begin to appreciate and adopt feminist views.

Exercises and Questions for Discussion

1. Women had to struggle to obtain the right to vote. What factors were responsible for men's having had the sole privilege of voting prior to this?

2. Suppose that back in 1870 the average household wealth in a U.S. state was $20 + w$ under coverture, where w is the average wage rate a married woman earned for market work in that state. Under the wife's "self-ownership," suppose that the total household wealth was $10 + 4w$. Assume, as do Geddes and Leuck (2002), that under coverture the household was like a firm managed and owned by the husband, whereas under self-ownership it was like an equal partnership between wife and husband.

    (a) Explain why the household wealth increased more rapidly through the wife's market wage under self-ownership than under coverture.

    (b) Comparing the average husband's wealth under coverture and the wife's self-ownership, explain why he would have preferred coverture for low values of his wife's wage but self-ownership for high values.

    (c) Draw a graph to identify the value of wives' wage rate beyond which husbands would have been willing to voluntarily abandon coverture in the state.

    (d) In this model, would American states with low levels of female literacy in any given year have been more likely or less likely to have abolished coverture? Why?

    (e) The states that had active movements in favor of women's rights were more likely to have abandoned coverture. Offer a possible explanation, using this model.

3. In an upcoming municipal election, the population of the city of Xanadu (400 thousand adults) has to vote for a mayor. The only issue that is relevant is the annual spending of the municipal government on school education. There are just two candidates, James Mellow and Susan Sharpe, who simultaneously announce their platforms. (Assume that they cannot change their positions later.) Each wants to adopt a platform that maximizes his or her votes.

(a) Suppose, first, that the opinions of the adult population regarding annual spending are spread out uniformly over the range between $10 million and $40 million. What is the Nash equilibrium level of educational spending that Mellow and Sharpe will choose? Explain your reasoning carefully, identifying how it relates to the median voter theorem.

(b) Now suppose that 100 thousand adults want spending to be precisely $40 million, whereas the opinions of the remaining 300 thousand adults are uniformly spread out over the range between $10 million and $40 million. What is the Nash equilibrium level of educational spending that Mellow and Sharpe will choose now? Explain your reasoning.

4. Consider Graciella Bertocchi's (2011) model of how women attained suffrage as applied to a small democratic country with male and female populations of 1,000 each. Initially the country is underdeveloped and only males work outside the home, earning an income of $1,000 each. All males desire the total government spending for various services to be $100,000. If women's opinions were included, this desired total government expenditure would rise to $200,000. The government charges a fixed tax rate of t per dollar earned to cover the cost of providing its services. Suppose that initially only males can vote, but they face a "cultural cost" of $70 each for seeing women as second-class citizens with no voting rights.

(a) When only men can vote, what is the tax rate t that will prevail in the country? Explain.

(b) Suppose that women also have the right to vote. What tax rate will prevail now? If men had to vote for universal suffrage, would women receive suffrage in this country according to Bertocchi? Why or why not?

(c) Now suppose that economic development increases the income of men somewhat and provides work for women. Men now earn $1,500 each, and women earn $1,000 each. If only men can vote, what will the prevailing tax rate be? (Assume that the desired levels of government expenditures for men and women are the same as before.)

(d) What will the tax rate in part c be if women can also vote?

(e) In Bertocchi's model, will men amend the constitution so that women will receive suffrage in this country after the economic development in part c has taken place? Why or why not?

5. In the light of Bertocchi's model, how would you expect women's education to determine the timing of women's suffrage? Can you suggest why the causality might go both ways? Explain the mechanisms involved.

6. Outline the theory of Doepke and Tertilt (2009) as to why women received suffrage. In their view, in what sense was it the traditional role of women that was responsible for the outcome?

7. Women and men in the developed world have different preferences for government services. Explain the reasons for these differences. Why did these differences become manifest (at least in the United States) only after women gained suffrage?

8. Explain the concept of the "political gender gap." What are the reasons behind this gap? Why do you think this gap seems to be manifest only in the developed countries?

9. Do you think the effects of the political gender gap might enable married women to exercise more autonomy within their households? If yes, explain how.

10. The political opinions of parents in the developed world seem to be influenced by the sex composition of the children in their family. Discuss the empirical evidence for this. What is the observed direction of influence? What are the reasons for this phenomenon?

11. If parents of daughters are pulled one way in their political opinions and parents of sons are pulled the other way, is there reason to believe that the net effect will not wash out at the level of the whole society? If so, can you argue why at least some feminist views might find broader acceptance among men over time?

CHAPTER ELEVEN

How Can Women Be Empowered?

I. Introduction

This final chapter addresses some of the important ways in which women can be empowered through government action. I interpret *empowerment* in a broad sense here. Not only does it refer to an increased say in household matters, it also means greater engagement by women in economic, social, and political affairs outside the home. As we might expect, there are potentially a large number of measures that can be put in place to accomplish this goal. Which ones are the most pertinent will depend on the social, cultural, political, and economic environments under consideration. To argue that one or a few policies would be the best for all environments would be ludicrous. Nevertheless, we shall discuss half a dozen broad government measures that warrant serious attention, bearing in mind that in practice we can devise many policies that must be tailored to the specific circumstances.

In the year 2000, under the auspices of the United Nations, over 190 countries agreed that they should collectively work toward achieving some important goals, called the Millennium Development Goals, by 2015. Broadly, there are eight such goals: eliminating extreme poverty; establishing universal primary education; promoting gender equality and empowering women; reducing child mortality rates; improving maternal health; combating HIV/AIDS, malaria, and other diseases; ensuring environmental sustainability; and promoting a global partnership for economic development.[1] All of these are relevant to women, but especially the second through the sixth, which not only target women but also require their active participation. Although the specific quantitative targets for each of these goals are ambitious—and

---

[1] See, for example, United Nations (2012), *The Millennium Development Goals Report 2012*, New York.

at the moment the world is falling far short of achieving most of them—the list identifies issues that most countries agree are of high priority. Women's issues figure prominently in these.

Esther Duflo (2012) has recently pointed out that there is a two-way causality between economic development and the empowerment of women.[2] To the extent that there is economic development in a country, for example, at least some of the poverty is reduced. When this happens, women benefit disproportionately compared to men because women are over-represented among the poor. This tends to empower women and also to narrow the gender gap along various dimensions. Working in the other direction, empowering women—by ensuring that they have better health and education, for example—contributes to the country's economic development. Could economic development induce a "virtuous circle" whereby the attendant empowerment of women would spur further economic development, which in turn would further empower women, and so on? Could the process initiated by economic development ultimately eliminate the various gender gaps? If so, promoting economic development would of its own accord solve the problem of gender disparities. Duflo argues that this is unlikely. I cannot but agree with her conclusion; as we have seen in the various chapters of this book, a gender gap persists in even the richest countries along various dimensions. This observation brings home the importance of government policies in actively intervening to empower women instead of passively expecting economic development to bring this about.

Because human capital enhances productivity, education opens up opportunities. In the developed world, there is not much difference between the educational accomplishments of women and those of men. In fact, in some advanced countries like the United States there are more women than men at the bachelor's and master's levels at universities. Nevertheless, on average, differences in education do not significantly handicap women in acquiring employment these days. In the developing world, however, the educational gap between women and men is substantial. In this chapter we shall discuss what cultural and economic factors are responsible for this. We shall then go on to examine why diverting some funds from educating boys to educating girls is not only equitable but also more efficient. Closing the education gap between women and men in the developing world is a very powerful way of empowering women. Furthermore, there are many externalities to educating women (benefits bestowed on society that they themselves do not capture) that are absent or weaker for men, and this provides an additional rationale for closing the gender gap in education.

As we saw in Chapter 3, the bargaining power of women within their households depends in a very important way on their earning power. Even if

---

[2] Duflo, E. (2012), "Women Empowerment and Economic Development," *Journal of Economic Literature* 50, pp. 1051–1079.

they choose to restrict themselves to housework, having the option of earning a good income makes a difference. Entrepreneurial activities typically require credit, and, especially in developing countries, women do not have adequate access to credit. This is largely because they do not have the collateral needed to gain access to credit. This chapter discusses innovative measures taken by the Grameen Bank in circumventing the difficulties faced by women in the credit market and the success the bank has met in empowering women. The success with which the essential methods of the Grameen Bank have been emulated in many developing countries demonstrates the importance of access to credit in enhancing the well-being of women.

Affirmative action policies to help minorities that have been disadvantaged over long periods of time have been put in place in many developed and developing countries. The idea here is that these policies will level the playing field somewhat so that the effects of gross inequities of the past can be gradually eliminated. One concern regarding affirmative action is that, by favoring certain minorities, it might institute de facto reverse discrimination against the majority—especially if affirmative action requires explicit quotas for minorities. In this chapter we assess theoretical arguments for and against the use of affirmative action to empower women and assess the evidence on the effects of affirmative action as implemented in the United States and India.

Next we extend the consideration of affirmative action into the political arena. The representation of women in politics is abysmal even in the developed world; in the developing countries, it is worse. Whether women are represented in political office would be an irrelevant consideration if their preferences were truly represented in democratic politics. But the evidence suggests that this is not necessarily so. We examine the effects of affirmative action policies in India (and Italy) that have sought to ensure the presence of women in politics. The empirical findings reviewed provide some evidence for the claim that such policies empower women by ensuring that the public goods of their preference are better delivered by electing female politicians. The lesson for other democracies is that affirmative action policies favoring women in politics may be empowering.

Family planning expenditures by governments have many benefits, as we have seen in Chapter 9. Not only do they enable women to avoid unwanted pregnancies, they also facilitate better timing and spacing of children. Furthermore, to the extent that men want more children than women, providing free contraceptives gives women a means to avoid pregnancies when their bargaining power is weak. Some contraceptives also prevent the spread of sexually transmitted diseases. Importantly, as we have seen, the avoidance of unwanted pregnancies prevents maternal mortality arising from them, whether in natural childbirth or from unsafe abortions. Government expenditures in the form of health insurance in poor countries also benefit female children disproportionately, as Duflo (2012) points out. For all these reasons, this chapter examines the issue of the government provision of family practice services and health insurance.

Finally, we shall discuss the importance of reforming inheritance and property laws. In developing countries, property in the form of land is very important and the inheritance laws regarding this form of property are grossly inequitable across genders. We shall examine the evidence for the benefits to women of a recent amendment to the inheritance laws in India that requires more equitable treatment of women. This also enables us to bring out some of the unintended adverse consequences of well-meaning reforms, which require accompanying complementary reforms to render the former more efficacious. In the developed world, too, property laws are important. Relatively recent changes in divorce laws and the accompanying property laws have altered the bargaining power of married women. We shall examine the consequences of these.

II. Educating Women

One of the most important routes through which women in developing countries can be empowered is greater education. Although education levels may not differ greatly by gender in the developed world (consult Figure 1.5 in Chapter 1), in developing countries, there is often a huge gender gap. Women tend to be far less educated than men. Paul Schultz (2002) has persuasively argued that governments in developing countries should spend more money to educate girls.[3] There is an equity aspect to this, he points out, as well as an efficiency aspect. The equity aspect has to do with fairness, with the fact that women and men ought to be treated similarly and should have similar opportunities open to them. Because most civilized societies place considerable weight on fairness, equity considerations alone provide good reasons for correcting the gender gap in education. The efficiency aspect of educating more women has to do with increasing the size of a nation's output or GDP by redressing the gender imbalance. If biasing educational resources toward men and away from women lowers the country's GDP, we have good efficiency reasons for correcting the inequity in education. Are there such efficiency reasons? Yes, there are several.

Let us first consider the private returns earned on resources devoted to education. The return to an additional year of schooling depends on the increase in income the extra education makes possible in comparison to the cost. Suppose that a person incurs an expenditure of $10,000 on an extra year of education in the present and, as a result, her income increases annually by $1,600 forever. Her private return to education is computed as

[3] Schultz, T. P. (2002), "Why Governments Should Invest More to Educate Girls," *World Development* 30, pp. 207–225.

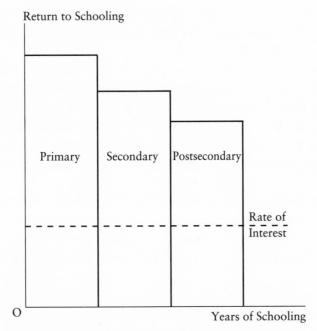

FIGURE 11.1 Relative returns to education

$1,600 ÷ $10,000 × 100 = 16% per year. Suppose, further, that saving the $10,000 in a bank is the next-best alternative use of her money and that the rate of interest the bank offers is 3% per year. It is clearly worthwhile for her to undertake that extra year of educational investment because its rate of return exceeds the opportunity cost of the money.[4]

Studies on the returns to education have shown that there are substantial private returns to primary, secondary, and postsecondary education.[5] Although all of these returns exceed the opportunity cost of money, the returns are highest for primary schooling and often (but not always) lowest for postsecondary education. Figure 11.1 schematically displays these returns. The declining rate of return to education reflects the diminishing returns to the acquisition of human capital. As can be seen, investment in all levels of education is privately profitable because it exceeds the interest rate. In reality, these returns to education are marginally higher for women than for men.[6] But here we shall assume that they are the same across the sexes. However, in developing countries fewer women than men are educated. Furthermore, there is also a difference in the distribution of education

[4] We can also arrive at this conclusion by computing the present value of the stream of extra income the investment generates and seeing that this exceeds the initial investment of $10,000.

[5] This literature has been well summarized in Psacharopoulos, G. (1994), "Returns to Investment in Education: A Global Update," *World Development* 22, pp. 1325–1343.

[6] The overall rate of return for women is 12.4%, and for men it is 11.1%; Psacharopoulos (1994), Table 6.

by gender. In particular, many men have secondary and postsecondary education, whereas many women don't even have primary education.

The facts that the returns to education differ by level of education and that men and women have different amounts of education suggest that there are good efficiency reasons for increasing the education of women. Suppose that the private returns to primary, secondary, and postsecondary education are 15%, 12%, and 8%, respectively, all of which exceed the rate of interest (3%, say). Clearly all levels of education are privately profitable. Now suppose that there are many women who do not have primary education, fewer have secondary education, and none have postsecondary education. Let us further assume that all men have primary and secondary education and a fair number have postsecondary education.

A dollar spent on postsecondary education earns a return of 8%, irrespective of gender. This return will be forgone if that dollar is diverted to some other use. If that dollar is used toward educating a woman who is currently illiterate, it will earn a return of 15%. In other words, diverting the dollar from giving someone postsecondary education and to giving someone else primary education will increase the nation's income. But we have assumed that there are many women who do not even have primary education, whereas all men have primary and secondary education and some have postsecondary education. So reducing the amount of postsecondary education for men and diverting the resources to educating women would enhance efficiency. Therefore, redressing the gender imbalance in education is not only equitable but also efficient.

Why are women less educated than men in developing countries? There are many reasons. For one, cultural biases often place greater weight on sons than on daughters. Because it is most often the social norm that lineage is transmitted through sons, it is deemed more important that sons rather than daughters be equipped with the skills and assets needed to do well in life. Furthermore, men may be seen as the breadwinners of their families, whereas women are seen as being devoted to housework. So educational expenses incurred on behalf of daughters are often perceived as a waste. Finally, as we saw in Chapter 8, in many cultures (like those in South Asia) parents in their retirement live with their sons. In underdeveloped economies in which there are no government pension plans, this reliance of parents in their old age on their male children is responsible for a strong preference for sons over daughters. Scarce resources are directed toward the healthcare and education of sons at the expense of daughters.

The returns to education considered above were explicitly recognized as private, that is, as the returns that accrue to an individual receiving education. Education, however, frequently has benefits to people other than the recipient. In a village with many illiterate people in a developing country, for example, an educated person will confer benefits on others. Many people may rely on his reading and writing skills to learn about matters that are individually profitable to them. Furthermore, this person may be able to teach others to read and write. When such benefits are conferred on others (called positive externalities), the benefits to society from educating an individual will exceed the private benefit that accrues to that person alone. In other words, the *social return* on education will exceed the private return. So if the private benefit to an individual is such that investment in extra education is warranted, the investment will be even more warranted on the basis of its social benefit. In some cases, even education conferring private benefits lower than the opportunity cost of funds may be desirable from society's point of view because the social benefit may well be great.

In the presence of positive externalities, the social returns will exceed the private returns if individuals bear the full costs of their education. However, in most countries education is subsidized, sometimes highly. The calculation of the private rate of return uses only that part of the expenditure that individuals incur, whereas the calculation of the social return incorporates *all* the expenditures associated with education. So the social returns may deceptively appear to be smaller than the private returns. Thus, for example, in Asia the private rates of return for primary, secondary, and postsecondary education are 39.0%, 18.9%, and 19.9%, respectively, whereas the social rates of return are computed to be 19.9%, 13.3%, and 11.7%, respectively.[7] The former are higher because the government heavily subsidizes education.

The externalities associated with the education of women are often more important than those associated with the education of men. There is considerable evidence that educating women reduces child mortality rates. This is because educated mothers are more knowledgeable about hygienic practices and foods that are nutritious for their children. Also, they can better identify their children's illnesses and quickly take steps to deal with them. Furthermore, educated mothers can help with their children's education. Educated fathers can also confer these benefits on children, but the effect is greater for mothers because they tend to spend more time with their children. Women's education can benefit the health status of daughters especially. Using data from Brazil, Ghana, and the United States, Duncan Thomas (1994) has shown that educating mothers improves the health outcomes of daughters (as measured by height for age).[8] Finally, the education of women also contributes to reductions in fertility. Better-educated women have better outside options, and the higher opportunity cost of their time induces them to have fewer children. If their husbands have pref-

[7] Psacharopoulos (1994), Table 1.
[8] Thomas, D. (1994), "Like Father Like Son; Like Mother Like Daughter: Parental Resources and Child Height," *Journal of Human Resources* 29, pp. 950–988.

erences for more children, these women are better able to counter them by asserting themselves because education increases their bargaining power. This reduction in a family's fertility confers a net benefit on society in over-populated developing countries.

How can more girls in developing countries be educated when parents are unwilling to educate them? The fact that there are externalities associated with education—and with the education of women in particular—suggests that there are good *efficiency* reasons (apart from the more obvious equity one) for governments to intervene. One way the state can help is by subsidizing the tuition fees of girls more than those of boys. Another is to offer scholarships to girls for school attendance. Segregating schools by gender may go a long way toward alleviating the concerns of conservative parents who do not wish to send their daughters to schools in which boys also study.

If governments in poor countries manage to increase the earning power of women by educating them, they will also contribute to reducing the number of "missing women," a serious problem that we discussed in Chapter 8. There we saw that earning power counters cultural biases against girls. Recall that the work of Nancy Qian (2008) revealed that in those regions of China where women had a comparative advantage (in tea production), the sex ratio was less biased toward boys than in the regions where men had a comparative advantage (in orchards). Wherever women are enabled to become productive in market work, it is less likely that they will be seen as a burden or as being less important than men. By educating girls, governments can offset the considerable weight of cultural norms that favor educating only boys and thereby enable girls to survive and lead more fulfilling lives as women.

III. Giving Women Access to Credit

In developing countries, it is men who largely own personal assets. In Chapter 5 we demonstrated that in order to gain access to credit one must usually own assets that can be offered as collateral. This feature of the credit market is why one needs to already have some wealth before one can borrow. Because women in developing countries have few assets, their access to credit is limited. This restricts the scope of entrepreneurial activities that could generate income for them. One of the most powerful ways to empower women is to make credit accessible to them.

If commercial banks could profitably lend money to women or, more generally, to the poor, they would do so. The reason they typically do not is that the poor lack wealth to offer as collateral. We have seen that the need for collateral in credit markets arises due to two problems, both of which stem from the fact that it is usually infeasible for creditors to collect the full amount owed (the principal plus the interest). Usually borrowers are under limited liability, that is, under some circumstances they can walk away without paying the full amount they owe.

Let us briefly recall from Chapter 5 the nature of the difficulties that arise from this. The first problem that arises from limited liability (the moral hazard problem) is that people are less careful with money that does not belong to them. If they have invested borrowed money, they may not exert the same amount of effort to make the investment pay off because not all the money invested is their own. Under limited liability, if the enterprise fails they can default on their loans. In the worst-case scenario, the borrowers may abscond with the borrowed money or embezzle it.

The second problem that arises from limited liability (the so-called adverse selection problem) stems from the fact that borrowers and lenders may have different information about the project that will be undertaken with the borrowed money. With this asymmetric information, borrowers may invest in risky projects that offer the prospect of huge profits but also carry a high probability of failure. They get to keep the profits (after paying off the loan) in the former case but walk away from their obligations in the latter due to limited liability. So borrowers may opt to invest the borrowed money in risky projects, forgoing the opportunity of investing in safer projects that offer more modest returns. The moral hazard and adverse selection problems are less problematic if borrowers can offer more collateral to creditors. This increases the extent of their liability and reduces the scope of cheating and of exploiting asymmetric information. This is why commercial banks do not lend to people without collateral and the poor are excluded from credit markets.

The Efficacy of Group Lending

Lack of collateral presents a serious problem for people who are poor and, in particular, for women of developing countries: they cannot get access to the much-needed credit that would enable them to escape poverty. In Bangladesh, a perceptive activist named Muhammad Yunus started the Grameen Bank, which offered small amounts of credit (called *microfinance* or *microcredit,* typically less than $500) to people without collateral, especially women.[9] To circumvent the problems associated with the absence of collateral, he used an ingenious mechanism. He introduced a practice called *group lending.* The Grameen Bank lent money only to individuals who belonged to groups that were voluntarily formed. These groups did not consist of strangers; rather, they usually comprised neighbors living in

---

[9] An excellent source for details about the Grameen Bank and other banks operating along similar lines is Morduch, J. (1999), "The Microfinance Promise," *Journal of Economic Literature* 37, pp. 1569–1614. So is Armendariz, B., and J. Morduch (2005), *The Economics of Microfinance,* MIT Press, Cambridge, MA.

the same geographical areas, and so they knew each other very well. The essential feature of the lending program peculiar to this bank was that not all members of a group received loans at the same time; the lending was staggered. For example, in a group of four people, the bank would first lend to, say, only two of them. Only if they repaid their loans did the other members of the group receive loans. Sometimes if the entire group received loans and any one member could not repay the loan, the others were held liable for the amount owed. In other words, the entire group was liable for the default of any group member (called *joint liability*). This meant that, if the group did not make up the deficit for the defaulting member, the entire group would be denied loans in the future.

How does the institutional innovation of group lending solve the two problems plaguing credit transactions? Consider, first, the problem of moral hazard. There are various ways in which the fact that someone else's money is at stake can impinge on a borrower's incentives. But the crucial fact is that, because of limited liability, the borrower does not face the full consequences of deliberate choices that may involve shirking, putting the borrowed money to uses other than those agreed upon, and so on. The borrower will be less negligent if the money invested is entirely his own. The extent of the negligence will depend on the trade-off between its costs and benefits. The cost of negligence is the lower probability that the enterprise will succeed, and the benefit to the borrower is the extra leisure he can consume by shirking. The borrower will tolerate some decline in the probability of success because the money invested is not entirely his own. However, too much shirking will lead to an unviable enterprise, and that will hurt the entrepreneur, too. In other words, the borrower will choose an optimal amount of effort that balances the extra benefits of shirking against the extra costs. Nevertheless, this effort is likely to be less than he would apply if the money were entirely his.

The introduction of group lending changes the borrower's trade-off. If she defaults on the loan, other members of the group may not get a loan from the bank. Because she personally knows these members (who are likely neighbors, friends, relatives, and so on), the denial of credit to them is an additional cost to the defaulting borrower. As a result, she will be wary of defaulting. A person may not mind defaulting on an agreement with an impersonal bank but will be very averse to willfully putting friends and neighbors in difficulty. In this way, the institution of group lending invokes social ties (*social capital*, as it is called) to substitute for the financial capital that would have served as collateral. This, of course, works only in regions where the culture promotes strong personal ties between people. In the rural areas of developing countries, people rarely move, so ties between neighbors last not just for years but for generations. In the developed world or in the urban areas of developing countries, dealings between people are more impersonal. In these places, group lending is less viable.

Group lending also reduces moral hazard through another route. It provides incentives for group members to monitor each other.[10] Members who do not have credit right now but expect to receive credit from the bank in a couple of months will have a stake in ensuring that group members who currently have credit will not default. So the former will monitor the latter to ensure that the money they borrowed is put to good use and that the right amount of effort is applied. If, on the other hand, the problem is that entrepreneurs can divert the borrowed funds to more risky projects, group members will monitor each other to prevent this switch if the bank holds them jointly liable for an individual group member's default.[11] This monitoring is also something they can do better than the bank because group members have much more information about each other than the bank does. In this way, group lending transfers some of the bank's supervisory activity to the group.

What about the scenario in which different borrowers have projects of different riskiness? We have dealt with this at length in Chapter 5 and review it only briefly here. Suppose that there are only two projects available with the same expected value: a safe one with a low default probability and a risky one with a higher default probability. A creditor who knows for sure that the project available to a borrower is the risky one will charge a higher interest rate than for the safe one. This is because the creditor must account for the higher probability that the loan will not be repaid. If creditors cannot distinguish between borrowers with safe projects and those with risky ones, they have to charge the same interest rate to everyone. So that they can cover their costs, this rate will have a value lying somewhere between the interest rates for safe and risky projects. At this interest rate, the borrowers with safe projects are subsidizing those with risky projects. If this average rate is sufficiently high, those with safe projects will not borrow, that is, they will drop out of the market. This is the classic problem of adverse selection that we studied earlier.

How does group lending solve this problem of adverse selection?[12] Because group members have more information about each other than the bank does, they will know whether each member's project is safe or risky. And because the formation of groups is voluntary, people with safe projects will not team up with those with risky projects because *all* group members are liable to the bank in the event of an individual member's default. A group with safe projects will not admit a person with a risky project. Groups will be such that either all members have safe projects or all members have risky projects.

[10] The pioneering analysis of this view is in Varian, H. (1990), "Monitoring Agents with Other Agents," *Journal of Institutional and Theoretical Economics* 146, pp. 153–174.

[11] This point was first made in Stiglitz, J. E. (1990), "Peer Monitoring and Credit Markets," *World Bank Economic Review* 4, pp. 351–366.

[12] See Ghatak, M. (1999), "Group Lending, Local Information and Peer Selection," *Journal of Development Economics* 60, pp. 27–50.

The bank, however, still does not know whether a group has safe or risky projects. So it will have to charge all groups the same interest rate. Nevertheless, joint liability can improve matters by lowering the default rate: if one borrower cannot repay the lender, the other group members will. So the average interest rate the bank needs to charge in order to cover its costs will be *lower* under group lending with joint liability. If the rate is sufficiently lower, the people with safe projects who would have dropped out of the market under individual contracts may now opt to borrow. In this case, the adverse selection problem will be resolved.

These are some of the reasons that the Grameen Bank reduced the default rates of its borrowers to only about 5%. But there are other reasons. One of these is that the bank requires borrowers to start repaying the debts right away, on a weekly basis. This facilitates the early detection of problem cases so remedial measures can be undertaken. Furthermore, the fact that loans that are responsibly repaid open the door for future borrowing will naturally provide strong incentives for avoiding default. The success of the Grameen Bank has resulted in its replication, with some variations, in a whole host of developing countries such as Indonesia, Bolivia, and India.

The default rate of borrowers varies by gender. As Jonathan Morduch (1999) points out, the Grameen Bank did not start out lending mostly to women, even though it now does (94% of the loans were given to women by 1992). The reason it does now is that in the bank's early years women defaulted less frequently than men. This is because women are less mobile, so they cannot seek credit elsewhere if they burn their bridges by defaulting. This concentration on lending to women, however, serves a useful social purpose. For one thing, women are in greater poverty than men, so they benefit more from having access to credit. Furthermore, if the credit increases women's income, more of it will be spent on their households' nutrition than if the extra income accrued to men. For example, as we saw in Chapter 3, Brazilian data revealed that an increase of $1 in the nonlabor income of mothers was 20 times more effective in lowering child mortality than an equal increase in the income of fathers.[13] So it is not only the women receiving credit who benefit from it; the benefit extends to their whole families.

The Benefit of Group Lending

Does access to microcredit really improve the well-being of the women who receive it? Research on this issue offers conflicting opinions, which are comprehensively summarized by Naila Kabeer (2001).[14] On the one hand, some

---

[13] See Thomas, D. (1990) (cited in Chapter 3). Recall also the study by Duflo (2003) (cited in Chapter 3) on the effect of women's pension incomes on their grandchildren's health.

[14] Kabeer, N. (2001), "Conflicts over Credit: Re-evaluating the Empowerment Potential of Loans to Women in Rural Bangladesh," *World Development* 29, pp. 63–84.

researchers have claimed that women with access to loans merely hand them over to their husbands. In this view, microcredit offered to women plays into the hands of already entrenched patriarchal interests. Often the husbands of these women may be unable, and sometimes unwilling, to repay the loans—leaving the women in a quandary. The crucial issue is one of control; women may gain access to credit, but they may not have control over its use. On the other hand, some researchers find that access to credit has managed to increase women's economic contributions, made them more aware of their rights, and even increased their participation in politics. Final conclusions on whether the effects of microcredit are better for women than for men warrant some caution, however. A careful recent study conducted in the Philippines by Dean Karlan and Jonathan Zinman (2011) has found that although microcredit does have some benefits, they do not seem to accrue disproportionately to women.[15]

Recall from our discussion in Chapter 3 that it is earnings from their own labor that empowers women. As we saw from the research conducted by Anderson and Eswaran (2009) using data from the Matlab area of Bangladesh, when women helped their husbands earn income it did not contribute to their autonomy. These women did not have control over that income. It is outside options that determine bargaining power within the household, and for the women in the Matlab area these outside options were curtailed by purdah restrictions. So by working on their husbands' farms, they acquired no additional autonomy relative to women who specialized in housework. It is only by working for themselves and controlling their income that women acquire a greater say relative to their husbands.

In interviews that Kabeer (2001) conducted in Bangladesh, she found, however, that women with access to credit did benefit in some ways. For one thing, they were less subject to domestic violence from their spouses. Furthermore, even if they merely channeled their credit to their husbands, these women seem to have acquired greater self-respect. These are nontrivial benefits in the context.

IV. Using Affirmative Action to Benefit Women

When various forms of discrimination have worked to the disadvantage of specific groups for long periods of time, one obvious avenue for addressing this is to implement laws that ban such discrimination. Many countries have put in place such laws, but it is in the United States that their effects have been documented in the greatest detail. In the United States the Equal Pay Act, which was legislated in 1963, banned discrimination by sex in the payment of wages. The civil rights movement, in which Martin Luther King Jr.

[15] Karlan, D., and J. Zinman (2011), "Microcredit in Theory and Practice: Using Randomized Credit Scoring for Impact Evaluation," *Science* 332, pp. 1278–1284.

played a pivotal role, led to a landmark piece of legislation in 1964 called Title VII, which banned discrimination by sex, color, race, religion, and country of origin. This was followed by equal employment opportunity legislation, in particular the Equal Employment Act passed in 1972, which attempts to ensure that all people have the same access to jobs if they have the necessary qualifications.

These measures, however, do not necessarily guarantee a level playing field. For if discrimination has been in effect for many decades, it is unlikely that all groups have had equal access to the institutions that provide the requisite qualifications. Affirmative action is a policy that is intended to go beyond giving equal access to everybody; it attempts to redress the damaging effects of discrimination against some minorities in the past. As a consequence, many countries that have historically disadvantaged groups have instituted affirmative action policies. Examples include India, the United States, Malaysia, Brazil, and South Africa.

In the United States, as in India, affirmative action has been a contentious policy. On the one hand, there are arguments against it because preference for one group implies discrimination against other groups. In effect, this argument suggests that affirmative action results in reverse discrimination. For example, in the United States a qualified white male applicant may be denied a job because it has been given to a less qualified black person or a woman. On the other hand, there are arguments suggesting that reverse discrimination does not necessarily obtain—it depends on how affirmative action is applied in practice. We shall assess these arguments and the empirical evidence for and against them. In particular, we shall focus on the effects of affirmative action on women's employment.

Other than at educational institutions, affirmative action in the United States has typically been applied to federal contractors. This is because these contractors receive money from the federal government for various government projects. They have to either comply with the government's dictates regarding affirmative action or risk forfeiting these lucrative contracts. A good way to test for the employment effects of affirmative action, then, is to compare changes in the employment of minorities among contractors with those among noncontractors. Any difference can presumably be attributed to affirmative action. Jonathan Leonard was the first economist to take this approach to examine the issue.[16] Over the period 1974–80, he compared the growth in the employment of women by a large sample of federal contractors (where women comprised 28% of the workforce in 1974) with that of women employed by noncontractors (where women comprised 39% of the workforce). Fewer women were employed among contractors because con-

[16] His work is summarized in Leonard, J. S. (1989), "Women and Affirmative Action," *Journal of Economic Perspectives*, Winter, pp. 61–75.

tractors are more likely to operate in the manufacturing sector as opposed to the retail sector, and fewer women than men take up work in the former. This difference, in itself, is not relevant to the issue of affirmative action. The crucial question is how the growth rates in the employment of women among the two types of firms differed after affirmative action was put in place.

Leonard found that between 1974 and 1980, the employment of women increased by 0.6% among noncontractors and by 1.2% among contractors.[17] Thus the rate of increase was twice as large among the latter type of firms. He also found that the effect of affirmative action on the employment of blacks (men and women) was greater than that on white women. In large corporations, the threat of lawsuits under Title VII (which bans discrimination) may have been responsible for increases in the employment of minorities; affirmative action per se probably had a small effect. This is because, when a firm's employment numbers are large, statistical techniques can be used to establish possible discrimination and Title VII can be invoked in such lawsuits. It is in small firms that this is not possible, so affirmative action may have had more bite there.

A concern that is often raised about affirmative action is that it might ultimately become entrenched as a rigid quota system in which a given proportion of jobs has to be reserved for minorities. Looking at the behavior of large contractor firms, Leonard further found that their hiring of minorities consistently fell short of goals. This could not have occurred had the goals been viewed as rigid quotas. Affirmative action did influence hiring, though. For white women the actual hiring was about a fifth of the intended goal; it was higher for black women.

The evidence that affirmative action seems not to have been implemented as a quota system is reassuring to some because it counters concerns about large-scale reverse discrimination. If firms are choosing unqualified women over more qualified men, the profitability of these firms should decline and so should the productivity of women. As Leonard reports, using data from manufacturing firms in 1966 and 1977 (respectively, before and after affirmative action was put in place), no evidence of such a decline is found. We might wonder how this could be possible. Was there a need for affirmative action, then, if productive women were in abundant supply?

One answer to this question comes from the distinction between the intensity of the search for appropriate candidates and the criteria used for hiring from the group of potential applicants. Harry Holzer and David Neumark (2000) examined the hiring practices in the early 1990s of a sample of firms in four large cities (Atlanta, Boston, Detroit, and Los Angeles) of the United

---

[17] If these percentages seem small, it must be noted that the numbers employed in aggregate are large, so small changes in percentage translate into substantial changes in absolute numbers.

States.[18] In particular, their survey focused on the extent to which affirmative action or the Equal Employment Opportunity Act influenced how the firms (a) recruited potential candidates for a position, and (b) hired for the position. As Holzer and Neumark point out, affirmative action may entail a greater effort on the part of firms to identify qualified people among minorities than they might have exerted before. This is particularly so if there is imperfect information about potential applicants' qualifications. Furthermore, firms can make up for perceived deficiencies through training programs. If this is the case, affirmative action need not entail a decline in quality of the hired choices. Rather, it may simply provide qualified women with better access to employment opportunities and facilitate better use of women with the right abilities but nonstandard qualifications. This is precisely what the authors of the study found. As a result of affirmative action, employers broadened the scope of the searches and screening in their recruitment efforts and, as a result, saw a more diverse group of recruits for potential hiring. Consequently, the productivity of workers hired under affirmative action was no lower than that of other workers.

Rulings by the U.S. Supreme Court have found implementation of affirmative action as a quota system to be unconstitutional.[19] By explicitly making race or gender salient, a quota (reverse) discriminates against individuals of the majority. Economists take the view that it is not possible to espouse affirmative action or even the less controversial policy of nondiscrimination without also embracing quotas or quota-like restrictions. Roland Fryer and Glenn Loury (2005) have argued that the distinction between affirmative action and quotas is a mythical one.[20] To understand their argument, suppose that a government agency wishes to enforce not affirmative action but only nondiscrimination against a particular group—say women—using the threat of severe punishments. Under-representation of women in a firm could be due to the firm's discrimination or to the fact that qualified women have not applied. The government agency usually has less information about the true state of affairs than the firm but can observe the actual number of women hired. If the firm cannot credibly communicate to the enforcement agency that fewer qualified women have applied, it may appear that it is discriminatory. To evade punishment, the firm may behave *as if* there were a quota in place and employ more women. So quota-like restrictions will obtain in practice even if the enforcement agency's mandate is only to root out discrimination.

[18] Holzer, H. J., and D. Neumark (2000), "What Does Affirmative Action Do?," *Industrial and Labor Relations Review* 53, pp. 240–271.

[19] The first challenge to affirmative action as a rigid quota was resolved in 1978. The case involved a white student who was denied admission to medical school by the University of California. See *Regents of the Univ. of Cal. v. Bakke,* 438 U.S. 265, pp. 275–276, 1978.

[20] Fryer, R. G., and G. C. Loury (2005), "Affirmative Action and Its Mythology," *Journal of Economic Perspectives* 19, Summer, pp. 147–162.

Even in the absence of reverse discrimination by rigid quotas, however, arguments have been made that affirmative action hurts the people it is intended to help. Evidence on some of the possible negative effects of affirmative action comes more from its race aspect than from its gender aspect. An argument has been made that affirmative action implemented in educational institutions in the United States may in fact be harming the very people to whom it is applied. When blacks, for example, are admitted to top schools under affirmative action it is possible that fewer of them may actually end up graduating because of a mismatch between their academic preparation and the requirements of these schools. A recent study analyzed data from the University of California system, which has several campuses, on students who went into programs in science, technology, engineering, or mathematics (STEM).[21] The study showed that minority students (blacks and Hispanics) who went to the Berkeley and Los Angeles campuses of the University of California would have had higher graduation rates had they gone to the lower-ranked campuses at Riverside or Santa Cruz. Thus students with weak academic preparation are mismatched when they attend the more demanding academic institutions, and this works to these students' disadvantage.

There is compelling experimental evidence, however, that in certain contexts the costs of affirmative action in practice can be much smaller than may be anticipated. In Chapter 2 we discussed experimental results showing that women may be willing to compete with one another but that they tend to shy away from competitions that are of mixed gender. We also discussed evidence suggesting that men are more overconfident than women and opt for tournaments (where the winner takes all) in favor of piece rates (in which the payment they receive depends only on their own performance). Even high-ability women choose not to compete in mixed-gender tournaments, whereas even men with mediocre abilities opt for them.

In a very interesting experimental setup in which participants with similar distributions of skills by gender had to perform some mental tasks, Muriel Niederle, Carmit Segal, and Lise Vesterlund (2013) examined the effect of an affirmative action type of quota.[22] Individuals in groups of 6, comprising 3 women and 3 men, were given the option of picking a piece-rate game or a tournament, both involving simple arithmetic skills. Fewer women than men participated in the tournament. Next the authors imposed an affirmative action quota in the experiment: the woman with the highest score would necessarily be a winner, and there would be an additional winner who had the top score among the rest. This, of course, raised the probability that a woman would be

[21] Arcidiacono, P., E. Aucejo, and V. J. Hotz (2013), "University Differences in the Graduation of Minorities in STEM Fields: Evidence from California," NBER Working Paper 18799, National Bureau of Economic Research, Cambridge, MA.

[22] Niederle, M., C. Segal, and L. Vesterlund (2013), "How Costly Is Diversity?: Affirmative Action in Light of Gender Differences in Competitiveness," *Management Science* 59, pp. 1–16.

a winner and so increased the number of women competing in tournaments. The proportion of women entering tournaments rose for an additional reason: women (who don't mind same-gender competitions) perceived that they would be competing against more women. In particular, the affirmative action quota aspect of the experiment attracted high-ability women who would have stayed away from tournaments in the absence of affirmative action.

The above finding suggests that the argument that favoring women through affirmative action quotas would lower the average quality of employees at firms is not necessarily correct. If the quota draws higher-ability women into the competition, it need not be the case that the women employed are displacing men of higher ability. These experimental results of Niederle, Segal, and Vesterlund provide a novel argument in favor of quotas for women in competitive scenarios. This mechanism may well justify an affirmative action policy of Norway requiring that the boards of directors of state-owned and public limited corporations comprise at least 40% of each sex.[23]

India is a country that has implemented a strong affirmative action program based on caste. Ashwini Deshpande (2006) offers an account of the differences between affirmative action in the United States and in India.[24] To lend a hand to the Scheduled Castes or Dalits (previously deemed untouchable), the Scheduled Tribes (who were not integrated into society), and other backward castes, the Constitution of India had quotas for these groups written into it. Fixed proportions of seats in educational institutions and jobs in government organizations are reserved for these groups. Furthermore, as of 1992 the constitution was amended to extend reservations for these groups (and also for women) to the political arena. By comparing the standards of living across people by caste, Deshpande argues that the equalization of opportunities across castes requires affirmative action.

As we shall see in the next section, affirmative action in the political arena has had positive effects in India—on the backward castes and on women. The effects of quotas in the arenas of employment and education are less clear. Recently, in a careful statistical analysis Victoria Hnatkovska, Amartya Lahiri, and Sourabh Paul (2012) found that over the period 1983–2005, there was considerable convergence between the lower and upper castes in educational levels, occupations, and standard of living.[25] The median wage

[23]The evidence on the efficacy of this is mixed, however. For a review, see Pande, R., and D. Ford (2011), "Gender Quotas and Female Leadership: A Review," background paper for *World Development Report 2012,* http://scholar.harvard.edu/rpande/publications/gender-quotas-and-female-leadership-review.

[24]Deshpande, A. (2006), "Affirmative Action in India and the United States," background paper for *Equity and Development, World Development Report 2006,* https://openknowledge.worldbank.org/handle/10986/9038.

[25]Hnatkovska, V., A. Lahiri, and S. Paul (2012), "Castes and Labor Mobility," *American Economic Journal: Applied Economics* 4, pp. 274–307.

premium of the upper castes relative to the disadvantaged groups (Scheduled Castes and Scheduled Tribes) declined from 36% in 1983 to 21% in 2005.[26] However, the authors found that little of the convergence between the castes can be attributed to quotas per se; most of it appears to have been due to the improved educational attainments of the lower castes.[27]

Under what conditions can we expect affirmative action (with or without rigid quotas) to work? In an illuminating theoretical article, Stephen Coate and Glenn Loury (1993) (cited in Chapter 4) inquired into one aspect of this, namely, whether affirmative action could eliminate negative stereotyping by employers. In other words, suppose that people believe that women, blacks, or some other minority has lower productivity even though that may be incorrect. Will the implementation of affirmative action tend to eliminate the negative stereotyping? If it does, affirmative action may be needed only temporarily; after it has accomplished its purpose, it can be dismantled without loss to the targeted minorities.

But how can negative stereotyping exist among rational employers to begin with? If employers believe that women are less productive than men, for example, how can such beliefs persist in the face of evidence to the contrary? Coate and Loury demonstrate that employers' beliefs may set up expectations among the affected minorities in such a way that these prior beliefs are confirmed by outcomes. To understand this, suppose that employers, given their beliefs, assign women or blacks to lower-level jobs that require less human capital and therefore have lower wages associated with them. As a result, these minorities have less incentive to acquire human capital because the returns to that investment will be lower for them. Thus the outcome will confirm the prior beliefs of the employers. However, these minorities may be induced to undertake the required investments if affirmative action is put in place because they now know that, by investing in themselves, they will get the better jobs.

It seems, from the above argument, that affirmative action will eliminate negative stereotyping by employers. But Coate and Loury demonstrate that this does not necessarily obtain. They show that, under some conditions, affirmative action may make matters worse instead of better. Suppose that employers hold firm to their stereotypical views but, in order to meet the requirements of affirmative action, they lower the standards expected of the targeted minorities. In this case, minorities will receive the signal that they need not undertake

---

[26] As the authors point out, this compares well with the fact that in the United States the premium of the median wage of whites relative to that of blacks has remained around 30% for several decades.

[27] Ironically, affirmative action along caste lines in access to educational institutions seems to have harmed women. In educational institutions focused on engineering, more women belong to the group displaced by these policies than to the group of displacers. See Bertrand, M., R. Hanna, and S. Mullainathan (2010), "Affirmative Action in Education: Evidence from Engineering College Admissions in India," *Journal of Public Economics* 94, pp. 16–29.

the needed investment because their present skills are adequate. So the patronizing view of employers could eliminate the incentives of minorities to acquire the skills needed for the better jobs. The outcomes, then, will continue to confirm the lower expectations that employers have of minorities because the latter will indeed have lower levels of skill than the majority. For affirmative action to eliminate stereotyping, employers must hold all employees responsible for meeting the requisite standards; there should be no dilution of standards.

The U.S. experience summarized above has lessons for other countries. Judicious application of affirmative action can have beneficial effects for women without necessarily hugely discriminating against men. However, if employers are required to lower their standards of acceptable performance or if they are patronizing in their attitude toward women, affirmative action policies may dissuade women from acquiring the requisite skills and the policies may end up implementing de facto reverse discrimination.

V. Improving Women's Political Representation

One important way in which women can be empowered is by increasing their presence in elected political offices. Even in the developed world, where women have made substantial inroads into paid employment and into previously male-dominated occupations, women are greatly under-represented in politics. This representation is the highest in Scandinavian countries. For example, on average the proportion of seats in the lower and upper houses of the Swedish national parliament occupied by women is around 43%. In sharp contrast, in the United States the corresponding proportion is only about 14%.[28] In the developing world, the representation of women in politics is generally even lower. Why is this? Part of the problem is that until economic development releases women from household chores and enables them to participate in paid employment, entering politics is a far cry. As Pippa Norris and Ronald Inglehart (2001) point out, it is only when women go into occupations like journalism and law that they can hope to have the kind of exposure that would make politics a viable option.[29] Furthermore, they point out that there are cultural barriers that prevent the entry of women into politics. People seem to believe that men make better leaders than women. However, there is a generational effect here: the attitudes of the more recent generations tend more toward equality along this dimension, but this is more the case in the developed world.

Why would we expect the entry of women into politics to empower them in general? After all, the number of elected political leaders constitutes a

[28] See Norris, P., and R. Inglehart (2001), "Cultural Obstacles to Equal Representation," *Journal of Democracy* 12, pp. 126–140.
[29] Ibid.

minuscule proportion of the entire population, and even if women managed to win 50% of these positions, these women would still be a trivial proportion of the entire female population in any country. One reason to think that electing women is important for their empowerment is that they are more likely to represent the interests of women in general. We have seen in Chapter 10 that women and men tend to have different preferences with regard to important issues like the role of government in the economy. In general, women prefer greater government involvement than men, that is, women are more "left-wing" than men—particularly in the developed countries.

Even if men and women differ in their policy preferences, we may further wonder why it is necessary for women to be *elected* to political office for women's preferences to be represented. As long as women have suffrage, their vote will be taken into account by politicians hoping to win elections. If in democracies the elected politicians have to implement the policies preferred by the electorate, why does the gender of the politicians matter? In a two-party system, for example, we have seen that the median voter theorem predicts that the preferences of the median voter will be implemented—irrespective of the genders of the competing politicians. Is there reason to believe that the outcomes are not entirely determined by the preferences of the electorate? Do politicians have some leeway to indulge their own preferences, possibly?

This question was addressed by Steven Levitt (1996).[30] Using data from the voting behavior of U.S. senators over the period 1970–90, he sought to identify the weights that senators put on voters' preferences, their own parties' preferences, their supporters' preferences, and their own ideologies. He found that senators placed no more than 25% of the weight on voters' preferences. Among voters, they placed more weight on the preferences of their supporters than the rest; they gave supporters' preferences three times the weight of those of nonsupporters. Furthermore, the senators also put some weight on the preferences of their respective parties. Finally, they placed the greatest weight on their own ideologies. This evidence suggests that politicians have considerable leeway in getting around representing the preferences of the members of their constituencies. However, Levitt did find evidence to suggest that when reelections are looming on the horizon, senators pay attention to the preferences of nonsupporters—especially if their reelection prospects are unclear.

Michelle Swers (1998) has provided evidence from the 103rd Congress of the United States, which met between 1993 and 1995, showing that women in the legislature vote differently from men on bills that are relevant to women's issues.[31] On legislation pertaining to women's health, abortion, and

---

[30] Levitt, S. (1996), "How Do Senators Vote?: Disentangling the Role of Voter Preferences, Party Affiliation, and Senator Ideology," *American Economic Review* 86, pp. 425–441.

[31] Swers, M. L. (1998), "Are Women More Likely to Vote for Women's Issue Bills Than Their Male Colleagues?," *Legislative Studies Quarterly* 23, pp. 435–448.

children, for example, women are more likely than men to vote across party lines in favor of more liberal positions. A difficulty with evidence such as this, however, is that constituencies or states that vote for female politicians may differ systematically from those that do not. As a result, we cannot be sure that the voting behavior on legislative bills that is attributed to women politicians truly reflects gender differences and not the preferences, say, of the voters who elected them. Recently Marit Rehavi (2013) has corrected for this problem by looking at women elected in the United States in *closely contested* state elections against men.[32] Because the vote counts were very close in these selected elections, we can be sure that the subsequent behavior of the elected women in the legislature does not reflect differences between the voters in these states and that it truly reflects the preferences of the women politicians. Rehavi finds that female politicians at the state level do indeed vote differently than male politicians on some bills—especially those pertaining to health issues.

Using data from India over the period 1967–2000, Irma Clot-Figueras (2011) examines whether women in state legislatures vote differently from men.[33] She finds that women favor public expenditures that are different from those favored by men, but the extent of this depends on their caste and class. Women legislators from disadvantaged groups—the Scheduled Castes and Scheduled Tribes—favor pro-women and pro-poor policies such as land redistribution and expenditures on primary school education. Women from upper castes and classes, in contrast, oppose land redistribution and favor investments in secondary and higher education, reflecting their class interests. Although there is evidence of gendered preferences, in other words, these preferences are also influenced by economic interests.

Now that we see why the representation of women's preferences may require women to be elected, we have to ask how this can be accomplished. Because women have typically been unable to break into political office even in many developed countries, what measures might be put in place to expedite the process? And if women do manage to get into elected positions, do they really make a difference? We address these questions now.

Regarding the second question, it might seem that establishing an answer should be quite easy. All we need to do is compare various outcomes in which women are the elected leaders with the corresponding outcomes in which men are the leaders and see if there are differences. The procedure, unfortunately, cannot be quite so simple. If we compare the outcomes in Norway (where there is a substantial number of elected women) to those in

---

[32] Rehavi, M. M. (2013), "Sex and Politics: Do Female Legislators Affect State Spending?," unpublished manuscript, University of British Columbia, Vancouver.

[33] Clot-Figueras, I. (2011), "Women in Politics: Evidence from the Indian States," *Journal of Public Economics* 95, pp. 664–690.

Pakistan (where there are few elected women in its intermittent democracy), how can we be sure that the differences in economic outcomes can be attributed entirely to women? It is possible, for example, that liberal values were responsible for more women being elected in Norway, and the same liberal values may also be responsible for differences in outcomes relative to Pakistan. To correctly identify the effects of women per se, we need to be more careful. To isolate such effects, economists often use what are called natural experiments. These are situations that arise for reasons that have nothing to do with the issues under consideration, as the following discussion clarifies.

Before focusing on women, I first allude to the effect of quotas (referred to as reservations) for disadvantaged groups in India. Rohini Pande (2003) has asked in the context of India whether the political representation of these groups mandated at the state level by the Indian Constitution improved their well-being.[34] In jurisdictions reserved for such groups, only members of these groups can be put up as potential candidates in an election. Pande statistically examines whether reservations for Scheduled Castes and Scheduled Tribes have influenced policies at the state level. Her finding is that reservations (quotas) have increased the targeted flow of resources to these groups. The greater presence of mandated Scheduled Caste politicians in a state is correlated with higher job quotas, and the greater presence of mandated Scheduled Tribe politicians is correlated with higher welfare spending on this group. Political quotas seem to help the targeted groups.

Now consider political quotas for women. In an amendment to its constitution in 1992, India sought to ensure that one-third of the village-level councils or gram panchayats (GPs) elected village chiefs (pradhans) who were women. In these reserved GPs, political parties could field only women candidates. The GPs that were to be headed by female village chiefs were selected *at random*. This choice by randomization is crucial for assessing the effectiveness of female village chiefs because we cannot argue that these chiefs were chosen because the GPs were particularly liberal or for some such reason. The only reason these GPs had female pradhans was because a constitutional amendment required it. This natural experiment was exploited by Raghabendra Chattopadhyay and Esther Duflo (2004) (cited in Chapter 1) to directly compare economic outcomes in these reserved GPs with those that obtained in GPs that were not reserved.

The GPs had political authority to make some public goods investments in their jurisdictions. Chattopadhyay and Duflo made detailed comparisons of these investments between reserved and unreserved GPs in two districts, one in the state of West Bengal and the other in the state of Rajasthan. One

[34] Pande, R. (2003), "Can Mandated Political Representation Increase Policy Influence for Disadvantaged Minorities?: Theory and Evidence from India," *American Economic Review* 93, pp. 1132–1151.

goal of the investigation was to see if women's preferences were more likely to be met in the reserved GPs. As a measure of women's preferences, the authors used the frequency with which complaints were lodged by women regarding various public goods. In the West Bengal district that was studied, women complained more frequently than men about drinking water and about roads. This was because collecting water for the family's daily use was considered women's work and women were employed in the building of roads. In the Rajasthan district that was studied, women complained more often than men regarding the water supply but not about roads. The difference from West Bengal was that although women in the Rajasthan district were also responsible for collecting water, they neither worked on the roads nor used them often. (One might reasonably conjecture that the culture in Rajasthan is more patriarchal than in West Bengal, so women's movements are more restricted in the former state. As a result, they would have less use for roads.)

What did Chattopadhyay and Duflo find in the comparisons of public investments in the reserved and unreserved GPs? They found that in West Bengal the GPs with female pradhans invested more in drinking water and roads. In Rajasthan these reserved GPs invested more in drinking water but less in roads. These findings are in conformity with women's preferences in the two districts. Thus the gender of the pradhan matters. To the extent that women's preferences are under-represented in India's democracy, the constitutional amendment requiring reservation of a third of the GPs for the election of women pradhans was undoubtedly a good move.

There are other benefits to implementing quotas for women in politics. Lori Beaman, Raghabendra Chattopadhyay, Esther Duflo, Rohini Pande, and Petia Topalova (2009) have offered a compelling argument based on statistical discrimination.[35] Suppose that initially mostly men are elected to public office (as has been true in all countries). As a result, voters have more information about men's ability to lead. About women's abilities they have only conjectures, probably unfavorably biased ones at that. If voters are averse to taking risks, given their prior biases, in the absence of new information they will statistically discriminate against women in the manner we discussed in Chapter 4. Implementing mandatory quotas will offer more direct evidence on women's ability to be political leaders. As a result, prejudiced and misinformed prior views can be updated. The authors tested this conjecture using the experiment in India on political reservations that we described above. They found that, in those village councils of West Bengal that had never been reserved for women pradhans, in the election of May 2008 11% of the pradhans chosen were women. By contrast, this figure was 18% in

[35] Beaman, L., R. Chattopadhyay, E. Duflo, R. Pande, and P. Topalova (2009), "Powerful Women: Does Exposure Reduce Bias?," *Quarterly Journal of Economics* 124, pp. 1497–1540.

villages that were continuously reserved for 10 years prior to the election (but were not reserved in 2008). Thus mandatory exposure to female political leaders increases the chances of subsequent female representation in politics. One of the avenues through which this occurs is the updating of voters' beliefs regarding the competence of female politicians.

However, not all the evidence from India on the effects of political quotas for women is so positive.[36] Radu Ban and Vijayendra Rao (2008) examined data for the four southern states (Andhra Pradesh, Karnataka, Kerala, and Tamil Nadu) on the effectiveness of women village chiefs compared to that of the (mostly male) chiefs in unreserved village councils.[37] Using data from 2002, the authors found that on a broad spectrum of performance measures pertaining to the delivery of public goods, women did no better (or worse) than men. They did not seem to especially represent the preferences of women (surprisingly), and when they were up against entrenched patriarchal interests, they did poorly. However, the study did find that women learned quickly through experience in politics. This bodes well for the future.

Pranab Bardhan, Dilip Mookherjee, and Monica Torrado (2010) studied the effectiveness of women pradhans using data drawn from the Indian state of West Bengal for the period 1998–2004.[38] The question they asked was how effectively women targeted local government programs to households that were poor—in particular, those that were landless, low caste, or female headed. The authors found that, when women were pradhans in reserved GPs, the targeting of female-headed households worsened relative to those in unreserved GPs (but the targeting to low castes improved). The authors point out that inexperience may have been the reason for the adverse effects on female-headed households—in which case, this outcome will be temporary.

One may conjecture that establishing quotas that allow women to enter politics might be a good move even in developed countries. Maria De Paola, Vincenzo Scoppa, and Rosetta Lombardo (2010) have recently provided persuasive evidence from Italy for this conjecture.[39] In Italy, as in most countries in the world, women likely face barriers because of negative stereotyping: voters may think that women are not suitable for political office. If this is so,

[36]This literature is well summarized in Mansuri, G., and V. Rao (2013), *Localizing Development: Does Participation Work?*, World Bank, Washington, DC.

[37]Ban, R., and V. Rao (2008), "Tokenism or Agency?: The Impact of Women's Reservations on Village Democracies in South India," *Economic Development and Cultural Change* 56, pp. 501–530.

[38]Bardhan, P. K., D. Mookherjee, and M. P. Torrado (2010), "Impact of Political Reservations in West Bengal Local Governments on Anti-Poverty Targeting," *Journal of Globalization and Development* 1 (1), article 5.

[39]De Paola, M., V. Scoppa, and R. Lombardo (2010), "Can Gender Quotas Break Down Negative Stereotypes?: Evidence from Changes in Electoral Rules," *Journal of Public Economics* 94, pp. 344–353.

political parties will not put up women candidates in elections. For a short period (April 1993–September 1995), there was a unique natural experiment in Italy with regard to gender: the law required that political parties in municipal elections field candidates of a given gender as no more than two-thirds of their candidates. This forced parties to field some female candidates. The new reform, which was implemented in April 1993, was repealed in September 1995. Because not all municipalities in the country held elections during this period, there was a sample of municipalities that never had gender constraints imposed on them.

In their study De Paola et al. compared the political representation by women in the municipalities that were constrained with that in municipalities that were not. They found, first, that there was an increase in female representation on municipal councils during the period 1993–95. This is perhaps not surprising given the implementation of the law, but it was by no means inevitable. (The law only required the political parties to field a certain proportion of female candidates; election of these candidates was not guaranteed.) What is more interesting and important is that even after the law was repealed, the political representation by women in the municipalities affected by the short-lived reform continued to increase relative to those in municipalities that were never constrained by the quotas. This suggests that, even in developed countries, affirmative action in the political arena may go a long way toward reducing negative stereotyping in this arena.

We have alluded to the fact that women legislators take greater interest in bills pertaining to women's and children's issues. In this they are very likely representing not merely their own preferences but also the preferences of other female voters. Compelling evidence that giving women a voice in politics has beneficial effects not only for them but for society at large is seen in the effect of women's suffrage on child mortality. This interesting analysis was done by Grant Miller (2008) for the United States.[40] Scientific knowledge about how bacteria spread and how simple hygienic practices like washing hands and boiling milk could reduce the transmission of diseases was originally communicated to the American public by women who campaigned door to door. As we saw in Chapter 10, by an amendment of the U.S. Constitution all women in the country were granted suffrage in 1920, though many individual states had started granting women suffrage several decades earlier. Once women received suffrage, politicians had to cater to their preferences. Because women worry about children's health more than men, states subsequently increased their expenditures on local health. This enabled women to intensify their door-to-door hygiene campaigns. Miller

---

[40] Miller, G. (2008), "Women's Suffrage, Political Responsiveness, and Child Survival in American History," *Quarterly Journal of Economics* 123, pp. 1287–1327.

found that, as a result, the child mortality rate fell in the United States by around 10% between 1900 and 1930.

The evidence cited in this section suggests that there are good reasons to believe that expediting the representation of women in politics empowers a country's women. Furthermore, the benefits of this empowerment extend to children also. However, more research is warranted on this issue.

VI. Increasing Family Planning and Healthcare Expenditures

As we saw in Chapter 9, contraception has many benefits for women and society. First, by preventing unwanted pregnancies it reduces the maternal mortality associated with childbirth, a serious problem in developing countries. Second, by averting the need for abortions it reduces the maternal mortality from unsafe abortions, which is also a serious cause of death for women. Third, by preventing unwanted pregnancies it reduces the wear and tear on women's bodies even when childbirth is not fatal to them. Fourth, by preventing unwanted pregnancies of the poor it increases the resources available to other children in the family and positively affects their health and educational opportunities. Fifth, some contraceptives (like condoms) can prevent the spread of serious diseases like HIV/AIDS that are transmitted through contact with bodily fluids. Sixth, by preventing pregnancies contraceptives reduce the risk that women in some cultures will be put to death at the hands of their own family members because these individuals perceive that their "family honor" has been besmirched by the women's out-of-wedlock pregnancies. Seventh, by potentially reducing fertility contraception reduces the rate of population growth. This enables overpopulated countries to develop faster. Eighth, in the developed world (where fertility rates are already low), contraception enables appropriate timing of children. This offers women the opportunity to invest in their own human capital and plan their careers accordingly. Ninth, having access to safe birth control improves women's bargaining power relative to their spouses; given mothers' stronger preferences for the welfare of children relative to those of fathers, women's negotiating power is undermined by children. Tenth, by preventing accidental pregnancies contraception reduces the chances that women will have to settle into unhappy marriages with ill-matched spouses. There are plenty of other benefits that can be listed here.

Given these enormous benefits to women and society, it is imperative that all countries offer family planning services to their populations irrespective of individuals' ability to pay. A role for government is essential, because nongovernmental organizations can do only so much. Developing countries have recognized this in the past three decades or so and have increased government provision of these services, although a few developed (European) countries have gone in the opposite direction in order to counter below-replacement fertility rates.[41] Inadequate supply of family planning services is captured by the notion of an "unmet demand" for contraception. The demand for contraception stems partly from the desire to increase birth spacing and partly from the desire to curtail fertility. In developing countries, this unmet demand can be quite high, reaching a maximum regional average of 57% in Sub-Saharan Africa.[42]

There is some skepticism that the provision of family planning services will actually result in fertility reduction. As we saw in Chapter 8, many economists believe that economic development, by raising the wages of women, will increase the opportunity cost of having children and thereby automatically reduce fertility. In this view, fertility is determined by the demand side; increasing the supply of family planning services will not do much. Grant Miller (2009) examined the role of family planning services in fertility reduction by analyzing data from Profamilia, which is the oldest such service in Colombia.[43] This country had undergone a demographic transition in the 30 years between the early 1960s and the early 1990s. Miller found that the availability of contraceptives explained only 6%–7% of the fertility reduction during Colombia's demographic transition. Although this percentage of fertility reduction was undoubtedly small, its importance comes from the fact that by postponing the birth of the first child, it facilitated greater acquisition of human capital by young women.

The manner in which contraceptives are made available to women also matters in terms of whether they will be used even when they are supplied free. An interesting field experiment was conducted by Nava Ashraf, Erica Fields, and Jean Lee (2012) in Lusaka, Zambia.[44] Two groups of women were offered vouchers for free access to a desirable form of contraceptive (the injectable kind); to one group of women the offer was made in private, and to the other it was made in the presence of their husbands. In the latter group, the authors found, women were less likely to take up the offer and the reduction in fertility was significantly less. This suggests that the preferences of women and men as to the number of children are likely to be different (at least in the short run) and that women might have a greater unmet need for contraceptives than men. Here again, the evidence is suggestive of the possibility that bargaining power within households is an important determinant of contraceptive use.

Contraception is of tremendous value in containing the spread of HIV/AIDS. Consistent use of condoms by heterosexual couples reduces the risk of

[41] In 2001, only a third of the world's countries remained noninterventionist in this regard. See United Nations Secretariat (2003), *Fertility, Contraception, and Population Policies*, Population Division, New York.

[42] Westoff, C. F. (2006), *New Estimates of Unmet Demand Need and the Demand for Family Planning*, DHS Comparative Report 14, Macro International, Calverton, MD.

[43] Miller, G. (2009), "Contraception as Development?: New Evidence from Family Planning in Colombia," *Economic Journal* 120, pp. 709–736.

[44] Ashraf, N., E. Fields, and J. Lee (2012), "Household Bargaining and Excess Fertility: An Experimental Study in Zambia," BREAD Working Paper 282, Bureau for Research and Economic Analysis of Development, Duke University, Durham, NC.

HIV transmission by about 80% relative to the scenario in which no condoms are used.[45] Furthermore, the use of condoms prevents the transmission of a host of other sexually transmitted diseases like gonorrhea, syphilis, genital herpes, and genital HPV. Because prevention of these diseases is far less expensive than curing them, making condoms readily available is a strategy that makes a great deal of sense. The gender aspect of the transmission of infections comes from the fact that patriarchal values in many societies find it acceptable for men to have many sexual partners. So infected males can pass on sexually transmitted diseases to many females. Furthermore, because men tend to have sex with younger women, the need to promote condom use is even greater.

It must be emphasized that, although useful, increasing the supply of condoms to prevent the spread of such diseases does not guarantee their use. Men may refuse to use condoms, partly because they reduce the pleasure from sexual activity and also partly because of machismo. As mentioned above, if women's bargaining power is weak, they may not be able to prevail on their male partners to use condoms. Thus the effectiveness of condoms in preventing the spread of sexually transmitted diseases depends nontrivially on other policies (discussed in the other sections of this chapter) that increase the bargaining power of women.[46]

In Chapter 9 we discussed the serious problem of maternal mortality in developing countries. Around the globe, the maternal mortality rate varies drastically by region. Recall that this mortality rate is highest in Sub-Saharan Africa and Asia and lowest in the rich countries. Most of this mortality is due to hemorrhage during childbirth, and greater access to timely surgical interventions, control of infectious diseases, and better training of midwives, among other things, are crucial to reducing the deaths of mothers. Making abortion legal, as we saw earlier, is also important for this purpose. The best scientific studies available on the subject show that the proportion of maternal deaths due to unsafe abortions (which occur mostly in developing countries) has a median value of 16%.[47] If abortions were made legal in such countries, they would become available under much more hygienic conditions and would be performed by qualified professionals, and these deaths could be avoided.

It must be noted, however, that even in the developed world there is still some opposition to contraception and abortion. Much of this is based on

[45] Holmes, K. K., R. Levine, and M. Weaver (2004), "Effectiveness of Condoms in Preventing Sexually Transmitted Infections," *Bulletin of the World Health Organization* 82, pp. 453–464.

[46] In the case of sex workers, who tend to have unusually high incidences of HIV, the practice of unprotected sex is partly compensated for by the higher prices that they are paid. See Gertler, P., M. Shah, and S. M. Bertozzi (2005), "Risky Business: The Market for Unprotected Sex," *Journal of Political Economy* 113, pp. 518–550.

[47] Gerdts, C., D. Vohra, and J. Ahern (2013), "Measuring Unsafe Abortion–Related Mortality: A Systematic Review of the Existing Methods," *PLOS ONE* 8 (1), e53346, doi: 10.1371/journal.pone.0053346.

religious or ideological grounds. Because women's views on birth control tend to be more liberal than men's, the brunt of the fight for safe contraception (and, of course, the cost of its unavailability) is being largely borne by women. In the United States, for example, even four decades after *Roe v. Wade*, this landmark ruling of the Supreme Court is still in danger of being overturned.[48] If this were to actually occur, what happens to women with unwanted pregnancies in developing countries will also happen in the United States: many women will die because dire economic circumstances will force them to opt for abortions that are unsafe.

More generally, devoting resources to enabling greater and subsidized access to healthcare can have huge payoffs for women and children. Where healthcare is either unavailable or too expensive, child mortality rates are high. We saw in Chapter 8 that when child mortality rates are high, risk-averse parents overcompensate by having too many additional children, and this contributes to high rates of population growth. Apart from the adverse effects on economic development, having too many children also has deleterious effects on the health of women. We have seen that a reduction in child mortality is one of the observed triggers of the demographic transition to low levels of population growth.

When nutrition for young children is heavily subsidized in poor countries (for instance, by providing midday meals in schools), all school-going children will benefit, but female children will benefit disproportionately. This is because, first, it is more likely that girls will be sent to school for the free meal, so they will receive an education as an additional benefit. (More boys than girls are sent to school in the absence of such inducements.) Second, when resources are scarce, parents economize on the nutrition given to girls and spend what they can afford on boys. Elaina Rose (1999) has shown, using data from 16 states of India during the period 1967–71, that, particularly during droughts, the nutrition received by girls suffers relative to that received by boys.[49] Lack of nutrition makes children more vulnerable to diseases and therefore to premature death. Parental discrimination against girls also manifests when they are sick: it is less likely that parents will incur the expense of a doctor for girls than for boys.[50] For this reason, Duflo (2012) suggests that providing healthcare insurance would disproportionately benefit girls.

By reducing maternal mortality and the mortality of female children relative to male children, policies that increase expenditures for family planning

[48] For example, Mitt Romney, the Republican candidate in the 2012 presidential election, called for overturning *Roe v. Wade*.

[49] Rose, E. (1999), "Consumption Smoothing and Excess Female Mortality in Rural India," *Review of Economics and Statistics* 81, pp. 41–49.

[50] Female infant mortality in India, for example, is 30% higher than male infant mortality, and for easily preventable diseases like diarrhea, it is 100% higher. See Khanna, R., et al. (2003), "Community Based Retrospective Study of Sex in Infant Mortality in India," *British Medical Journal* 327, pp. 126–128.

and healthcare in developing countries will also contribute to reducing the number of "missing women."

VII. Reforming Inheritance and Property Laws

Inheritance has been a source of inequality across individuals in all societies and of gender inequality in particular. Historically, even today's developed countries had inheritance laws that favored sons, but these have now largely been changed to promote greater equity. In the developing world, as we saw in our discussion of Bina Agarwal's (1994) work in Chapter 5, bequests are still not egalitarian across all children. The ownership of assets, we have seen, confers many advantages on the wealthy: it facilitates better education, better earnings, entrepreneurship, greater exercise of autonomy, and other benefits. Traditional inheritance norms in developing countries, therefore, greatly militate against gender equality and are in need of reform. We discuss below a recent experience with changing inheritance laws that is very informative about how such changes play out in practice.

The recent experience in India provides a useful window on the consequences of reforms in property laws. The particular reform we shall discuss is that to the Hindu Succession Act (HSA). This act was the law passed in 1956 that governed the inheritance of property that is acquired by a father, as opposed to what is called "ancestral property."[51] The latter is property that is jointly owned, and sons had a right to a share of it but not daughters. The HSA required that acquired property be allocated to sons and daughters in an egalitarian manner. Because ancestral property is often a huge share of the property in India, the fact that daughters were excluded from consideration made inheritance laws very unfavorable for women.

Between 1976 and 1994, several Indian states amended the HSA at different times in order to remedy the gender imbalance.[52] The amended law required that daughters, too, be a given a share of the ancestral property. The consequences of this change have been investigated independently by Sanchari Roy (2013) and by Klaus Deininger, Aparajita Goyal, and Hari Nagarajan (2013).[53] The basic issue is whether and how the change in the inheritance law has improved the well-being of Indian women.

---

[51] Despite the term "Hindu" in the title, the act also applies to Buddhists, Jains, and Sikhs.

[52] These states, from the earliest to the latest in enacting the amendment, are Kerala, Andhra Pradesh, Tamil Nadu, Karnataka, and Maharashtra. In 2005 the entire country amended the law in a similar fashion.

[53] Roy, S. (2013), "Empowering Women, Inheritance Rights, Female Education, and Dowry Payments in India," Centre for Competitive Advantage in the Global Economy (CAGE) and Department of Economics, University of Warwick, Coventry, UK, and Deininger, K., A. Goyal, and H. Nagarajan (2013), "Women's Inheritance Rights and Intergenerational Transmission of Resources in India," *Journal of Human Resources* 48, pp. 114–141.

The findings of these two studies are similar in some respects. Both find that investment in the education of young girls in landowning households increased by about half a year, and this effect is expected to increase over time. In contrast to Deininger et al., however, Roy finds that there has been very little transfer of land to daughters since the amendment to the HSA.[54] Households find various ways of "gifting" the ancestral property to their sons so as to circumvent bequeathing it to their daughters. Roy's argument is that parents opted to increase the human capital investment in their daughters but continued to deny them a share of their land. So the amendment to the inheritance law did improve the well-being of women but not in the manner one would have expected.

Furthermore, Roy finds that, compared to girls in nonlandowning households, those in landowning households received greater dowries if they were in the 11–15 age group and smaller dowries if they were in the under-10 age group. The latter group of girls received more education (and probably had smaller dowries as a result). Roy explains this finding with an argument analogous to that made about dowries by Maristella Botticini and Aloysius Siow (2003) that we first encountered in Chapter 7. Recall that their interpretation of a dowry is that it is a "premortem" (before-death) bequest that parents give to their daughters. In the same manner, the increase in human capital of younger daughters following the amendment to the HSA can possibly be construed as at least partial compensation in lieu of receiving their share of the land. Older daughters received no education, probably because it was too late for them to acquire education before marriage.

There is an important point about the unintended consequences of changes in inheritance law that we should note here. Siwan Anderson and Garance Genicot (2012) studied the effect of the amendment to the HSA on male and female suicide rates in India during the period 1967–2004.[55] This duration brackets the period 1976–2004, during which some but not all the states of India had an amended law. (In 2005, the entire country passed the amended law.) Thus the authors could compare suicide rates in states that had amended the law and those that had not. After controlling for other possible factors that could have impinged on suicide rates, the authors found that the amendment to the HSA increased suicide rates for both males and females but more for males. They also found a correlation between increased domestic violence and the amended law. Anderson and Genicot make the reasonable conjecture that the amendment to the law may have increased conflict within landowning households and led to a greater incidence of suicide and domestic violence.

[54] This is also found in Brule, R. (2012), "Gender Equity and Inheritance Reform: Evidence from Rural India," Department of Political Science, Stanford University, Stanford, CA.

[55] Anderson, S., and G. Genicot (2012), "Suicide and Property Rights in India," BREAD Working Paper 353, Bureau for Research and Economic Analysis of Development, Duke University, Durham, NC.

A study undertaken by Daniel Rosenblum (2013) on female child mortality rates in India has also unearthed an unexpected adverse effect of the amendment to the HSA.[56] Rosenblum argues that, in a culture with a strong preference for sons, the amendment has made daughters more costly. This could have led to an increase in female mortality through subtle means such as reduced nutrition so that the ancestral land could accrue with greater probability to children of the favored sex. By examining data for the four states of India other than Kerala that had amended the HSA before 2005, Rosenblum found that the law did indeed increase female mortality rates.

The implication of the findings of Anderson and Genicot (2012) and of Rosenblum (2013) is *not* that equalizing rights to ancestral land by gender is a bad thing. Rather, the point is that when laws that tilt against ingrained social norms are implemented there may be an unexpected backlash. Policy makers need to anticipate such adverse effects and have in place additional policies that will prevent or reduce these effects.

Persuasive evidence of a very different sort on the importance of property law comes from the recent work of Siwan Anderson (2013) on the prevalence of HIV in Sub-Saharan Africa.[57] The colonies in Africa, depending on which nation usurped their land, inherited either common law (which is English in origin) or civil law (which is continental European in origin). These laws gave different degrees of security in property ownership, with common law offering greater security. However, married women had very few rights to property under common law in the event of divorce if their main contribution to their households was nonmonetary in nature. Civil law, on the other hand, recognized property in marriage as more or less communal, so women had equal rights to property in the event of divorce. Although these laws had been drastically amended in England and in Europe since they had colonized countries in Sub-Saharan Africa, the laws in the colonies still suffer from the hangover of the previous versions of the law that were imposed on them. This means that the bargaining power of women is greater in the former colonies that had civil law than in those that had common law. Anderson reasons that, as a result, they should have more autonomy in insisting on practices of safe sex with their husbands and in curtailing male behavior that is conducive to spreading HIV (like having multiple partners). This should result in a lower prevalence of HIV among women relative to men in the colonies that inherited civil law as opposed to common law. This is exactly what she finds. Discoveries such as these bring home, in the starkest possible manner, how important it is for property law to be egalitarian in its treatment across genders.

[56] Rosenblum, D. (2013), "Unintended Consequences of Women's Inheritance Rights on Female Mortality in India," forthcoming in *Economic Development and Cultural Change*.
[57] Anderson, S. (2013), "Legal Origins and HIV," unpublished manuscript, University of British Columbia, Vancouver.

In the developed world, gross gender inequities in property laws are more or less things of the past. (Recall, from our discussion in Chapter 5, that English and North American laws regarding property underwent a transformation in the nineteenth century.) Nevertheless, changes in property laws still impinge on the well-being of women. This is particularly the case in the realm of divorce. In the past it was typically the case that upon divorce property went to the person who had the title to it. Recently there has been a trend toward equal division of property regardless of who has the title when a married couple files for divorce. As we might expect, how property is going to be divided upon divorce affects the behavior and choices of a couple even while they are married. This is because property determines outside options in the event of divorce, and these, in turn, determine bargaining power within marriage.

Alessandra Voena (2012) examined married couples' behavioral response to the equal division of property that, in some states, accompanied the switch to unilateral divorce laws in the United States in the 1970s and 1980s.[58] These laws permitted divorces even if only one member of a couple unilaterally wished to dissolve the marriage. To isolate the effect of the equal division of property, Voena used data spanning the period from the late 1960s through the 1990s to compare behavior before reform to that after. She found that, compared to married couples in states in which the division of property was by title and not equal, couples in those states with equal division of property accumulated more assets. This was because, in the former states, spouses without title had little incentive to accumulate assets that would accrue to someone else in the event of divorce. Furthermore, in states with equal division of property, married women worked less after the reform in the divorce law. This was presumably because married women's bargaining power increased within marriage as a result of their more secure outcomes in the event of divorce.

So we see that, whether in poor countries or in rich ones, the distribution of property has an important effect on the well-being of women. Ownership of property opens doors that would have remained closed in the absence of wealth; it also enhances women's autonomy. Therefore, it is important to ensure that property laws are equitable.

VIII. Does Empowerment Make Women Happier?

We finally come to a discussion of the effect of empowerment on what is arguably the goal of all human endeavors, namely, achieving happiness. In recent decades economists have started addressing this issue through various

---

[58] Voena, A. (2012), "Yours, Mine, and Ours: Do Divorce Laws Affect the Intertemporal Behavior of Married Couples?," Kennedy School, Harvard University, Cambridge, MA.

measures intended to capture what is called *subjective well-being*. This refers to the well-being of a person as measured not by objective measures such as employment, income, wealth, and so on, but rather by a subjective feeling of happiness as reported by the person herself or by her evaluation of how she believes her life is going. Various surveys are now routinely conducted, such as the General Social Survey in the United States, the Eurobarometer in Europe, and the World Value Survey across the globe, which inquire into the subjective well-being of a random sample of people at different points in time. (Recall that I briefly alluded to such surveys in Section II of Chapter 7.)

The surveys vary somewhat in the exact framing of the inquiry, but a typical question is "Taken together, how would you say things are these days—would you say that you are very happy, pretty happy, or not too happy?"[59] The response is then put on a quantitative scale, with higher numbers reflecting greater subjective happiness. The numbers for the sample can then be averaged by country, by gender, and so on to yield an overall measure of subjective well-being for the entire country or a subgroup of interest. One may wonder whether subjective measures of well-being are accurate representations of actual well-being. There is ample evidence to suggest that they correlate with body language and also that the emotions determining well-being correlate with brain activity.[60] Further, to take an extreme example, the same factors that are seen to promote subjective well-being are the very factors that are seen to reduce suicide rates in a country.[61] So measures of subjective well-being should be taken seriously.

Women all over the world report subjective happiness levels that exceed men's. But what would we expect regarding trends in happiness levels in the past few decades? Throughout this book we have seen that, although a gender gap remains along many dimensions in developed countries, women have made remarkable progress in the past several decades. In the OECD countries, women's labor market participation has increased, the gender wage gap has narrowed, fertility has declined, the consumption of leisure has increased, and women's educational levels have risen to the point that more women than men now attend college. In view of all this, we would certainly expect women's subjective well-being in rich countries to have increased substantially in the past few decades. We would also expect that, at least in the important domain of happiness, the gender gap would have further increased in favor of women. The data, however, show that these expectations are wrong.

---

[59] This is the question posed in the General Social Survey of the United States.

[60] See, for example, Davidson, R. J. (2004), "Well-being and Affective Style: Neural Substrates and Biobehavioural Correlates," *Philosophical Transactions of the Royal Society of London B* 359, pp. 1395–1411. See also Layard, R. (2006), *Happiness: Lessons from a New Science,* 2nd ed., Penguin, New York, Chap. 2.

[61] See Helliwell, J. F. (2007), "Well-being and Social Capital: Does Suicide Pose a Puzzle?," *Social Indicators Research* 81, pp. 455–496.

A study by Blanchflower and Oswald (2004) that we alluded to in Chapter 7 examined the trend in subjective happiness in the United States (1972–98) and in Britain (1975–98). After accounting for a whole host of factors that could impinge on happiness, the authors found that American women's well-being declined over the period, whereas that of American men held steady. So both in terms of their absolute level of well-being and in terms of their well-being relative to men's, women's happiness declined over the period 1972–98. In Britain the average levels of life satisfaction of men and women were more or less flat; they showed no significant trend.[62]

Betsy Stevenson and Justin Wolfers (2009) have examined the trend in subjective well-being in the United States over a 35-year period and in a dozen or so OECD countries over various periods starting from the early 1970s.[63] The authors find that in the United States women's self-reported well-being not only has declined relative to men's but has declined absolutely. Because women have typically reported that they are happier than men, over the past three and a half decades this gap has been narrowing. The authors find that this narrowing has occurred across all demographic groups—by marital status, by fertility, by employment status, by age, and so on. In European countries, Stevenson and Wolfers find that the subjective well-being of both men and women has been increasing over time, but the rise has been slower for women. So in Europe, too, women's well-being has been declining relative to men's.

These are very surprising findings. Why is women's self-reported well-being declining (absolutely or relative to that of men) in the face of so many objective improvements in their lives (absolutely and relative to men)? There are some possible explanations, a few of which the studies referred to above allude to. But none have been nailed down yet by research as being definitive. Let us discuss a couple of possibilities.

One potential explanation has to do with the tendency to make comparisons. Humans seem to invariably measure their well-being by comparing themselves with others in a reference or comparison group. Employees in an organization compare their salaries with those of others in the same organization and feel dissatisfied if they think they are being underpaid. People belonging to the same club compare themselves with other club members and wonder if their own homes are as expensive as those of others, and so on. The tendency to make such comparisons with a reference group was first highlighted more than a century ago by Thorstein Veblen in his clas-

[62] Life satisfaction is captured in the Eurobarometer survey by the following question: "On the whole, are you very satisfied, fairly satisfied, not very satisfied, or not at all satisfied with the life you lead?"

[63] Stevenson, B., and J. Wolfers (2009), "The Paradox of Declining Female Happiness," *American Economic Journal: Economic Policy* 1, pp. 190–225.

sic *Theory of the Leisure Class*.[64] In this view, it is not a person's absolute income that determines her happiness, for example, but her income relative to that of a reference group.[65] Sixty years ago, when women traditionally stayed home, their comparison group would have been other housewives. Now that women have entered the labor force in a big way and are opting for careers, their comparison group has broadened. In particular, it is possible that this group includes men (who have fewer constraints on pursuing their goals). This change in the reference group may be leading women to feel less satisfied now—even though by objective measures they are much better off today.

Another reason may have to do with the decline in meaningful social interactions. Such interactions have an important effect on well-being. The community's collective social networks, comprising friends, relatives, co-workers, members of the same church congregation, and so on—which promote interactions that build trust and empathy—constitute what has been referred to as *social capital*. In an influential book, Robert Putnam (2000) has made the argument that the declining sense of community in America has reduced the social capital of people in this country and has led to many adverse consequences.[66] Social capital has been shown to be an important determinant of subjective well-being.[67] Participation in voluntary organizations such as parent and teacher associations and church congregations has been on the decline. To the extent that women participated more in such voluntary organizations, the loss of the attendant social interactions would conceivably have had a more adverse effect on their well-being than on men's.

Do the disconcerting empirical findings on the declining self-reported happiness of women suggest that the enormous strides they have made in the developed world are futile? Hardly. It is one thing to live in a world oppressed by patriarchy; hemmed in by family, social, and religious norms; and deprived of the means to allow one's abilities and capabilities to find expression. It is quite another to live more freely, to pursue what one thinks is worthwhile, to develop one's innate abilities, and to embrace a career that one finds meaningful. If one's subjective well-being declines as a consequence, it is more likely because of *self-imposed* standards instead of externally imposed patriarchal barriers. Frustration has invariably been an accompaniment of any worldly

[64] Veblen, T. (1899), *The Theory of the Leisure Class: An Economic Study of Institutions*, Macmillan, New York.

[65] Blanchflower and Oswald (2004) (cited in Chapter 7) provide evidence for this in their paper. There is well-established literature on this human proclivity to make comparisons.

[66] Putnam, R. D. (2000), *Bowling Alone: The Collapse and Revival of American Community*, Simon and Schuster, New York.

[67] Helliwell, J. F., and R. D. Putnam (2004), "The Social Context of Well-being," *Philosophical Transactions of the Royal Society of London B* 359, pp. 1435–1446.

achievement. Nevertheless, it is important to inquire what exactly is responsible for the declining absolute or relative subjective well-being of women in the developed world. Ironically, now that women have broken into domains that were once mostly men's preserves, the gender gap in happiness is also disappearing.

Perhaps it is not appropriate to use subjective well-being as a summary index of the progress women are making in the quality of their lives. Another influential approach is that pioneered by Nobel laureate Amartya Sen (1999), who espoused what he dubbed the "capabilities approach."[68] The basic idea is that we should be focusing on the capabilities that people have to be what they value and to perform certain functions that they value. Capabilities are important because they facilitate being and functioning. One may value being in good health and functioning as a researcher but may lack the capabilities to achieve these states of being and functioning. A Brahmin woman in India, for example, may belong to the elite, may be educated, and may even be wealthy. But she may not be able to function in her society as an advocate for the downtrodden because family and societal norms constrain her mobility and cause her actions to be scrutinized. So focusing on material things (like income and automobiles) is not entirely appropriate. Nor is a focus on subjective well-being adequate. Sen's reason for the latter is that people who live under appalling conditions may adapt to them and say that they are happy. From the point of view of society, however, their conditions are nevertheless very deprived. Likewise, someone else may live in opulence and yet feel miserable. Such scenarios of subjective well-being are not overemphasized if we focus on capabilities; subjective well-being could itself be included as one of the capabilities. Martha Nussbaum (2000), whose work we referred to in the previous chapter, has been very influential in applying the capabilities approach in general and especially to gender issues. She has suggested a list of 10 core or central capabilities that she argues are universal and should be incorporated into any application.[69] An index based on such a methodology (instead of the one based exclusively on subjective well-being) would very likely show that women in the developed countries are much better off today than they were four decades ago.[70]

[68] Sen, A. (1999), *Development as Freedom,* Oxford University Press, Oxford, UK.

[69] See also Nussbaum, M. C. (2003), "Capabilities as Fundamental Entitlements: Sen and Social Justice," *Feminist Economics* 9 (2–3), pp. 33–59.

[70] The Human Development Index attempts to capture attainments in a few basic capabilities of a population: life expectancy, education, and standard of living. The index is put on a numerical scale from 0 (worst) to 1 (best). The Gender-related Development Index (GDI) corrects this index for gender inequities and offers a more gender-sensitive measure. The GDI for the United States, for example, was 0.901 in 1995 (the earliest year for which GDI is available) and 0.937 in 2007/2008. Over the same period, China's GDI went from 0.578 to 0.776 and India's from 0.401 to 0.600. See United Nations Development Programme, *Human Development Report,* New York, for the respective years.

IX. Summary

We began this chapter with the recognition that gender disparities are fewer in the developed countries than in developing ones, but we noted that we cannot rely on economic development to eliminate the gender gap. We brought together the policy lessons that follow from the various aspects of women's issues we discussed in earlier chapters. We began with education, a source of considerable gender disparity in developing countries. We saw that there are both efficiency and equity grounds for government involvement in the education of girls and women. Furthermore, the education of women has external benefits for children.

Because women in poor countries have title to few assets, they are typically constrained in their ability to borrow and to become entrepreneurs. This restricts their ability to earn independent incomes and thereby undermines their bargaining power within their households. We examined the innovation of the Grameen Bank in circumventing the need for collateral and its consequences for women.

Because women have been disadvantaged relative to men for long periods of time, not only in the poor countries but also in the rich, we discussed the case for affirmative action. Drawing on the experiences of one rich country (the United States) and one poor country (India), we studied the pros and cons of such a policy, especially with regard to quotas for women. We saw that, although affirmative action can be useful for empowering women in the labor market, this outcome is more assured when certain conditions are met.

There are many barriers confronting women's entry into politics. Affirmative action policies with quotas for women in the political arena have been implemented in many countries. We studied the outcomes of these policies and saw why they are needed. The qualified verdict on this subject is that a quota for women in politics is potentially a useful instrument for women's empowerment.

Excess deaths of female children and adults relative to males and maternal mortality are two of the immediate reasons that sex ratios are biased in favor of males in developing countries. Furthermore, part of the reason for excessive fertility and the poor timing of children is the poor bargaining power of women compared to their husbands. We examined how government expenditures in developing countries on family planning services to reduce the unmet need for contraceptives and abortions, and for healthcare in general, can reduce the female disadvantage.

Next we addressed the fact that inheritance and property laws are highly inequitable in developing countries. By examining the effect of a recent reform of inheritance law in India, we saw how this change impinges on the well-being of women. The importance of property laws is brought out quite dramatically in a study we discussed on the prevalence of HIV in

Sub-Saharan Africa. We also examined how changes in property laws accompanying divorce in the developed countries impinge on the well-being of women.

Finally, we examined the evidence on the subjective well-being of women in affluent countries. It revealed that, despite the strides women have made toward achieving equality with men, their subjective well-being does not seem to be improving over time—an issue that warrants future research.

Exercises and Questions for Discussion

1. Explain why in developing countries transferring a dollar from postsecondary education to primary education would increase these countries' GDP. How does gender equality enter into this argument?

2. What are some of the reasons that the educational attainments of women are far lower than those of men in developing countries? What policies would you recommend to eliminate the gender imbalance in education?

3. What are some of the social benefits that the education of women can confer? Can you suggest reasons that it may be beneficial to society to educate women in developing countries even if the private returns are negative (which they are not)?

4. Explain the manner in which microfinance organizations such as the Grameen Bank do away with the need for collateral in order to extend credit. Why are women deemed to especially benefit from such banks?

5. Why might you expect the bargaining power of women within their households to increase with access to microcredit? Will this necessarily obtain? Under what conditions will the autonomy of women not improve when they receive microcredit?

6. In what respect do affirmative action policies for women differ from policies designed to prevent discrimination against them? When do you think affirmative action policies are morally justified?

7. Do affirmative action policies for women necessarily result in reverse discrimination against men? Identify conditions under which this need not be the case. What is the empirical evidence on this issue?

8. It is often believed that implementing an affirmative action policy for women will lower the output of firms. Why? In the light of experimental evidence provided by Niederle, Segal, and Vesterlund (2013), why is this belief not necessarily correct?

9. What are the reasons for using affirmative action in politics for women in the form of quotas?

10. Discuss the empirical evidence on the efficacy of assigning quotas for women in elected office in developing countries that are democracies. Explain why such quotas may be relevant for developed countries, too.

11. What are the various reasons that increasing the government expenditures devoted to family planning services and healthcare would disproportionately benefit girls and women?

12. In the developing world, inheritance laws are biased in favor of sons. Why? What are the consequences of this bias for married and unmarried women?

13. Discuss the empirical evidence on the benefits (or lack thereof) of the amendment to the Hindu Succession Act of India that granted even daughters equal access to their families' ancestral property.

14. Based on empirical evidence, what can we learn about unintended consequences from the above experiment on changes in inheritance laws in India?

15. Interpret the findings of Siwan Anderson (2013) on the incidence of HIV in Sub-Saharan Africa in terms of the bargaining power conferred on women by common law and civil law. What is the mechanism through which this bargaining power operates?

16. Outline some reasons that, though economic development may benefit women, by itself it is unlikely to eliminate all gender gaps completely.

INDEX

Page numbers for entries occurring in figures are followed by an *f;* those for entries in notes, by an *n;* and those for entries in tables, by a *t.*

abortion laws: in developed countries, 12, 276–77; effects of, 293–300; in United States, 12, 276–77, 291–92, 293, 298–300, 364; unsafe abortions and, 277, 280, 282, 363

abortions: access to, 12, 280–83, 287; crime rates and, 299–300; in developed countries, 280–81, 281t; in developing countries, 280, 281–83, 281t; history of, 276; of low-income women, 298–99; maternal mortality in, 280–81, 281t, 363; motives for, 281–82; number of, 280; opposition to, 276, 291, 293, 363–64; safety of, 277, 280, 281–82; sex-selective, 11, 266, 267–68, 270, 271, 272

abuse, domestic. *See* spousal violence

Adams, Renee, 35

adverse selection, in credit markets, 148, 149–50, 343, 345–46

affirmative action: debates on, 348, 349, 350–51; in education, 351, 352, 353n27; effects of, 348–54; in

employment, 16, 348–51, 352–54; empowerment through, 337; goals of, 337, 348; in India, 16, 352–53, 353n27, 357–59; in politics, 16, 337, 352, 357–60; quotas, 349, 350, 351–53, 357–60; for racial minorities, 351; reverse discrimination and, 16, 348, 350; in United States, 348–51, 354

Africa: abortions in, 281, 281t; bride prices in, 204, 221–22; fertility rates in, 11t, 260; globalization effects in, 173–74; maternal mortality in, 279, 279t, 281, 281t, 282; parliamentary seats held by women in, 17t; sex ratios in, 12t, 272. *See also* developing countries; *individual countries*

Agarwal, Bina, 137–38, 159, 365

agriculture: autonomy of women and, 92–93; development of, 92; gender roles in, 65–66, 93–94, 95, 213; inputs in, 173–74; labor productivity of women in, 216–18; plow technology in, 93, 94; productivity of, 92;

shifting and settled, 92–93; surplus of, 92–93

Ahern, J., 363n47

AIDS. *See* HIV/AIDS

Aidt, T. S., 323

Akerlof, George A., 55n51, 148, 231n51, 287–90

alcohol: consumption of, 208–9; prohibition in United States, 191, 316

Alesina, Alberto F., 94, 325

Allen, D. W., 240n67

Almond, Douglas, 267

altruism: explanations of, 36–37; gender differences in, 22, 24–26, 28–30, 35, 36; in prisoners' dilemma game, 31–33

Ananat, Elizabeth, 242–43, 294–95

Anderson, Siwan, 79, 84, 224, 272, 347, 366, 367

Angrist, Joshua, 86, 294

Anthony, Susan B., 2, 306

Arcidiacono, P., 351n21

Armendariz, B., 343n9

Aronson, J., 44n37

Arrow, Kenneth, 7–8, 105, 108n6, 113, 114

Ashenfelter, Orley, 110

Ashraf, Nava, 362

Ashton, John R., 215

cooperation: benefits of, 62; evolution of, 36–37; gender differences in, 28–29, 33–34; in households, 62; in prisoners' dilemma game, 33–34

cooperative bargaining models, 79. *See also* Nash bargaining model

Cornwall, Marie, 321

Cornwell, C. M., 234n56

Côte d'Ivoire: household spending preferences by gender in, 83, 263; polygyny in, 219

coverture, 309–12, 310f

credit access: benefits of, 134, 346–47; in developing countries, 159–60; discrimination and, 156–60; empowerment through, 342; by entrepreneurs, 8, 144–50, 156–60; firm sizes and, 156, 157; by gender, 8–9, 146, 149, 152, 156–60; increasing, 16, 343–46; labor market effects of, 152; microcredit, 160, 343–47; wealth as factor in, 133, 135, 143–46, 148–49, 342–43. *See also* collateral; financial institutions; interest rates

credit markets: adverse selection in, 148, 149–50, 343, 345–46; asymmetric information in, 144, 146–48, 343; default risk in, 134–35, 143, 145, 156–57, 158, 344; disadvantages of women in, 160; exploitation of women by, 133; gender discrimination in, 9, 156–60; incentive problem in, 144–46, 150; limited liability of borrowers, 143–44, 146, 147, 342–43, 344

Cremer, David, 34

criminal activity: abortion legalization and, 299–300; age differences in, 207; evolutionary view of, 207–8; homicides, 208; marriage effects on, 206–8; of poor, 208; sex ratios and, 269. *See also* trafficking

Croson, Rachel, 23, 43

cultural norms: changes in, 270; on divorce, 241–42; education investments and,

340; gender discrimination, 318; legal change and, 367; on political leadership, 354; preferences for sons, 11, 85, 264–68, 270, 271, 340, 342, 367; seclusion of women, 84, 93–94, 172, 219, 347. *See also* patriarchy

Dahlin, Eric C., 321

Daly, Martin, 207, 214, 215

Darwin, Charles, 43, 50

Das Gupta, Monica, 266, 268, 270

daughters: education of, 340; health status of, 181, 266, 272, 341, 364; influences on fathers' political views, 14, 321–22, 327–31. *See also* children; sex ratios at birth

Davidson, R. J., 369n59

Davies, M., 297n29

death rates. *See* mortality rates

debt. *See* credit access

Deere, Carmen D., 136

default risk, 134–35, 143, 145, 156–57, 158, 344

Deininger, Klaus, 365–66

DeMartino, R.,155n28

democracy. *See* legislatures; voting

demographics. *See* fertility rates; missing women phenomenon; mortality rates; population growth

demographic transition: autonomy of women and, 264; birth control access and, 277, 362; economic benefits of, 10, 249; fertility reductions in, 258, 259f, 262, 362; mortality rate reduction and, 258–60, 259f; in United Kingdom, 253, 254

Denmark, prostitution legalization in, 192

De Paola, Maria, 359–60

Deschenes, Olivier, 242

Deshpande, Ashwini, 352

developed countries: abortion laws in, 12, 276–77; abortions in, 280–81, 281t; birth control access in, 275–77, 283–87, 291–92; corporate boards in, 3, 4f, 35, 352; earnings by gender in, 6–7, 7f; education in, 336; entre-

preneurs in, 8, 9t, 134; fertility choice in, 250–54; fertility rates in, 10, 249, 260, 285–86, 298; gender wage gaps in, 178–79; labor market participation by gender in, 5–6, 6f, 229, 230–31; maternal mortality rates in, 279t, 283; sex ratios in, 265, 267–68; well-being in, 369–72; women's suffrage in, 306–7, 317, 319, 321–22. *See also* demographic transition; Europe; *individual countries*

developing countries: abortions in, 280, 281–83, 281t; birth control access in, 275, 276, 277–83; contraceptives in, 276, 361–63; credit access in, 159–60; education in, 338, 339–42; entrepreneurs in, 9t, 159–60, 172; fertility choice in, 254–56; fertility rates in, 10, 11t, 249, 254–56, 260–61, 268; foreign direct investment in, 171–72; gender wage gaps in, 178–79; healthcare spending in, 16, 364–65; labor market participation by gender in, 6, 61, 62; marriage practices in, 204; maternal mortality rates in, 12–13, 272, 279t, 282–83, 363; population growth in, 249, 257–58; sex ratios in, 249, 265–66, 268, 272; wealth distribution in, 137–38. *See also* Africa; Asia; Latin America and Caribbean; *individual countries*

dictator game, 29–30

discrimination, gender-based: in credit markets, 156–60; cultural norms on, 318; evidence of, 46, 47; by fellow employees, 113; in inheritance laws, 78; mortality rates and, 265, 266; by parents, 11, 266, 271–72, 364; profit effects of, 159; reducing, 46–48; by women, 47

discrimination, labor market: ability standards and, 124–28, 127f; in concentrated industries, 110–13; definition of, 7, 105; efficiency wage theory, 121–24, 184; evidence for, 110–14, 118–21; laws on, 347–48; prejudice against women, 7, 47, 105–14; profit effects of, 109, 110; by sexual orientation, 113–14; social networks as factor in, 105; statistical, 114–21; wage effects of, 106–8, 108f, 114–17; wealth accumulation effects of, 143. *See also* earnings by gender

discrimination, racial, 113, 118, 348

division of labor: in agriculture, 93–94, 95, 213; in households, 62, 76, 84; in hunter-gatherer societies, 88–89, 95, 213; in marriage, 204–5, 211–13, 234, 237–38, 326; in primitive communism, 87, 88. *See also* gender roles

divorce: autonomy of women and, 205; bargaining costs in, 239, 240; consequences of, 212–13, 237–38, 240, 242–43; cultural norms on, 241–42; earnings differences and, 232; increase in, 205, 237, 237f; laws, 78–79, 205, 213, 238, 239, 240–41, 319, 368; political impact of, 317, 319, 322–23, 325–26; property division in, 367, 368; threat of, 74, 75, 76–77; utilities compared to marriage, 238–39, 238f

Dixit, Avinash, 80

Doepke, Mattias, 311n10, 321–22

domestic violence. *See* spousal violence

Donohue, John J., 299–300

Doss, Cheryl, 136

dowries: in Asia, 204, 224–25, 366; compared to bride prices, 224, 269–70; costs of, 264–65; definition of, 204; explanations of, 222–24; poverty and, 224–25; as premortem inheritance, 222–24, 225, 244, 366; welfare of wives and, 225

Draper, Patricia, 88–89

Dreher, Axel, 192

Dreze, Jean, 208

Drolet, M., 103n1

drug use: criminal activity and, 207; marriage and, 208–9

DuBois, E. C., 306n4

Dubuc, Sylvia, 267

Duflo, Esther, 2n2, 16n15, 83, 134n2, 336, 338, 346n13, 357–59, 364

Duncan, Greg J., 208–9

Dutta, Jayasri, 323

Dyson, Tim, 262

earnings: bargaining on, 3, 35; of entrepreneurs, 150; human capital investments and, 226–29, 226f, 338–40, 339f; marriage premium, 233–34; savings from, 134, 138–39; women's control over, 66, 79. *See also* incomes; wages

earnings by gender: ability levels and, 124–28, 125t; antidiscrimination laws and, 347; comparative advantage and, 318–19; compensating differentials and, 104; competitive effects on, 111–12; in developed countries, 6–7, 7f; factors in differences, 22–23, 35–36, 103–4, 228–29; human capital and, 103, 228–29; industrialization and, 318; marital division of labor and, 204–5; marital status and, 228–29; in marriages, 232; by occupation, 178–79; of parents, 228–29; psychological differences and, 3, 35–36; sex ratios and, 268–69; of top executives, 22, 37; trade effects on, 111–12, 170, 178–80. *See also* discrimination, labor market

East Asia: gender wage gaps in, 179–80; globalization effects in, 173–74; parliamentary seats held by women in, 17t; preferences for male children in, 264–67, 270; sex ratios at birth in, 12t, 265–66, 268–69, 270. *See also* Asia; *individual countries*

Eaton, B. C., 27n7, 122n23

Eckel, Catherine, 26–27, 28–29

economic development: empowerment of women and, 2, 336; fertility rates and, 249, 256–58, 362; in polygynous societies, 221–22. *See also* developed countries; industrialization

Edlund, Lena, 187–88, 267, 269, 270n30, 325

Edmonds, Eric V., 182–83

education: child mortality rates and, 266; compulsory, 254, 262; costs of, 182–83; in developed countries, 336; in developing countries, 338, 339–42; economics courses, 195–96; efficiency gains from, 340, 342; empowerment through, 14–15, 338; externalities of, 15–16, 340–42; fertility rates and, 15, 254, 262, 341–42; funding of, 320; gender gap in, 138, 180, 336, 338, 339–40; globalization effects on, 180–83; government subsidies of, 341, 342; household spending on, 84; marginal returns to, 227–28; opportunity cost of, 227, 341; returns on investment in, 260–61, 338–42, 339f; school enrollments by gender, 14, 14f, 180–83; single-sex schools, 55, 342; social return on, 14–15, 341–42; women's suffrage and, 320–22. *See also* higher education; human capital

efficiency wage theory, 121–24, 184

Ekinci, Neslihan A., 44–45

elected officials. *See* legislatures; political representation

elections. *See* political gender gap; voting

Ember, C. R., 219n22

Ember, M., 219n22

empathy, 33, 36–37

employment: affirmative action in, 16, 348–51, 352–54; birth control effects on careers, 13, 283–85, 284f, 286–87; competition for jobs, 37–38; globalization effects on, 172–73, 174–78, 182, 183; hiring decisions, 37–38, 47–48, 105, 348–50;